PEARSON
my World
Social Studies ®

Building Our Country

PEARSON

Boston, Massachusetts
Chandler, Arizona
Glenview, Illinois
Upper Saddle River, New Jersey

ISBN-13: 978-0-328-63929-8
ISBN-10: 0-328-63929-X
23 17

Program Consulting Authors

The Colonial Williamsburg Foundation
Williamsburg, VA

Dr. Linda Bennett
Associate Professor, Department of Learning, Teaching, & Curriculum
College of Education
University of Missouri
Columbia, MO

Dr. Jim Cummins
Professor of Curriculum, Teaching, and Learning
Ontario Institute for Studies in Education
University of Toronto
Toronto, ON, Canada

Dr. James B. Kracht
Byrne Chair for Student Success
Executive Associate Dean
College of Education and Human Development
Texas A&M University
College Station, TX

Dr. Alfred Tatum
Associate Professor, Director of the UIC Reading Clinic
Literacy, Language, and Culture Program
University of Illinois at Chicago
Chicago, IL

Dr. William E. White
Vice President for Productions, Publications and Learning Ventures
The Colonial Williamsburg Foundation
Williamsburg, VA

Consultants and Reviewers

PROGRAM CONSULTANT

Dr. Grant Wiggins
Coauthor, *Understanding by Design*

ACADEMIC REVIEWERS

Bob Sandman
Adjunct Assistant Professor of Business and Economics
Wilmington College–Cincinnati Branches
Blue Ash, OH

Jeanette Menendez
Reading Coach
Doral Academy Elementary
Miami, FL

Kathy T. Glass
Author, *Lesson Design for Differentiated Instruction*
President, Glass Educational Consulting
Woodside, CA

Roberta Logan
African Studies Specialist
Retired, Boston Public Schools/ Mission Hill School
Boston, MA

PROGRAM TEACHER REVIEWERS

Glenda Alford-Atkins
Eglin Elementary School
Eglin AFB, FL

Andrea Baerwald
Boise, ID

Ernest Andrew Brewer
Assistant Professor
Florida Atlantic University
Jupiter, FL

Riley D. Browning
Gilbert Middle School
Gilbert, WV

Charity L. Carr
Stroudsburg Area School District
Stroudsburg, PA

Jane M. Davis
Marion County Public Schools
Ocala, FL

Stacy Ann Figueroa, M.B.A.
Wyndham Lakes Elementary
Orlando, FL

LaBrenica Harris
John Herbert Phillips Academy
Birmingham, AL

Marianne Mack
Union Ridge Elementary
Ridgefield, WA

Emily L. Manigault
Richland School District #2
Columbia, SC

Marybeth A. McGuire
Warwick School Department
Warwick, RI

Laura Pahr
Holmes Elementary
Chicago, IL

Jennifer Palmer
Shady Hills Elementary
Spring Hill, FL

Diana E. Rizo
Miami-Dade County Public Schools/Miami Dade College
Miami, FL

Kyle Roach
Amherst Elementary, Knox County Schools
Knoxville, TN

Eretta Rose
MacMillan Elementary School
Montgomery, AL

Nancy Thornblad
Millard Public Schools
Omaha, NE

Jennifer Transue
Siegfried Elementary
Northampton, PA

Megan Zavernik
Howard-Suamico School District
Green Bay, WI

Dennise G. Zobel
Pittsford Schools–Allen Creek
Rochester, NY

Social Studies Handbook

The First Americans

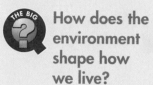

How does the environment shape how we live?

Native Americans of the Northwest carved totem poles like this one.

Age of Exploration

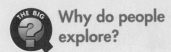 Why do people explore?

*Explorers used the magnetic compass
to help them find their way.*

Settlements Take Root

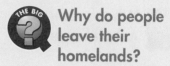

Why do people leave their homelands?

New Amsterdam

Chapter 4

Life in the Colonies

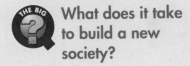

What does it take to build a new society?

Horn books helped colonial children learn to read.

The American Revolution

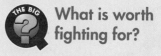

THE BIG **What is worth fighting for?**

The Townshend Acts angered the colonists.

A New Nation

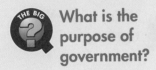

What is the purpose of government?

The United States Constitution

The Young Nation Grows

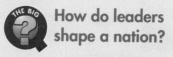

THE BIG ? How do leaders shape a nation?

1793 one cent coin

Chapter 8

Moving West

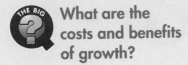 What are the costs and benefits of growth?

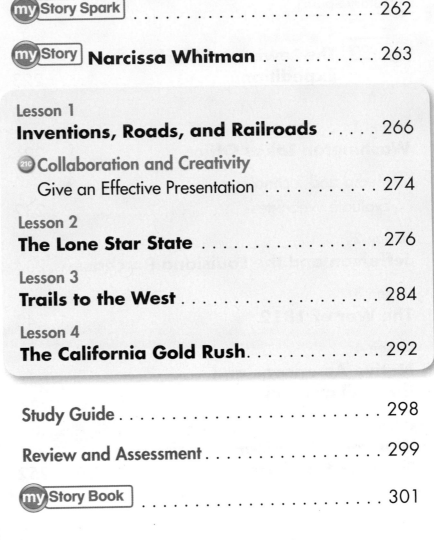

Posters urged people to move to San Francisco, California, during the mid-1800s.

Civil War and Reconstruction

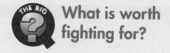 **What is worth fighting for?**

A Confederate soldier's hat, shoes, and gloves

⊙ # Reading Skills

RI.5.5. Compare and contrast events, ideas, concepts, or information.

RI.5.7. Draw on multiple sources to answer questions or solve problems.

Compare and Contrast

To compare and contrast is to look for similarities and differences in things.

Draw Conclusions

When we draw conclusions, we make decisions or form opinions about what we read.

Classify and Categorize

When we classify and categorize, we look at how things are related based on their characteristics.

GLASS

RECYCLING

PAPER

PLASTIC

The **Main Idea** is the most important idea about a topic.

Details support the main idea.

Reading Skills

Sequence

Sequence refers to the order of events. We use sequence when we list the steps in a process.

21st Century Learning Online Tutor Checklist

You can go online to myworldsocialstudies.com to practice the skills listed below. These are skills that will be important to you throughout your life. After you complete each skill tutorial online, check it off here in your worktext.

◉ Target Reading Skills

- ☐ Main Idea and Details
- ☐ Cause and Effect
- ☐ Classify and Categorize
- ☐ Fact and Opinion
- ☐ Draw Conclusions
- ☐ Generalize
- ☐ Compare and Contrast
- ☐ Sequence
- ☐ Summarize

Collaboration and Creativity Skills

- ☐ Solve Problems
- ☐ Work in Cooperative Teams
- ☐ Resolve Conflict
- ☐ Generate New Ideas

Graph Skills

- ☐ Interpret Graphs
- ☐ Create Charts
- ☐ Interpret Timelines

Map Skills

- ☐ Use Longitude and Latitude
- ☐ Interpret Physical Maps
- ☐ Interpret Economic Data on Maps
- ☐ Interpret Cultural Data on Maps

Critical Thinking Skills

- ☐ Compare Viewpoints
- ☐ Use Primary and Secondary Sources
- ☐ Identify Bias
- ☐ Make Decisions
- ☐ Predict Consequences

Media and Technology Skills

- ☐ Conduct Research
- ☐ Use the Internet Safely
- ☐ Analyze Images
- ☐ Evaluate Media Content
- ☐ Deliver an Effective Presentation

Keys to Good Writing

The Writing Process

Prewrite
- Choose a topic, gather details about it, and plan how to use them.

Draft
- Write down all your ideas, and don't worry about making it perfect.

Share
- Share your writing with others.

Edit
- Check your spelling, capitalization, punctuation and grammar.
- Make a final copy.

Revise
- Review your writing, looking for the traits of good writing.
- Change parts that are confusing or incomplete.

The Writing Traits

Good writers look at six qualities of their writing
to make it the best writing possible.

Ideas	Share a clear message with specific ideas and details.
Organization	Have a beginning, middle, and end that are easy to follow.
Voice	Use a natural tone in your writing.
Word Choice	Choose strong nouns and verbs and colorful adjectives.
Sentence Flow	Vary your sentence structures and beginnings to create writing that is easy to read.
Conventions	Follow the rules of spelling, capitalization, punctuation, and grammar.

Geography is the study of Earth. This study can be divided into five themes that help you understand why Earth has such a wide variety of places. Each theme reveals something different about a place, as the example of the Everglades shows.

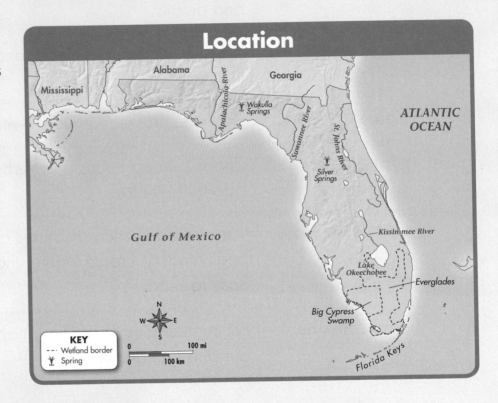

Location

Where can the Everglades be found?

The Everglades are located in southern Florida.

Mississippi

Alabama

Georgia

Apalachicola River

Wakulla Springs

Suwannee River

St. Johns River

ATLANTIC OCEAN

Silver Springs

Gulf of Mexico

Kissimmee River

Lake Okeechobee

Everglades

Big Cypress Swamp

Florida Keys

KEY
- - - Wetland border
Spring

0   100 mi

0   100 km

Place

How is this area different from others?

The place is wetlands where a plant called sawgrass grows. There are dry islands called hammocks that are covered with trees.

Human/Environmental Interaction

How have people changed the place?
Highways have made the Everglades a place visitors can explore more easily.

Movement

How has movement changed the region?
Population growth and tourists have led to increased use of the area.

Region

What is special about the region that includes the Everglades?
There are vast areas where many endangered species live.

Reading Maps

Reading maps is an important skill for learning about the world, past and present. To read maps, you'll need to recognize some of their most important features.

A **compass rose** looks a bit like an arrow and shows the directions: north, south, east, and west. A **map key** helps readers interpret the symbols that appear on maps. Look at the map key on the next page. You can see that the star marks the state capital. The **scale** on a map shows distance. A map might show a scale in which 1 inch on the map represents 100 miles.

Some maps are marked with **latitude** and **longitude** lines. Latitude lines run east and west and measure distance north and south of the equator. Longitude lines, sometimes called meridians, run north and south and measure distance east and west of the prime meridian. A **locator map** is a simple map usually set in the corner of a larger one. It shows the location of the larger map in the country or the world.

1. What line would you find at 0° longitude?

....

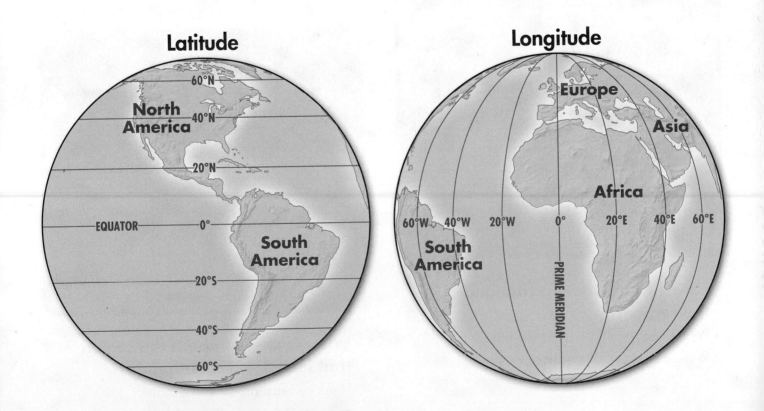

Political Maps

Not all maps are created for the same reason. Some maps are called **political maps**. They show political information, such as the location of state or national borders or the location of capitals and other cities. Using the map below, you can locate the state capital of Florida. You can also locate other important cities. The areas that are not part of the subject of the map are sometimes tinted a shade of gray or brown. On this map, the states of Georgia and Alabama are tinted tan to show that they are not the main subject of the map. The locator map on the upper right shows where Florida is located in the United States

Vocabulary

compass rose

map key

scale

latitude

longitude

locator map

political map

2. Use the map. **Name** the capital city of Florida.

....

3. **Name** two other cities marked on the map.

....

....

4. **Circle** the map key. Put a **square** around the compass rose.

5. Estimate the distance between Jacksonville and Miami.

....

6. In which part of the country is Florida located?

....

Florida, Political

Alabama
Georgia
Tallahassee ★
Pensacola
Jacksonville
Gainesville
Daytona Beach
ATLANTIC OCEAN
Orlando
Gulf of Mexico
Tampa
St. Petersburg
Sarasota
West Palm Beach
Fort Myers
Fort Lauderdale
Naples
Miami

KEY
★ Capital city
• City

N W E S

0   100 mi
0   100 km

7. On a separate sheet of paper, draw a political map that includes your city or town. Include some of the surrounding cities and towns.

Physical Maps

A **physical map** has a different purpose from a political map. A physical map shows the physical characteristics of a place. It can show mountains and valleys. It can also show bodies of water, including rivers, lakes, and oceans.

A physical map shows the **relief** of an area. Relief shows high and low places through different colors and shading. On the map below, the relief shows the high mountains. The flat plains have no relief. Blue areas of most maps are bodies of water.

This physical map includes labels for important landforms. A valley is a low area, usually between mountain ranges. A peninsula is an area of land that is almost completely surrounded by water. An island is an area of land that is completely surrounded by water.

8. **Circle** the state made up of islands on the map. Put an **X** on one valley on the map. **Draw** a box around a peninsula on the map. **Draw** a row of triangles on two mountain ranges.

9. Which mountain ranges would have made it difficult for pioneers to travel from east to west during the settlement of America?

....

....

....

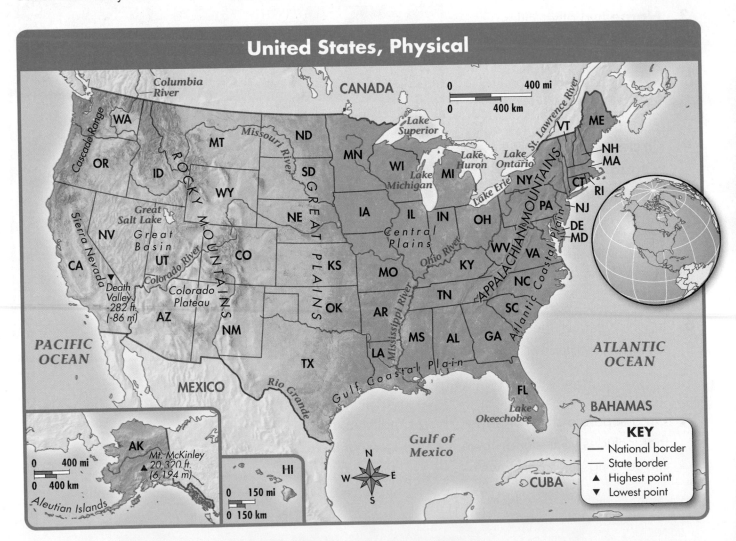

United States, Physical

Elevation Maps

An **elevation map** also shows physical characteristics of a land area. **Elevation** is the distance or height above sea level. Using an elevation map, you can compare and contrast different landform regions, such as mountains, river valleys, and plains The map below uses different colors to show the differences in elevation. Areas shaded purple are the highest.

An elevation map may help engineers decide where to build roads, bridges, and tunnels. For example, look at the map of Colorado. It shows where flatter areas run into steep areas in the Rocky Mountains. When Coloradans were planning ways to improve travel, they used elevation maps to find the right spots to build tunnels for railroads and highways.

Vocabulary

physical map
relief
elevation map
elevation

10. Which area of Colorado has the highest elevations, the eastern part or the western?

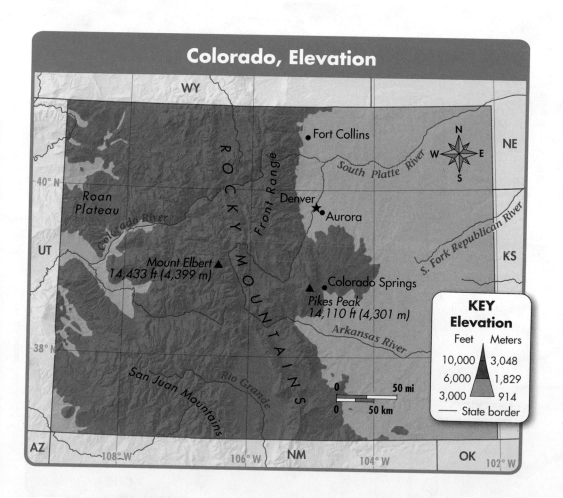

Colorado, Elevation

KEY
Elevation

Feet	Meters
10,000	3,048
6,000	1,829
3,000	914
— State border	

Regions

A **region** is an area that shares physical or human characteristics. A regions map shows areas that have common features. Regions might be based on population. They might be areas that share a language or religion in common. Five regions of the United States are shown below. These regions are based on their geographic location.

11. **Circle** your state. **Draw** a box around the region where you live.

12. Which states belong to the region where you live?

....

....

....

....

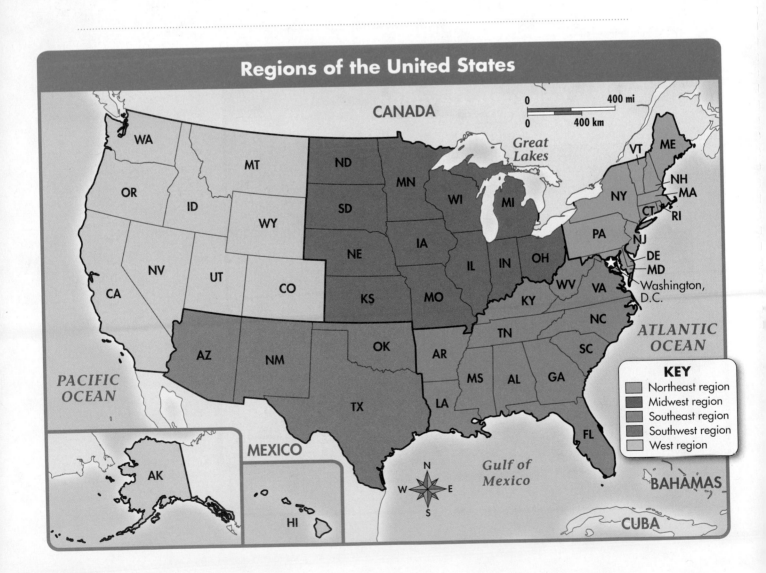

Regions of the United States

Historical Maps

Sometimes maps are useful for providing historical information. This kind of map is called an **historical map**.

Historical maps sometimes include dates that tell when events took place. They often use special symbols to show where battles or other types of events took place. They might include arrows to show movements of people or armies. They might be designed to show the changing borders of states or countries. Historical maps of the United States, for example, show how the country grew from the original 13 colonies to a nation of 50 states.

Look at the historical map on the right. This map gives information about the "express riders" during the days before the American Revolution. Colonial leaders needed a way to share news with each other across the 13 colonies. They formed committees that wrote letters about what the British were doing and what protests were planned. These letters were delivered by "express riders" who rode fast horses to carry messages between committee members in different cities. This map helps tell the story of the express riders.

Vocabulary

region

historical map

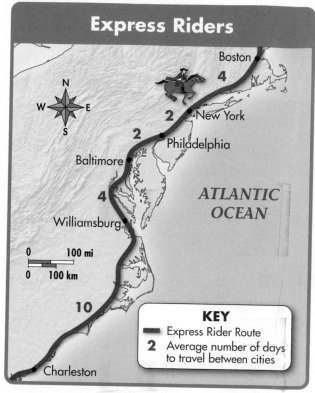

13. **List** two things about the express riders' routes that this map shows.

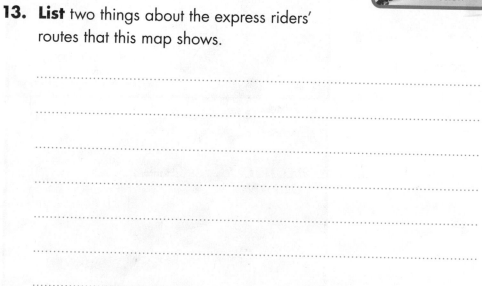

Special-Purpose Maps

A special-purpose map gives information related to a certain theme. For example, a **population-density map**, like the one of California on this page, shows the average number of people who live in an area. You could use it to compare how many people live in the coast as opposed to inland.

There are many other kinds of special-purpose maps. A **satellite map** shows a picture of the land and cities from space. An immigration map could show which states have the highest rates of immigration. A zip-code map shows the zip codes of each area of a state or country. Weather maps are used to track storms. Knowing the path of a storm helps people be prepared.

Special-purpose maps contain a lot of information. You can use the information to compare different places or to gather details about one place. You could draw a special-purpose map of your neighborhood. It might show your home, your friends' homes, your school, and your favorite places to visit.

14. What special information does this map show?

....

....

....

15. Which city has a greater population density, Hanford or San Jose?

....

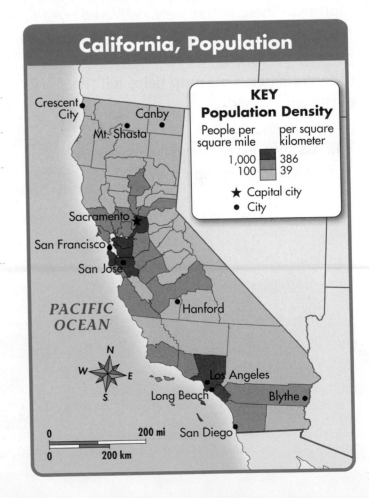

California, Population

KEY
Population Density

People per square mile	per square kilometer
1,000	386
100	39

★ Capital city
• City

Crescent City
Canby
Mt. Shasta
Sacramento ★
San Francisco
San Jose
PACIFIC OCEAN
Hanford
N W E S
Los Angeles
Long Beach
Blythe
San Diego

0   200 mi
0   200 km

Current-Events Maps

Some special-purpose maps deal with current events. They help people decide what laws to make or how to work for change. They can also show the outcome of an election. The map below shows the results of the 2010 senatorial elections.

Vocabulary

population-density map

satellite map

2010 Senatorial Election Results

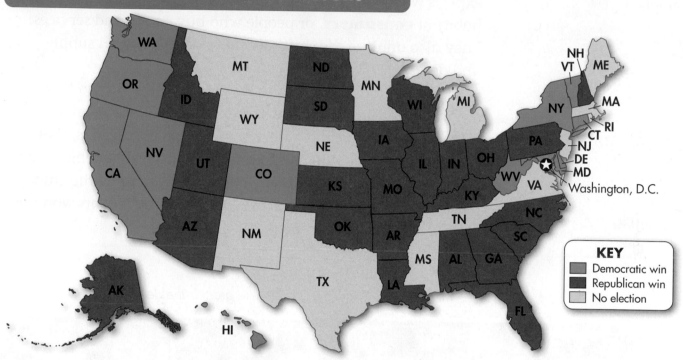

KEY
- Democratic win
- Republican win
- No election

16. On a separate sheet of paper, **make** a bar graph to show how many states elected Republican senators and how many states elected Democratic senators.

Got it?

17. **Look** at the current events map above. On a separate sheet of paper, describe election results for your region.

18. How is the special-purpose map on the previous page different from a physical map of California?

....

....

Our Market Economy

Vocabulary

consumer
demand
supply

Supply and Demand

Economics is the study of the production, distribution, and consumption, or use, of goods and services. Economists are experts who study those processes. They analyze the changing habits of **consumers**, or people who buy goods and services. They also analyze the shifting relationship between supply and demand.

In economics, **demand** means consumers' desire to buy a particular thing or service. For example, if the students at a school start admiring a fancy new brand of sneakers, they might create a high demand for them. The level of demand for a product is related to its price. Therefore, if some of the students at school can't afford the new sneakers, those students won't be part of the demand for sneakers.

The more people who want an item, the greater the demand.

The term **supply** means the amount of goods or services that are available. For example, suppose that a store owner receives a big shipment of the fancy new sneakers. She has a large supply. She might worry that she won't be able to sell all those shoes. So she lowers the price. Suddenly, the quantity demanded goes up. Those students at school who could not afford the shoes before, now are able to pay the lower price. The addition of these students to the group who is buying the shoes adds to the demand.

1. Suppose there are 100 students who want to buy sneakers. The store, however, only has 50 pairs. Should the store owner raise or lower the price of the sneakers?

    ....

2. Suppose a store has 100 pairs of sneakers, but only 50 students want to buy them. Should the store owner raise or lower the price of the sneakers?

    ....

3. Based on your answers to the questions above, **circle** the correct answer.

    When demand goes up, prices go up/down.

    When supply goes up, prices go up/down.

    When demand goes down, prices go up/down.

    When supply goes down, prices go up/down.

The Marketplace

The United States has a **free market economy**. In this economic system people, not the government, own the factories, businesses, and stores that make, sell, and distribute goods or services. In a free market, businesses can make most decisions about what to produce and what prices to charge. Individuals choose what to buy in the marketplace. In a free market, these types of decisions are made all the time by millions of people. A free market works by meeting the needs and wants of individuals.

Competition is the struggle among producers for the money consumers spend. In a free market, competition usually makes prices lower. High demand for goods means businesses need to hire more workers. When people work, they have money to buy goods. This increases demand and causes businesses to increase supply. More people working is good for a free market economy.

4. **Circle** the marketplace that would be the right place for you to offer your babysitting services.

Buyers and sellers exchange goods and services in a marketplace.

Scarcity and Opportunity Cost

We want many things and, in general, more and more of those things. Yet, we can't always have everything that we want because of scarcity. **Scarcity** means that there is a limit to what we can have. We must make choices, for example, about how and where we spend our money.

All choices have a cost. If a student chooses to spend his allowance on a book, he might not be able to go to the movies with friends. The trip to the movies is the **opportunity cost**. It is the thing you have to give up to get the thing you want.

Vocabulary

free market economy

competition

scarcity

opportunity cost

5. In each row, **circle** the option you would choose. **Write** the option you would not choose, or the opportunity cost, in the third column.

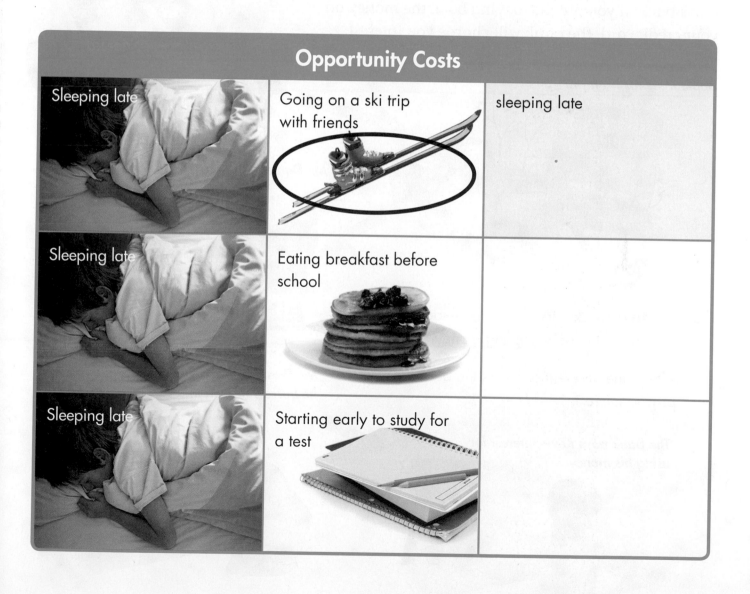

Opportunity Costs

Sleeping late	Going on a ski trip with friends	sleeping late
Sleeping late	Eating breakfast before school	
Sleeping late	Starting early to study for a test	

Banks

Many people put their money into a bank to keep it safe or to earn interest. This is called having a **bank account.** You might think that a bank saves each dollar you give it in a special, hidden place. That is partly true. But banks also lend their customers' money to businesses and individuals. Borrowers promise to pay the bank back according to a schedule and for a small fee called **interest.** In exchange for using your money, the bank pays you some of the interest.

Sometimes banks offer a credit card to their customers. A **credit card** is a card that allows its holder to use it for small loans. The cardholder may buy things with the card, based on the promise to pay the bank back. If you are late paying back the money on your credit card, the bank will charge you interest.

Mr. Daniels uses the money to buy more apple trees for his farm.

6. **Write** a checkmark next to the image that shows the bank lending money.

7. **Circle** the image that shows the bank paying interest.

The bank pays Kevin interest for using his money.

How Banks Work

Kevin deposits money in his bank account.

The bank uses the money deposited by Kevin and other customers to loan Mr. Daniels money.

Mr. Daniels sells the apples from his new trees.

Mr. Daniels pays the bank back the money he borrowed with interest.

The Economy Today

Every day we make economic decisions that affect the economy. We decide what to buy based on what we can afford. We consider what we have to give up in order to get what we want. The government also influences the economy. It helps people who lose their jobs or homes. It helps very poor people find food and shelter. It makes rules about how banks should lend money to businesses. It enforces legal contracts, and it provides currency, or money, for the country to use.

One of the most important economic decisions that our government makes is called a **trade agreement.** These agreements make it easy for businesses to **import** (bring in) or **export** (send out) goods to and from these countries. As a result, goods made in those places are cheaper to buy in America than goods made in other countries that do not have favorable trade agreements. The United States has trade agreements with individual countries such as China and India. Both China and India have become economic superpowers partly because of their trade agreements with the United States.

Vocabulary

bank account

interest

credit card

trade agreement

import

export

U.S. Trade Partners

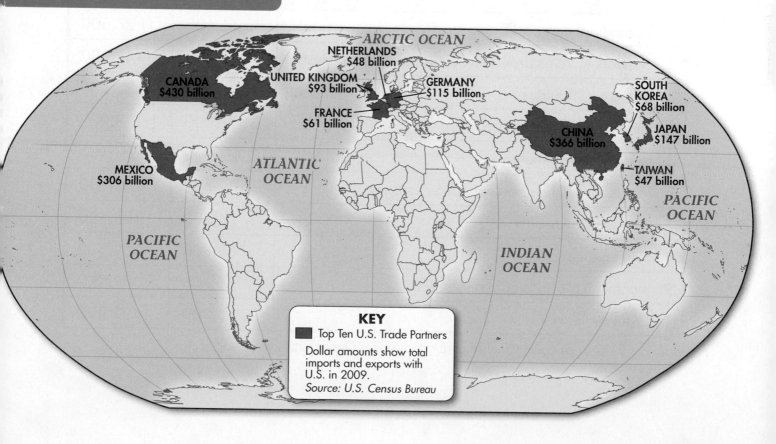

ARCTIC OCEAN

NETHERLANDS
$48 billion

CANADA
$430 billion

UNITED KINGDOM
$93 billion

GERMANY
$115 billion

SOUTH KOREA
$68 billion

FRANCE
$61 billion

CHINA
$366 billion

JAPAN
$147 billion

MEXICO
$306 billion

ATLANTIC OCEAN

TAIWAN
$47 billion

PACIFIC OCEAN

PACIFIC OCEAN

INDIAN OCEAN

KEY

Top Ten U.S. Trade Partners

Dollar amounts show total imports and exports with U.S. in 2009.
Source: U.S. Census Bureau

Jobs

Some economic conditions make it cheaper for companies to hire workers in countries such as China and India to **manufacture**, or make, goods. As a result, many manufacturing jobs are moving to those and other Asian countries. Many American businesses used to make manufactured goods like televisions and clothing. Now more businesses offer services instead. Service jobs include nursing, teaching, and sales. However, some services, such as technology help, are now also performed overseas.

8. Name three additional service jobs not listed in the chart.

....

....

....

Most of the 10 fastest-growing jobs are jobs in which people offer a service to other people.

10 Fastest-Growing U.S. Jobs		
Occupation	**Number of People Employed**	
	2008	**2018**
1. Biomedical engineers	16,100	27,600
2. Network-systems and data-communications analysts	292,000	447,800
3. Home health aides	921,700	1,382,600
4. Personal and home-care aides	817,200	1,193,000
5. Financial examiners	27,000	38,100
6. Medical scientists, except epidemiologists	109,400	153,600
7. Physician assistants	74,800	103,900
8. Skin-care specialists	38,800	53,500
9. Biochemists and biophysicists	23,200	31,900
10. Athletic trainers	16,400	22,400

Source: Bureau of Labor Statistics, United States Department of Labor

Technology and Specialization

Businesses make decisions that help them earn more money or lower their costs. Some businesses become more competitive by improving their technology. Others become more competitive by specializing in one product or having their workers specialize in one job. To **specialize** is to concentrate in one particular area.

Vocabulary

manufacture

specialize

These workers are trained to do a specialized job. The business runs smoothly when people know their jobs well.

9. What are some specialized jobs needed to make a movie?

....

....

10. Circle a worker using technology to make a movie.

Got it?

11. Name at least three factors that influence the price of goods.

....

....

....

Participating in Our Government

Vocabulary

representative
  democracy

constitution

separation of powers

checks and balances

article

amendment

What Is Government?

Government is a system for running a community, state, or country. The government of the United States is a republic, or **representative democracy.** That means we elect people to act as our representatives, or people who express our ideas and opinions, in the government.

We expect a lot from our government. For example, we expect all people to be treated equally, no matter what their race, religion, or gender is. We believe that people deserve to make free choices about what they believe and how they live. As a nation, we agree to follow the lead of a majority, or the largest number of people, as long as the rights of the minority, or the smallest number of people, are respected.

The U.S. Constitution

A **constitution** is a written plan for government. The United States Constitution was written more than 200 years ago by a group of leaders now known as the Founding Fathers. The Constitution set up the plan for our government by creating three branches to govern the nation: the executive, legislative, and judicial branches. The executive branch includes the President of the United States and the officials who work with him or her. The legislative branch, also known as Congress, is made up of members of the Senate and the House of Representatives. The judicial branch includes the Supreme Court, which is made up of nine justices. They ensure that the nation's laws are interpreted according to the Constitution. Other courts in the judicial branch help settle conflicts.

The Constitution also established a separation of powers. The **separation of powers** means that each of the three branches of our government has its own responsibilities and powers. Also, each branch can check, or limit, the powers of the others. This plan is called a system of **checks and balances.** It is designed to make sure that the powers of the three branches of government are balanced, or equal.

Three Branches of Government

Branch	Duties	Checks
Executive	• Makes sure laws are carried out • Commands the armed forces	• Can veto, or reject, laws passed by Congress • Appoints judges
Legislative	• Makes laws • Establishes taxes	• Can reject vetoes • Can refuse to confirm judges appointed by the President
Judicial	• Interprets laws • Decides if laws follow the Constitution	• Can overturn President's actions if these actions go against the Constitution • Can stop laws that go against the Constitution

1. Who is the head of the executive branch?

....

2. How does the judicial branch check the other branches?

....

....

The Bill of Rights

The Constitution is divided into laws called **articles**. One of the most important parts of the Constitution is its plan for making changes to those laws. A change to an article in the Constitution is called an **amendment**. Just after the Constitution was ratified, or approved, its authors added ten very important amendments. They are called the Bill of Rights.

To write the Constitution, the Founders relied on English law and its concept of **individual rights**, or freedoms protected by law. The rights protected in the U.S. Bill of Rights are based, in part, on those granted to English subjects under the Magna Carta of 1215 and the English Bill of Rights of 1689. The U.S. Bill of Rights protects free speech, freedom of religion, and other important rights.

To amend the Constitution, two-thirds of the members of both houses of Congress must vote for the proposed change. Or, two-thirds of state legislatures may call for a constitutional convention. Three-fourths of the states must approve the amendment before it becomes law. Since the Bill of Rights was added, the Constitution has been amended 17 times. In 1870, an amendment extended voting rights to all men, regardless of race. In 1920, an amendment gave voting rights to women.

Federalism: National, State, and Local Government

The U.S. Constitution also divides power between the national and state governments. This system is called **federalism** and it is another factor limiting the power of the federal government. The national government may print money, declare war, or make treaties with other nations. States may not, but they may establish local governments and conduct elections. Local governments run many of the other services we use every day.

Federal	**State**	**Local**
• military forces	• state police	• police force and fire fighters
• interstate highways	• state highways	• neighborhood roads
• national parks	• state parks	• town recreation areas
• provides some financial assistance to schools	• sets school standards and provides financial assistance	• makes day-to-day decisions for schools

3. **Circle** the government duty that you think is the most important. On a separate sheet of paper, **write** a paragraph explaining your choice.

Popular Sovereignty

The Constitution includes other important ideas about how the government works and how its powers are limited. One key concept is the rule of law. The **rule of law** means that the law applies equally to all people, no matter how powerful or wealthy they are. Everyone, including the President, must obey the laws of the land. Another important idea is popular sovereignty. **Popular sovereignty** means that the citizens of a country have a right to choose what kind of government they have.

Voting is an important right. It gives citizens a right to choose their representatives in government.

4. Draw a line between each term and its definition.

separation of powers	The idea that the government exists because the people of a country want it to exist and agree to follow its rules
federalism	The idea that the law applies equally to all people no matter how powerful or wealthy people are
popular sovereignty	Freedoms protected by law
checks and balances	The system of government in which powers are divided between cities, states, and the nation as a whole
rule of law	The system that separates the jobs and powers of government among three branches
individual rights	The system that gives each branch different powers and allows each branch to limit the power of the others

Government in Action

The state and national governments have big responsibilities. They operate schools, keep the nation and cities safe, and protect parks for everyone to enjoy. Americans pay money every year to the state and national governments to help pay for the services they receive. This money is called **taxes.**

Sometimes, the government makes laws that prevent people from hurting animals, the environment, or one another. For example, there is a law that people riding in a car must wear a seat belt. Many cities and states require residents to recycle glass bottles, metal cans, and plastic containers. City, state, and national governments all have laws that protect the environment. These laws protect what is called the common good. The **common good** means what is good for everyone.

Government Workers

Postal Worker

Teacher

Firefighter

5. **Circle** the picture if you have ever used the services of this government job.

6. **Name** the job of two or more government workers you saw today.

Politics

Of course, not everyone agrees with how the government does its job. Some people join groups in order to share their ideas about government. Many voters join a political party to try to influence government decisions. A **political party** is a group of people who have similar beliefs about how government should be run.

Each political party nominates a **candidate**, a person who runs for a particular office, or job. The members of the party try to convince others to vote for their candidate. Then, on election day, voters decide which candidates they want to lead the government.

Of course, after an election, the losing political party is disappointed because its candidate has not been elected. However, elections in the United States are peaceful. Although voters may feel strongly that the common good would be better served if their candidates had won, they accept the decision of the majority. This is a key principle of a stable democracy.

Vocabulary

tax
common good
political party
candidate

Barack Obama was the first African American to run for President on a major party ticket. He was elected to office in 2008.

Being a Good Citizen

Democracy, even more than other forms of government, depends on good citizenship. The government can best serve the people of a country when they stay involved. There are a number of important ways to be a good **citizen**.

This group of volunteers in Miami, Florida, is painting a mural to decorate a local elementary school.

7. **Circle** the actions on the chart that you can do now as a good citizen.

Ways to Be a Good Citizen	
Obeying the Law	Good citizens respect the rights of others by obeying the law.
Voting	Citizens cast their ballots to tell who they want to serve as government leaders. Voters must be at least 18 years old.
Paying Taxes	Every citizen benefits from the services of the city, state, and federal government. These services are paid for by people who pay taxes on the money they earn.
Volunteering to Do Community Service	Volunteering to help one's town and helping one's neighbors are great ways to be a good citizen.
Petitioning Government Leaders	Good citizens make their voices heard by writing letters and letting their elected officials know what they think.

How We Participate in Government

Vocabulary

citizen

Good citizens do more than exercise their most basic rights and responsibilities. To improve our government and society, they stay informed about issues by reading or watching the news. Many citizens volunteer or join organizations that work on issues they care about. Others run for political office. Still others write letters to the newspaper to share their views on a subject.

Communicating with your elected representatives is an important way to participate in government. You can find the name and address of your elected representatives by calling the offices of your town, or searching the Internet. Most elected officials are glad to receive letters or e-mails, and they try to write back to explain how they think about your issue.

8. **Make** a list of three things you would like to do to participate in government.

....

....

....

....

....

Got it?

9. **Name** three rights that are held by citizens of the United States.

....

....

10. **Explain** why it is important to be a good citizen in a democracy.

....

....

The First Americans

THE BIG ?

How does the environment shape how we live?

What is the oldest thing you have ever seen or touched? **Write** about where it came from and how it connects you to the past.

....

....

....

....

....

Mesa Verde, Colorado, built around 1100

Ancient Farmers
Builders in Stone

my Story Video

Today is a special day for December! She is visiting Mesa Verde National Park for the first time. December is a member of the Navajo Nation in Gallup, New Mexico. She is also part Zuni. Her home is a few hours south of this fascinating 52,000-acre park.

At Mesa Verde more than 600 cliff dwellings tell the story of the Ancient Puebloan, or Anasazi (ah nuh SAH zee), people. Hundreds of years ago, these ancient farmers created communities in the cliffs. Some archaeologists (people who study the way ancient people lived) believe the cliff dwellings were built for protection. Others think they let the native people escape the heat in the area.

Ranger Linda, December's park ranger for the day, explains that the people used natural resources to live. "Food, water, shelter. It's as simple as that. The Ancient Puebloans farmed corn, beans, and squash on the top of these mesas. They created reservoirs to store water. They made shelters in these cliffs."

Mesa Verde is located in southwestern Colorado. This mountainous region ranges in elevation from 6,100 to 8,500 feet. It's believed that more rain fell here than nearby places, giving ancient farmers water for their crops and and a good place to live.

December is wearing traditional clothing and jewelry of the Navajo people.

1

Ancient Puebloans dug pithouses such as this for shelter on the mesas. This was before they moved into cliff dwellings.

Ancient Puebloans used these stones to grind corn to make flour. The large stone is called a *metate*. The smaller one is called a *mano*.

Still, keeping families warm, safe, and dry was challenging. The people had to make shelters. In the earliest times, starting in about A.D. 550, families lived in pithouses. Pithouses were deep pits, dug into the ground, with walls of wood and mud. As time went on, the communities outgrew the pithouses. By A.D. 750, the Ancient Puebloans were building pueblos. The pueblos were above-ground buildings made mostly of stone.

Many of the pithouses became kivas. "The kivas were like ceremonial living rooms with fire pits and brick walls," explains Ranger Linda. "Families would gather here and celebrate."

Archeologists think that by A.D. 1100 the people had moved to cliff dwellings. These stone towns featured storage space, work areas for preparing food and clothing, fire pits for cooking, and kivas for special celebrations.

Mesa Verde contains many kivas. Ancient Puebloan families would build fires in the kivas and hold celebrations there.

"Wow, it's so peaceful here. I can understand why they chose this area to live. Life must have been very hard, though," whispers December. The soft-spoken young lady is in awe. Realizing her ancestors lived here is remarkable to imagine. When she sees the grand Cliff Palace for the first time, December says, "That is way cool!"

Cliff Palace is Mesa Verde's largest cliff dwelling. She now has a sense of how life may have been for the ancient people.

December and Ranger Linda explore a path between two low stone walls.

Ancient Puebloans painted pictures like these on the walls of many cliff dwellings.

"How did they communicate?" asks December.

Ranger Linda and December have stopped to look at some strange and beautiful drawings and carvings on the canyon's stone wall.

"Petroglyphs are found pecked into walls and pictographs are found painted on the walls," answers Ranger Linda. "We know they communicated and told stories this way but what they say for sure may never be known."

If the language of these ancient farmers is a mystery, the reason they left the ancient pueblos is also hard to explain. Some archeologists think a long drought caused the communities to break up. Others think the land was over-farmed. Whatever the reason, much about the pueblos of Mesa Verde National Park remains a mystery today.

December learned so much on her tour that she became a Junior Park Ranger. Ranger Linda led her through the pledge and awarded her a badge. "I'm coming back again soon," December vows. "And I promise to take care of all national parks!"

December and Ranger Linda discuss when this ancient stone wall may have been built.

Think About It Based on this story, how do you think the land and climate affected the way the Ancient Puebloans lived? As you read the chapter ahead, think of the ways in which the environment shapes people, and the ways people shape their environment.

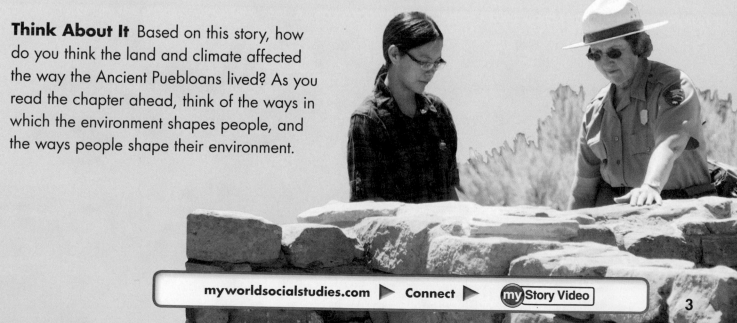

Ancient American Civilizations

This photograph shows an environment similar to what ancient people settled thousands of years ago.

People have not always lived on the continents of North and South America. Scientists say that about 15,000 years ago, people began traveling here from Asia. Many Native Americans have different ideas about how people first came to live on these continents. The Tlingit (TLIHN ket) people, for example, tell how a character called Raven created people and animals in the area of the Pacific Northwest. Other Native American groups tell different stories.

People Arrive in the Americas

Some scientists and historians think that people first came to North and South America by boat. These first people may have sailed across the Atlantic or Pacific Ocean. Most experts, though, think that people first crossed into North America from Asia over what is today the Bering Strait. A strait is a narrow body of water.

In search of food, ancient people followed animals into North America.

4

Draw what you think an ancient dwelling would look like in this environment. Write a caption for your drawing.

UNLOCK THE BIG ?

I will know that ancient people migrated to and settled the Americas.

Vocabulary

migrate   agriculture

culture   civilization

hunter-gatherer   irrigation

Thousands of years ago, temperatures were much colder than today. Much of the world's water formed thick sheets of ice on land. This made the seas shallower.

As a result, the Bering Strait was not a strait at all. It was a dry bridge of land that people today call Beringia. Experts think that the first Americans may have been hunters who tracked animals across this land bridge. In this way, people were able to **migrate**, or travel, from Asia to North America.

Once in North America, people continued to migrate. Over time, hunters chased animals south and east across North America, looking for food to feed their families and groups. People also moved into Central America and then into South America. In this way, humans settled most areas of the two continents.

1. **Circle** the most southern area where early Americans migrated after they arrived in North and South America.

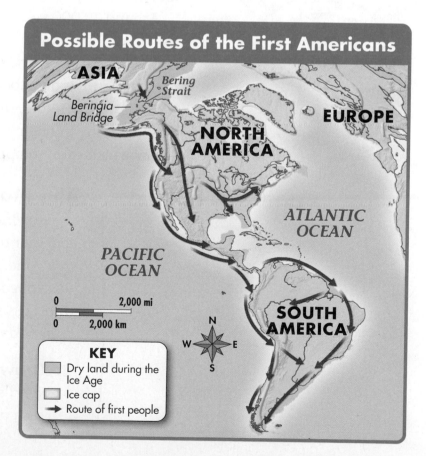

Possible Routes of the First Americans

ASIA

Bering Strait

Beringia— Land Bridge

NORTH AMERICA

EUROPE

PACIFIC OCEAN

ATLANTIC OCEAN

SOUTH AMERICA

0   2,000 mi

0   2,000 km

N W E S

KEY

☐ Dry land during the Ice Age

☐ Ice cap

→ Route of first people

sun

water

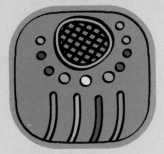

snake

Learning to Use the Land

Settling the Americas took thousands of years. As people pushed slowly into new areas, they faced new challenges. In some places, there were high mountains. In other places, there were deep forests or vast grasslands. Some people lived near large bodies of water, such as sea coasts, rivers, or lakes. Others lived in dry, hot deserts.

Wherever they settled, people developed special ways of living. They used the materials they found to build shelters. They made clothing to protect against the conditions they faced. As a result, in different areas, people dressed and behaved differently. Their dwellings looked different from those in other areas. They even developed different languages.

As people learned to survive in the different lands where they lived, their cultures changed, too. A **culture** is a set of beliefs and way of life that is special to a certain group. Historians think that the people who first came to the Americas were **hunter-gatherers.** Instead of staying in one place, they traveled to hunt and gather food. They hunted wild animals, fished, and caught insects. They also gathered food from wild plants, including fruits, seeds, and roots.

Around 10,000 years ago, people in what is now Mexico in the southern part of North America took a big step. They began to practice **agriculture,** which means they planted and raised their own food. Native peoples planted corn, beans, sweet potatoes, and other crops. Agriculture allowed people to stay in one place year-round. Larger, permanent settlements began to appear.

The Mayan and Aztec Worlds

Growing settlements needed rules for living together and making decisions that affected everyone. So, they formed governments. They developed religions and systems for learning and passing on knowledge. Cultures with these complex ways of life are called **civilizations.**

2. **Draw** your own picture to represent a word such as *cloud* or *river* or an idea such as *peace.*

The Mayan civilization rose about 4,000 years ago in what we now call Central America. It reached its peak between A.D. 300 and 900. The Mayas created systems for writing and for doing advanced math. They watched the skies carefully. Then they charted movements of the sun, moon, and stars. The charts helped them create a highly accurate calendar.

By A.D. 1200, the Mayan civilization was fading. Around the same time, another great civilization arose in Central America. This was the Aztec civilization. The Aztecs are also known as the Mexica (meh SHEE kah). They controlled an area from southern Mexico through Central America.

The heart of the Aztec world was the city of Tenochtítlan (te nahk TEE tlahn), located where Mexico City stands today. As many as 300,000 people lived there. Government leaders in the capital ruled over millions of other people throughout the area who were not Aztecs.

The Aztecs were skilled farmers. They built systems for bringing water to dry fields. This is called **irrigation.** They also invented a brilliant system for growing crops on large reed mats covered with mud. The mats were placed in the watery swamps that surrounded the city.

3. Tenochtítlan, the Aztec capital city, was a center for business and religion. **Circle** parts of the picture that show trade taking place.

Other North American Cultures

Elsewhere in North America, other native cultures emerged. One example is the Inuit (IN oo iht). This culture began 2,500 years ago in the frozen far north. Inuit ways centered on the struggle to live in a harsh place. For example, the Inuit developed the kayak, a kind of small watertight canoe. Kayaks are ideal for hunting whales, seals, and other sea animals. The Inuit also built winter homes out of blocks of snow.

Far to the south, the Mound Builders developed a civilization some 3,000 years ago. This culture spread across a wide area around the Mississippi River. The Mound Builders were known for their huge earthen structures. Some mounds served as graves. Others were sites for religious ceremonies. Building these mounds took skill and organization. The Mound Builders were also active traders. They set up a large network in which goods from all over North America were actively traded.

The Ancient Puebloan or Anasazi (ah nuh SAH zee) culture first appeared about 2,000 years ago. Its people lived in the area where the states of Utah, Colorado, Arizona, and New Mexico now meet. The Ancient Puebloans were farmers, growing corn, beans, and squash. They used irrigation to water their crops in the dry land. They also made beautiful painted pottery.

The Ancient Puebloans were skillful builders, too. On the flat tops of high hills, called mesas, they built large apartment-style houses. Then, around A.D. 1100, they began to build dwellings under the shelter of cliffs. Mesa Verde in Colorado is an example.

4. **Write** one benefit and one challenge about living in a cliff dwelling.

....

....

....

....

....

....

Some cliff dwellings at Mesa Verde were villages with multi-story buildings.

Sometime around A.D. 1300, the Ancient Puebloans abandoned the cliff dwellings. Scattering, some of them became part of the Pueblo people, a culture that still thrives in the American Southwest today.

5. ⊙ **Compare and Contrast Fill in** the chart contrasting the structures built by three different native peoples.

Native American Structures

Inuits	Mound Builders	Ancient Puebloans

Got it?

6. ⊙ **Compare and Contrast Explain** several differences between a hunter-gatherer culture and one that practices agriculture.

....

....

....

7. ❓ You are hiking with your parents to explore an Ancient Puebloan ruin where you find artifacts (but leave them there!). **Write** about the feeling of seeing something that may be hundreds of years old.

my Story Ideas

....

....

⬛ **Stop!** I need help with ....

⏸ **Wait!** I have a question about ....

▶ **Go!** Now I know ....

Work in Teams

When Native Americans hunted for food, they often worked in groups, or teams. They understood that one person acting alone might have less success. Working together, they could accomplish much more.

Working as a team involves finding ways to use everyone's skills and abilities. When you work in a team, you hear ideas you might not have thought of yourself. You learn ways of solving problems that you might not have tried.

Working as a team is not easy. To do it, follow these key steps:

Identify the tasks. Break the assignment down into separate tasks that team members can handle.

Assign roles. Think of the skills each team member has and decide who should get to handle each task.

Involve everyone. Make sure everyone takes part. Each person's job should be necessary to the success of the group.

Get help. Part of working in a team is learning to solve problems together. However, if you face challenges that keep your team from doing its work, ask for help.

A Native American team works together to hunt buffaloes and feed their families.

Suppose that you need to prepare a report on a Native American group. The report must include an oral and a visual presentation. You have been assigned to a group of four students to complete this project.

1. Start by figuring out the tasks that the team needs to do. What jobs need to be accomplished to complete the entire assignment?

....

....

....

2. Once you know the tasks to complete, you can assign roles for carrying out the tasks. How can you make sure team members are all involved and a good fit for their job?

....

....

....

3. What can you do if you have concerns about the way the team is working to get the job done?

....

....

....

4. Apply Remind yourself that success depends equally on each member. **Explain** why good team work is necessary for your success.

....

....

....

Adapting to Different Places

Envision It!

This scene shows what a Native American village with longhouses might have looked like long ago.

1. To make a canoe, the Powhatans burned a large log and then dug out the charred wood. **Write** two ways this canoe shows how the Powhatan people used the resources that were around them.

_____

_____

_____

_____

_____

No one knows how many people lived in North America 600 years ago. There may have been 10 or 15 million, or even more. People lived in camps, villages, and towns all across the continent. Many of them traveled long distances to hunt, trade, and make war. The land they lived in shaped the way they lived. In turn, they shaped the land.

The Native Americans of North America

There were hundreds of Native American groups in North America. Native peoples differed because the places in which they lived were different. Each group invented tools and developed skills suitable to the land around them. They learned to **adapt,** or change, to survive in the conditions they faced. For example, the Powhatans (pou HAT unz) lived in what is now Virginia. Streams and rivers run through the woods there. To travel by water, the Powhatans learned to build canoes using large trees. They made sharp tools for carving out canoes from animal bones and stones. They depended on the rivers for food, too, and made traps, nets, and other tools to catch fish.

While each Native American group was different, people in the same areas often shared ways of doing things. Experts call these culture areas. Within each culture area, people lived under similar conditions.

UNLOCK THE BIG ?

I will know that Native American groups adapted to their environments.

Vocabulary

adapt
bison
economy

List ways in which the people used natural resources for their homes and clothing. Circle examples in the picture.

For this reason, people from the same culture areas often had similar cultures. For example, Native Americans from the Great Plains lived on the grasslands that cover the middle part of North America. Many of them depended on the bison, or buffalo, to meet their needs. The **bison** was a large animal that once roamed the plains by the millions.

2. **Circle** a Native American group that lived near the Cherokees and was part of the same culture area. **Draw** a box around a group that lived near the Yokuts.

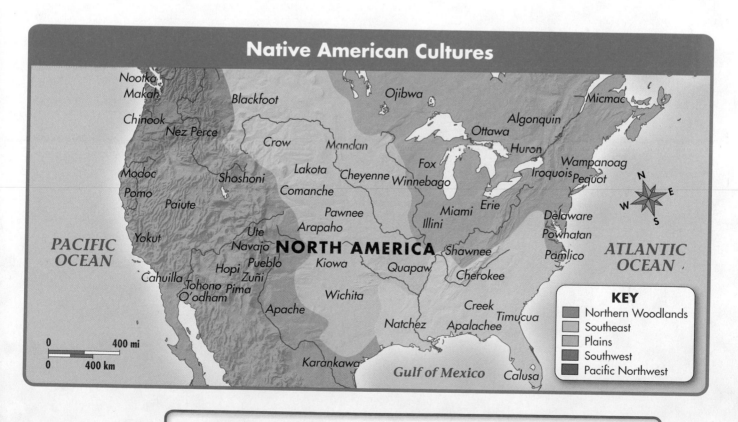

Native American Cultures

Nootka
Makah
Blackfoot
Ojibwa
Micmac
Chinook
Algonquin
Nez Perce
Ottawa
Crow
Mandan
Huron
Modoc
Lakota
Fox
Wampanoag
Shoshoni
Cheyenne
Winnebago
Iroquois
Pequot
Pomo
Comanche
Paiute
Pawnee
Miami
Erie
Arapaho
Illini
Delaware
Yokut
Ute
NORTH AMERICA
Shawnee
Powhatan
Navajo
Hopi Pueblo
Kiowa
Quapaw
Pamlico
PACIFIC OCEAN
Cahuilla
Zuñi
Cherokee
ATLANTIC OCEAN
Tohono O'odham
Pima
Wichita
Creek
Apache
Natchez
Timucua
Apalachee
Karankawa
Gulf of Mexico
Calusa

0   400 mi
0   400 km

KEY
Northern Woodlands
Southeast
Plains
Southwest
Pacific Northwest

Native American Economies

The bison was key to the economy of many Plains peoples, such as the Cheyennes (shye ANZ) and Lakota. An **economy** is the system by which a group makes, shares, and uses goods. While some people farmed on the plains, life for many Native Americans there depended on bison. The animals supplied food, fuel, clothing, and coverings for tepees. People moved often, following bison herds across the plains.

Native Americans of the Northern Woodlands, such as the Iroquois, often combined farming with hunting and gathering. Their housing styles varied. Two examples are longhouses and wigwams that were made from small trees, animal skins, and bark.

In the Pacific Northwest, peoples such as the Makah and Nootka depended on the sea. They were experts at catching fish, whales, and seals. These animals provided food, tools, and clothing. Everything the people in this area needed was nearby.

3. This painting shows a camp with tepees near the Great Lakes. **Write** how the people in the painting used the resources listed below.

water ....

....

animal hides ....

....

trees ....

....

plants ....

....

....

As a result, they often lived in settled villages for at least part of the year. Using wood from the forests, they built sturdy wooden houses. They also used wood to carve impressive totem poles that displayed symbols of the natural world.

Hunting and gathering were central to many groups living in the Southwest near what is now California and Nevada, such as the Cahuilla (kuh WEE uh). Often, food was hard to find. Some groups traveled long distances to search for wild plants and animals. During the winters, they built homes partly underground. When they traveled, they often built simple shelters made of brush. That way, they could move quickly from one temporary home to another.

The Southwest area that is now Arizona and New Mexico is a dry land. Its resources, including water and trees, are often scarce. The Pueblo people of this area grew much of their food, including squash, corn, and beans. They also grew cotton to make into clothing.

Farming was also the main activity for the Cherokees and other groups in the Southeast. Native farmers planted corn, beans, and squash. After picking the foods, they dried and burned the remaining stalks and leaves. This added nutrients to the soil. People in this area were also expert hunters. They ate the meat of the animals they caught and made tools from the bones.

Trade was another way Native Americans got the goods they needed and wanted. People from one area often traveled long distances to trade with Native Americans in other areas.

Native Americans Change the Land

Native Americans were skilled at using what the land gave them. They made and used tools to help them hunt and gather food or to make farming easier. They also found ways to change the land so that it could better supply the things they needed.

The Pueblo people had limited water available to them and used it carefully. They dug irrigation canals to bring water to their crops. Their use of irrigation shows that the Pueblos did not just adapt to the land. They actually changed it for their needs.

4. The Makah in the Pacific Northwest carved totem poles from huge trees found there. **Circle** the parts of the pole that symbolize birds.

15

Some Native Americans used fire to change the land to help improve hunting or get rid of pests.

Another way Native Americans changed the land was by setting fires in forests or grasslands. The fires helped in many ways. In California, native peoples burned shrubs to help grow grasses that attracted deer and other animals. In the Southeast, burning forest underbrush also made deer hunting easier. Other groups used fire to get rid of pests. Some experts think that these fires forever changed the types of plants that grow in many parts of North America.

In Florida, the Calusa people actually made some of the land on which they lived. Mound Key, an island, is thought to have been the site of the main Calusa town. The island itself is a mound of shells collected by the Calusas!

Changing Ways of Life

Native Americans changed not only the land, but their own ways of living. Groups that were successful farmers could stay in one place for long periods of time. They developed permanent types of homes. An example is the large longhouse built by the Iroquois in the Northern Woodlands.

Native Americans on the Plains changed their way of life dramatically, too, in the 1500s. That was when they first traded with Spanish explorers for horses. The Plains people became expert at using horses for hunting and in warfare. They gave up being farmers and kept on the move. This new means of transportation greatly changed their lives.

5. For each culture area, **write** one major activity that made up the economy of the native peoples who lived there.

Culture Areas and Their Economies

Plains	Depended on bison
Northern Woodlands	Both farming and hunting-gathering
Pacific Northwest	
Southeast	
Southwest	

6. ⊙ **Compare and Contrast Draw** pictures to contrast the foods eaten by Native Americans who were hunter-gatherers with those eaten by native peoples who were farmers.

Got it?

7. ⊙ **Compare and Contrast Contrast** the type of housing used by Native Americans who moved around frequently with that used by peoples who stayed in one place.

....

....

....

....

8. ❓ You are hiking with your parents in the Southwest. You notice how hot and dry the land is. **Write** about how the land might have been challenging to ancient people in the area.

my Story Ideas

....

....

....

▪ **Stop!** I need help with ....

▮ **Wait!** I have a question about ....

▶ **Go!** Now I know ....

Native American Cultures

Native Americans today still teach their children important adult skills, such as weaving and planting.

The lives of Native Americans included much more than gathering food and making shelters. Like people everywhere, they had families, friends, and ways of learning. They told stories, played games, and created music and art. Native Americans had deep religious beliefs and practices, and formed complex governments. In other words, they had rich and varied cultures.

What Is Culture?

Culture is the way of life of a group of people. It includes their art, rules, beliefs, and history. Culture is what people learn from their community.

Tlingit (TLIHN ket) dancers at a modern-day potlatch (PAHT lach) in Alaska wear traditional clothing and perform stories of their people.

Draw a picture of a skill you will need to learn to become an adult in your culture. Explain why the skill is necessary.

UNLOCK THE BIG ? I will know that cultures varied widely among Native American peoples.

Vocabulary

nomad   ancestor
government
council
league

One part of culture is the way people work. The tools and skills one group uses set it apart from other groups. For example, the Cherokees' practice of farming in the Southeast had little in common with the bison-hunting of the Blackfoot people in the Plains.

Native American cultures differed in many other ways as well. People from different groups spoke different languages and practiced different arts and crafts.

Clothing and hairstyles are other features of culture. Feathered headdresses, such as the one pictured here, were used by some Native Americans. Some peoples wore some version of the Mohawk hairstyle, where stiff hair stood on end down the middle of the scalp.

Different cultures have their own celebrations. Groups in the Northwest held great feasts called potlatches. At these events, hosts showered guests with food and gifts. The event was a way of showing off a person's wealth and rank in the community.

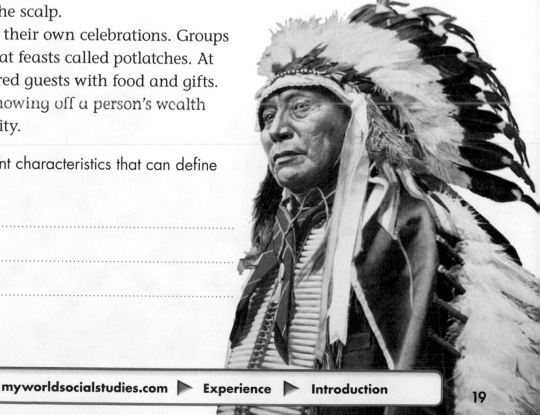

Sioux chief Hollow Horn Bear wears a feathered headdress.

1. **Identify** three different characteristics that can define a culture.

   ....

   ....

   ....

Daily Life for Native Americans

In general, Native American men and women had clear roles. Both roles were vital to a group's survival.

Women played the central role in gathering and preparing food. If there were farm fields or gardens, women were responsible for them. They also gathered wild foods, such as nuts and berries. After a successful hunt, the women butchered the bison or cleaned the fish.

Women were also in charge of family and home life. A key task was caring for children. In addition, women made clothing and other household goods. On the Plains in the north-central part of the United States, this task included preparing and sewing bison skins. In the Pacific Northwest, a woman might make clothes using cedar bark. For **nomads,** who moved often to search for food, household work meant moving the house, too. Plains women, for example, took down the tepees and put them up in the new camping place.

Native American men did the hunting and fishing for their village and family. While women usually tended crops, men handled some key agricultural tasks. For example, they helped clear fields for planting.

Men's work also included protecting the community when different groups came into conflict over land. Men also traveled from the village on trading missions.

This Zuni storyteller is passing on history and traditions to children in his village.

2. ◉ **Compare and Contrast List** two roles that women played in feeding their families.

....

....

....

....

List two roles that men played in feeding their families.

....

....

....

....

Children's Roles

Native Americans treasured children and believed they had a special connection to the spirit world. Young children were watched carefully by their parents and the whole village. They stayed close to their mothers to be fed and protected. They helped mothers in their work.

Childhood, however, was short. Children became adults in their early teenage years. Boys and girls began training early to learn the roles of men and women. Boys had to prove themselves in difficult tests, such as spending time alone in the wilderness. Girls also learned wilderness skills, such as how to gather food. Both boys and girls learned from storytellers, who passed on the group's traditions.

Of course, both Native American children and adults also had fun! Some groups held celebrations to mark key events in a child's life, such as the first fish caught. Children also played many games, some of which taught skills they would need. For example, the people of the Northern Woodlands played a form of lacrosse. Playing the game prepared young men to be hunters and warriors.

Playing lacrosse with equipment such as these sticks helped Native Americans learn key life skills.

3. **Fill in** the chart with details about the roles of Native American men, women, and children.

Roles of Native American Family Members

Women	Men	Children
	Men hunted and did some farm chores. They protected the village and went on trade missions.	

A Sioux chief speaks to the group's council and family members to help make a decision.

Native American Leaders and Rules

Most Native Americans believed that individuals were responsible for acting properly and making good choices. They also developed systems for making rules and decisions to help guide the group. That is, they developed systems of **government.**

A group's government usually fit its way of life. For example, nomads often traveled in small family units. The top male, who was often the father, served as leader. Other family members could challenge the leader's decisions.

Settled groups had more formal systems of government. Often, they had a decision-making body called a **council.** A council might be made up of leaders from the group's main families. Councils often followed a single leader, or chief. A chief worked with the other leaders; he did not rule the group like a king. The chief's power was sometimes passed down in a family. At other times, it was given to those who did great deeds. Some groups had separate chiefs for wartime and peacetime.

22

In the Southwest, a Pueblo town's government was led by its religious leader. This person had the power to give other villagers important jobs, such as governor or war chief. In turn, the people in these positions took advice from a council. This council was made up of men who had served as leaders at other times.

Governments of Large Nations

Small groups often combined with other groups to form large nations. Sometimes the groups were forced to join the larger nation. The Powhatans are an example. They included many groups controlled by a single, powerful chief.

In what is today New York state, five different nations joined forces to form a league. A **league** is a group whose members share the same goals. The members of the League of the Iroquois (EAR uh kwoy) called themselves the People of the Longhouse, or Haudenosaunee (haw duh noh SAW nee).

The League of the Iroquois had clear rules to make sure the members worked together in peace. A 50-person council of men made the League's decisions. The council members were chosen by leading women from each member group. These women could also remove and replace council members. All League decisions needed the consent of all five groups.

4. **Fill in** the graphic organizer with the rules of the council of the Iroquois. **List** the roles of men and women in the government.

The Government of the League of the Iroquois

How the Council Worked
- Included representatives from all five groups

Role of Men
- Discussed problems and made decisions

Role of Women
- Chose council members

Native American Religion

Most Native Americans were deeply religious. They still are today. Many Native Americans in the past worshipped a god or gods. For example, some groups believed the sun was a god who brings warmth and light.

In many groups, people believed that animals and the earth had spirits. It was important to seek their help and favor. For example, hunters might ask permission from the spirits before killing animals or catching fish. Southeast and Northern Woodlands peoples held religious festivals to celebrate the harvest. They danced, sang, and prayed. The celebrations were a time for people to give thanks and make themselves worthy of the land's gifts.

In the Southwest, Pueblo people, such as the Hopi, sought help and advice from kachinas (kuh CHEE nuhs). These are spirits that represent natural forces, such as wind and storms, or ancestors. An **ancestor** is a relative who lived in the past. Pueblo artists carved beautiful kachina dolls. These helped children learn the important traditions and beliefs of the group. For some group celebrations, dancers dressed as kachinas. They performed special dances meant to call forth the kachinas into the presence of the group. Such dances are still held today.

The Jemez, a Pueblo group in the Southwest, performed a Green Corn Dance at harvest time.

Many Native American groups had religious leaders called shamans. People believed shamans had special knowledge or skills, such as the ability to heal the sick or to communicate with the gods. In some groups, shamans were men; in others, both men and women held the role.

This kachina doll represents one of the Hopi people's gods.

5. **Explain** how kachina dolls were important to Pueblo culture.

....

....

....

....

....

Got it?

6. ● **Compare and Contrast** **Explain** some of the similarities and differences among Native American governments.

....

....

....

....

7. ❓ You visit a pueblo to learn more about the links between past and present Puebloan cultures. **Write** a list of things you would like to learn to see how today's Pueblo culture is like ancient Puebloan life.

my Story Ideas

....

....

....

◻ **Stop!** I need help with ....

❚❚ **Wait!** I have a question about ....

▶ **Go!** Now I know ....

Study Guide

Lesson 1

Ancient American Civilizations

- Scientists think the first humans came to the Americas thousands of years ago, crossing from Asia to North America.
- As they migrated, these early Americans formed different cultures.
- Civilizations included the Mayas and Aztecs.

Lesson 2

Adapting to Different Places

- By the late 1400s, hundreds of Native American groups existed in North America.
- Native Americans learned ways of adapting to the land.
- They also adapted the land to meet their needs.

Lesson 3

Native American Cultures

- Among Native Americans, many different cultures emerged.
- Daily life featured clear roles for men, women, and children.
- Native American groups developed religions and formed governments to serve their needs.

Review and Assessment

Lesson 1

Ancient American Civilizations

1. According to most experts, in what way did people first come to the Americas?

....

....

....

....

....

2. What is one reason people who settled different parts of North and South America developed different cultures?

....

....

....

....

3. **Put** the letter of each culture next to one of its key characteristics.

   a. Inuits

   b. Mound Builders

   c. Ancient Puebloans

   .... learned to farm in a dry climate

   .... developed kayaks for hunting in icy waters

   .... built huge earthen structures

Lesson 2

Adapting to Different Places

4. What were two types of economies found among different Native American groups?

....

....

....

....

5. What was the most important resource for people of the Plains?

....

....

....

....

6. **Complete** the sentences below with the correct word or words.

   a. Native American groups used .... as a way to improve hunting or to clear land to help certain plants grow.

   b. The Calusa people of present-day Florida used huge amounts of shells to

   ....

   c. The Pueblo people used .... to grow crops in a dry land.

Lesson 3

Native American Cultures

7. **Circle** the correct answer.

   Which was a key role of Native American women in feeding their families?

   A. Taking down and setting up tepees

   B. Planting and harvesting crops

   C. Hunting and fishing for food

   D. Trading with other groups

8. ◉ **Compare and Contrast** How did the government structure of small and large Native American groups differ?

   ....

   ....

   ....

   ....

   ....

9. What do kachina dolls represent to the Pueblo people?

   ....

   ....

   ....

   ....

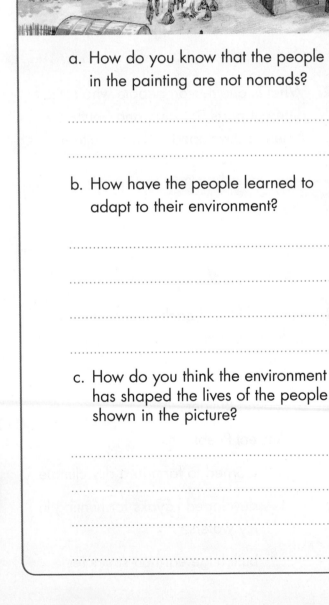

10. ❓ **How does the environment shape how we live?**

    Use the illustration and questions below to think more about this chapter's Big Question.

    a. How do you know that the people in the painting are not nomads?

    ....

    ....

    b. How have the people learned to adapt to their environment?

    ....

    ....

    ....

    ....

    c. How do you think the environment has shaped the lives of the people shown in the picture?

    ....

    ....

    ....

Go online to write and illustrate your own **myStory Book** using the **myStory Ideas** from this chapter.

How does the environment shape how we live?

Native Americans lived in lands with a wide range of climates and resources. Some lived in desert regions where water, plants, and animals were scarce. Others lived in woodlands filled with usable plants and game animals. The places people lived shaped how they lived. The same is true today. People live in many types of environments, which affects the choices they make every day.

Think about the environment where you live. **Write** about how it affects the life you live. Then, **draw** a picture that shows one example of how people in your community have adapted to their environment.

....

....

....

....

While you're online, check out the **myStory Current Events** area where you can create your own book on a topic that's in the news.

Age of Exploration

THE BIG **?** Why do people explore?

Describe a time you explored a new place. Then **write** why you explored it and how you felt about it.

....

....

....

....

....

....

An explorer climbs in an
underground cavern.

Álvar Núñez Cabeza de Vaca
Explorer of Florida and Texas

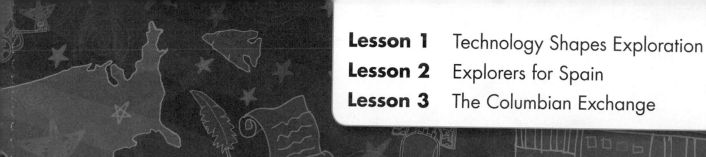

my Story Video

The story of Álvar Núñez Cabeza de Vaca is one of adventure and exploration, of seeing new lands and meeting new people. It is also a story of hardship. His journey was full of challenges—storms, hunger, slavery, and more.

Not much is known of Cabeza de Vaca's early life. He was born in Spain in the year 1490. He spent the first part of his career in the military and began exploring when he was nearly 40 years old.

In 1527, Cabeza de Vaca sailed from Spain on his first voyage, as an officer under the command of Pánfilo de Narváez (PAHN fee loh deh nahr VAH ehs). The goal of the voyage was to take control of land in North America. European rulers were eager to claim land in North America and expand their country's power.

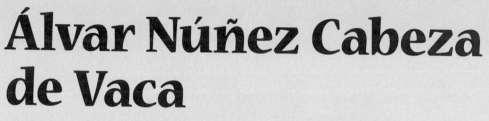

Cabeza de Vaca left Spain to explore the Americas.

31

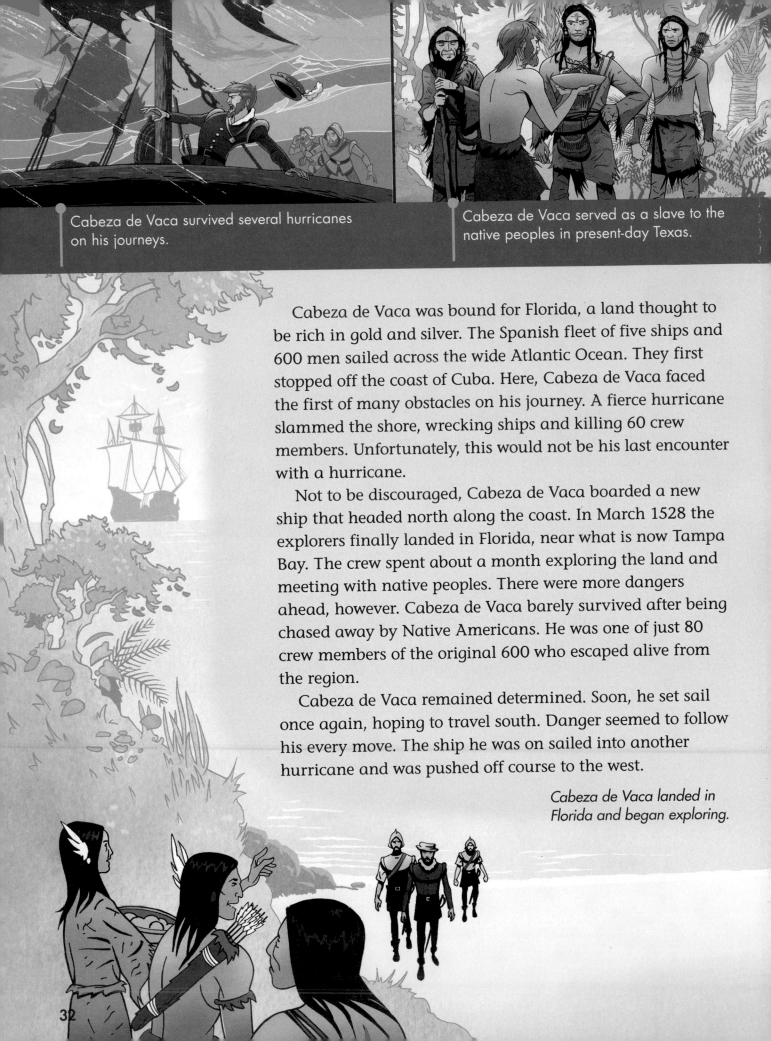

Cabeza de Vaca survived several hurricanes on his journeys.

Cabeza de Vaca served as a slave to the native peoples in present-day Texas.

Cabeza de Vaca was bound for Florida, a land thought to be rich in gold and silver. The Spanish fleet of five ships and 600 men sailed across the wide Atlantic Ocean. They first stopped off the coast of Cuba. Here, Cabeza de Vaca faced the first of many obstacles on his journey. A fierce hurricane slammed the shore, wrecking ships and killing 60 crew members. Unfortunately, this would not be his last encounter with a hurricane.

Not to be discouraged, Cabeza de Vaca boarded a new ship that headed north along the coast. In March 1528 the explorers finally landed in Florida, near what is now Tampa Bay. The crew spent about a month exploring the land and meeting with native peoples. There were more dangers ahead, however. Cabeza de Vaca barely survived after being chased away by Native Americans. He was one of just 80 crew members of the original 600 who escaped alive from the region.

Cabeza de Vaca remained determined. Soon, he set sail once again, hoping to travel south. Danger seemed to follow his every move. The ship he was on sailed into another hurricane and was pushed off course to the west.

Cabeza de Vaca landed in Florida and began exploring.

Spanish explorers were surprised to see Cabeza de Vaca dressed in rags and traveling with native peoples.

The accounts Cabeza de Vaca wrote of his journeys are filled with valuable information about the Texan land and people.

Cabeza de Vaca spent the next four years living with native peoples near present-day Galveston, Texas. In order to obtain food and shelter, he served them as a slave. At times, Cabeza de Vaca pretended to be a healer, hoping this would earn him better treatment. He also worked as a trader, bringing shells and beans from the coast to trade for animal skins in the interior of the country.

By 1532 Cabeza de Vaca was one of only four members of his crew still alive. He convinced his three companions to walk hundreds of miles to reach Spanish land in Mexico. Their route likely passed through present-day Texas, New Mexico, Arizona, and then into Mexico. They became the first Europeans to travel in the American West.

In July 1536, Cabeza de Vaca finally met a group of Spanish explorers in Mexico. He was thrilled to see them after so many years living among native peoples. Later he wrote about the meeting:

"[The Spaniards were] dumbfounded [amazed] at the sight of me, strangely dressed and in company with Indians. They stood staring for a long time."

Cabeza de Vaca returned to Spain in 1537 and wrote about his experiences. A true adventurer at heart, he later traveled to South America to explore new lands.

Think About It Based on this story, do you think Cabeza de Vaca's reasons for exploring were worth the dangers he faced? As you read this chapter, draw conclusions to explain what Cabeza de Vaca's story tells about why people explore.

myworldsocialstudies.com ▶ Connect ▶ my Story Video

Technology Shapes Exploration

Envision It!

Explorers used a magnetic compass such as this one to help them know in which direction they should sail.

Because the sea surrounds Europe on three sides, Europeans long ago learned to travel the ocean. At first, most European sailors stayed close to land. Then new types of ships and new sailing instruments improved sea travel. Brave sailors set out for new lands and riches. Most looked for routes to trade with Asia. A few explorers found their way to North America.

Viking Explorers

The Vikings were from Scandinavia, a region in northern Europe that includes Norway. Beginning in the ninth century, the Vikings sailed the northern seas. The Vikings raided European towns. They also explored and settled new lands. One well-known Viking was Eric the Red, a red-headed adventurer. He sailed from Norway to Iceland and then to Greenland. His son, Leif Ericsson, was an explorer, too. Ericsson and his crew were likely the first Europeans to land in North America.

Leif Ericsson

1. This map shows Viking travels. **Complete** the route that Eric the Red might have taken from Norway to Greenland.

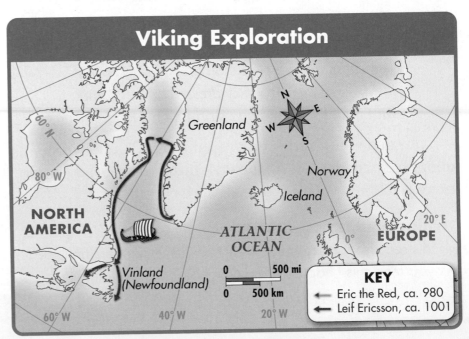

Viking Exploration

Greenland

Norway

Iceland

NORTH AMERICA

ATLANTIC OCEAN

EUROPE

Vinland (Newfoundland)

| 0 | 500 mi |
| 0 | 500 km |

KEY
← Eric the Red, ca. 980
← Leif Ericsson, ca. 1001

I will know that advances in technology helped Europeans explore trade routes and settle in new places.

Draw and label a tool you might use today to find your way.

Vocabulary

merchant   caravel

navigation   trading post

astrolabe   slave trade

technology

In 1001, Ericsson founded a settlement in what is today Canada. This Viking outpost did not last long. It would be hundreds of years before Europeans returned to North American shores. Europeans did not take an interest in sea exploration again until the 1400s. What caused explorers to sail beyond the familiar ocean waters around them?

Searching for Riches

By the 1400s, trade between Europe and Asia had increased. European **merchants**, people who buy and sell goods, bought popular Asian goods, such as silk and spices. Traders shipped these goods thousands of miles over rough, dangerous roads. Thieves sometimes attacked the traders, stealing their property. Even with these problems, trade with Asia made many people rich. European nations began to compete for control of trade routes. Some European rulers wanted to find a sea route to Asia to obtain its riches more easily.

2. ◉ **Draw Conclusions**
Fill in the conclusion based on the facts given.

New Routes to Asia

Fact
Goods from Asia were in demand in Europe.

Fact
Land routes to Asia were long, dangerous.

Conclusion

Explorers used astrolabes, such as this one, to help them find their way through unfamiliar waters.

Better Navigation Tools

Although a sea route from Europe to Asia would be longer than the land route, traveling by sea was faster. Sailors had begun using navigation tools that improved sea travel. **Navigation** is the process sailors use to plan their course and find their location far from land.

The Chinese had invented the magnetic compass centuries earlier. European sailors relied on it to know in which direction they were headed. The needle of a compass always points north so sailors could know their direction in relation to north. Another invention was the **astrolabe** (AS truh layb) from North Africa. This navigation tool measures the height of the sun or a star above the horizon. Astrolabes helped sailors tell how far north or south of the equator they had sailed.

These navigation tools also helped Europeans improve maps. Mapmakers learned to chart more accurately the locations of places such as harbors, mouths of rivers, and coastlines. Sailors felt more confident traveling in unfamiliar waters when they could follow routes already explored by other sailors.

3. **Explain** the purpose of these navigation tools, used by sailors during the 1400s.

Tools for Exploring

Tool	How the Tool Helped Sailors
Astrolabe	
Magnetic compass	
Maps	

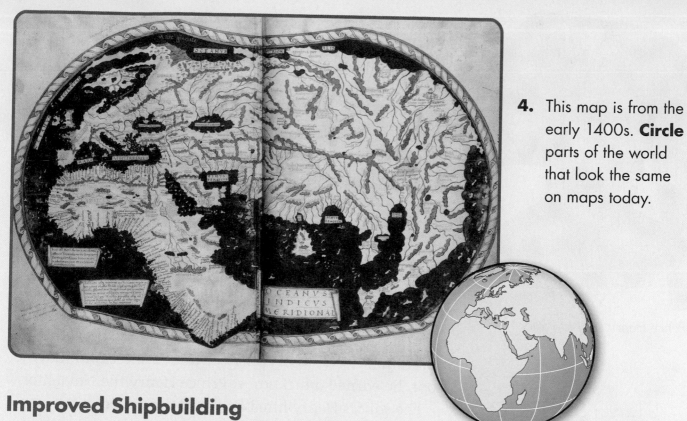

4. This map is from the early 1400s. **Circle** parts of the world that look the same on maps today.

Improved Shipbuilding

New shipbuilding technology made ocean travel easier in the 1400s. **Technology** is the use of scientific knowledge and new ideas to create practical tools that improve lives. In earlier times, heavy ships moved slowly, propelled by square sails. In the early 1400s, Portuguese shipbuilders invented a new kind of sailing ship called the **caravel**.

The smaller, lighter caravel had triangular sails to better control the wind. There were other improvements as well. Portuguese shipbuilders built the wooden decks without gaps and waterproofed the wood, covering it with tar and other materials. They braided stronger ropes and made long-lasting sails from canvas. Larger cargo areas in the ship could carry enough supplies for longer voyages. Later, builders added a square sail to the caravel, giving it better control.

This caravel is a replica of a fifteenth-century sailing vessel.

Prince Henry the Navigator

Portuguese Explorers

Portugal led the search to find a sea route to Asia. Its location on the western coast of Europe made it a perfect place for sailors to start their journeys. Also, Portuguese rulers encouraged exploration. They often provided the money sailors needed to make expensive sea voyages.

Prince Henry, the son of Portugal's king, started a school to teach navigation and mapmaking in about 1419. He had several reasons for opening the school. Henry wanted to know more about the world around him and to gain wealth by trading for African gold and ivory. As a Christian, he also wanted to spread his religion in Africa.

At Henry's school, sailors, scholars, mapmakers, and shipbuilders worked together to improve sea travel and invent new tools. Henry's school was so successful that soon he earned a nickname, Prince Henry the Navigator.

The sailors Henry hired explored the west coast of Africa. They scouted the region and set up forts and **trading posts**, which were stores and small settlements where goods could be bought and sold. Portuguese sailors also searched for a route to Asia around the southern tip of Africa. They wanted to be the first Europeans to reach Asia by sea in order to control trade there.

The Portuguese used forts such as this one in western Africa.

5. Circle details in the painting of Prince Henry's school that show it is a navigation school.

Gold and ivory were not the only items being traded in Africa. The Portuguese also took part in the **slave trade**. Slave traders bought and sold humans as property. While other countries also captured and enslaved small numbers of Africans, the Portuguese made slave trade an important business activity. As a result, the African slave trade grew. This cruel practice would continue for many centuries and expand to European colonies across the Atlantic Ocean.

6. Fill in the boxes with details about Portuguese exploration.

Facts About Portuguese Exploration

What made Portugal a good place for sea exploration?	Why did Prince Henry open his school?	What were the main accomplishments of Henry's voyages?
• •	• to learn about the world • to gain wealth through trade • to spread his religion • to improve sea travel	• •

Vasco da Gama

Reaching India

Prince Henry spent nearly 40 years providing money for voyages to Africa's western coast. However, his expeditions never managed to sail all the way around the tip of Africa. After Henry died in 1460, other Portuguese sailors continued searching for a sea route to Asia.

In 1487, Bartolomeu Dias (bar too loo MEH oo DEE uhs) led an expedition of three ships to explore Africa's western coast. As they neared the southern tip of the continent, fierce storms struck the ships. When the weather cleared, Dias made an exciting discovery. His ships had actually sailed around the tip of Africa! Finally, a Portuguese sea captain had achieved Prince Henry's goal of reaching Africa's east coast. The Portuguese named the tip of Africa the Cape of Good Hope.

Ten years later, Vasco da Gama followed Dias's route around Africa. Sailing even farther than Dias, he crossed the Indian Ocean and reached India. Da Gama's voyage allowed Portugal to take a leading position in India's rich spice trade.

7. **Draw** clouds where Dias encountered storms. **Write** *S* where da Gama traded for spices.

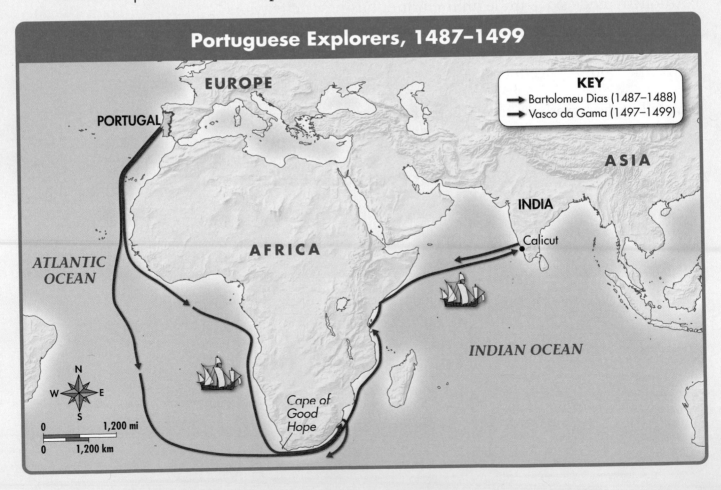

Portuguese Explorers, 1487–1499

KEY
→ Bartolomeu Dias (1487–1488)
→ Vasco da Gama (1497–1499)

EUROPE

PORTUGAL

ASIA

ATLANTIC OCEAN

AFRICA

INDIA

Calicut

INDIAN OCEAN

Cape of Good Hope

N W E S

0   1,200 mi
0   1,200 km

8. Draw a picture to illustrate each caption.

Dias's ships run into fierce storms off the coast of Africa.

With their triangular sails, caravels were lighter and faster than European ships had been before.

Got it?

9. ◉ **Draw Conclusions** Portuguese rulers paid the expenses of exploring for trade routes. How did Portugal benefit from Vasco da Gama's voyage to India?

....

....

....

10. ❓ You've just graduated from a school of navigation in Portugal and have been assigned to a voyage. **Write** a brief diary entry about your hopes for the future as an explorer.

my Story Ideas

....

....

....

⬛ **Stop!** I need help with ....

⏸ **Wait!** I have a question about ....

▶ **Go!** Now I know ....

Use Timelines

A timeline is a diagram that shows the sequence, or order, of a group of events. You can use a timeline to understand whether events happened before or after each other. Timelines also help you see whether events happened at almost the same time or were far apart in time.

Timelines are divided into sections. Each section shows an equal period of time. The timeline on this page covers a 500-year time span and is divided into periods of 100 years. Its subject is early European exploration from the time of the Vikings until the voyages of famous Portuguese explorers. Four events are shown on the timeline. A line is drawn from each event to its correct location on the timeline.

1001
Leif Ericsson founds settlement in Canada

1419
Prince Henry opens school

1487
Dias rounds Cape of Good Hope

| 1000 | 1100 | 1200 | 1300 | 1400 | 1500 |

1497
Da Gama sails to India

You can also use timelines to measure the amount of time between two events. Use the one above to calculate how much time passed between the voyages of Portuguese explorers Bartolomeu Dias and Vasco da Gama. Find the dates of the two events, and subtract the earlier one from the later one. The dates are 1487 and 1497, so there were 10 years between the voyages of Dias and da Gama. As you will see on the next page, Christopher Columbus set out on his first voyage in 1492. That was exactly halfway between the voyages of Dias and da Gama.

Try *it!*

Read the following paragraph about Christopher Columbus's first three voyages. Then, use the information to make a timeline.

Christopher Columbus sailed from Spain on his first voyage in August 1492. He made landfall later that year on an island in the Caribbean Sea. Columbus made a second voyage in September 1493 to explore more of the region. In 1494 Columbus founded La Isabela in the present-day Dominican Republic. He returned to Spain in 1496.

List the four dates mentioned in the paragraph. Then **write** a short description of the event that happened on each date.

Date: ....

Date: ....

Date: ....

Date: ....

1. Use your list to fill in the missing dates and events in the timeline below.

2. **Apply Create** your own timeline. **List** at least four major events that have happened to you during your life. **Draw** a timeline and place each event on it.

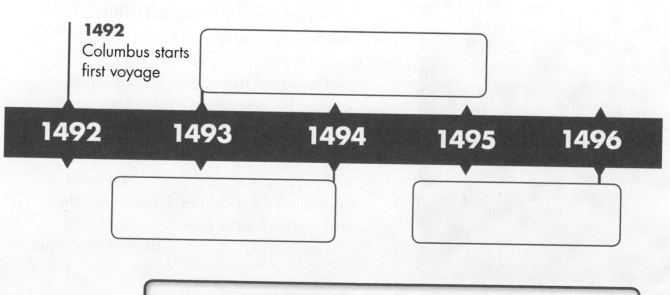

Explorers for Spain

Envision It!

An explorer meets with the king of Spain before leaving on a voyage of exploration to the Americas.

1. This painting shows the Tainos meeting Columbus and his crew at their landing. **Circle** details that show contrasts between the Tainos and the Europeans.

Christopher Columbus was a man with a bold plan. By the late 1400s, explorers had already reached Asia by sailing east from Europe. Columbus wanted to find a new route to Asia by sailing west across the Atlantic Ocean. Columbus had a lot of courage but not much money for the voyage. Who would help pay for such a dangerous trip?

Columbus Sets Sail

Columbus asked Portugal's king to fund his voyage. The answer was no. Next, he asked Spain's rulers. After several requests, King Ferdinand and Queen Isabella agreed to become Columbus's patrons. A **patron** gives financial support to another person or cause.

The Spanish rulers hoped to earn money from the gold and spices that Columbus expected to trade for in Asia. They needed money to pay for a war Spain had recently fought. Ferdinand and Isabella also hoped to spread Christianity in Asia and to start new Spanish settlements.

Columbus sailed from Spain with 90 men on three ships. After five weeks at sea, his weary crew spotted land and then reached shore on October 12, 1492. Columbus wrote in his journal:

"The crew . . . saw signs of land, and a small branch covered with berries. Everyone breathed afresh and rejoiced at these signs."
—Christopher Columbus

Write what the king might be saying to the explorer. What does the king want the explorer to do?

Vocabulary

patron

conquistador

expedition

empire

circumnavigate

colony

Columbus believed they had reached Asia. Instead, his ships had landed on an island in the Caribbean Sea, which is part of North America. Because he thought they were near India, Columbus named the region the West Indies and called its people Indians. The people he met had a different name for themselves. They were the Tainos (TYE nohz).

Columbus made three more voyages to the Americas. On these trips, he traded animals and crops with the Tainos. He also claimed land for Spain and started settlements. In 1494, he founded La Isabela in what is now the Dominican Republic. This was the first European town in North America.

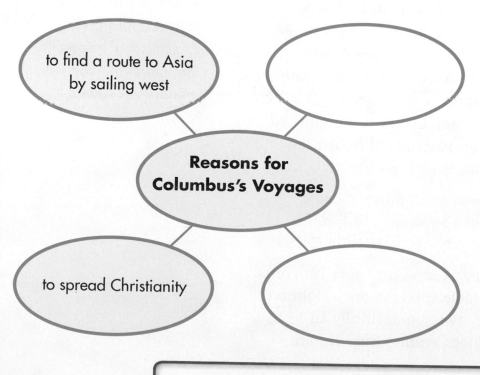

to find a route to Asia by sailing west

Reasons for Columbus's Voyages

to spread Christianity

2. ◉ **Main Ideas and Details Write** two more reasons for Columbus's voyages in the ovals.

Cortés and the Aztecs

News of the discovery of a land between Europe and Asia spread quickly throughout Europe. Soon, other Europeans set sail for the Americas. In the early 1500s, a group of Spanish soldiers, later called **conquistadors** (kahn KEES tuh dorz), or conquerors, arrived.

One conquistador, Hernán Cortés (er NAHN kor TEZ), led an **expedition**, or organized journey, to Mexico in 1519. Cortés had heard of the Aztec empire and its riches. An **empire** is a group of nations or peoples ruled by a single group or leader. Cortés planned to conquer the Aztecs.

Cortés gathered an army of Spanish soldiers and native peoples. He led them into the grand city of Tenochtitlán (tay noch tee TLAHN), the Aztec capital. Cortés was impressed by the city and the Aztec leader, Moctezuma (mahk teh ZOO muh). He wrote to the Spanish king:

". . .Of Moctezuma, and the wonderful grandeur and state that he maintains, there is so much to be told."
—Hernán Cortés

At first, Moctezuma welcomed Cortés and gave him gifts. Cortés responded by taking Moctezuma prisoner. Fighting broke out and lasted for nearly two years. Finally, in 1521, the Spaniards defeated the Aztecs, ending their empire.

3. This painting by a Spanish missionary in the 1500s, shows a battle between Cortés's soldiers and Aztec warriors near Tenochtitlán. The Aztecs are using spears and wearing quilted cotton armor. **Circle** the weapons and clothing that helped the Spaniards win the war against the Aztecs.

Ferdinand Magellan

In 1519, another explorer set sail from Spain. Ferdinand Magellan, an expert navigator, commanded five ships. Like Columbus, he hoped to reach Asia by sailing west. Magellan traveled south along the coast of South America until he found a strait, or narrow waterway, leading to the Pacific Ocean. From there, he thought the journey to Asia would be a short one. He was wrong. His ships sailed four months before spotting land. His men were weak and exhausted when they finally reached land in the Philippines, off the east coast of Asia.

Weeks later, Magellan was killed in a battle with native peoples in the Philippines. His crew continued sailing west back to Spain. Only one ship made it home, however. It was the first to **circumnavigate**, or sail completely around, the world.

Ferdinand Magellan explores near the tip of South America in a small boat from his fleet.

4. ◎ **Compare and Contrast Fill in** the Venn diagram with information about the voyages of Cortés and Magellan.

Comparing Voyages

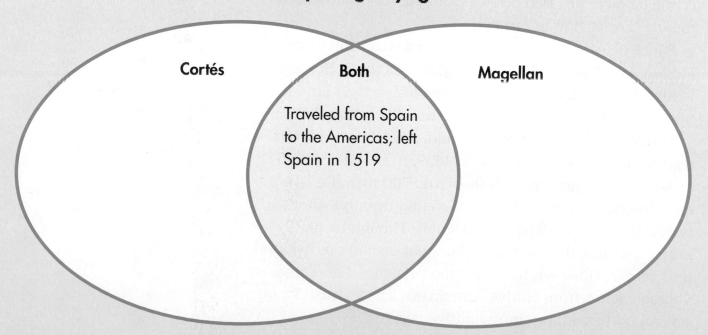

Cortés | Both | Magellan

Traveled from Spain to the Americas; left Spain in 1519

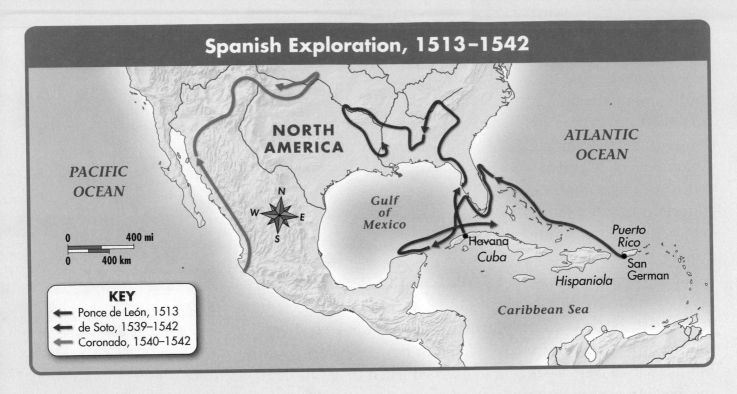

Spanish Exploration, 1513–1542

NORTH AMERICA

ATLANTIC OCEAN

PACIFIC OCEAN

Gulf of Mexico

0   400 mi
0   400 km

KEY
← Ponce de León, 1513
← de Soto, 1539–1542
← Coronado, 1540–1542

Havana
Cuba

Hispaniola

Caribbean Sea

Puerto Rico
San German

Exploring the North

Spanish conquistadors explored other parts of North America in their search for riches. Juan Ponce de León (hwahn PAHN suh day LEE awn) settled the island of Puerto Rico in 1508. There he heard myths about a magical spring that could turn old people young. The stories were not true.

Hoping to find this fountain of youth, Ponce de León led an expedition out of Puerto Rico in March 1513. A month later, at Easter time, he landed in present-day Florida. The name he gave this rich and colorful land, *Pescua Florida*, means "Easter flowers" in Spanish.

Ponce de León was probably the first European to visit Florida. Later, he tried to start settlements there. However, Native Americans in the area feared losing their land to the armed newcomers. They attacked, and the settlers left.

Other Spaniards explored Florida, sometimes with terrible results for the native peoples. In 1539, Hernando de Soto sailed to the region with 10 ships and 700 men. De Soto's expedition spent several years traveling through what is now the southeastern United States. Though he never found treasure, de Soto learned a great deal about the land and people. However, the expedition stole food and other valuable items from Native Americans. The Spanish fought several battles, killing many native peoples.

5. Write the answer to each question about the Spanish Explorers.

a. What led Ponce de León to travel north from Puerto Rico?

....

....

....

b. Who began an expedition on the Pacific coast?

....

48

Coronado's Expedition

Another Spanish explorer, Francisco Vásquez de Coronado, also wanted to search for treasure in the Americas. While serving as a Spanish leader in Mexico, he had heard rumors of a rich kingdom to the north called Cíbola (SEE buh luh). This mythical land was supposed to be filled with gold, silver, and jewels. Others had looked for it, but none had found it.

Coronado set out to find Cíbola in 1540. Hundreds of Native American soldiers and servants took part in the expedition along with several hundred Spanish soldiers. During their travels through present-day New Mexico, Arizona, and other southwestern states, Coronado claimed land for Spain. He also attacked and killed many native peoples. Like de Soto, Coronado found no treasure, and he returned to Mexico very disappointed. His men did discover several important landmarks in the Southwest. For example, one scouting party became the first Europeans to see the Grand Canyon in Arizona.

Francisco Coronado leads hundreds of Spanish and Native American soldiers in search of a mythical land filled with riches.

6. **Draw Conclusions** **Write** a conclusion based on the facts.

Measuring Spanish Accomplishments

Fact
Ponce de León explored Florida, but his settlements in the new land failed.

Fact
De Soto never found treasure, but he learned much about the people and land in the Southeast.

Fact
Coronado opened the Southwest to the Spaniards, but he never found great riches.

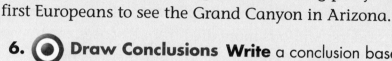

Conclusion

Settling in the Americas

In 1535, Spain established the colony of New Spain in North America. A **colony** is a settlement or area far from the country that rules it. New Spain became an important part of the Spanish Empire. Over time, New Spain would expand to include many islands in the Caribbean, as well as large parts of North and South America.

Towns sprang up throughout New Spain. In 1565, St. Augustine was founded in what is today Florida. It is the oldest town established by Europeans in the United States. Across the continent, in 1610, Spanish leaders founded Santa Fe in what is now New Mexico.

The settlers who arrived in New Spain came for several different reasons. Spanish officials moved to the colony to set up a government. Roman Catholic priests came to teach Native Americans about Christianity. Other colonists came to start farms and businesses or to search for gold and silver.

The Spanish takeover of New Spain brought harsh changes to Native Americans who had lived in the area for hundreds of years. Many native people were killed battling the conquistadors. Millions more died from diseases, such as smallpox, brought unknowingly to the Americas by the Spaniards. Native peoples who survived often lost their lands and property. Spanish settlers forced many of the Native Americans to work against their will in mines and on farms in New Spain.

This church, built on the Caribbean island of Cuba in the 1500s, reflects building styles from Spain. The bell tower and its arches are Spanish in design.

7. ⊙ **Cause and Effect Fill in** the missing effects in the graphic organizer.

Effects of Spanish Colonization

Cause		Effect
Spain sets up the colony of New Spain.	→	
Native American land is taken over by Spanish settlers.	→	

Got it?

8. ⊙ **Draw Conclusions** What conclusion can you draw about life for Native Americans in New Spain? **Explain** your answer.

....

....

....

9. ❓ You are in Spain and have signed on with Columbus for a voyage he is planning. **Describe** how you feel when you find out that Columbus wants to sail west across the Atlantic Ocean.

my Story Ideas

....

....

....

◻ **Stop!** I need help with ....

❚❚ **Wait!** I have a question about ....

▶ **Go!** Now I know ....

The Columbian Exchange

Plants and animals such as these were exchanged between people in the Eastern and Western Hemispheres.

1. Spanish explorers melted down Native American artifacts such as these to make gold bars to send to Europe. **Explain** how you know these objects were valuable to native peoples.

....

....

....

....

....

....

When Christopher Columbus landed in the Americas in 1492, he changed history. His arrival set in motion the **Columbian Exchange**. This was a movement of people, animals, plants, cultures, and even disease between the Eastern and Western hemispheres. The Columbian Exchange led to powerful changes around the world.

Changing Ways of Life

The arrival of Europeans in the Americas transformed Native American life. Conquistadors not only killed native peoples in battle, they also took over their cities. Then, settlers from Spain and later from other European countries arrived in the Americas to take their land.

These newcomers imposed more changes on Native Americans. Priests persuaded many native people to give up their old beliefs and become Christians. Colonists started large farms, growing sugar cane and other crops. They forced Native Americans to work in the fields. Native peoples were also compelled to work in dangerous, underground mines. The gold, silver, and other minerals they took from the earth were shipped back to Europe. As a result, countries such as Spain and Portugal gained both wealth and power from the Americas.

Label those you think came from the Eastern Hemisphere with E; label those from the Western Hemisphere with W.

UNLOCK THE BIG ?

I will know that the Columbian Exchange resulted in the exchange of useful crops and animals, as well as deadly diseases.

Vocabulary

Columbian Exchange

epidemic

devastation

Harmful Effects

Native peoples suffered in another way as well. Without knowing it, Europeans brought disease germs with them that had a terrible impact. Most Native Americans had no defense against diseases such as smallpox, measles, and malaria. Epidemics occurred among the native peoples. An **epidemic** is an outbreak of disease that spreads quickly and affects many people. The **devastation**, or great harm, was enormous. Millions of people died.

The exploration and colonization of the Americas affected Africans, too. As native populations decreased in the Americas from sickness and overwork, Europeans looked for new sources of labor. They turned to the slave trade. Captured Africans were enslaved, forced onto ships, and transported across the Atlantic Ocean. Many Africans died on the journey. Those who survived were forced to labor in the Americas, just as Native Americans had been.

2. ◉ **Cause and Effect**
Write the effect of colonization of the Americas on each group of people.

Effects of Colonization

Europeans	Native Americans	Africans
		captured, enslaved, and transported to the Americas to work

The Columbian Exchange

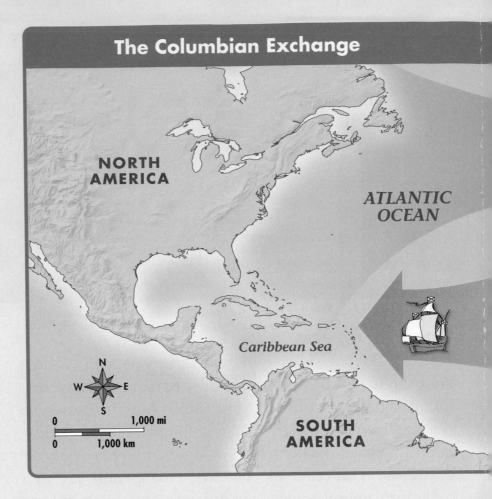

NORTH AMERICA

ATLANTIC OCEAN

Caribbean Sea

SOUTH AMERICA

N
W E
S

0   1,000 mi
0   1,000 km

A Powerful Exchange

When Europeans first landed in the Americas, they found plants and animals they had never seen before. Foods from the Americas, such as corn, peanuts, potatoes, squash, and pineapples became part of their diet. Turkeys, guinea pigs, and llamas were also new to them.

The Europeans, in turn, brought with them plants unknown in the Americas. These included wheat, rice, peaches, and lettuce. Some of the crops the Europeans brought, such as onions, coffee, bananas, and sugar cane, originally came from Africa or Asia. Animals common in Europe but new to the Americas also came by ship. They included horses, pigs, chickens, and cattle.

The arrival of the horse had an enormous impact on some Native American cultures. Horses transformed the way these Native Americans lived. Now, they could travel farther in search of food and hunt their prey more easily. Horses also allowed them to use bigger travois, or sleds, and to carry heavier loads than before. Native Americans became experts at riding horses and moving quickly across open territory to hunt or to fight against enemies.

3. **Circle** foods and animals that are mentioned in the text on these two pages. **List** the ones sent from the Americas in the box to the left of the map. **List** the ones sent from Europe, Africa, and Asia in the box to the right of the map.

54

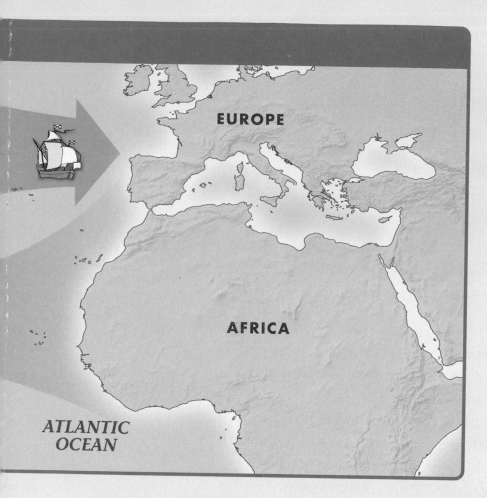

EUROPE

AFRICA

ATLANTIC
OCEAN

New Crops, Changing Diets

The Columbian Exchange transformed the way people on
both sides of the Atlantic farmed and ate. For example, potatoes
had been the main crop of the Incas in parts of South America.
Spanish explorers learned about potatoes and sent them back
to Europe. Over time, European farmers found potatoes to be an
easy-to-grow, nutritious crop. Along with corn, potatoes allowed
European populations to increase as people became healthier
and better fed.

Native American farmers learned to grow
European and African crops such as
wheat, rice, and sugar cane, and added
them to their diets. However, the arrival
of sugar cane had a harmful result, too.
The crop grew well in the warm, moist
climate of the Caribbean. Spanish settlers
in the Americas began growing huge
amounts of sugar cane to sell in Europe.
First they forced Native Americans to labor
in the sugar cane fields. Later, they made
enslaved Africans do the work.

*Horses brought by
Spaniards to the
Americas in the 1500s
dramatically changed
how many Native
American groups lived.*

55

Cultures combined at this wedding ceremony. Two Native American women wearing European style clothing married two Spanish men. Guests at the wedding included both Spaniards and Native Americans.

Cultures Collide

Plants, animals, and diseases were not the only things shared during the Columbian Exchange. People from the Western and Eastern Hemispheres also exchanged culture.

Europeans, Africans, and Native Americans had very different cultures. They wore different clothing, spoke different languages, and practiced different religions. Each culture had their own distinct styles of music, dance, and celebrations.

As the groups mixed, they shared parts of their cultures with one another. In some instances, they began to use words from other languages. Some cultural exchanges were forced, however. For example, Europeans forced many Native Americans to practice Christianity. When Native Americans resisted such changes, deadly conflicts sometimes occurred.

Even today, the exchange between cultures continues to affect people around the world. People eat foods and use goods from across the globe every day. Most places on Earth possess a mixture of cultures.

As this chart shows, many words that we use today in English began in other cultures that came together in the Americas.

Sharing Language		
European Words	**Native American Words**	**African Words**
coffee (Turkish)	canoe	banjo
guitar (Spanish)	hurricane	jazz
mosquito (Spanish)	moose	yam
sugar (French)	skunk	zebra

4. ⊙ **Draw Conclusions Read** the facts and **fill in** a conclusion on how the Columbian Exchange affected some native peoples.

Fact	Fact	Conclusion
Many Native Americans died from diseases brought by Europeans.	Deadly conflicts broke out when Native Americans resisted some changes.	

Got it?

5. ⊙ **Draw Conclusions Write** a conclusion based on these facts: (1) the introduction of horses changed how many Native Americans lived; (2) the introduction of potatoes changed how many Europeans ate.

....

....

....

6. You are on one of Columbus's ships that lands in the Americas. **Write** a letter to a friend telling about the strange and wonderful things you've seen and tasted.

my Story Ideas

....

....

....

....

⬛ **Stop!** I need help with ....

⏸ **Wait!** I have a question about ....

▶ **Go!** Now I know ....

Study Guide

Lesson 1

Technology Shapes Exploration

- Europeans sought sea routes to Asia to trade for valuable goods.
- Navigation tools and new ship designs made sea travel easier.
- Prince Henry of Portugal paid for voyages to Africa.
- Vasco da Gama was the first European to reach India by sea.

Lesson 2

Explorers for Spain

- Spain's rulers paid for voyages to find riches and to spread Christianity.
- Christopher Columbus landed in North America by sailing west.
- Spanish conquistadors searched for gold and glory in the Americas.
- In 1535, Spain established the colony of New Spain in the Americas.

Lesson 3

The Columbian Exchange

- Columbus's voyages sparked huge changes for Europeans, Native Americans, and Africans in the Western and Eastern hemispheres.
- As groups mixed, they shared parts of their cultures with one another. Animals and crops, as well as deadly diseases, were exchanged.

Review and Assessment

Lesson 1

Technology Shapes Exploration

1. What did people learn and do at Prince Henry's school?

....

....

....

2. Number the following events in the order, or sequence, that they happened.

_____ Bartolomeu Dias rounds Africa.

_____ Prince Henry starts his navigation school.

_____ Leif Ericsson founds a settlement in North America.

_____ Vasco da Gama reaches India.

3. **Complete** the word web. Give examples of advances in technology that improved sea travel during the 1400s.

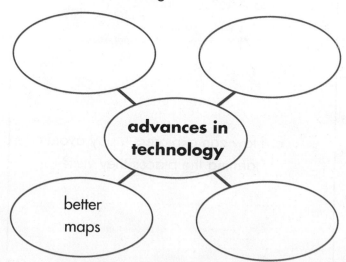

Lesson 2

Explorers for Spain

4. **Circle** the correct answer. Coronado and de Soto were disappointed because they

   A. lost battles to Native Americans.

   B. failed to find gold and riches.

   C. failed to spread Christianity.

   D. were not chosen to lead expeditions.

5. ◉ **Draw Conclusions Write** two facts to support this conclusion: The Spaniards treated the Aztecs harshly.

Fact: ....

....

....

Fact: ....

....

....

6. What was the significance of Ferdinand Magellan's voyage?

....

....

....

....

Lesson 3

The Columbian Exchange

7. **Fill in** the blanks in the paragraph below.

   Europeans introduced crops such as

   .... and animals such as

   .... to the Americas. They

   returned to Europe with vegetables such

   as .... and ....

8. What effect did the Columbian Exchange have on Africans?

   ....

   ....

   ....

   ....

9. **Complete** the chart. Give examples of useful and harmful effects of the Columbian Exchange on native peoples.

Useful Effects	Harmful Effects

10. ? **Why do people explore?**

Explorers left Europe to travel to distant places. Use these questions to think more about exploring.

a. Why were European rulers willing to pay for expensive explorations?

   ....

   ....

   ....

b. If you were an explorer in the 1500s, why might you explore the Americas or look for a new route to Asia?

   ....

   ....

   ....

c. How can explorers today avoid harming the places they visit?

   ....

   ....

   ....

Go online to write and illustrate your own **myStory Book** using the **myStory Ideas** from this chapter.

Why do people explore?

During the 1400s and 1500s, people knew little about the world beyond their shores. Even though we know much more about the world now, there is still much to discover. Deep ocean trenches, dense rainforests, and dark caverns are just a few of Earth's unexplored places. People still explore to see new places, learn about new cultures, and just to have fun!

List details about an unusual place you have explored on a trip or in your neighborhood. Then, **describe** your adventure. Explain why you explored the place and how you felt about it.

....

....

....

....

....

Now **draw** an image that shows something interesting you saw while exploring.

While you're online, check out the **myStory Current Events** area where you can create your own book on a topic that's in the news.

Settlements Take Root

THE BIG ? **Why do people leave their homelands?**

Describe your feelings about your home. Then **write** about what might cause you to leave it and start a new life somewhere else.

....

....

....

....

Plimouth Plantation in Plymouth, Massachusetts, recreates the life of English settlers.

Jamestown Settlement
Three Cultures Meet

my Story Video

"Welcome to Jamestown, Kaylee," says Julie. Julie is Kaylee's guide at the Jamestown Settlement in what is now Virginia. Jamestown, explains Julie, was home to a group of people who came from England in 1607. That was thirteen years before the Pilgrims arrived in Massachusetts.

"There were 104 original settlers, all men and boys," Julie adds. "Women came later. It took them 144 days to sail here on three different ships." The settlers were sent by the Virginia Company in London. Its investors hoped to find riches in the Americas. They hoped to find a route to India and its spices, too.

Julie and Kaylee board the *Susan Constant*, a replica of an original ship. "Wow," says Kaylee, "this seems really old!"

Kaylee gets ready to board a replica of one of the ships that brought the settlers to Jamestown.

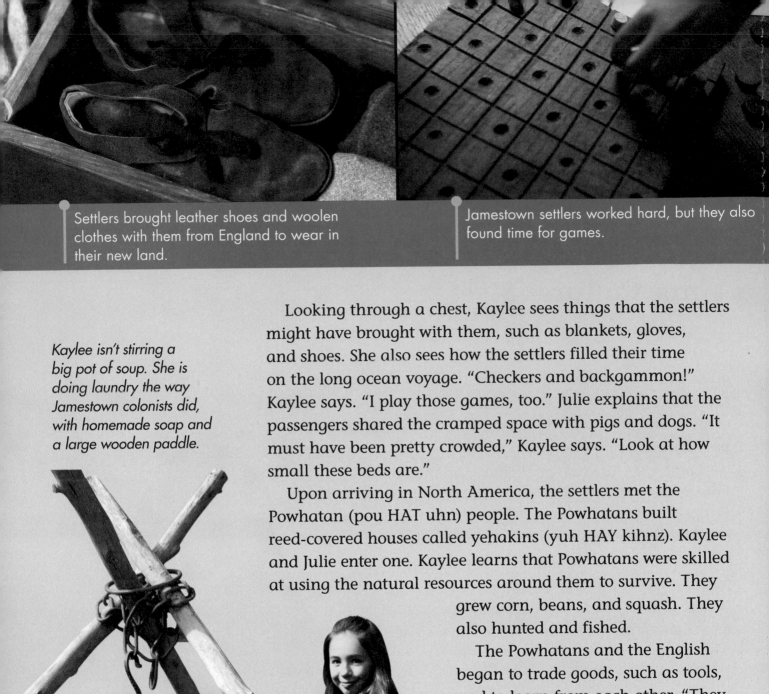

Settlers brought leather shoes and woolen clothes with them from England to wear in their new land.

Jamestown settlers worked hard, but they also found time for games.

Kaylee isn't stirring a big pot of soup. She is doing laundry the way Jamestown colonists did, with homemade soap and a large wooden paddle.

Looking through a chest, Kaylee sees things that the settlers might have brought with them, such as blankets, gloves, and shoes. She also sees how the settlers filled their time on the long ocean voyage. "Checkers and backgammon!" Kaylee says. "I play those games, too." Julie explains that the passengers shared the cramped space with pigs and dogs. "It must have been pretty crowded," Kaylee says. "Look at how small these beds are."

Upon arriving in North America, the settlers met the Powhatan (pou HAT uhn) people. The Powhatans built reed-covered houses called yehakins (yuh HAY kihnz). Kaylee and Julie enter one. Kaylee learns that Powhatans were skilled at using the natural resources around them to survive. They grew corn, beans, and squash. They also hunted and fished.

The Powhatans and the English began to trade goods, such as tools, and to learn from each other. "They had a complicated relationship," Julie says. The settlers began to take over land the Powhatans considered their own. This led to fighting between the groups.

Julie explains that the settlers mostly worked the land, did chores, and guarded the fort. Occasionally, they had time for recreation. Kaylee got to try her hand at ring toss.

Standing inside a reconstructed yehakin, Kaylee examines items used by colonists and Native Americans.

A modern-day actor at Jamestown Settlement makes metal tools in a blacksmith shop.

"It must have been a pretty tough life for the English, especially after what they were used to," says Kaylee. "But walking around the settlement, I can see how exciting it must have been to start a new life in a different land."

The Powhatans and the English were not the only ones living in or near Jamestown, Kaylee learns. Africans who had been forced into slavery in West Africa arrived in the colony and were made to work for the settlers. The Africans introduced new techniques for toolmaking and fishing. Kaylee and Julie compare tools made by the English, Powhatans, and Africans. "They were all pretty handy," Kaylee points out.

The meeting of three different cultures was not easy. The English gave up a more comfortable life to come to Jamestown, dreaming of wealth but facing starvation. The Africans, brought to North America against their will, endured the horrors of slavery. The Powhatans found themselves being forced to share land they had considered their home for hundreds of years.

"Here in Jamestown, these three cultures met and came together," Julie says. "Their ideas and technologies blended together to form the culture of colonial Virginia."

Think About It Based on this story, how do you think the English settlers felt about their decision to move across the Atlantic Ocean? As you read the chapter ahead, think about why people crossed the Atlantic to come to the Americas and how their lives and the lives of others would have changed.

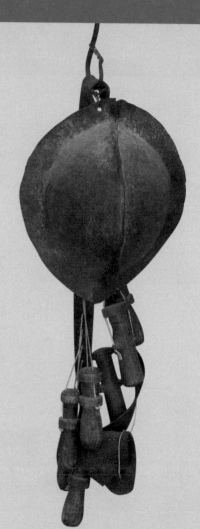

Colonists kept their gunpowder dry by hanging wooden powder flasks and musket ball pouches from nails on the walls of their cabins.

Lesson 1

The Spanish Colony in the Americas

Envision It!

The Spaniards set up a colony in the Americas that changed the lives of Native Americans.

Spain conquered and settled the Americas for several reasons. Spain's **monarchs,** or rulers, saw an opportunity to gain great wealth and power. The Spanish Catholic Church also hoped to persuade native peoples to accept the Catholic faith. However, first Spain had to take control of the lands they came to call New Spain. These lands were already settled by Native Americans.

The Colony of New Spain

In what is today Mexico, the Spaniards fought and conquered the Aztec people living there. They also defeated other Native Americans who stood in their way. By the mid-1500s, Spain controlled a large colony in the Americas.

As Spanish leaders had hoped, New Spain was rich in gold and silver. Soon the colony was shipping tons of treasure back to Spain. Enslaved Native Americans did most of the hard mining work. It was the Spanish, however, who benefited from selling the gold and silver.

Ranching and farming were also important in New Spain. At the heart of these businesses was the encomienda (en koh mee EN duh). An **encomienda** was a grant from the Spanish government that gave a Spanish settler the right to control local Native Americans.

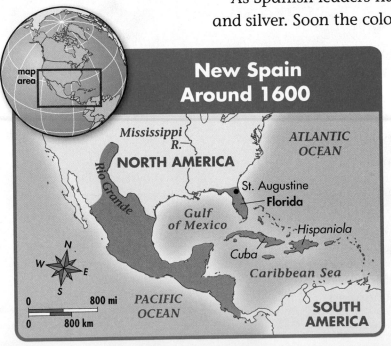

New Spain Around 1600

map area

Mississippi R.

NORTH AMERICA

Rio Grande

ATLANTIC OCEAN

St. Augustine

Florida

Gulf of Mexico

Hispaniola

Cuba

Caribbean Sea

N W E S

0 800 mi
0 800 km

PACIFIC OCEAN

SOUTH AMERICA

Draw a picture that shows an event or incident that would change your life.

UNLOCK THE BIG ?

I will know that Spain created a large colony in the Americas.

Vocabulary

monarch
encomienda
class structure
missionary

Native Americans in New Spain had very little control over their lives. The settlers were supposed to protect and care for native people and teach them Christianity. The native people were expected to repay the settlers with free labor, gold, silver, and other goods.

Native Americans, along with enslaved people brought from Africa, ranked lowest in the colony's class structure. A **class structure** is a system for ranking people, often according to power or wealth. There were three classes above Native Americans. The most powerful people in New Spain were Spaniards born in Spain. They were known as *peninsulares* (pay neen soo LAHRS). They held most of the highest government and Church positions. Next were the *creoles* (KREE ohls). These were people born in New Spain to Spanish parents. Many creoles owned land. Below them were *mestizos* (me STEE zohs), people who were of mixed Spanish and Native American background. The *mestizos* were the largest class.

1. ◉ **Categorize Complete** the diagram by labeling the different classes of society in New Spain, with the highest rank at the top.

mestizos

The Settlement at St. Augustine

Spanish explorers traveled deep into North America in the early 1500s. Spain also tried several times to establish settlements in Florida. However, bad weather, conflict with Native Americans, and other problems stopped these efforts.

Then, in 1565, Spain decided to try again. A year before, settlers from France had built a fort in northern Florida at present-day Jacksonville. Spain saw France as a rival for control of the Americas. So Spain sent a small fleet to destroy the French fort. Then they built their own fort and town a little farther south. They called it St. Augustine (saynt AW guhs teen). Unlike earlier colonies, this one survived. Today it is the oldest European settlement in the United States.

Supporting St. Augustine was expensive, and Spanish officials talked of abandoning the colony. Its governor, Gonçalo Méndez de Canço (gahn SAH loh MEN dez day KAHN soh), convinced the officials that the fort protected both lives and property. St. Augustine survived because Spain needed a fort and safe harbor in Florida.

The settlement was near the route followed by Spanish ships that carried treasures from the Americas to Spain.

2. **Circle** parts of the picture of St. Augustine that show it was designed to protect Spanish settlers and travelers.

These ships were tempting targets for pirates from rival countries. By keeping soldiers in St. Augustine, Spain could protect its shipping. Later, Saint Augustine would also become an important port for slave trading.

Most of the citizens of St. Augustine were Spanish soldiers. Besides protecting and rescuing Spanish ships, these soldiers also helped protect missionaries. A **missionary** is someone who travels to a new land to persuade others to believe in a particular religion. In Florida, missionaries usually worked with Native American leaders. After the founding of St. Augustine, Spanish missionaries traveled through much of Florida and nearby areas. They set up villages called missions. The missions had two goals. One goal was to teach Native Americans the Catholic religion. The other goal was to introduce Native Americans to the Spanish way of life.

In order to survive, Spanish settlers in Florida depended on Native Americans such as the Timucuas (tim uh KOO uhs). In fact, the Spaniards near St. Augustine relied on the Timucuas to help provide food and labor. So the Spaniards gave native leaders many gifts and did not challenge their right to govern their own people. In return, native leaders let missionaries teach their religion and let the Timucuas work on Spanish farms.

3. **Write** to complete the following statement about how the Spanish settlers and Timucua people got along in St. Augustine:

The Spaniards received help from the Timucua people to raise their food. The Timucua people received

....

....

....

Timucua warrior

69

Cooperation and Conflict

Over time, Spain built many missions and forts. In the 1700s, it founded colonies in what is now Texas, California, and other parts of the southwestern United States.

As you have read, sometimes the Spaniards and Native Americans worked together peacefully. In general, though, contact with the Spaniards harmed Native Americans. One serious problem was disease. In some places, illness carried by Spaniards wiped out entire Native American communities. Native Americans also suffered from harsh treatment. At St. Augustine and many other missions, many Native Americans died of overwork.

Sometimes Spanish missionaries used force to change the way Native Americans lived, worked, and worshiped. Many Native Americans did not like this and fought back. One rebellion occurred in Florida in the 1650s. In 1680 an uprising of Pueblo people in present-day New Mexico left 400 Spaniards dead and forced the remaining Spaniards to leave the area. Some years later the Spaniards returned, but bad feelings remained in parts of New Spain.

Spanish Missions, 1600–1650

NORTH AMERICA

Florida

ATLANTIC OCEAN

Hispaniola

Gulf of Mexico

New Spain

Cuba

Caribbean Sea

Trinidad

PACIFIC OCEAN

SOUTH AMERICA

KEY

New Spain, 1600

• Spanish mission, 1600–1650

0   400 mi

0   400 km

4. The Spanish built missions like the one shown below to help control their colony and spread their religion. On the map, **circle** the missions located in modern-day Florida. **Put** a **square** around the missions farthest north in New Spain.

70

5. (◉) **Categorize Label** each of the following statements as *cooperation* or *conflict*.

Native Americans helped Spanish settlers raise food.	
The Spaniards forced Native Americans to become Christians.	
The Timucuas were allowed to govern themselves.	
The Spaniards overworked Native American workers.	
The Spaniards took land from Native Americans.	
The Spaniards gave gifts to Native Americans.	

Got it?

6. (◉) **Generalize Describe** the relationship between the Spaniards and Native Americans in New Spain.

....

....

....

....

7. (?) You have been selected to go with a group of settlers to a distant   **my Story Ideas**
island. Should you join the expedition or choose to stay home? **Make a chart**
in which you list reasons for going in one column and reasons for staying in the other.

....

....

....

■ **Stop!** I need help with ....

❚❚ **Wait!** I have a question about ....

▶ **Go!** Now I know ....

The English Colonies in Virginia

Envision It!

English settlers at Jamestown sought a good location for their colony. However, the site they chose had problems.

1. **Write** what Queen Elizabeth I might have said to Sir Walter Raleigh about attempting to start a colony in North America.

....

....

....

....

In the late 1500s, England and Spain were bitter rivals. England envied Spain's rich American colony. Queen Elizabeth I of England hoped to establish an English colony in North America. It took many years, and several failures, before a successful colony took root.

The English in North America

Sir Walter Raleigh (RAW lee), an advisor to Queen Elizabeth I, led England's attempt to set up a North American colony. With the queen's support, he sent an exploring party across the Atlantic Ocean in 1584. They landed in what is now North Carolina. Back then, however, they called the whole area Virginia. The next year, Raleigh sent 117 settlers to the same area. They settled on a place called Roanoke (ROH uh nohk) Island.

1585
Raleigh first sends settlers to Roanoke Island.

1584	1585	1586

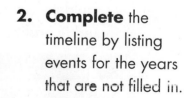
Vocabulary

drought
investor
cash crop

House of
Burgesses
representative

Draw what you think would be the perfect location for a settlement in a land that is new to you.

The colonists depended on local Native Americans for food. Then, a **drought**, or a long period without rain, may have caused the Native Americans to stop providing supplies. Many colonists starved. In 1586, the survivors returned to England.

Raleigh sent another 150 settlers to Roanoke Island the next year. They also sought help from Native Americans. However, arguments between the two groups led to more food shortages.

John White, the colony's leader, decided to go back to England to get help. He could not return until 1590 because England was at war with Spain. When White finally arrived at Roanoke, no settlers could be found. Adding to the mystery was a carving on a tree: CROATOAN. This was the name of friendly Native Americans nearby. White never found the missing colonists. The failed Roanoke settlement became known as the Lost Colony.

2. Complete the timeline by listing events for the years that are not filled in.

1587
Raleigh sends new group to settle at Roanoke.

1588
England and Spain are at war.

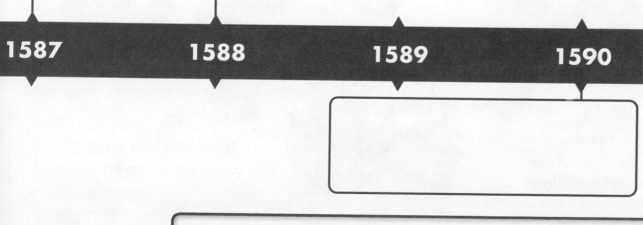

| 1587 | 1588 | 1589 | 1590 |

Success at Jamestown

More than a decade would pass before the English began making serious plans to start another American colony. After Queen Elizabeth died, the new king, James I, became interested in setting up an English colony. In 1606, he gave an organization called the Virginia Company the power to carry out the project.

The Virginia Company wanted to start a colony that earned money. In order to fund the project, the company invited investors to buy shares, or part ownership of the company. An **investor** gives money to a business hoping to earn more money in return. If the Virginia Company earned a profit from minerals or products exported from Virginia, investors would receive a share of the profits. Meanwhile, the company could use investors' money to pay for the project.

3. **Complete** the sentences to explain how the Virginia Company worked.

Investors provided

....

....

Colonists exported

....

....

How the Virginia Company Worked

① Investors paid for shares in the Virginia Company.

② The company financed three ships to take settlers to Virginia.

③ The settlers built the colony at Jamestown.

④ Lumber, tobacco, glass, tar, and pitch were exported to England.

⑤ After products were sold, investors shared in profits.

Soon, the Virginia Company was ready to begin its project. In late 1606, three ships and more than 100 colonists set sail for America. The ships carried strict orders from company leaders. These told the colonists what kind of site to choose for the colony. It was to be on a river inland from the ocean. That way, ships from rival countries could not easily spot it. It should also be easy to defend from attack. The English were especially worried about the presence of Spanish ships sailing from Cuba and Florida. These might pose a threat to a Virginia colony.

The Jamestown instructions also spelled out how many colonists should build houses and how many should plant crops. Others were to hunt for gold or to search for rivers that might be a shortcut to the riches of Asia. The colonists even received tips on how to treat Native Americans. They were told,

"... you must have great care not to offend the naturals [Native Americans]."

—*Virginia Company pamphlet, 1606*

For the most part, the colonists followed the instructions. They chose what they thought was a safe and healthy spot. They went about the work of building their colony. They named it Jamestown, after their king. Jamestown would become the first lasting English colony in North America.

4. Study the Rival Settlements map. **Write** why English settlers wanted to hide their colony from Spaniards.

....

....

....

....

....

....

This old map shows the inland location of Jamestown. Notice all of the Native American settlements located near Jamestown.

Rival Settlements, Early 1600s

KEY
■ Spanish colonies
→ Route of Spanish treasure fleet

Jamestown

NORTH AMERICA

35° N

ATLANTIC OCEAN

30° N

St. Augustine

Florida

0   200 mi
0   200 km

25° N

80° W

Havana

85° W   75° W

Cuba   75

Hard Times in Jamestown

Unfortunately, the Jamestown colonists soon found that their settlement was not in a healthy location. The water was unfit to drink, and clouds of mosquitoes attacked from the nearby swamps. Many colonists died from diseases carried by the insects.

Also, the local Powhatan people were not always friendly. They worried about having newcomers settle in their territory. The Powhatans made several attacks on the colony.

After the first year, John Smith became leader in Jamestown. He pushed the settlers to improve the colony. He tried to improve relations with the Powhatans and their chief, whom the colonists called Powhatan. According to Smith's journal, he also made friends with Pocahontas, the chief's young daughter.

5. The colonists at Jamestown seldom had enough food for everyone. **Circle** the sources of food shown in this painting. Why might colonists have needed help to find and grow food?

....

....

....

Smith wrote that Pocahontas once saved his life after the Powhatans had taken him prisoner. This story may not be true. What is true is that Pocahontas made friends with the colonists. For a time, the two groups got along much better.

In the fall of 1609, Smith was hurt in an accident. He had to return to England. Around that time, a new group of English settlers arrived. They were supposed to help the colony. Instead, they stretched food supplies to the limit. The result was disaster. The freezing winter of 1609–1610 was called the Starving Time.

The colony survived only because more colonists and supplies arrived from England in the spring. However, Jamestown faced still another problem: it was not earning money. The colonists had not found gold. The goods they produced did not sell well in Europe. The investors in the Virginia Company were getting impatient.

"Of five hundred within six months after Captain Smith's departure, there remained not past sixty men, women, and children."

—John Smith, 1609

6. ⊙ **Categorize Read** each statement below. In the blank, **write** whether it shows what the colonists *expected* or what they *found*.

The English colonists would find riches in Virginia.	
The colonists realized that the nearby swamps were full of mosquitoes.	
The settlement had poor water that was unfit to drink.	
Jamestown would be a good location for a settlement.	
Colonists could build good relations with Native Americans.	
The Native Americans often were not friendly.	

Jamestown Moves Forward

In 1612, colonist John Rolfe introduced something new to Virginia, namely, a new type of tobacco plant. The Powhatans already grew a type of tobacco, but Rolfe's was different. He hoped it would be more to the liking of people in England.

The new plants grew well in the Virginia soil, and the tobacco was of high quality. People in England were willing to pay a high price for it. The Virginia Company at last had a way to make money from their colony. Soon, the cash crop filled the colony's fields. A **cash crop** is a crop raised for sale, not for use by the people who farm it.

Rolfe also played a part in another key event in Jamestown history. In 1614, he married Pocahontas. The marriage helped keep the peace between the English and Powhatans for several more years. This peace would not last, but it did give the colony a chance to grow larger and stronger.

To attract more settlers, the Virginia Company began giving land away. Many settlers became landowners. In England, landowners had the right to take part in government. In 1619, the Virginia Company gave the colonists this right, too. It set up a special legislative body called the **House of Burgesses.** In England, a burgess represented a town. The members of this body included 22 **representatives,** or people chosen by voters to speak and act for them. The House of Burgesses made laws and decisions for the colony. It made sure that the colonists had a say in their own government. We still have a representative form of government today.

Self-government remained an important custom in Virginia. It also developed in other English colonies in North America.

7. The members of the House of Burgesses helped make rules for the Virginia colony. **Write** two things you notice about the representatives in this painting.

....

....

....

....

8. **◎ Cause and Effect Complete** the graphic organizer about the Jamestown colony.

Causes

Rolfe plants tobacco.	

Effects

Better relations occur between colonists and the Powhatans after 1614.

The colonists and Powhatans live together peacefully for a while.	

Got it?

9. **◎ Compare and Contrast** How were the earliest English attempts at colonization similar to and different from the Jamestown effort?

....

....

....

....

10. **❓** You've just arrived as a colonist on a new island. What are the first things you must do to survive? **Explain** why.

my Story Ideas

....

....

....

⬜ Stop! I need help with ....

⏸ Wait! I have a question about ....

▶ Go! Now I know ....

Pilgrims and Puritans in New England

Envision It!

Some of these foods were probably served at the first Thanksgiving celebration.

This ship is a replica of the original Mayflower *that carried the Pilgrims to New England.*

For 102 English passengers packed into the *Mayflower*, there was good news and bad news. After two stormy months at sea, they were nearing land. Unfortunately, that land was not in the northern part of Virginia, which had been their goal. Storms had blown the ship farther north. Now they were weary and short of supplies. Winter was coming, so they decided to find a place to come ashore.

The Pilgrims Arrive

The year was 1620. The land the *Mayflower* was nearing was not completely mysterious. English explorer John Cabot had sailed there more than 100 years before. Since that time, many English ships had come to take codfish from local waters. In fact, the *Mayflower* passengers already had a name for the land that lay before them: Cape Cod. It was part of a larger area they later called New England.

The Jamestown settlers had hoped to find riches in North America or to earn money from products sent back to England. The *Mayflower* settlers also expected to earn money, but they had a more important goal. They wanted freedom to practice their religion. They belonged to a group known as Separatists. They wanted to separate, or break off, from the Church of England. At that time, all people in England had to belong to that church. The Separatists wanted religious independence.

Draw or list foods eaten at Thanksgiving that are different from those eaten at the first Thanksgiving.

Vocabulary

Pilgrim   indentured
Mayflower   servant
Compact   Puritan

Because these Separatists set off to build a new religious life in America, they later became known as the Pilgrims. A **pilgrim** is a person who goes on a religious journey.

Because they were on their own in an unfamiliar land, the Pilgrims decided that they needed a strong and fair government. So before they even left the *Mayflower*, the male Pilgrims wrote a compact, or agreement, about how they would govern themselves. It was known as the **Mayflower Compact.** In it, the group promised to work together to make "just and equal laws." No person or group would have power over the others. The Pilgrims agreed to hold town meetings at which all important issues would be discussed. Town meetings are still an important part of self-government in many New England communities.

1. **Fill in** the Venn diagram to compare and contrast goals of the Pilgrims and the Jamestown settlers.

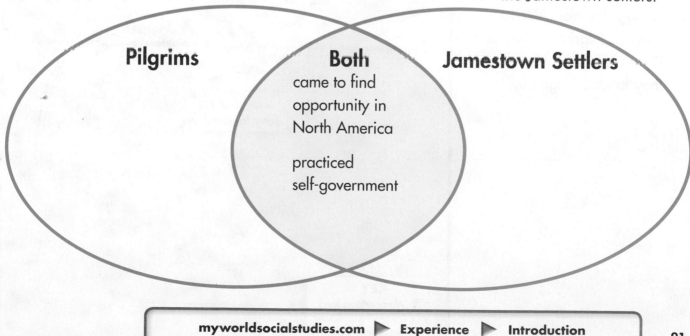

Pilgrims   Both   Jamestown Settlers

came to find opportunity in North America

practiced self-government

The Pilgrims and Native Americans

After making landfall at Cape Cod, the *Mayflower* continued west. The Pilgrims settled at a place they called Plymouth (PLIH muth). This land was once home to the Wampanoag (wahm puh NOH ag) people. However, the area seemed empty at first. Many of the native people had died from diseases caught from earlier visitors or had moved away.

That first winter at Plymouth was dreadful. The Pilgrims suffered from hunger, cold, and disease. Half of them died. Spring brought warmer weather and several visitors. The first was a Native American named Samoset. Surprisingly, he spoke some English words, which he had learned from traders who had visited the area earlier. Samoset introduced the Pilgrims to Tisquantum (tih SKWAHN tum), or Squanto, a member of the Wampanoag people. Squanto spoke English very well. He had once been captured by an Englishman and taken to England. Squanto helped the Pilgrims. William Bradford, the Pilgrims' first chosen leader, wrote about Squanto in his journal:

"He directed them how to set their corn, where to take fish, and procure [get] other commodities [materials], and was also their pilot to bring them to unknown places."

—William Bradford, 1646

William Bradford thanks Squanto for helping the Pilgrims.

2. **Study** the map. **Write** why the Pilgrims settled in Plymouth rather than where they landed originally.

....

....

....

....

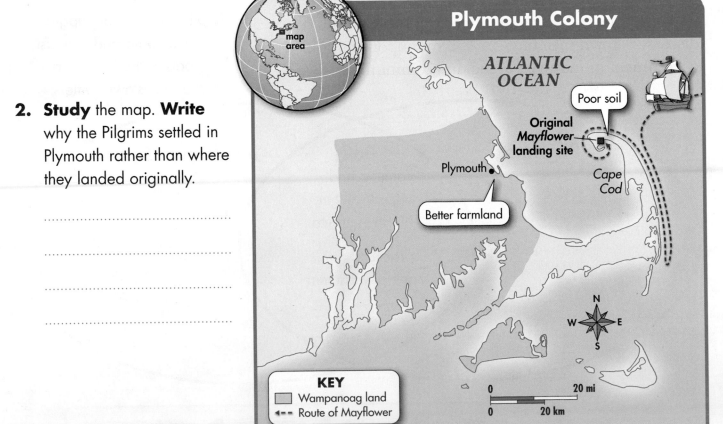

Plymouth Colony

map area

ATLANTIC OCEAN

Poor soil

Original Mayflower landing site

Plymouth

Better farmland

Cape Cod

N W E S

KEY
- Wampanoag land
- Route of Mayflower

0   20 mi

0   20 km

Two Different Cultures

	Pilgrims	Wampanoag
land ownership	property owned by whole group; later, families owned home and field	lands for hunting and fishing belonged to group
religion	Christianity based on the Bible	believed living things had a spiritual connection
clothing	men: jackets, knee pants, stockings, boots; women: skirts, tops, aprons, stockings, low-heeled shoes	men: breech cloths, moccasins, leggings; women: deerskin skirts and shoulder wraps, fur coverings in cold weather
food	biscuits, fish, meat from game	corn, squash, beans, fish, deer, turkeys, and other game

William Bradford

Massasoit

Working and Celebrating Together

Squanto also served as a translator. A translator helps people who speak different languages to understand each other. Squanto helped the Pilgrims and the Wampanoag leader, Massasoit (mas uh SOYT), make an agreement that benefited both groups. The Pilgrims received help starting farms and raising food, such as corn and pumpkins. For their part, the Wampanoag feared attack from other native peoples in the area. They were happy to gain military support from the Pilgrims.

With Native American help, the Pilgrims enjoyed a good harvest in 1621. So, in the fall, the Pilgrims held a feast of thanksgiving. They invited their Wampanoag friends to celebrate with them. For three days, the colonists and Native Americans relaxed and ate together. The menu included the corn Squanto had helped the Pilgrims plant. They also probably ate deer, duck, fish, pumpkin, beans, nuts, and more. It is possible that wild turkeys were on the menu, too.

3. **Study** the chart. Then **answer** this question: Why did the Wampanoag and Pilgrims get along despite their differences?

....

....

....

....

....

....

....

Life at Plymouth Plantation

The Pilgrims had much to celebrate after their first year in Plymouth. They also had much work to do. It was not easy building a new life in an unfamiliar land.

The Pilgrims had to work hard to grow food. Clearing trees took backbreaking effort. Planting and tending crops was also demanding. Men, women, and children worked in the fields and gardens.

Plymouth was a colony of families. A number of children traveled with their parents on the *Mayflower*. Once on land, however, the children had little time for play. Although they did not have to attend school, young people were expected to work. Even small children ran errands or did other small chores. Older children had harder jobs.

The Pilgrims grew food to feed their families. They also grew it to trade. The Pilgrims exchanged corn with Native Americans for animal furs. These they shipped to England for sale. The fur sales helped the Pilgrims pay their large debts. They owed money to a company in England that had financed the colony.

4. Pilgrims built their small houses out of materials they found nearby. Study the picture below. **Write** a list of materials the Pilgrims may have used for their houses.

....

....

....

....

....

Pilgrim houses and clothing might have looked like these modern reconstructions.

Some people came to Plymouth as indentured servants. An **indentured servant** is someone who agrees to work without pay for someone else for a set time. In return, the servant receives food, clothing, and shelter. An indentured servant's term might last from a few months to ten years or more. At the end of the term, the servant is free. He or she might receive more food, clothing, or even land. For many poor English people, becoming an indentured servant was the only way to start a new life in America.

Church was a big part of life in Plymouth. Remember, the Pilgrims had come to America so they could practice their religion freely. Everyone was expected to take part in worship services and to follow the basic church teachings. The Pilgrims did not permit much dissent, or disagreement, with their religious views.

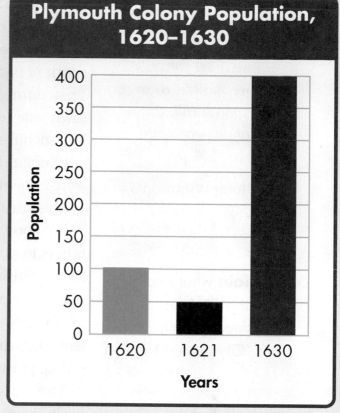

Plymouth Colony Population, 1620–1630

Source: Population of Plymouth Town, Colony, and Country 1620-1690

5. **Read** the information in the graphic organizer. Then **answer** the following question: If you were a young person in England, why would you become an indentured servant?

After that first difficult winter, the population of Plymouth Colony grew slowly but steadily.

....

....

....

....

Costs and Benefits of Indentured Servants

	For Indentured Servant	For Landowner or Business Person
Costs	unpaid labor; lack of freedom	housing, food, and clothing for the servant
Benefits	passage to America; eventual freedom	cheap labor

The Massachusetts Bay Colony

In 1630, a group of 700 English settlers left their homes to sail to New England. They established a new colony north of Plymouth called the Massachusetts Bay Colony. They named the main settlement Boston, after the English town where many of them had lived. In many ways, the Massachusetts Bay Colony was like Plymouth. Its founders left England so they could practice their religion freely. They were known as **Puritans.**

The Puritan leader was John Winthrop. He wanted the new colony to be "a City upon a Hill," or an example for others to follow. Religion was at the heart of daily life in the Massachusetts Bay Colony. Church leaders governed, and colonists had to obey church teachings. Everyone had to go to church services. Those who disobeyed could be forced to leave the colony. Rule breakers might also be shamed with public punishment or even be put to death.

The Puritans believed strongly in education, and they built America's first public schools and libraries. They felt all colonists should be able to read the Bible and understand church teachings. The Puritans also founded Harvard College to train church leaders.

Compared to Plymouth and Jamestown, the new colony had a smooth start. It did not face starvation or disease.

> *"... we must consider that we shall be as a City upon a Hill, the eyes of all people are upon us."*
>
> —John Winthrop

6. **Explain** what kind of behavior John Winthrop expected in this "City upon a Hill."

....

....

....

....

Disobeying the rules in Massachusetts Bay often led to public punishment like this.

However, the Puritans did create some problems for themselves, especially among local Native Americans. At Plymouth, the Pilgrims had not tried to spread their religion to the Wampanoag. The Puritans had less respect for Native American ways. The first seal of the colony showed a Native American saying, "Come over and help us." This attitude led to conflict and even to war later in the 1600s.

Still, the Massachusetts Bay Colony and all of New England grew quickly. By 1640, there were 16,000 settlers living in many different parts of New England.

Got it?

7. **Categorize Circle** any answers that would belong in a paragraph about the Massachusetts Bay Colony.

    a. established schools for children and even a college

    b. always had good relations with Native Americans

    c. were very strict if people broke rules

    d. had to deal with starvation and disease

8. You and your friends have just set up a new colony and need a way of governing yourselves. How do you decide who's in charge and what the rules will be?

my Story Ideas

....

....

....

....

Stop! I need help with ....

Wait! I have a question about ....

Go! Now I know ....

Make Decisions

Suppose you lived in Europe in the 1500s or early 1600s. You have heard that colonists can own land and perhaps become wealthy in North America. There are also great risks. Should you become a colonist or not? How do you go about making this life-changing decision?

Making decisions is a process. By following these steps in order, you can increase your chances of making the right decision.

1. **Identify the issue.** To make a good decision, you must first recognize the problem or question you face. What is the outcome that you want?

2. **Think of options.** Write down all the ways you can think of to solve the problem or answer the question. These are your options.

3. **Test the options.** Focus on each of your options. Ask yourself: What might happen if I choose this option? What are the possible good and bad outcomes?

4. **Choose an option.** Choose the option that has the greatest chance of meeting your goals. By choosing the option you think is best, you have made your decision.

Once you have made a decision, you can act on it. Develop a plan to carry out the option you chose. Keep your mind open, however. You should be willing to change your decision if the action you take does not work out as well as you hoped.

The Pilgrims wanted to practice their religion in their own way. How do you think the Pilgrim leaders in the early 1600s made the decision to leave Europe? Follow the decision-making process to determine how the Pilgrims may have made their decision.

1. What is the issue?

....

....

2. What are their options?

....

....

....

3. How does each option work?

....

....

....

4. Which option is best?

....

....

5. Apply Think about a decision you might face in your life today. On a separate sheet of paper, **write** down your answers to questions 1–4.

1. What is the issue?

2. What are my options?

3. How does each option work?

4. Which option is best?

The French and Dutch in North America

Envision It!

The French built close ties with many Native American groups in North America.

The French began exploring the Americas a few years after the Spaniards. In the 1530s, Jacques Cartier (zhahk kar tee AY) made two trips to what is now Canada. He was looking for a **Northwest Passage**, a shortcut by water across North America to Asia. He didn't find the shortcut, but he did claim the region for France. On his third voyage, in 1541, Cartier believed he had found gold and diamonds. He loaded samples of this great treasure onto his ship and returned to France.

French Traders and Settlers

Cartier had been fooled. His gold and diamonds were only worthless rocks. Therefore, France saw no reason to send settlers to Canada. In the 1560s, the French started a settlement in Florida, but the Spaniards quickly destroyed it. French leaders decided that settling North America was too much trouble.

The French were still interested in the region's resources, however. French fishing boats sailed into North American waters. Rugged outdoorsmen also arrived to buy valuable animal furs. Furs were greatly prized in Europe. Beaver and other furs were used mainly to make a popular type of hat.

The French became interested in expanding their fur trade in Canada. By 1608, explorer and businessman Samuel de Champlain (sham PLAYN) formed a French trading post at what is now the city of Quebec. It was the first successful French settlement in North America. Several other trading posts followed in the area.

Quebec in the early 1700s

UNLOCK THE BIG ?

I will know the key events surrounding the establishment of French and Dutch colonies in North America.

Key Terms

Northwest Passage

commerce

Write a dialogue between the French trader and the Native American selling an animal fur.

Champlain was mostly interested in trading with local Native Americans. He worked to build close relationships with the Huron people. Champlain even joined with Huron fighters against their enemies, the Iroquois.

Over the next few years, Champlain and other French traders worked to expand their trade network. Fur traders in canoes paddled the region's rivers and streams, carrying goods such as beads, knives, and metal pots to exchange for furs. The network they created soon reached all the way to the Great Lakes.

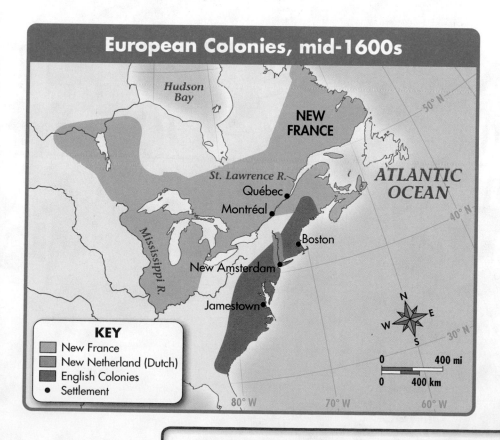

European Colonies, mid-1600s

Hudson Bay

NEW FRANCE

50° N

St. Lawrence R.

ATLANTIC OCEAN

Québec

Montréal

40° N

Mississippi R.

Boston

New Amsterdam

N
W   E
S

Jamestown

30° N

KEY
- New France
- New Netherland (Dutch)
- English Colonies
- • Settlement

0   400 mi
0   400 km

80° W   70° W   60° W

1. **Look** at the map. **Write** why New France stretched so far to the west.

....

....

....

....

French Settlements Grow

The colony of New France grew slowly. By the 1660s, only a few thousand French people lived there. Some settlers came to the colony to find farmland, establish villages, and raise families. Others roamed the land trading for furs. French missionaries arrived to convert Native Americans to Christianity. The French settlers were not always welcome. Iroquois people remained bitter foes of the French and their Native American friends. Warfare between these groups made life very dangerous.

In 1663, France's king Louis XIV took control of the colony. He sent soldiers to deal with the Iroquois. Once peace was established, the king encouraged families to move to New France and settle the colony.

French exploration also increased. In 1681–1682, Robert de La Salle, a daring and proud man, led a team of French and Native Americans all the way to the mouth of the Mississippi River. This is where the city of New Orleans is located today.

2. **Write** what the Native Americans might be thinking as La Salle claims the Mississippi River valley for France.

....

....

....

....

Along the way, La Salle claimed the entire river valley for France. He also claimed all the land of all the river valleys flowing into the Mississippi. This vast area covered much of North America. La Salle called it Louisiana to honor King Louis.

The Dutch Arrive

In the early 1600s, the Netherlands was another powerful country in Europe. Its people, the Dutch, also hoped to find a Northwest Passage. This would help them profit from the valuable trade with Asia. So, in 1609, Dutch business leaders sent an English sailor named Henry Hudson to search for such a route.

Hudson found a river that seemed promising. Today, we call it the Hudson River. Hudson entered the river's mouth, near what is now New York City. He sailed north for 150 miles or so. Hudson was finally forced to turn back when the water became too shallow. He had not found a shortcut to Asia. However, he had found a rich fur-trading area.

The land Hudson explored and claimed for the Dutch became the colony of New Netherland. The most important settlement of this colony was New Amsterdam. It was located on what is now the island of Manhattan. In 1626, Dutchman Peter Minuet bought the island from Native Americans. It became the center of a thriving trade.

The Hudson River was deep enough to allow ships to travel far inland. It remains an important river today.

3. ◉ **Categorize Read** each statement. **Write** in the column on the right whether the statement refers to the English, French, or Dutch colonists.

At first, they thought they had found the Northwest Passage.	
They raised crops and made products to sell in Europe.	
Missionary work was important to them.	
They fought deadly wars against the Iroquois.	
Many came seeking freedom of religion.	
Most settled in or near New Amsterdam.	

Life in New Netherland

Like Jamestown, New Netherland was based on commerce. **Commerce** is the business of buying and selling goods. A Dutch company ran the colony. Shareholders and settlers all hoped the colony would make them rich.

Many of the settlers took part in the fur trade. Some started farms. Others worked as craftspeople, making furniture and tools. One coastal village depended on the hunting of whales.

The population of New Netherland grew steadily. By the mid-1660s, 9,000 people lived there. Many were not Dutch. Company officials invited settlers from Germany, Sweden, Denmark, and elsewhere. New Netherland was home to a small number of Jews, or people who practiced the Jewish religion. There were also many enslaved Africans forced to work in the colony. More than 18 different languages were spoken there. One visitor in the 1640s wrote,

Peter Stuyvesant (STY vuh sahnt) was an important Dutch colonial leader in New Netherland.

> *"On the island of Manhattan . . . there may well be four or five hundred men of different sects [religious groups] or nations."*

—Father Isaac Jogues, 1646

The Native Americans in the area included the powerful Iroquois. In the northern parts of the colony, settlers depended on Native Americans to supply furs. They tried to build close relationships with these neighbors. To the south, settlers wanted to take over Native American land to farm. Many conflicts took place. Both sides used violence to settle disagreements.

Conflict between the Dutch and English increased as English settlers moved west into what is now Connecticut and western Massachusetts. Dutch efforts to settle these areas led to threats of war. In time, the English would take over all of New Netherland.

4. **Circle** an object in this painting of New Amsterdam that might remind Dutch settlers of their home in the Netherlands.

5. ⊙ **Cause and Effect Complete** the graphic organizer.
Write an effect for each cause.

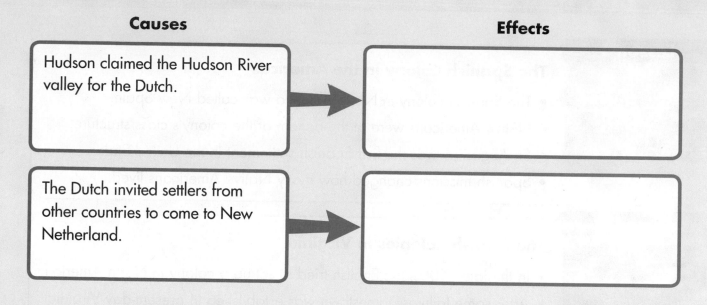

Causes	Effects
Hudson claimed the Hudson River valley for the Dutch.	
The Dutch invited settlers from other countries to come to New Netherland.	

Got it?

6. ⊙ **Categorize Write** why each of these colonies was started: New Spain, Jamestown, Plymouth Plantation. Was it for money-making reasons, religious freedom, or both?

....

....

7. (?) You are a colonial leader, and your sponsors back home want you to start earning money for them. How will you establish trade with your home country, and what will you send? What do you want to receive in return?   **my Story Ideas**

....

....

....

⬜ **Stop!** I need help with ....

⏸ **Wait!** I have a question about ....

▶ **Go!** Now I know ....

Study Guide

Lesson 1

The Spanish Colony in the Americas

- The Spanish colony in North America was called New Spain.
- Native Americans were at the bottom of the colony's class structure.
- St. Augustine was the first Spanish settlement in the United States.
- Spanish missions changed how many Native Americans lived.

Lesson 2

The English Colonies in Virginia

- In the late 1500s, the English tried to set up a colony in North America.
- After some failures, Jamestown was established in present-day Virginia.
- The colonists made peace with the Powhatans, and the colony grew.
- Tobacco became the cash crop that helped the colony succeed.

Lesson 3

Pilgrims and Puritans in New England

- The Pilgrims came to New England to be free to practice their religion.
- The Pilgrims survived with the help of local Native Americans.
- The Puritans also came to North America for religious reasons and settled in what is now Boston.

Lesson 4

The French and Dutch in North America

- The colony of New France was started with a trading post in Quebec.
- France claimed a huge portion of North America.
- The Dutch colony of New Netherland grew around the Hudson River valley and what is today New York City.

Review and Assessment

Lesson 1

The Spanish Colony in the Americas

1. Why did Spain establish a settlement at St. Augustine?

....

....

....

2. What was the purpose of the Spanish missions in New Spain?

....

....

....

....

3. **Circle** the correct answer.

The uprising of the Pueblo people in 1680 shows how

A. Native Americans accepted mission life.

B. Spanish colonization sometimes angered Native Americans.

C. the Spanish class structure was very successful.

D. peninsulares rejected the social system of New Spain.

Lesson 2

The English Colonies in Virginia

4. What was the role of the Virginia Company in the settling of Jamestown?

....

....

....

5. How did the colonists get along with the Powhatan people near Jamestown?

....

....

....

6. **Write** a sentence explaining the role of each of the following in the English colonization effort:

a. Sir Walter Raleigh

....

....

b. John Rolfe

....

....

c. House of Burgesses

....

....

....

Pilgrims and Puritans in New England

7. What was the Mayflower Compact?

....

....

8. ⊙ **Categorize Check** the category in which you think the colonies at Plymouth and Massachusetts Bay best belong.

_____ Colonies based on commerce

_____ Colonies based on religion

The French and Dutch in North America

9. Describe the French relationship with Native Americans in New France.

....

....

....

....

....

10. Briefly describe the population of the colony of New Netherland.

....

....

....

....

....

11. ❓ **Why do people leave their homelands?**

Use the questions below to think more about this chapter's Big Question.

a. Why did Spanish colonists travel to New Spain?

....

....

b. Why did English colonists move to Jamestown or to New England?

....

....

c. What enterprise did both French and Dutch colonists pursue?

....

....

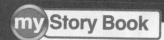 **my Story Book**

Go online to write and illustrate your own **myStory Book** using the **myStory Ideas** from this chapter.

Why do people leave their homelands?

Today, as in earlier times, people are often on the move. They leave the places where they were born to move to other parts of the world. There are many reasons people make this move. Some are seeking opportunity for a better life in a faraway place. Others are fleeing something that threatens them in their homeland.

Think about your home town and your future. **Write** about what might cause you to leave your home town to begin a new life somewhere else.

....

....

....

....

Now, **draw** a picture that shows what you would bring with you if you moved to a new home in some other part of the world.

While you're online, check out the **myStory Current Events** area where you can create your own book on a topic that's in the news.

Life in the Colonies

What does it take to build a new society?

Suppose you are moving to a faraway new home. What will you bring with you to start your new life? What would you leave behind?

....

....

....

....

....

This modern-day reconstruction of a colonial stage wagon shows how many colonists traveled in the 1600s and 1700s.

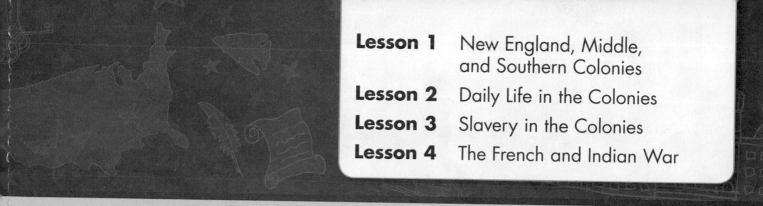

Benjamin Franklin
Young Apprentice

my Story Video

Benjamin Franklin was a remarkable man with a wide range of talents. As a printer and writer, he helped to shape the ideas of American colonists. As a scientist and inventor, he conducted important experiments and created useful tools, such as bifocals and the Franklin stove. As a civic leader, he set up America's first public library and fire department.

Born in the city of Boston in 1706, Benjamin Franklin came from a large family. He had 16 brothers and sisters! His father's job as a candlemaker earned the family enough to live on. Still, the Franklins could not afford to send their bright son Benjamin to college. Instead, Ben needed to learn a trade so that he could earn a living.

Before being apprenticed at age 12 to learn the printing trade, Benjamin Franklin sometimes helped his father make candles.

101

While Ben was an apprentice to his brother (and master), he was not always treated well.

Even as a teenager, Ben Franklin showed a sharp wit in his newspaper articles, which readers enjoyed.

When Ben Franklin turned 12 years old, he did what many young people his age did. He became an apprentice. In the 1700s, young people learned trades by becoming apprentices to skilled "masters." They might learn to make shoes or build furniture or bind books. An apprentice left home to live and work with a master tradesperson. Working without pay for up to seven years, he or she received food, clothing, and shelter. At the end of the training, the apprentice was ready to start a career.

Benjamin and his father decided that he would learn the printing trade, apprenticed to his older brother. James Franklin ran a shop in Boston, where he printed a popular newspaper as well as pamphlets and posters. Working for him, Ben learned to set type, taking metal letters from cases and arranging them on frames into words and paragraphs. He learned to ink the type and print pages one sheet at a time.

A printer's apprentice needed to learn how to set type for newspapers and how to operate a printing press properly.

Ben abandoned his apprenticeship and sailed away from Boston at the age of 17.

Within a few years, Ben Franklin owned a successful printing business in Philadelphia.

Ben's life as an apprentice was not easy. The work was hard, and hours were long. Sometimes his brother would yell at him or even beat him. This was not unusual for those times. Still, Ben felt that his brother did not always treat him fairly.

Ben did learn to be a printer. For a time, he even helped run his brother's business. He also began writing articles for the newspaper, using the pen name of "Silence Dogood." Even though Ben was a teenager with little education, people loved the clever things he wrote about life in the colonies.

When Ben was 17, he decided that he was ready to set out on his own before his seven-year apprenticeship was complete. In those days, apprentices did not break their agreements. So what did Ben do? He hopped a ship to New York City to look for work.

Soon he moved on to Philadelphia. Using the skills he had learned during his apprenticeship, Frankin found work in a local print shop. Later, he sailed to Great Britain to learn more about the printing business.

Finally, Franklin returned to Philadelphia. Through hard work, he built a successful printing business there. While Franklin explored interests in many other fields, printing and writing were always important to him. He became famous for the columns he wrote and the witty sayings he published yearly in *Poor Richard's Almanack*. Benjamin Franklin became a symbol of the genius and spirit of the hardworking American colonies.

Think About It Based on the story, what qualities did it take to be successful in the American colonies? As you read the chapter ahead, think about what Benjamin Franklin's story tells you about colonial society.

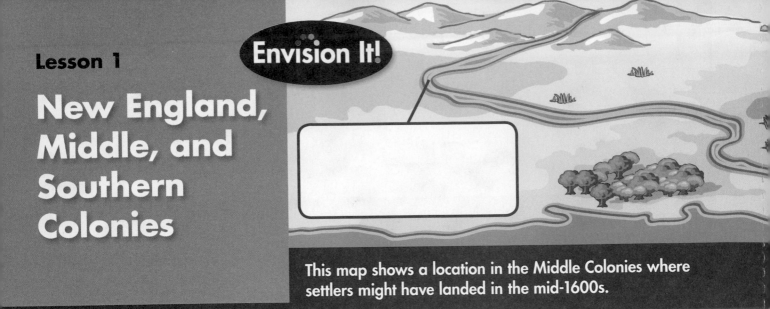

New England, Middle, and Southern Colonies

Envision It!

This map shows a location in the Middle Colonies where settlers might have landed in the mid-1600s.

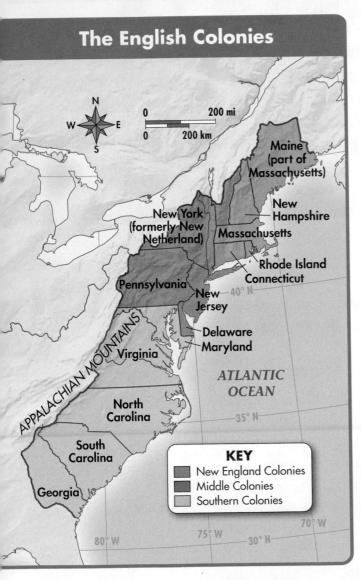

The English Colonies

N W E S

0   200 mi
0   200 km

Maine (part of Massachusetts)

New York (formerly New Netherland)

New Hampshire

Massachusetts

Pennsylvania

Rhode Island
Connecticut

New Jersey

40° N

Delaware
Maryland

APPALACHIAN MOUNTAINS

Virginia

ATLANTIC OCEAN

North Carolina

35° N

South Carolina

KEY

■ New England Colonies
■ Middle Colonies
□ Southern Colonies

Georgia

70° W

80° W   75° W   30° N

By the 1730s, there were 13 English colonies covering a narrow strip between the coast and the mountains.

The early colonists in North America were influenced by their environment. Settlers in Jamestown faced swarms of mosquitoes from nearby swamps. The Pilgrims at Plymouth Plantation suffered through freezing winter weather. The Dutch in New Amsterdam used their location to become a center for trade. Geography would continue to shape life as the colonies grew.

Geography of the English Colonies

Settlers from England came to North America throughout the 1600s. By the 1730s, colonies stretched from present-day Maine to what is now Georgia. These colonies can be grouped into three geographic regions. A **region** is an area defined by common features or conditions. The colonists lived in New England, the Mid-Atlantic region, and the South.

In New England, people farmed the thin, rocky soil, but farming was not the region's main business. Instead, many local merchants traded goods with England and with other colonies. Others earned their livings cutting timber from dense forests. Along the coast, they built ships, fished, or hunted whales.

UNLOCK
THE BIG
?

I will know the role of geography in the settling and development of the English colonies.

Vocabulary

region   proprietor
climate   diverse
dissent

Explain whether each feature labeled on the map might be helpful or pose difficulties for the new settlers.

The Middle Colonies had rich soil and a warmer climate. **Climate** is the pattern of weather in a place over a long period of time. Many colonists in this region raised wheat to sell. Iron dug from the ground was another key resource.

Colonies in the Southern region had an even warmer climate. Along the coast, the land was flat, and the soil was rich. Farmers in this region planted cash crops, such as tobacco and rice. Their large farms were called plantations.

In all regions, water was a key means of transportation and trade. Settlements clustered near rivers and on the coast.

While the land shaped how the settlements grew, settlers also changed the land. They cleared trees for farming and harvested timber. They changed the soil by growing crops year after year. Settlers also built roads and bridges.

1. **Complete** the chart with information about the connection between geography and settlements in the colonies.

Geography and Settlements

How the Land Shaped Settlements	How Settlers Changed the Land
•	•
•	•

The New England Colonies

In New England, the Puritans established towns throughout the region. Settlers built homes and farms on land that they saw as vacant. However, local Native Americans did not fence or use land in the way that English people did. The land that colonists assumed was empty, was often absolutely necessary to Native Americans. Such differences sometimes led to conflict.

In each New England town, the meetinghouse was the center of town life. It was usually a large, simple building located on the town common area. The meetinghouse was used for religious services and for town meetings. Government decisions and actions were decided at town meetings. Only church-going men who owned property could vote at these meetings.

Male settlers had a say in government, but Puritan leaders did not put up with **dissent**, or disagreement. Roger Williams discovered this when he came to the Massachusetts Bay Colony in 1631. Williams was a church leader, but he believed in freedom of religion.

In most New England towns, houses were clustered around a common area, where the meetinghouse and often artisan shops were located.

2. How are the town residents using the common area?

....

....

....

....

....

Shops and houses

Meetinghouse

The Common

106

Williams argued that civil leaders did not have the right to require everyone to worship in exactly the same way. Top Puritan leaders in Boston called Williams's ideas "new and dangerous." In 1636, he was banished, or forced to leave the colony. He started a new settlement that he called Providence. Settlers in Providence were free to practice religion in their own way. This was the start of what would become the colony of Rhode Island.

Anne Hutchinson was also forced to leave Massachusetts. She offended Puritan leaders by speaking out on religious matters and insisting that faith in God was more important than church rules. In 1638, she went to Rhode Island.

Thomas Hooker, a Puritan minister, wanted more political freedom. He felt that all men should be allowed to vote, not just church members or property owners. His ideas led him to leave Massachusetts in 1636 to start a colony that would become Connecticut.

Anne Hutchinson was banished from Massachusetts because she did not agree with church leaders in the colony.

3. ◎ **Main Ideas and Details Fill in** the graphic organizer below with the missing details.

Dissent in the Puritan Colonies

Main Idea
Dissent was not tolerated in Puritan colonies.

Supporting Detail

Supporting Detail

Supporting Detail
Thomas Hooker left Massachusetts to find more political freedom.

The Middle Colonies

After its founding by the Dutch in the 1620s, New Netherland became a thriving trade center. The colony soon included a settlement made by Swedes in the New Jersey area in the 1630s. Then in 1664, England sent a fleet to capture New Netherland. The colonists refused to fight, so governor Peter Stuyvesant surrendered to the English without firing a shot. The Dutch did try later to recapture the colony. However, by 1674, England was in full control.

England's king gave the colony to his brother, the Duke of York. The colony was renamed New York. This name was also given to the city that had been called New Amsterdam.

The Duke of York gave some of his lands in New York to two friends. Their names were George Carteret and John Berkeley. The land they received would become the colony of New Jersey. The Duke of York, Carteret, and Berkeley were known as proprietors (pruh PRYE uh turz). A **proprietor** is someone who owns land or property. New York and New Jersey were called proprietary colonies.

Log cabins such as this one built by Swedish settlers in New Netherland in 1637 became a popular style of building in the Middle Colonies.

Roof shingles were split off of logs.

Square-cut logs formed the walls.

New York and New Jersey had a **diverse** population. That is, there were people from many different countries and backgrounds living there. People in these colonies belonged to many different religious groups, too. This remained true even as the colonies grew.

People of different religions were also accepted in the colony of Pennsylvania. This colony began in 1681. England's king gave the land for the colony to William Penn, who was a Quaker. Quakers were opposed to war and felt people could pray in their own way. Penn believed strongly in protecting each person's right, or freedom, to practice his or her religion. Penn also believed in the rights of Native Americans living on the land he had been given. He promised to pay them a fair price for it.

Delaware was also one of the Middle Colonies. It was part of Pennsylvania until 1704, when it became a separate colony.

As a Quaker, William Penn sought to maintain peaceful relations with Native Americans living near his new colony.

4. **Complete** each label on this timeline with facts about the founding of the four Middle Colonies.

Founding of the Middle Colonies

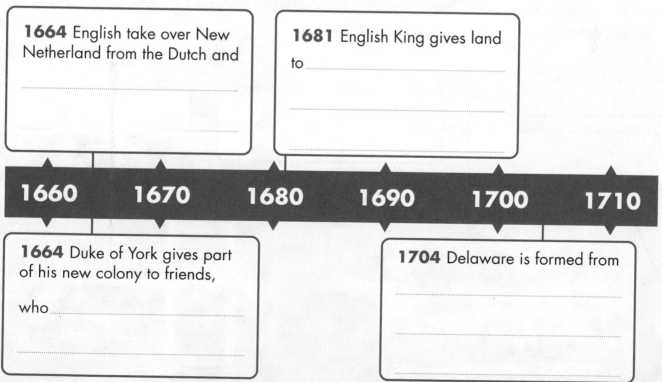

1664 English take over New Netherland from the Dutch and
....
....
....

1681 English King gives land to ....
....
....

| 1660 | 1670 | 1680 | 1690 | 1700 | 1710 |

1664 Duke of York gives part of his new colony to friends, who ....
....
....

1704 Delaware is formed from
....
....
....

Southern Colonies

In the South, the Virginia Company controlled Virginia at first. Then in 1624, King James I decided to take over the colony. He appointed a governor under his control to run Virginia. Becoming a royal colony under the king's rule did not really change Virginia much. Self-rule continued. The governing body, the House of Burgesses, continued to meet.

One big change did occur in 1632. Charles I, England's new king, gave part of Virginia to Lord Baltimore, one of his followers. This new proprietary colony was named Maryland. Lord Baltimore belonged to the Catholic Church. Maryland welcomed Catholics, who were not always accepted in other colonies.

Carolina also began as a proprietary colony. In 1663, King Charles II granted this land to eight of his supporters. The colony was split in 1729 into North and South Carolina. The Carolinas had good soil for farming. In South Carolina, plantations grew valuable crops, especially rice. They relied on enslaved workers to farm and do other work. Charleston, an important Carolina city with a fine harbor, became a key trading center.

Georgia was founded in 1732. King George II let James Oglethorpe start a colony there for English people jailed for debt. Oglethorpe was welcomed by Tomochichi (toh moh chee CHEE), chief of the Yamacraws. Georgia became known for its good relations with Native Americans. It also served a key military role, standing between Spain's Florida colony and the other English colonies.

5. Enslaved people did much of the work on plantations, such as this one in Maryland. **Write** a task that a worker might have done in the kitchen, the house, or the barn of this plantation.

Planter's house
....

Kitchen
....

Barn
....

6. Draw a line to match the detail in the right column with the colony it describes.

Describing the Southern Colonies

Virginia	**a.** It was a proprietary colony that welcomed Catholics.
Maryland	**b.** Colonists there had good relationships with Native Americans.
North and South Carolina	**c.** It became a royal colony when King James I took it over.
Georgia	**d.** Many rice plantations were located there.

Got it?

7. Main Ideas and Details Provide details to back up the main idea that several new colonies were formed from existing ones.

....

....

....

....

8. As a colonial sailor on a merchant ship, you make a stop in Boston. Before you sail away, you walk to the town common. How is the common used, and what did you find there?

my Story Ideas

....

....

....

Stop! I need help with ....

Wait! I have a question about ....

Go! Now I know ....

Daily Life in the Colonies

Envision It!

To communicate in colonial America, people wrote letters using quill pens, ink, and paper.

Today, you can shop at a mall or use the Internet to shop online. In colonial America, people did not have such choices. How did colonists earn a living? How did they feed and clothe their families? What did they do to try to improve their lives?

Colonies and Resources

People in different colonies had different answers for these questions. The land, climate, and natural resources differed from one colony to another.

Most colonial American families lived and worked on farms. They grew or made much of what they needed. They sold crops and products to pay for other necessities, such as tools, salt, and gunpowder. They also bartered with neighbors for some needs. **Barter** means to trade one good for another.

Other colonists worked in jobs related to their colony's location, land, or resources. Along the New England coast, many earned their living from the sea.

1. **Circle** the industry that was found in every region. Then **place a check** next to those found in more than one region.

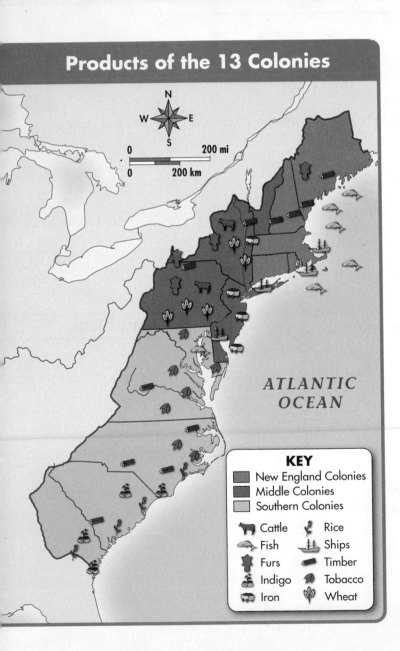

Products of the 13 Colonies

N
W E
S

0   200 mi
0   200 km

ATLANTIC OCEAN

KEY
New England Colonies
Middle Colonies
Southern Colonies

Cattle   Rice
Fish   Ships
Furs   Timber
Indigo   Tobacco
Iron   Wheat

UNLOCK THE BIG ?

I will know how the patterns of life and work in the colonies differed from the patterns today.

Vocabulary

barter   mercantilism

export   triangular trade

import   artisan

raw materials   class

Draw a tool you often use to communicate with others. Explain the benefits of the tool you drew.

New England industries sprang up to take advantage of the ocean's resources. Anglers caught and sold fish, such as cod. Whalers hunted whales to make products such as lamp oil, candles, and perfume. Shipbuilders used the region's timber to build boats for fishing and ships for whaling.

In the Middle Colonies, the region's sheltered harbors and deep rivers allowed ships to travel regularly over the waters and trade to thrive. Many colonists in cities such as New York and Philadelphia worked as merchants and traders. Others worked as sailors or dockworkers, people who loaded and unloaded ships.

People also changed the land to suit their needs. For example, some colonists dammed, or blocked, rivers and streams to create power from fast-flowing water. Millers often set up their businesses next to the river or stream. They used the water power for their gristmills. These were machines for grinding wheat into flour. The flowing water turned a water wheel, and the moving wheel turned the grinding stones inside the mill to crush the wheat.

2. **Explain** why gristmills were built next to rivers and streams.

....

....

....

Imports and Exports

American colonists traded goods among themselves. They also carried on trade with other countries, selling exports and buying imports. An **export** is a product sold to other countries. An **import** is a product bought from other countries.

Over time, England took steps to control colonial trade. The colonies provided England with **raw materials**, or resources that can be made into products, such as timber for making furniture. The English wanted colonists to buy manufactured goods, such as furniture and pottery, from England alone.

In fact, England passed laws limiting colonists' trade with other countries. The English government did this to protect its own industries. This practice is known as protectionism. As a result, colonists had to rely on England for many items. Such restrictions angered many colonists. They felt that these laws showed that England would treat the colonists unfairly to increase their profits from trade.

These trade laws were based on England's belief in the economic policy of mercantilism (MUR kun tihl ihz um).

Colonists were expected to buy pottery, such as this vase, only from England.

3. ● **Main Ideas and Details** **Add** details from the text that support the main idea.

How England Controlled Trade in the Colonies

Main Idea
England took steps to control trade in the American colonies.

Supporting Detail
Colonies exported raw materials to England.

Supporting Detail

Supporting Detail

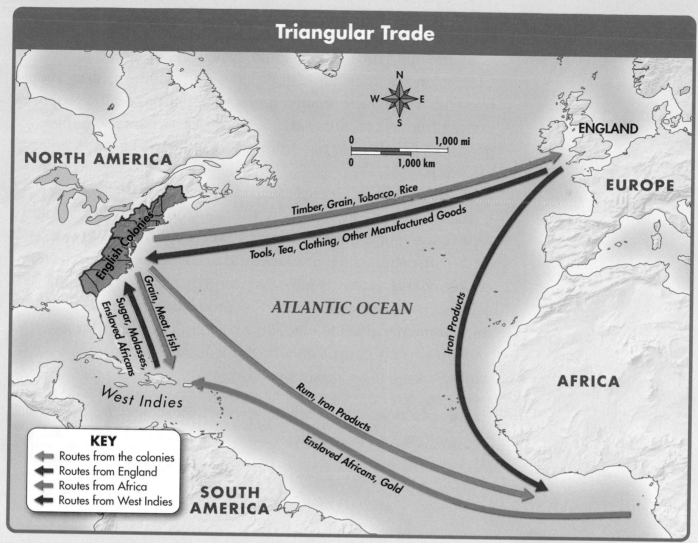

Triangular Trade

NORTH AMERICA

English Colonies

Timber, Grain, Tobacco, Rice

Tools, Tea, Clothing, Other Manufactured Goods

ATLANTIC OCEAN

ENGLAND

EUROPE

Iron Products

AFRICA

Grain, Meat, Fish

Sugar, Molasses, Enslaved Africans

West Indies

Rum, Iron Products

Enslaved Africans, Gold

SOUTH AMERICA

KEY
- Routes from the colonies
- Routes from England
- Routes from Africa
- Routes from West Indies

Triangular trade routes linked the colonies with Europe, Africa, and the West Indies.

Mercantilism was an economic idea popular in the 1600s and 1700s. People who supported this idea thought that countries benefited from trade when they exported more than they imported. In this way, a country earned more money from products it sold to other countries than it spent on products bought from other countries.

Over time, colonial trade took on a pattern known as **triangular trade.** *Triangular* means "three-sided." Triangular trade had three parts. Ships sailed to Africa, the Americas, and Europe. Some carried enslaved Africans to the West Indies and then to the English colonies. Ships from the colonies took fish, lumber, and tobacco to Europe. Tools, tea, and manufactured goods came from England. On both sides of the Atlantic, merchants and traders grew rich.

4. **Describe** the route that traders used to bring enslaved people from Africa to North America.

....

....

....

....

....

....

115

Artisans and Craftspeople

By the mid-1700s, Philadelphia, New York, Boston, and Charleston had grown into large cities and trading centers. People from the countryside brought goods to sell in these cities. Imports arrived from other countries. Merchants bought and sold these goods. As people grew rich from this trade, cities became centers of wealth.

In the countryside, people tended to do many different tasks. In the towns and cities, however, workers could specialize in one type of work, or a trade. These were **artisans,** or skilled workers and craftspeople, such as blacksmiths, carpenters, wigmakers, basketmakers, and tinsmiths. Working in a market economy, artisans could make their living by producing the goods people in their town wanted to buy. Some colonial cities grew large enough to support artisans who made luxury goods, such as watchmakers and silversmiths.

5. **Explain** what skill each artisan is demonstrating. Do people still perform these skills today?

....

....

....

....

Modern artisans keep alive the skills of the past at restoration sites such as Colonial Williamsburg in Virginia.

Colonial Society

Europeans in colonial society belonged to certain **classes**, or society groups, based on their wealth or importance. The highest class was known as the gentry. It included wealthy landowners and merchants as well as church officials. Often, government and community leaders came from this group.

The largest number of colonists belonged to the middle class. This class included small farmers, shopkeepers, and village artisans. These people were not rich, but they earned a living. They had little left over after meeting their basic needs. Most middle-class men were able to vote.

The lower class consisted of ordinary workers and servants. This group of people did not own property or businesses. Unlike today, in colonial times lower class members were not allowed to vote. A worker on a fishing boat or on a farm would belong to this class. So would an indentured servant or apprentice. Indentured servants worked without pay for a period of time in return for food, clothes, and transportation. Enslaved people were considered lower than these three classes of society.

In colonial life, class was important. Even at worship services, people usually sat according to their class. It was possible, however, for a hardworking person to move up in class.

6. Complete the diagram with information from this page.

Classes of Colonial Society

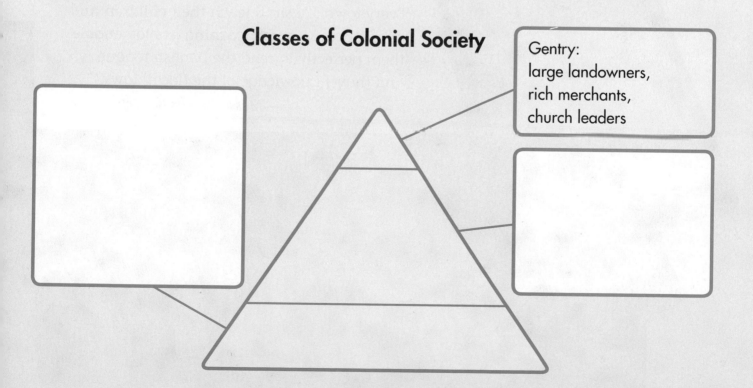

Gentry:
large landowners,
rich merchants,
church leaders

Daily Life in the Colonies

Work, of course, was a big part of daily life. Chores at home took a lot of time and skilled effort. Women made clothing, candles, and other household items. They grew, preserved, and prepared food. Most women cared for children. This could be a big challenge in families with more than a dozen children.

Most children also had work to do, starting at an early age. The chores became more demanding as the children grew older. Many children were sent away at age 12 to begin training in a trade. When they did have time for fun, children played with simple toys. These included metal hoops from barrels, dolls made of cornhusks, or tops made from scraps of wood and string. Children sometimes made work into a game. They might hold a contest to see who could carry the most wood or husk corn the fastest.

Some children did go to school. Most New England towns were required to have schools. There were schools in some other colonies, too. Sometimes, children were given lessons at home. Most children did not have a full education, however. By the time they were teenagers, they usually worked full time. Only a few young people went to college.

Colonial children of all ages often attended school together, sometimes in one large room. They learned to read from pages placed on wooden tablets and covered with a clear sheet of animal horn.

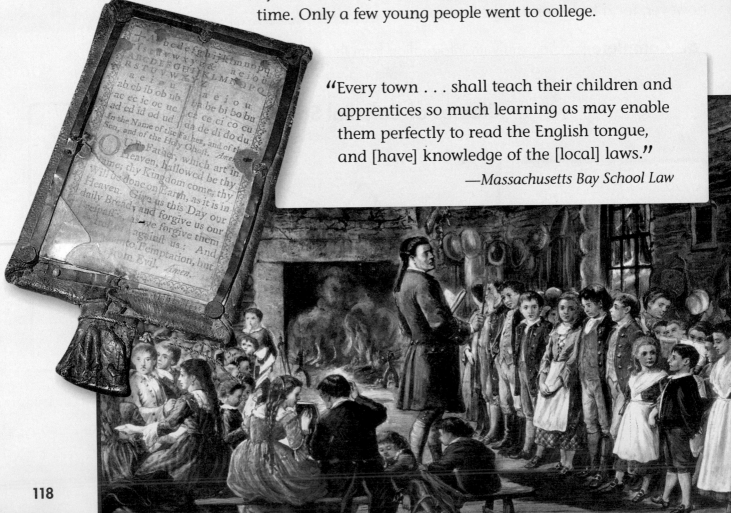

"Every town . . . shall teach their children and apprentices so much learning as may enable them perfectly to read the English tongue, and [have] knowledge of the [local] laws."

—*Massachusetts Bay School Law*

Religion was always important to colonial life. In the 1730s, however, an event called the Great Awakening took religious interest to a new level. Preachers traveled from town to town, giving fiery talks that inspired listeners. Large crowds of worshipers would gather for these talks. The Great Awakening helped spread religious feelings. At the same time, it weakened the power of church leaders who had previously directed life in some colonies. The movement stressed that people should develop their own connection to God. They did not have to rely upon a church leader to tell them how to live or worship.

During the Great Awakening, ministers such as George Whitefield inspired churchgoers to stronger religious feelings.

Got it?

7. **⊙ Main Ideas and Details Provide** two details to support the main idea that the life and work of a small farmer differed from that of an artisan living in a big city.

....

....

....

8. **?** You are visiting relatives in Philadelphia, Pennsylvania. Your 12-year-old cousin is an apprentice in a furniture workshop. Why did he sign up for an apprenticeship, and what is he learning?

my Story Ideas

....

....

....

▮ **Stop!** I need help with ....

❚❚ **Wait!** I have a question about ....

▶ **Go!** Now I know ....

Slavery in the Colonies

WALO
CAYOR
BAOL
MANDING
FULA
SUSU
FANTE
BENIN
TEKE
LOANGO

N
W E
S

0   500 mi
0   500 km

ATLANTIC OCEAN

map area

Enslaved people captured in western Africa brought some of their culture and language to the Americas.

In the summer of 1619, a Dutch ship carrying cargo that included a group of Africans landed at Jamestown. Local residents bartered for these Africans and put them to work. They were not paid and received only food and shelter for their work. A few may have gained their freedom after some time. Within a few years, new laws were passed in Virginia and Massachusetts that took away all rights from African servants. **Slavery**, a system in which people are bought and sold as if they were property, had begun in the English colonies.

The Slave Trade

What began that summer soon grew into a large and horrifying business. Many groups of people have been enslaved throughout history, often as a result of war. In the growing colonies, however, workers were wanted. Indentured servants met part of this need, agreeing to work for a time. Enslaved Africans, however, made no such agreement. They were captured and taken against their will without hope of freedom.

Africans were captured and then crammed side by side into ships. They were bound for sale in the Americas.

At first enslaved people came mostly from the western part of Africa. Other Africans captured them, marching the captives to the coast where European traders awaited in ships. In return for human captives, the Europeans offered guns and other goods. The African captors used the guns to enslave more people.

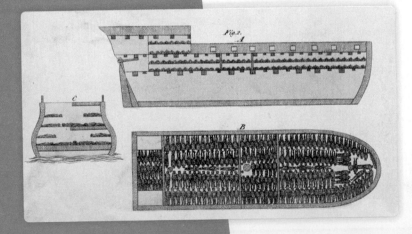

Vocabulary

slavery
Middle Passage
uprising

Draw a picture to illustrate one of these words of African origin: *banjo, gumbo, jazz, cola, tote, goober, jumbo.*

Next came the terrifying journey to the Americas. This was called the **Middle Passage.** The captured Africans were packed into boats. They were chained together, body to body, in the cargo holds. With little room to stand or stretch, they lay in darkness for weeks and months. Frightened and hungry, many people became sick and did not survive the trip. Many others wished they had died and were jealous of those who no longer had to suffer. As one survivor of the Middle Passage wrote about those who had died:

"I envied them the freedom they enjoyed, and as often wished I could change my condition for theirs."

—Olaudah Equiano

1. ◉ **Main Ideas and Details Write** two additional details that support the main idea.

Horrors of the Middle Passage

Main Idea
The Middle Passage was a terrifying experience.

Supporting Detail

Supporting Detail
The Africans lay in darkness for months and didn't know where they were being taken.

Supporting Detail

Slavery in the North

Following the Middle Passage, many enslaved Africans found themselves in the English colonies of North America. There, they were sold in auctions. An auction is a public sale in which the highest bidder makes the purchase. Once purchased, enslaved Africans became the property of colonists. They had very few basic rights.

Every colony practiced slavery. The Massachusetts Bay Colony passed the first law to allow it in 1641. Other colonies soon had similar laws. Slavery was most widespread in the South, but it existed throughout the colonies.

Many enslaved Africans in the North lived in cities and towns. In the 1750s, for instance, one out of ten residents in the city of Boston was African American. Most of them were enslaved. Some of them worked in shops, helping artisans with their work or doing skilled work themselves. Others worked in inns or as personal servants in the homes of wealthy people. In the cities, slaveholders rarely owned more than one or two enslaved people.

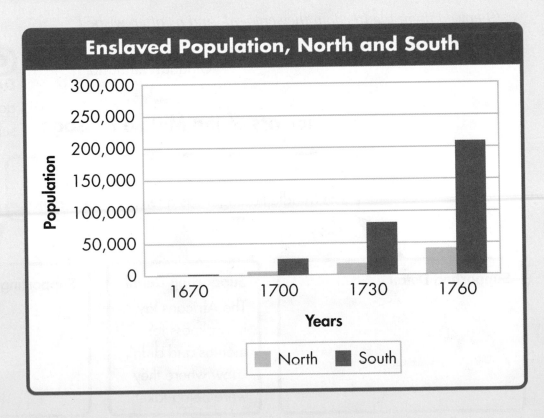

Advertisements for slave auctions used adjectives such as "valuable," as though human beings were mere objects.

To be SOLD by AUCTION,
On SATURDAY the 17th day of JANUARY inst.
At HAYNE HALL, near JACKSONBURGH,
Ninety valuable Negroes
Belonging to the Estate of the late
COLONEL ISAAC HAYNE.
Among the Men, are
DRIVERS, WHEELWRIGHTS,
CARPENTERS, COOPERS, &c.

Enslaved Population, North and South

Enslaved people worked in all of the American colonies. However, slavery in the North and in the South grew at different rates.

122

Some enslaved Africans worked on farms in the North. A successful farmer might keep only one or two of them. Mostly, though, northern farmers did not grow crops that required large numbers of workers. For that reason, there were fewer enslaved farmworkers in the North.

A very few African Americans in the northern colonies were free. Some bought their freedom by saving money from working in shops or selling produce from gardens. Sometimes, a slaveholder would set a person free. Free African Americans often lived in the cities of the North. Still, even free African Americans had few rights. For example, they could be kidnapped and taken back into slavery.

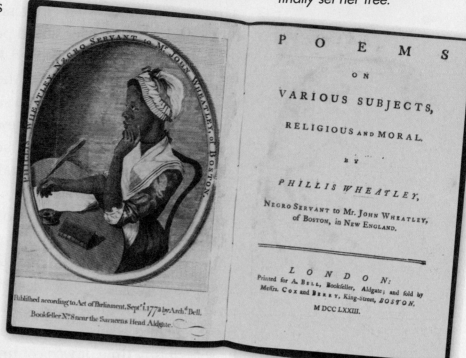

Phillis Wheatley was sold to a Boston family in 1761 at an auction. She learned to write and became a noted poet. Her owners finally set her free.

2. Using the graph on the previous page, **compare** and **contrast** how slavery grew in the North and South between 1670 and 1760.

Topic
Comparing Slavery in the North and South

Ways alike
*

*

Ways different
*

*

Slavery in the South

Slavery developed differently in the South from in the North. In the South, farmers grew tobacco or rice. Later, they grew cotton. These crops required many workers to tend, pick, and prepare the plants for shipping. Many southern planters relied on enslaved Africans to do this work. Planters with large farms might purchase hundreds of enslaved people. In parts of the South, there were many more enslaved Africans than Europeans.

Enslaved Africans did more than work in the fields. They brought special knowledge and skills from their African homes. For example, some Africans knew about planting and growing rice. Because of their skills, rice become a huge cash crop in the Carolinas. The success of rice had a bad result for many Africans, however. Rice plantations expanded, and their owners purchased many more enslaved Africans to work on them.

The way enslaved Africans lived in the South was different from in the North. In the South, enslaved Africans often lived together in large communities. In many cases, they formed families. The families provided support and happiness. However, they were also a source of pain because a family member could be sold at any time. It was common for slaveholders to separate husbands from wives or children from parents.

Plantation life was hard on African American families. Still, enslaved people developed a rich culture. In plantation villages, people from different parts of Africa met and mixed. African words, foods, and music blended with European languages and customs on the plantations. The result would have a long-lasting impact on American customs and music.

White slaveholders feared the growing slave culture. They often tried to crush it. For example, at times the playing of African music was outlawed in some places. Colonists felt that a united slave community would be strong and dangerous. They could not keep African Americans from forming a strong new culture, however. This culture helped support African Americans in difficult times. It also added to the way of life in the South.

3. **Explain** why a rice plantation in the South might require many workers and why enslaved Africans were used for this work.

....

....

....

....

Enslaved workers unload rice plants from barges. Both men and women toiled at this backbreaking work.

Fighting Back Against Slavery

No matter where an enslaved person worked, slavery was a brutal system. The enslaved people had almost no rights. They could be beaten or whipped or worse. Their families could be taken away. They could be kept from meeting with friends or learning to read. These are just some of the horrors with which they had to live.

Many enslaved people found ways to fight back. Some learned to read and write and used their new knowledge to encourage others to go against the rules. Others might break tools, set fire to property, or steal food. Some enslaved people saw justice in destroying or taking the property of people who had stolen their freedom. The extra food also helped them to survive their hard lives.

Enslaved people also tried to escape. Sometimes, runaways formed communities in swamps or forests far away from white settlements. In this way, they could avoid capture for long periods of time.

In a few cases, enslaved Africans fought back violently. Slave **uprisings,** or rebellions, occurred in several colonies, including New York, Virginia, and South Carolina. They were often bloody. In 1739, the Stono Rebellion in South Carolina left dozens of whites and blacks dead.

4. ◉ **Main Ideas and Details Complete** the graphic organizer by filling in two more details that support the main idea.

Resistance to Slavery

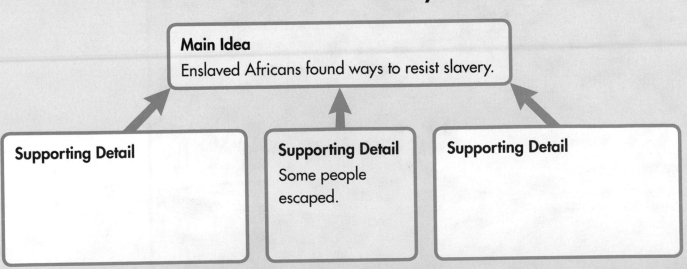

Main Idea
Enslaved Africans found ways to resist slavery.

Supporting Detail

Supporting Detail
Some people escaped.

Supporting Detail

126

These uprisings terrified white slaveholders. They sometimes responded by clamping down even harder on enslaved Africans. In 1741, for example, fear of a slave rebellion in New York City led to terrible violence against African Americans. Whites who were thought to be helping enslaved people were also killed.

Still, enslaved Africans kept up their resistance. On plantations, they came up with ways of staying together and sharing information. For example, they used songs to send secret messages among themselves. These songs helped enslaved Africans survive. With time, such songs became part of American culture.

Enslaved Africans played handmade banjos, such as this one, and sang songs to convey secret messages.

Got it?

5. **◉ Main Ideas and Details List** two details to support the main idea that both slave traders and slaveholders mistreated enslaved Africans.

....

....

....

6. **?** As part of your trip to the American colonies, you visit a rice plantation near Charleston. You have a chance to talk to some enslaved workers at the plantation. How did they get there? What is their life like?

my Story Ideas

....

....

....

⏹ **Stop!** I need help with ....

⏸ **Wait!** I have a question about ....

▶ **Go!** Now I know ....

Compare Viewpoints

A viewpoint is the way someone looks at or thinks about a subject. Often in the study of history, you will find that different people see the same subject in different ways. Comparing two viewpoints can help you understand how differences and conflicts happened. Read, for instance, these two views on colonization in North America.

Passage A

"And as for the general sort that shall go to be planters [in Virginia], be they [very] poor, so they be honest, . . . the place will make them rich."

—Virginia Company pamphlet, 1609

Passage B

"For we must consider that we shall be as a City upon a Hill. The eyes of all people are upon us. So that if we shall deal falsely with our God in this work we have undertaken . . . we shall be made a story and a by-word throughout the world. "

—John Winthrop, 1630

To compare viewpoints, first understand the subject. What idea do the two views have in common? Both writers discuss the reasons why English colonists might come to North America.

Next, consider how the viewpoints differ from one another. Passage A suggests that making money was the key goal of colonization in Virginia. The pamphlet explains that an honest, hardworking person could become rich there. Passage B suggests that colonists came to America to set an example. Through their actions in America, colonists would show others how to live a proper, religious life.

Read the two viewpoints from Native American leaders below.

Quote A

"Your forefathers [English settlers] crossed the great water and landed on this island. Their numbers were small. We took pity on them and they sat down among us. We gave them corn and meat. They gave us poison in return."

—*Sagoyewatha, Seneca*

Quote B

"When the Frenchmen arrived at these falls, they came and kissed us . . . . They never mocked at our ceremonies, [or harmed] the places of our dead."

—*Chippewa chief*

1. What is the subject of these two quotes?

   ....

   ....

2. What is the viewpoint expressed in Quote A?

   ....

   ....

3. What is the viewpoint expressed in Quote B?

   ....

   ....

4. **Apply Think** of a subject about which people have different viewpoints. For example, should students be allowed to have cell phones in school? **Write down** opinions on both sides of the subject. **Compare** the viewpoints.

   ....

   ....

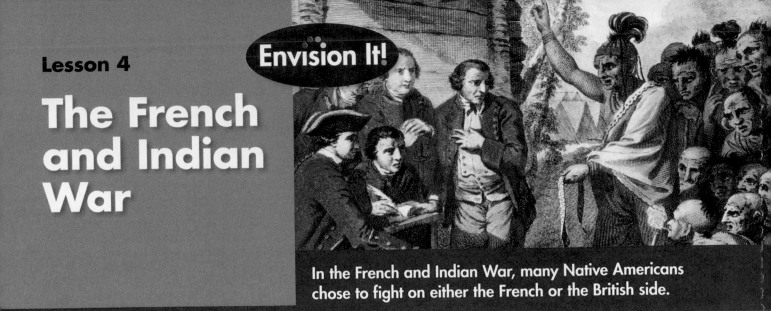

Lesson 4

The French and Indian War

Envision It!

In the French and Indian War, many Native Americans chose to fight on either the French or the British side.

1. **Circle** the part of the map where conflicts between the British and the French were most likely to occur in the 1750s.

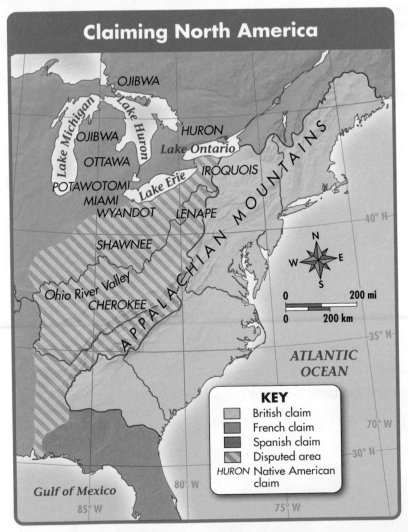

Claiming North America

OJIBWA

Lake Michigan

Lake Huron

OJIBWA

HURON

Lake Ontario

OTTAWA

POTAWOTOMI

MIAMI

Lake Erie

IROQUOIS

WYANDOT

LENAPE

APPALACHIAN MOUNTAINS

40° N

SHAWNEE

N
W   E
S

Ohio River Valley

CHEROKEE

0   200 mi
0   200 km

35° N

ATLANTIC OCEAN

KEY
British claim
French claim
Spanish claim
Disputed area
HURON Native American claim

70° W

30° N

Gulf of Mexico

80° W

85° W

75° W

It was a war with two names, fought on two continents. In Europe, it was called the Seven Years' War, one of many wars between France and Great Britain. In North America, it was called the French and Indian War. Here, the fighting included a third power. Native Americans, who had lived on the land long before the French or British arrived, took sides.

Conflicts Begin

Native Americans had always had a mixed relationship with Europeans. Sometimes, they helped struggling newcomers or traded actively with the colonists in their area. Sometimes, however, they attempted to drive European colonists away.

In 1675, Metacom, a Wampanoag leader in New England, began a war against the colonists in the region.

The British, the French, and Native Americans came into conflict in the Ohio River valley in the 1750s.

UNLOCK THE BIG ?

I will know how Great Britain became the greatest colonial power in North America.

Vocabulary

King Philip's War	Pontiac's Rebellion
ally	Proclamation of 1763
treaty	

List three ways you think Native Americans might help themselves by siding with a European force.

Metacom was called King Philip by settlers. The conflict became known as **King Philip's War.** The result was a defeat for Metacom in which many of his people died. Not all Native Americans supported Metacom. Some joined the colonists in the war.

Colonists accepted Native American help. Yet what they really wanted was their land. As the American colonies grew, settlers pushed west, clearing woods for farms and building towns. By the mid-1700s, many had crossed the Appalachian Mountains to reach the Ohio River valley. This rich land was home to many powerful Native American peoples. The French also claimed the area. The stage was set for a bloody fight.

2. ◎ **Main Idea and Details**
Fill in the graphic organizer with details that support the main idea.

Native Americans React to Settlers

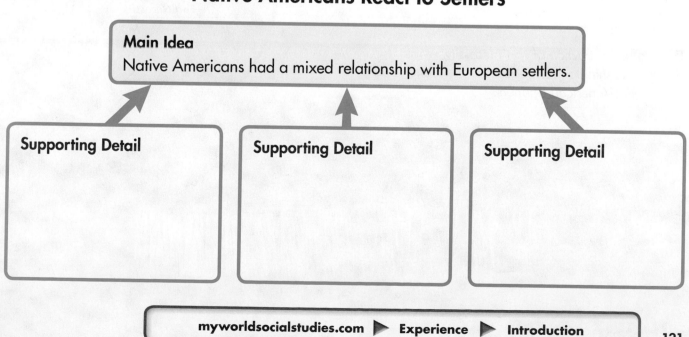

Main Idea
Native Americans had a mixed relationship with European settlers.

Supporting Detail

Supporting Detail

Supporting Detail

War Between Britain and France

The Ohio River valley was part of the huge region that French explorer Robert de La Salle had claimed for France. The French built forts in the area to protect their claim.

The British also thought the valley was theirs. Some British pioneers established a trading post near the site of present-day Pittsburgh in Pennsylvania. They considered this area across the Appalachian Mountains to be part of the Virginia colony.

The French would not give up their claim to the valley, however. French soldiers destroyed the British trading post and built a fort nearby. They called it Fort Duquesne (doo KAYN).

In 1753, the British sent a small force to the region. Its leader was a young soldier from Virginia named George Washington. Washington saw that Fort Duquesne was well guarded, so he decided not to attack. Instead, his men fought and defeated a small group of French soldiers in the woods nearby. Then, they built their own fort. They called it Fort Necessity.

French soldiers, joined by Native Americans, attacked the fort. Together, they beat the British. The French allowed Washington and his surviving soldiers to return to Virginia.

3. **Write** two reasons why this fort was probably easy for the French and Native Americans to capture.

....

....

....

....

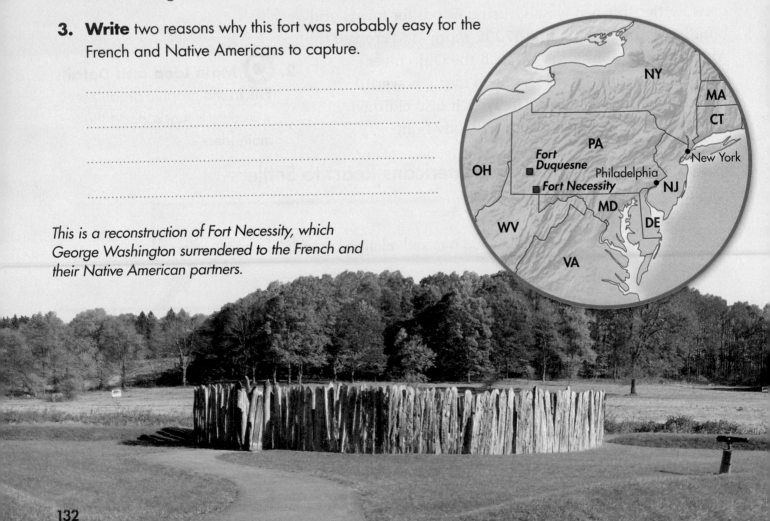

This is a reconstruction of Fort Necessity, which George Washington surrendered to the French and their Native American partners.

The French and Indian War had begun. The war's name came from the fact that in North America, the British army fought both the French and their Native American allies. An **ally** is a military partner. Many Native Americans supported the French. They feared the British, whose colonies were spreading. The British, in turn, sought the support of the powerful Iroquois as an ally. At first, the Iroquois resisted. One of their leaders said:

[The French and British] are both quarrelling about lands which belong to us, and such a quarrel as this may end in our destruction.

—Hendrick Peters, Iroquois leader

Later, the Iroquois decided to side with the British. They hoped this would help them keep control of their land.

4. **Complete** the sequence chart. **List** two other key events leading up to the start of the French and Indian War.

Events Leading to the French and Indian War

1. French and British claim land in Ohio River valley.

2. _____
_____
_____

3. _____
_____
_____

4. French defeat Washington at Fort Necessity with the help of Native American allies.

Lt. Colonel George Washington led a British force in the first battle of the French and Indian War when he was only 22.

The British Win

In 1755, the British returned, hoping to capture Fort Duquesne. This time, they sent a general, Edward Braddock. Washington served as his advisor. French and Native American fighters defeated the British again, killing General Braddock. The effort to capture the fort failed.

The British lost many early battles. For a while, it seemed that they would lose the war. Then, in 1757, British leaders sent reinforcements from Europe. Made stronger, the British army at last took control over Fort Duquesne in 1758.

The Iroquois decided to join the British side. This new force was unstoppable. In a key 1759 battle, the allies captured Quebec, the capital of New France. The next year, the British captured Montreal, another French settlement in present-day Canada. The French and their allies had been beaten. In 1763, France and England signed a **treaty**, which is a formal agreement between countries. France agreed to surrender much of its territory in North America east of the Mississippi River.

The Ohio River valley was now under British control. This upset many Native Americans. They knew that more colonists from the east would soon arrive. Unlike the French, British settlers built towns and roads, changing the land. In 1763, an Ottawa leader named Pontiac took action. He led an army that attacked British forts and villages in the Ohio River valley.

In 1763, Pontiac rallied Native American groups to fight together to make the British leave their lands.

After much fighting, the British crushed **Pontiac's Rebellion.** Still, the outbreak alarmed many British leaders, and the fighting had been very expensive. King George III issued a formal order, the **Proclamation of 1763.** It blocked colonists from settling lands west of the Appalachians. The king hoped this order would help keep peace with Native Americans.

The proclamation upset colonists eager to settle in the Ohio River valley. Many of them pushed west despite the order. This added to a growing strain between the colonies and Great Britain.

5. **Explain** what effect the Proclamation of 1763 had on colonization.

....

....

....

....

....

....

....

Got it?

6. **◉ Main Ideas and Details Describe** at least three details to support the following main idea: The British and French fought to control North America in the mid-1700s.

....

....

....

7. **❓** After the French and Indian War, you want to move westward to start a farm. Why do you think this is a good idea? How will you persuade your family to cross the mountains? What concerns do you have about this move?

my Story Ideas

....

....

....

◼ **Stop!** I need help with ....

⏸ **Wait!** I have a question about ....

▶ **Go!** Now I know ....

Chapter 4
Study Guide

Lesson 1

New England, Middle, and Southern Colonies

- The 13 English colonies were shaped by geography.
- In New England, the ocean and forests provided key resources.
- In the Middle Colonies, farming was a major economic activity.
- In the Southern Colonies, conditions were ideal for rice and tobacco.

Lesson 2

Daily Life in the Colonies

- Most colonists lived and worked on farms.
- Some colonists in cities were artisans who practiced skilled trades, such as printing, blacksmithing, or basket weaving.
- England tried to control colonial trade.

Lesson 3

Slavery in the Colonies

- The practice of slavery began soon after the settlement of Jamestown.
- Enslaved Africans worked in both the North and the South.
- Enslaved people suffered greatly but made valuable contributions.
- Enslaved people resisted their captivity in many ways.

Lesson 4

The French and Indian War

- British, French, and Native Americans clashed in the Ohio River valley.
- After early defeats, the British and their allies won the war.
- The Proclamation of 1763 tried to stop British settlement beyond the Appalachian Mountains.

Review and Assessment

Lesson 1

New England, Middle, and Southern Colonies

1. **Explain** how geography helped shape the English colonies.

   ....

   ....

   ....

   ....

2. What was the difference between a proprietary and a royal colony?

   ....

   ....

   ....

   ....

3. **Draw** a line to connect each of the following with the colony to which he is linked.

   A. Roger Williams   1. Georgia

   B. George Carteret   2. Maryland

   C. Lord Baltimore   3. Connecticut

   D. William Penn   4. Rhode Island

   E. James Oglethorpe   5. Pennsylvania

   F. Thomas Hooker   6. New Jersey

Lesson 2

Daily Life in the Colonies

4. Why did cities have more artisans than the countryside?

   ....

   ....

   ....

   ....

   ....

5. What kinds of people occupied the middle class in colonial life?

   ....

   ....

   ....

6. **Circle** the correct answer.
   Which of the following was a result of England's pursuit of mercantilism?

   A. The colonies grew very rich.

   B. The colonies became centers of manufacturing.

   C. The colonies focused on producing raw materials.

   D. The colonies were allowed to import goods only from England.

Chapter 4

Review and Assessment

Lesson 3

Slavery in the Colonies

7. **Main Idea and Details Fill in** the details to support the main idea given in the chart below.

Main Idea: Enslaved Africans lived in different housing in the North and the South.

8. What are some of the ways enslaved people resisted slavery?

9. What is the Middle Passage?

Lesson 4

The French and Indian War

10. The French and Indian War started in North America because of conflicts over which region?

11. What helped turn the tide of the war in favor of the British?

12. **What does it take to build a new society?**

a. How did enslaved Africans contribute to life in the colonies?

b. How did creating a community help enslaved Africans to cope with their lives?

Go online to write and illustrate your own **myStory Book** using the **myStory Ideas** from this chapter.

 # What does it take to build a new society?

When people live together in a community, they must figure out ways to meet their needs and wants, such as education and safety. They find ways to agree about important principles for getting along and working together to accomplish goals. They figure out how to govern themselves, too. The way people in a community make these decisions together helps build the society.

Think about the society you live in. **Write** about some part of this society, such as the government or schools, and how people are trying to work together to make the society work for everyone.

....

....

....

Now, **draw** a picture that shows what you could do to improve your society.

While you're online, check out the **myStory Current Events** area where you can create your own book on a topic that's in the news.

The American Revolution

What is worth fighting for?

Describe an idea or a group that you support. Then **write** about how you show your support for the group or idea.

....

....

....

....

....

Cannon on display at Valley Forge, Pennsylvania

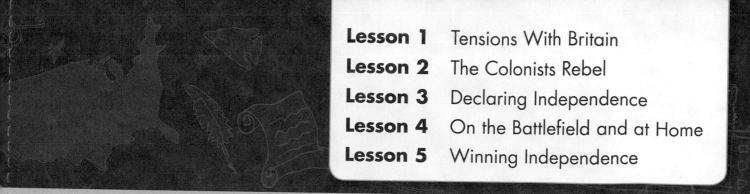

Samuel Adams
Champion of Liberty

my Story Video

The American Revolution was a war fought for liberty. It was a war that sparked greatness in a few ordinary people. George Washington is known as a heroic general. Thomas Jefferson is remembered for writing the Declaration of Independence and Paul Revere for warning of a British invasion. However, decades before the battles of the revolution, one man in Boston organized the movement that started the fight for liberty. He never used force against the British, but the British called him "the most dangerous man in Massachusetts." His fellow countrymen called him "the father of American independence." His name was Samuel Adams.

As a young man, Samuel looked more like a poor student than a dangerous revolutionary. After grammar school in his hometown of Boston, Massachusetts, he attended Harvard College and graduated at age seventeen.

In the 1700s, it was not unusual to have such an early start on a college education. Adams's family hoped he would become a minister, but he showed an interest only in politics. He loved to go around town debating how the colonies should be governed.

Samuel Adams speaking at Harvard College

141

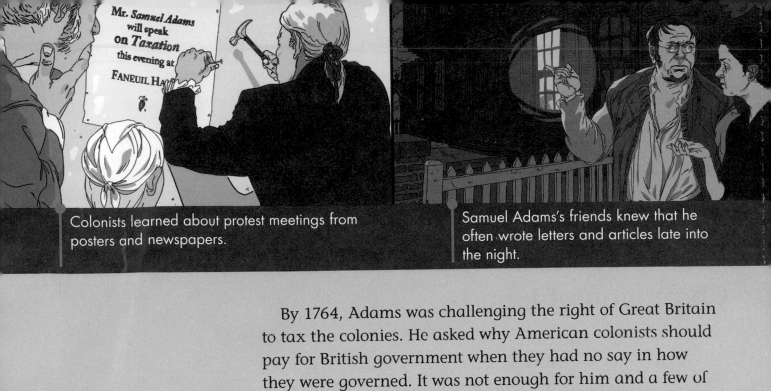

Colonists learned about protest meetings from posters and newspapers.

Samuel Adams's friends knew that he often wrote letters and articles late into the night.

Samuel Adams traveled throughout the colonies to spread the call of liberty.

By 1764, Adams was challenging the right of Great Britain to tax the colonies. He asked why American colonists should pay for British government when they had no say in how they were governed. It was not enough for him and a few of his friends to talk among themselves about colonists' rights. Adams needed to get the word out to as many working people as possible. Today, Samuel would be called a political activist, or someone who supports political change. He wrote thousands of letters to newspapers and other colonial leaders about British injustice. He spoke at hundreds of meetings. Sometimes he exaggerated what the British had done to make sure he got people's attention.

The Boston Harbor near Adams's home gave Great Britain a port for shipping trade goods and for landing troops.

Samuel Adams and his friend John Hancock watched the colonists' militia get ready to fight in 1775.

Adams spent so much time and energy on politics that he failed at almost every job he had. He was so determined to get his message out that he stayed up late at night, writing words to inspire people to join his cause.

Most of Adams's efforts focused on the theme of freedom. As a college student, he wrote an essay about whether the colonists should resist the royal government of Great Britain. Later he wrote in the *Boston Gazette* newspaper:

> "We cannot have forgotten that . . . Great Britain declared that they had right and authority to make any laws whatever binding on his majesty's [King George III's] subjects in America. How far this declaration can be consistent with the freedom of his majesty's subjects in America, let any one judge who pleases."
> —Samuel Adams

Adams wrote a steady flow of letters and articles for more than 30 years. Whenever groups of colonists got together, they discussed his ideas. Adams had hoped his ideas would cause the colonists to act to protect their rights and freedoms. Considering that Thomas Jefferson called Samuel Adams "the patriarch [father] of liberty," it seems that Samuel Adams got his wish.

Think About It Based on this story, what issues do you think Samuel Adams thought were worth fighting for, and how did he fight? As you read this chapter, remember that fighting for something doesn't have to occur on a battlefield.

Tensions With Britain

Envision It!

JOIN, or DIE.

This political cartoon shows the British colonies as separate parts of a snake.

The Stamp Act required that stamps like this be placed on all printed materials.

Great Britain had won the French and Indian War. As a result, Great Britain gained a huge amount of land in North America. However, it also gained a huge **debt**, which meant that it owed money. Britain also needed to send thousands of soldiers to North America to protect the new lands. Where would the British get money to pay for these troops and repay its debt?

Trouble Over Taxes

Leaders in Great Britain decided to tax American colonists to pay for part of the debt. The money raised from taxing colonists would also help pay the costs of defending the colonies.

George III was king of Great Britain and supported the idea of taxing colonists. So did many members of Britain's law-making assembly, Parliament (PAHR luh munt), which makes Britain's laws. The members of Parliament represented different areas in Great Britain. To them, the tax seemed fair.

In 1765, Parliament passed the Stamp Act. This law placed a tax on paper products in the colonies, such as legal documents, newspapers, and even playing cards. When the colonists bought these items they would have to buy a stamp.

1. **Circle** the part of the stamp that shows it is from a royal government.

Draw what the cartoon might look like if the colonies worked together, united. Write a new caption.

UNLOCK THE BIG ?

I will know that the colonists believed that fighting against unfair laws was worth the risk.

Vocabulary

debt   effigy
congress   boycott
repeal   tariff

No Taxation Without Representation!

When the colonists learned about the Stamp Act, they complained. None of Parliament's representatives came from the American colonies. Since colonists had no representatives in Parliament, they thought Parliament should not tax them. A common cry in the colonies was, "No taxation without representation!"

2. ◎ **Cause and Effect Fill in** the missing cause and effect.

Taxing the American Colonies

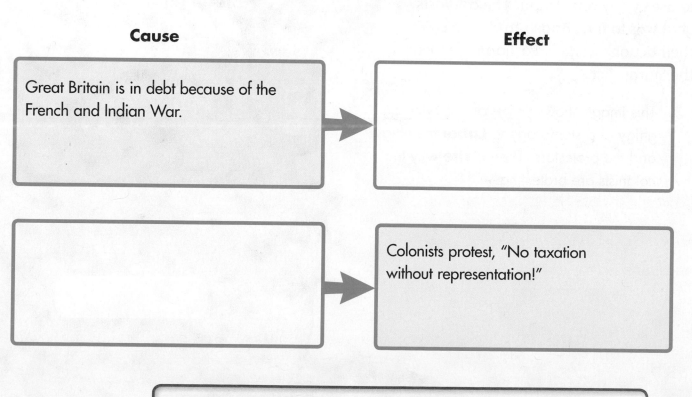

Cause		Effect
Great Britain is in debt because of the French and Indian War.	→	
	→	Colonists protest, "No taxation without representation!"

The Colonists Take Action

Patrick Henry was a young lawyer from Virginia. He opposed the Stamp Act. He gave a powerful speech to Virginia's lawmakers. Parliament had no right to tax the colonists, he argued.

Other leaders agreed with Henry. In October 1765, representatives from nine colonies met in New York City. They included lawyers, farmers, and businesspeople. The meeting they held was called the Stamp Act Congress. A **congress** is a formal meeting. It can also be a law-making body. The Congress asked Parliament to **repeal**, or cancel, the Stamp Act.

Patrick Henry

Individual colonists also opposed the Stamp Act. A group in Boston, called the Sons of Liberty, organized protests. Other groups formed throughout the colonies, taking actions that frightened the people who sold the stamps, called stamp agents. These groups burned stamps, threatened stamp agents, and sometimes attacked the agents' homes. In Boston, protestors created an **effigy,** or a life-sized puppet, of the local stamp agent and hung it from a tree. Soon no one was willing to sell the stamps.

In addition, some merchants, people who buy and sell goods for profit, decided to boycott British goods. **Boycotts** take place when people act together and refuse to use or buy something. The colonists' goal was to hurt British trade. By 1766, their actions worked. Parliament repealed the Stamp Act.

THE FOLLY OF ENGLAND AND THE RUIN OF AMERICA

3. This image shows protestors carrying an effigy of a stamp agent. **Label** the effigy and the protestors. Then **write** why the colonists are protesting.

....

....

....

New Taxes From Great Britain

Although Parliament had repealed the Stamp Act, Great Britain still needed money. King George III and Parliament also wanted the American colonists to understand that Great Britain had the right to tax them.

In 1767, a British leader named Charles Townshend called for a new set of laws to control the colonies. These were called the Townshend Acts. The laws placed a **tariff,** or tax, on many goods that the colonists imported from Britain. These goods included paper, wool, glass, paint, and lead.

Tariffs are usually placed on goods to control trade between nations. But the only purpose of the taxes of the Townshend Acts was to make money for Great Britain. The colonists had to pay these taxes, but people living in Great Britain did not.

In response to the new tariffs, colonists boycotted many of the taxed items. The boycotts were more widespread than they had been for the Stamp Act. In Boston, the Sons of Liberty organized protests. Leaders such as Samuel Adams and James Otis spoke out about colonists' rights.

Colonists boycotted British goods to protest the Townshend Acts.

4. **Fill in** the chart with details about the Townshend Acts.

All About the Townshend Acts

What were the Townshend Acts?	Why did Britain need a new tax?
	Britain needed a new tax to pay its debts from the French and Indian War.

Who was against paying this tax?	What effect did the tax have in the colonies?

Protests and boycotts spread throughout the colonies. More and more men and women joined the effort. Mercy Otis Warren, a writer from Boston, was the wife of a Massachusetts politician. Through her poems, plays, and historical writings, she promoted opposition to the British. In perhaps her most famous poem, she encouraged people to boycott tea and other imported goods. "We'll quit the useless vanities [unnecessary items] of life," she wrote.

In Newport, Rhode Island, a group of women known as the Daughters of Liberty began weaving their own cloth. They organized "spinning bees" where women would come together and spend hours spinning wool yarn. That way they wouldn't have to buy British wool. Others found ways to substitute homemade items for imported goods. For example, people began making "Liberty Tea," a tea using plants from North America. They drank it instead of imported British tea.

5. ◉ **Cause and Effect** **Fill in** the missing effects.

Boycotting Britain

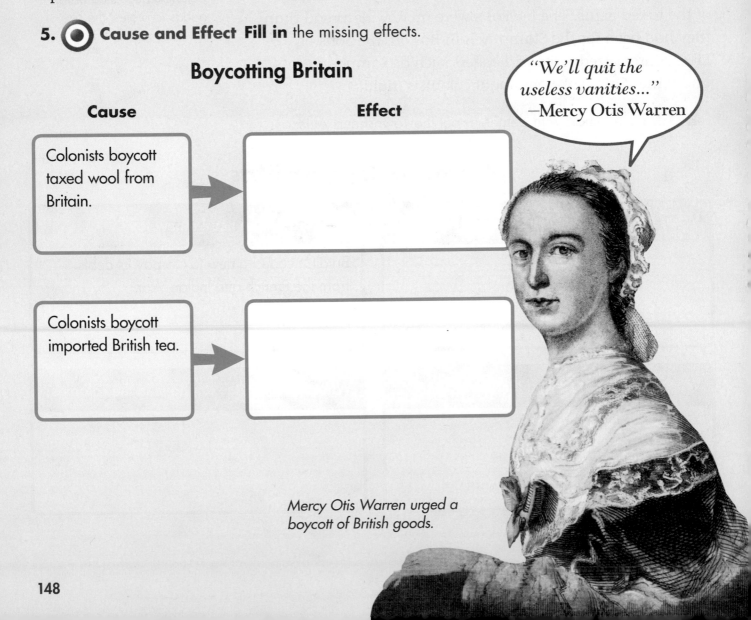

Cause	Effect
Colonists boycott taxed wool from Britain.	
Colonists boycott imported British tea.	

"We'll quit the useless vanities..."
—Mercy Otis Warren

Mercy Otis Warren urged a boycott of British goods.

Townshend Acts Repealed, Mostly

The boycotts were successful. Many British merchants lost money. In an attempt to limit the protests, the British government sent warships and troops to Boston Harbor in 1768.

The troops did not stop the colonists, and the British merchants continued to lose money. They asked Parliament to repeal the Townshend Acts. In 1770, Parliament agreed. It repealed all of the taxes except a tax on tea.

Though American colonists had won a victory over the British Parliament, problems remained. Tea was still taxed, British troops were still in Boston, and colonists were still angry. In the next few years, the trouble got worse.

British warships landed troops in Boston in 1768.

Got it?

6. **Cause and Effect** What was the effect of British taxation on the colonists?

....

....

....

7. Your family runs a printing shop. **Write** a letter to a friend in Great Britain telling him or her how your family feels about the Stamp Act.

my Story Ideas

....

....

....

....

Stop! I need help with ....

Wait! I have a question about ....

Go! Now I know ....

Use Primary Sources

A primary source is something written about an event, a place, or a time by someone who was there, or an "eyewitness." Eyewitness accounts can be letters, diaries, documents, newspaper articles, speeches, or even maps. These primary sources give information about events that only a witness would know.

Information by someone who was not present at an event is a secondary source. Secondary sources can collect and summarize information from many sources. Textbooks, some magazine and newspaper stories, encyclopedias, and some Internet sites are secondary sources.

The newspaper article represented below is a primary source because it was written by someone who was at the event. The subject of this newspaper article is the funeral for the victims of the Boston Massacre. The source is the *Boston Gazette and Country Journal*. The article was written on March 12, 1770.

Last Thursday, agreeable to a general request of the inhabitants and by the consent of parents and friends, were carried to their grave in succession the bodies of Samuel Gray, Samuel Maverick, James Caldwell, and Crispus Attucks, the unhappy victims who fell in the bloody massacre of the Monday evening preceding!

On this occasion most of the shops in town were shut, all the bells were ordered to toll a solemn peal, as were also those in the neighbouring towns of Charlestown, Roxbury, etc. The procession began to move between the hours of four and five in the afternoon, two of the unfortunate sufferers, viz. Messrs. James Caldwell and Crispus Attucks who were strangers, borne from Faneuil Hall attended by a numerous train of persons of all ranks; and the other two, viz. Mr. Samuel Gray, from the house of Mr. Benjamin Gray (his brother) on the north side the Exchange, and Mr. Maverick, from the house of his distressed mother, Mrs. Mary Maverick, in Union Street, each followed by their respective relations and friends, the several hearses forming a junction in King Street, the theatre of the inhuman tragedy, proceeded from thence through the Main Street, lengthened by an immense concourse of people so numerous as to be obliged to follow in ranks of six, and bought up by a long train of carriages belonging to the principal gentry of the town. The bodies were deposited in one vault in the middle burying ground. The aggravated circumstances of their death, the distress and sorrow visible in every countenance, together with the peculiar solemnity with which the whole funeral was conducted, surpass description. ■

As you read the newspaper article, think about what a primary source offers you that you might not get from a secondary source.

1. **Look** at the images in the newspaper article. Each black shape stands for a coffin, or narrow box for burying a dead body. Each coffin has initials on it. What do you think these stand for?

   ....

   Why do you think the newspaper chose to picture the coffins?

   ....

   ....

2. As you read the text in the newspaper, **underline** the words used to describe the mood, or feeling, of the day.

   How might this eyewitness account of the funeral be different from a secondary source of the same event?

   ....

   ....

   ....

   ....

3. How might a secondary source written years after the funeral be useful?

   ....

   ....

4. **Apply** Think about a recent current event and find a primary source that shows or describes the event. What can you learn from this primary source that you could not learn from a secondary source?

   ....

   ....

The Colonists Rebel

When ships or troops close off a city or harbor to keep people and supplies from getting in, a **blockade** occurs.

Crispus Attucks

What would life have been like for a British soldier in Boston in 1770? The Townshend Acts had been repealed, but many people in Boston were still angry. Some colonists were very angry that the British troops were in their city.

The Boston Massacre

On the night of March 5, 1770, a group of workers in Boston argued with a British soldier, throwing snowballs, and yelling insults. More soldiers arrived, but the crowd grew larger. Then unexpectedly, some soldiers fired gunshots into the crowd.

Five colonists were killed, including Crispus Attucks, a sailor who had escaped slavery years earlier. Others were wounded. Colonists called the shooting the Boston Massacre. A **massacre** (MAS uh kur) is the killing of many people.

1. **Write** a newspaper headline that describes this event.

....

....

....

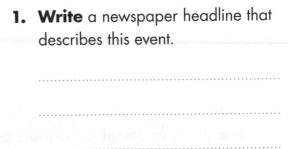

This image, made by Paul Revere, shows the colonists' view of the Boston Massacre.

152

UNLOCK THE BIG ?

I will know how fighting between the colonists and British soldiers began.

Vocabulary

massacre   Loyalist
quarter   neutral
martial law   militia
Patriot

Create a blockade on this map by drawing ships in position to close off the harbor.

The event shocked people throughout the colonies. The soldiers went on trial for murder. John Adams, a cousin of Sons of Liberty member Samuel Adams, defended the soldiers in court. Adams did not approve of British taxes, and he did not like having soldiers in Boston. Still, he thought they should have a fair trial. None was convicted of murder, but two soldiers were found guilty of a less serious crime.

Letters by "Express"

At the time of the Boston Massacre, some colonial leaders were looking for ways to share news about British actions and colonial protests. Samuel Adams and others in different colonies formed Committees of Correspondence. Letters and other written messages are kinds of correspondence.

Members of the committees sent letters to alert each other. The letters were delivered by "express riders" on fast horses. Paul Revere, a Boston silversmith, was one of the riders.

2. **Write** how long it would take a rider to carry a message from Boston to Philadelphia, get a response, and return to Boston.

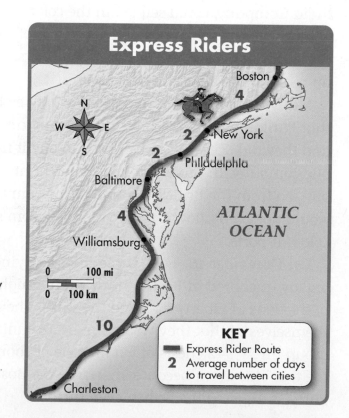

Express Riders

Boston
4
New York
2
2
Philadelphia
Baltimore
ATLANTIC
OCEAN
4
Williamsburg
0   100 mi
0   100 km
10
Charleston

KEY
— Express Rider Route
2 Average number of days to travel between cities

The Boston Tea Party

In 1773, Parliament passed a new law, the Tea Act. This law said that only one British company, the East India Company, could sell tea in the colonies. The law actually lowered the price of tea, but it kept the tea tax that was left over from the Townshend Acts. This ended up making the tea more expensive.

Many colonists opposed the Tea Act. They believed that Parliament did not have the right to tax the tea, and they did not want to be forced to buy it from only one company. In protest, colonial merchants refused to buy tea from the British East India Company. They would not even allow it to be unloaded from ships in colonial ports.

On December 16, 1773, three ships carrying British tea lay anchored in Boston Harbor. That night, members of the Sons of Liberty boarded the ships. They disguised themselves so that they would not be recognized. The group threw 342 chests of tea into the harbor, ruining the tea. This event became known as the Boston Tea Party. It angered the British even further.

3. This painting shows the Boston Tea Party. **Write** why you think some colonists disguised themselves and boarded the ships at night.

....

....

....

....

....

Great Britain Reacts

King George III and Parliament were furious when they heard about the Boston Tea Party. They passed a series of laws to punish the people of Boston. The colonists called these laws the Intolerable Acts. *Intolerable* means "unbearable." These punishments included,

- The colonists had to **quarter**, or give food and shelter to, British troops.
- The colony of Massachusetts was put under **martial law**. That meant it was controlled by the military, under British general Thomas Gage.
- British navy ships blockaded Boston Harbor. The port would stay closed until colonists paid for the tea they had destroyed.

As news of these laws spread, colonists began taking sides. Those who strongly opposed Britain's actions were called **Patriots.** Colonists still loyal to Britain were called **Loyalists.** Many colonists were "undecideds," or **neutral.** They did not choose one side or the other. Thomas Hutchinson, a Loyalist, was governor of Massachusetts at the time of the Tea Party. Samuel Adams was a Patriot.

4. Write what Samuel Adams and Thomas Hutchinson might have said about the Intolerable Acts.

Samuel Adams
Patriot

Thomas Hutchinson
Loyalist

Colonial Representatives Meet

In September 1774, representatives from all of the colonies except Georgia met to discuss the events in Boston. They called the meeting the First Continental Congress. The Congress agreed to stop all trade with Britain until the Intolerable Acts were repealed. The representatives also agreed to ask the king to help solve the problem of taxes.

The Congress hoped to settle the conflict peacefully, but they knew they might have to fight. Each colony agreed to train a **militia** (muh LIHSH uh), or a volunteer army. Some militias called themselves minutemen, because they needed to be ready to fight at a minute's notice.

Patrick Henry spoke out about the need to prepare for war.

Patrick Henry Speaks Out

In March 1775, Patrick Henry gave a speech at a church in Virginia. His goal was to convince people to prepare for war with Britain. He proposed that Virginia form a volunteer army. He said, "The war is inevitable—and let it come! . . . Gentlemen may cry Peace, Peace, but there is no peace. The war is actually begun!" Then he spoke the words he is most famous for: "I know not what course others may take; but as for me, give me liberty, or give me death!"

5. **Write** what you think Patrick Henry meant when he said, "Give me liberty, or give me death!"

....

....

....

Paul Revere's Ride

In April 1775, British leaders in Boston worried about the new militias. General Thomas Gage heard that Patriots were storing weapons in Concord, about 20 miles from Boston. He also knew that Samuel Adams and John Hancock, another Patriot leader, were staying in Lexington, between Boston and Concord.

On April 18, Gage decided to march some of his troops out of Boston. They would arrest Adams and Hancock and destroy the weapons in Concord. Gage tried to keep this plan a secret, but the Patriots found out. They hung lanterns in a church to alert others. Two men, Paul Revere and William Dawes, galloped off to warn the militias that the British soldiers were on the move.

Racing west from Boston, Revere and Dawes woke minutemen along the way. They reached Lexington in time to warn Adams and Hancock. Another rider, Samuel Prescott, joined them. British troops captured Revere, but Prescott reached Concord in time to warn the militia.

Paul Revere alerted minutemen and citizens as he raced ahead of British troops.

6. ⊙ **Cause and Effect Fill in** the missing effect.

March to Concord

Cause	Effect
British plan to march to Concord. →	

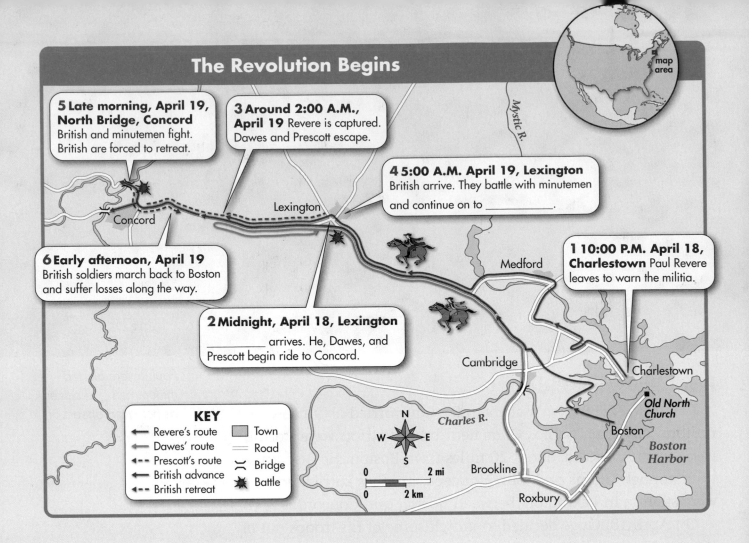

The Revolution Begins

5 Late morning, April 19, North Bridge, Concord British and minutemen fight. British are forced to retreat.

3 Around 2:00 A.M., April 19 Revere is captured. Dawes and Prescott escape.

4 5:00 A.M. April 19, Lexington British arrive. They battle with minutemen and continue on to _____.

1 10:00 P.M. April 18, Charlestown Paul Revere leaves to warn the militia.

6 Early afternoon, April 19 British soldiers march back to Boston and suffer losses along the way.

2 Midnight, April 18, Lexington _____ arrives. He, Dawes, and Prescott begin ride to Concord.

Concord

Lexington

Medford

Cambridge

Charlestown

Old North Church

Boston

Boston Harbor

Brookline

Roxbury

Mystic R.

Charles R.

KEY
- ← Revere's route
- ← Dawes' route
- ◄-- Prescott's route
- ← British advance
- ◄-- British retreat
- ▢ Town
- ═ Road
- ⊃⊂ Bridge
- ✸ Battle

N W E S

0   2 mi
0   2 km

The First Shots

The British soldiers reached Lexington at 5:00 A.M. on the morning of April 19, 1775. About 70 minutemen were waiting for them. The soldiers approached the colonists and told them to leave. Then someone, no one knows who, fired a gunshot. Both sides began shooting, and the British killed eight minutemen.

The British soldiers advanced to Concord to search for weapons. Patriot women in Concord helped hide the weapons, but the soldiers never made it to the center of Concord. A battle began at Concord's North Bridge. The militia, who outnumbered the soldiers, forced the British to turn back. As the soldiers marched back to Boston, Patriots began firing their weapons on them from behind trees and stone walls. By the time the British soldiers reached Boston, about 250 of them had been killed or wounded.

7. Fill in the missing events for boxes 2 and 4.

After those first battles, the British soldiers stayed in Boston. In order to keep them in the city, Patriot militias sneaked onto nearby Breed's Hill on the night of June 16 and built a fort.

The next morning, more than 2,000 British soldiers began marching up the hill to attack the Patriots. Twice the Patriots stopped the British advance. The third time, though, the Patriots ran out of ammunition and the British captured the hill. The fight became known as the battle of Bunker Hill, a hill that was next to Breed's Hill. Though it was a British victory, many more British soldiers were killed than Patriots. The battle of Bunker Hill showed the colonists that war with Britain had come.

Minutemen agreed to be ready to fight in a minute.

Got it?

8. ⊙ **Draw Conclusions** Why do you think most of the soldiers in the Boston Massacre were found not guilty?

....

....

....

9. ⊛ You can see the battle of Bunker Hill from the window of your home in Charlestown. Do you think the colonists should be fighting the British? Why or why not?

my Story Ideas

....

....

....

⬛ **Stop!** I need help with ....

⏸ **Wait!** I have a question about ....

▶ **Go!** Now I know ....

Declaring Independence

These are some of the signatures on the Declaration of Independence.

The fighting in 1775 forced American colonists to take sides. Many Loyalists disagreed with British laws, but they hoped to settle the conflict peacefully and remain part of Great Britain. Patriots, however, felt the colonies should govern themselves. It was time to become a separate country, they argued.

Thirteen Colonies

New Hampshire
Claimed by New Hampshire and New York
Massachusetts
New York
Rhode Island
Connecticut
Pennsylvania
Philadelphia
New Jersey
Delaware
Maryland
Virginia
North Carolina
South Carolina
Georgia

map area

ATLANTIC OCEAN

0   200 mi
0   200 km

N W E S

The Second Continental Congress

In May 1775, representatives from each of the colonies met in Philadelphia, just as they had met for the First Continental Congress the year before. This Second Continental Congress had many decisions to make. It chose John Hancock from Massachusetts to be president of the Continental Congress.

1. **Look** at the map of the 13 colonies. **Circle** the colony Patrick Henry came from, the colony John Hancock came from, and the city where the Second Continental Congress met. **Write** why you think the representatives met in that city.

....

....

....

I will know that by July 4, 1776, many colonists felt that independence from Great Britain was worth fighting for.

Circle the largest signature. Write why you think this person chose to write his name so large.

Vocabulary

Continental army   rights

petition   treason

independence

One of Congress's first acts was to create the **Continental army.** This was an army of paid soldiers from the colonies. George Washington, a wealthy planter from Virginia, was chosen to lead the army. Washington had fought in the French and Indian War and was a skillful soldier.

Although they planned for war, many representatives in Congress still wanted peace with Great Britain. To further this goal, Congress sent an official message directly to King George III. It was called the Olive Branch Petition. A **petition** is a written request for rights or benefits. An olive branch is a symbol of peace.

The petition said that the colonists wanted the king to help settle their conflict with Parliament. They asked for more freedom to govern themselves. King George refused even to read the petition.

Common Sense

Congress debated what to do next. To a Pennsylvanian named Thomas Paine, the choice was clear. In January 1776, Paine wrote a pamphlet called *Common Sense*. He used language that was easy for people to understand. He gave reasons why it was "time to part" with Great Britain. Paine's pamphlet convinced many colonists that it was time for **independence**, which means freedom from rule by others.

King George III

A Government of Our Own

Members of the Second Continental Congress also read *Common Sense*. By the spring of 1776, many of them agreed that it was time to declare independence from Great Britain. In June, Richard Henry Lee, a representative from Virginia, asked Congress to vote on independence.

Before holding the vote, Congress wanted to have a written document declaring independence and explaining why it was necessary. Thomas Jefferson, John Adams, Benjamin Franklin, Roger Sherman, and Robert Livingston were chosen as the committee, or group, to create the document. Jefferson was only 33 years old, but people knew he was intelligent, educated, and a good writer. Because of these qualities, the committee asked him to do the actual writing.

"You can write ten times better than I can," Adams told Jefferson.

"Well, if you are decided, I will do as well as I can," Jefferson replied.

Jefferson spent time crafting the document on his own. He then shared his draft with Adams and Franklin. They helped Jefferson, making comments and suggesting changes. Two weeks later, Thomas Jefferson presented the rewritten document to Congress. Congress then made its own changes, including removing a strongly-worded attack on slavery. Once these and other changes were made, Congress had its finished document. It was called the Declaration of Independence.

2. This painting shows Benjamin Franklin, John Adams, and Thomas Jefferson working together on the Declaration of Independence. **Write** why you think it was helpful to have a group work together to create this document.

....

....

....

....

....

....

....

The Declaration of Independence

Jefferson began by explaining why the colonies should become independent. He spoke about people's **rights**, or freedoms, that cannot be taken away. Many of his ideas were inspired by John Locke, an Englishman. Locke believed that governments are created in order to protect people's rights. Jefferson wrote,

> "We hold these truths to be self-evident, that all men are created equal, that they are endowed by their Creator with certain unalienable rights, that among these are life, liberty, and the pursuit of happiness."

3. Write three rights that Jefferson says that people are born with.

....

....

....

Jefferson then said that if a government tries to take away these rights, people should be able to create a new government. He wrote,

> "Whenever any form of government becomes destructive of these ends, it is the right of the people to alter or to abolish it, and to institute [put in place] new government."

4. Write what Jefferson said people have a right to do when their government stops protecting their rights.

....

....

....

Jefferson's list of grievances, or complaints, recorded ways that King George III had tried to take away the colonists' rights. These included,

> "He has refused to assent [agree] to laws, the most wholesome and necessary for the public good . . . .
>
> He has kept among us, in times of peace, standing armies, without the consent of our legislatures . . . .
>
> For imposing Taxes on us without our Consent: He has plundered [robbed] our seas, ravaged our coasts, burned our towns, and destroyed the lives of our people."

5. Choose one of these accusations against the king, and **describe** an event that fits this example.

....

....

....

....

The last part of the Declaration said that because Great Britain had tried to take away their rights, the colonies had the right to become a separate country, to be called the United States of America. These are the words Jefferson used:

> "We, therefore, the representatives of the United States of America . . . declare that these united colonies are, and of right ought to be, free and independent states . . . and . . . They have full power to levy [begin] war, conclude peace, contract alliances [partnerships], establish commerce [trade], and do all other acts and things which independent states may of right do."

6. Describe the powers that the new nation has, according to the declaration.

....

....

....

....

....

After this section, each of the members of the Second Continental Congress signed the Declaration of Independence. John Hancock, the president of the Congress, signed it first, with the largest signature.

A Brave Step

Congress voted to approve the Declaration of Independence on July 4, 1776. People throughout the colonies celebrated the event by cheering, ringing bells, and even tearing down statues of King George III. The members of Congress signed it in August.

The signers knew that what they were doing could cause them grave personal hardship. They could be accused of **treason**, which is the crime of fighting against one's own country. If they were found guilty, they could be hanged. The fate, or future, of the new country now depended on the Americans who would sacrifice to win the war for independence.

In 1776, the phrase "all men are created equal" did not apply to everyone in society. The rights of women, African Americans, and Native Americans were not recognized, as they are today. But the Declaration was a significant step forward for individual rights.

Colonists celebrated the Declaration of Independence by tearing down statues of King George III.

The Declaration established the idea that the United States government would be based on the ideas of freedom, equality, and protecting people's rights. The story of American history ever since 1776 has, in many ways, been the story of how the promise of the Declaration of Independence has shaped our nation.

7. This is a replica of the printing press used to print copies of the Declaration of Independence. Riders carried copies to people in distant colonies. **Write** how people share important documents today.

....

....

Got it?

8. ◉ **Summarize** In your own words, what is the main idea of the Declaration of Independence?

....

....

....

9. ❓ You have just heard the Declaration of Independence read aloud in your town. **Write** a journal entry describing whether you agree with the ideas in it.

my **Story Ideas**

....

....

....

....

⬛ **Stop!** I need help with ....

⏸ **Wait!** I have a question about ....

▶ **Go!** Now I know ....

Lesson 4

On the Battlefield and at Home

Envision It!

British soldiers, or "redcoats," would have worn uniforms like these.

When the fighting began between British and Continental soldiers, many people thought the colonists could not win. Great Britain's army was larger and better trained. The British also had money to hire German **mercenaries**, or soldiers who are paid to fight for another country. The Patriots had to gather an army quickly. Some troops did not even have proper uniforms. Still, the Patriots did have a cause they believed in. For many of them, that was enough to keep them fighting.

The First Victories

In 1775, a Vermonter named Ethan Allen led a group of soldiers called the Green Mountain Boys. On nearby Lake Champlain, British soldiers controlled Fort Ticonderoga. One morning in May, Allen and his men surprised the troops and captured the fort.

Capturing Fort Ticonderoga gave Allen control of 59 cannons, which General George Washington wanted. Washington's troops had surrounded the British soldiers in Boston. Washington could use the cannons to force the British out. But first he needed to get the cannons.

Fort Ticonderoga's position on Lake Champlain helped the British control the northeastern part of the country.

166

UNLOCK
THE BIG
?

I will know that even when conditions were difficult, Patriots continued fighting for their independence.

Vocabulary

mercenary   enlist

retreat   alliance

morale

Write a list of words that might describe a soldier who wears this uniform.

Washington sent Colonel Henry Knox from Boston to Fort Ticonderoga on a daring mission to bring the heavy cannons back. The cannons weighed over 120,000 pounds in all. Using sleds pulled by oxen, Knox's troops dragged the cannons over snow, mud, and ice. The 300-mile journey took two months.

Once the cannons arrived in Boston, Washington's troops quietly hauled them at night into the hills above the city. The next morning, British commanders were shocked to see the huge guns aimed and ready. They chose to leave rather than fight. On March 17, 1776, the British troops sailed out of Boston Harbor, first to Canada, later to the city of New York.

1. This painting shows Knox's men dragging the cannons to Boston. **Write** why Knox's men went to so much trouble.

....

....

....

....

One Life to Lose

Washington tried for months to drive the British out of New York City. In the summer of 1776, he wanted to send spies to the British camp to learn about their battle plans. Nathan Hale, a 21-year-old teacher and captain in the Connecticut regiment, volunteered for the job.

In the fall of 1776, Washington's army suffered defeats at White Plains, which is northwest of the city, and at the battle of Long Island, New York. Hale was captured by the British and condemned, or sentenced, to death. He met his fate bravely. He reportedly told the British, "I only regret that I have but one life to lose for my country."

Washington Crosses the Delaware

After their defeat at the battle of Long Island, the Americans retreated into New Jersey. To **retreat** is to move away from the enemy. The British army then forced the Patriots from New Jersey into Pennsylvania.

Washington and his men grew discouraged. Food and supplies ran low. The general knew they needed a victory, so he planned a surprise attack on Trenton, New Jersey. German mercenaries, known as Hessians (HESH unz), controlled the town for the British.

On the night of December 25, Washington and his men started to cross the icy Delaware River. Sailors from Massachusetts rowed soldiers across the river.

A snowstorm made the river icy and cold, and the crossing difficult and dangerous. However, Washington's troops landed safely. They arrived in Trenton the next morning and surprised the Hessians. With ease, the Patriots defeated the mercenaries, capturing more than 900 prisoners.

2. Do people today still feel that independence is worth possibly dying for? **Write** below how you know.

....

....

....

Nathan Hale

Soon after the battle of Trenton, Washington's troops gained another victory. In nearby Princeton, New Jersey, they drove back three British regiments. These victories improved the **morale**, or spirits, of the troops. Many of the Patriot soldiers had **enlisted**, or signed up for armed service, for only a short time. If they chose to, they could have left the army. The victories at Trenton and Princeton gave Patriot soldiers confidence that the Continental Army could win the war. Many of them enlisted again.

3. Choose colors to show the American and British victories. **Use** these to **color in** the battle symbols in the key and on the map.

....

....

....

....

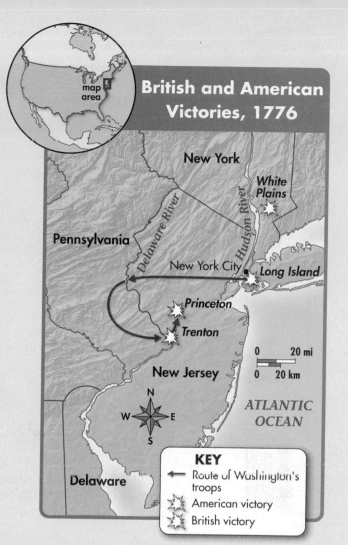

British and American Victories, 1776

map area

New York

White Plains

Delaware River

Hudson River

Pennsylvania

New York City   Long Island

Princeton

Trenton

New Jersey

0   20 mi
0   20 km

ATLANTIC OCEAN

Delaware

N W E S

KEY
← Route of Washington's troops
American victory
British victory

George Washington leads his troops across the Delaware River.

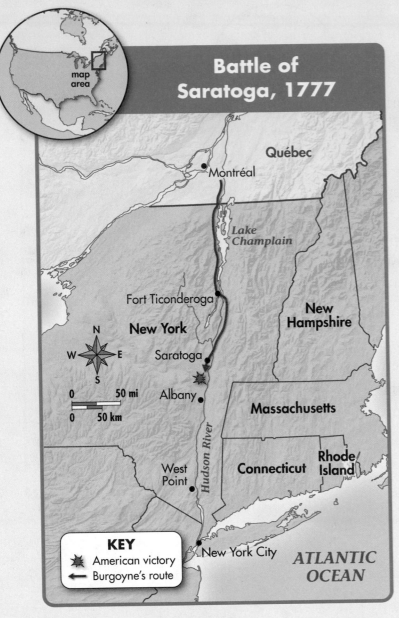

Battle of Saratoga, 1777

map area

Québec

Montréal

Lake Champlain

Fort Ticonderoga

New York

New Hampshire

Saratoga

Albany

Massachusetts

West Point

Hudson River

Connecticut

Rhode Island

New York City

ATLANTIC OCEAN

0   50 mi
0   50 km

KEY
⭐ American victory
← Burgoyne's route

The Battle of Saratoga

In 1777, the British had a new plan of attack. A year earlier, the Patriots had failed to defeat the British in Quebec. British General John Burgoyne took command of these northern troops and led them south from Quebec along Lake Champlain. He planned to capture Albany, New York. Burgoyne expected another British general, William Howe, to come north along the Hudson River to meet him. By controlling the entire river, the British hoped to cut the northeastern part of the country off from the rest of the United States.

Burgoyne and his men captured Fort Ticonderoga and then moved on to Saratoga. General Howe was unable to help Burgoyne. King George III had ordered Howe to capture Philadelphia, far to the south.

Burgoyne's route to Albany was blocked by Patriot troops. Thaddeus Kosciusko (kahs CHOOS koh), a Polish engineer, had helped the Patriots by building a temporary fort near Saratoga, New York. The two sides fought there in September and October. An American officer named Benedict Arnold led attacks on the British.

Burgoyne needed reinforcements, or extra troops. His supplies were running low. Without badly needed extra troops and supplies, Burgoyne and the British forces were in trouble. Meanwhile, more and more volunteers joined the Patriots. After two fierce battles, Burgoyne was forced to surrender.

4. **Trace** the route Burgoyne took to Saratoga. Then **write** what you think a victory at Albany would have meant to the British.

....

....

....

....

....

The battle of Saratoga was a turning point in the war. Before the battle, Benjamin Franklin had tried to convince French leaders to help the Americans. The French, however, weren't sure that the Americans could beat the British. After Saratoga, the French agreed to an **alliance,** a formal agreement of friendship between countries. They sent ships, troops, and money to help the United States.

Benedict Arnold, the hero of Saratoga, later betrayed the Patriots for money and for personal reasons. In 1780, he plotted to surrender the fort at West Point, New York, to the British. The plan failed. He became one of the most famous traitors in American history.

Washington at Valley Forge

In September 1777, soon after the battle of Saratoga, the British captured Philadelphia. The Continental Congress was forced to leave that city and move to York, Pennsylvania. Washington's army also retreated, setting up camp at Valley Forge, Pennsylvania, for the winter.

Camp life at Valley Forge was harsh. Scarce food and a lack of warm clothing added to that winter's hardship, or suffering. More than 2,500 men died of disease, hunger, or cold.

Washington worked hard to get the supplies his troops needed. By spring, soldiers had more food and clothing. They also had help from a German officer named Friedrich von Steuben. At Valley Forge, he taught officers how to train their own soldiers. The soldiers' improved skills turned them into a serious fighting force.

5. **Write** what a soldier at Valley Forge might say in a letter to his family.

....

....

....

....

....

....

A replica of the log cabins Washington's troops built at Valley Forge

Women of the Revolution

Many women played important roles in the war. Martha Washington traveled with her husband, visiting with troops and helping soldiers. Other women cooked, carried water, made clothes for troops, and served as nurses for the sick and wounded.

Women who carried water to soldiers on the battlefield earned the nickname Molly Pitcher. Mary Ludwig Hayes of New Jersey was probably one of them. As the story goes, when her husband was injured, Hayes took his place firing cannons at the British.

Other women worked as spies or messengers for the army. Deborah Sampson even dressed in men's clothes and secretly joined the army. She fought in several battles before anyone discovered she was a woman.

Women did not have to be close to the battlefield to help the war effort. Phillis Wheatley, a former slave, wrote poetry about the colonists' struggle for freedom and spoke out against slavery.

Abigail Adams, the wife of John Adams, believed strongly in independence and in rights for women. While John was at the Second Continental Congress, she wrote him letters saying, "In the new code of laws . . . remember the ladies."

6. **Fill in** the chart with facts about each woman and how she helped the revolutionary cause.

Revolutionary Women

Abigail Adams	Phillis Wheatley	Deborah Sampson

Native Americans in the Revolution

Different Native American nations fought on different sides during the war. Those who fought with the British, such as the Cherokees, wanted the colonists to stop taking their land. They hoped that the British would help them. Joseph Brant, a Mohawk leader, met with King George III before the war and told his people to side with the British. Other Native American groups, such as the Oneida (oh NYE dah) and many Tuscarora, fought on the Patriot side. Many other Native Americans remained neutral.

Joseph Brant

Got it?

7. ◉ **Cause and Effect Name** two effects of the Patriots' victory at the battle of Saratoga.

....

....

....

8. ❓ You live on a farm in Pennsylvania. The war has been going on for several years. How do you and your family support the ideas you believe in?

my Story Ideas

....

....

....

....

⬛ **Stop!** I need help with ....

⏸ **Wait!** I have a question about ....

▶ **Go!** Now I know ....

Winning Independence

Envision It!

Soldiers used powderhorns like this to keep their gunpowder dry.

Have you ever planned to do something that you thought would be easy and then found it was harder than expected? That's what happened to the British army. They expected to defeat the Americans quickly. After three years of war, however, things weren't going the way they had planned.

Advantages and Allies

One reason the Americans were winning the war was that they were fighting on their own land. They knew the geography and made good use of it. They could also get food and supplies more easily than the British, who had to ship goods more than 3,000 miles across the ocean.

The colonists had another advantage. Many people believed that independence was a cause worth fighting for. That cause attracted soldiers from other countries, such as Friedrich Von Steuben, who helped at Valley Forge. Another important friend to the Americans was the Marquis de Lafayette. He arrived in Philadelphia two years after the American Revolution began. The colonists made him a major general in the Continental army.

France was the United States's first ally, but as the war went on, other nations also gave support. The Dutch sent arms and ammunition, and made loans to the Americans. Spain, which claimed land west of the Mississippi River, declared war on Great Britain in 1779.

Friedrich Von Steuben

Draw other items you think soldiers would need to bring with them.

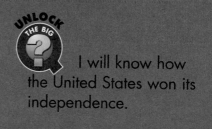
Vocabulary

strategy
peninsula
negotiate
Treaty of Paris

Bernardo de Gálvez, the Spanish governor of Louisiana, provided money and supplies to Patriot forces. He attacked British forts in Baton Rouge, Natchez, Mobile, and Pensacola. Spanish control of these forts kept the British from entering the Mississippi River.

The British had invaded the South and wanted to capture seaports. In 1778, they captured Savannah, Georgia. They expected to get support from southern Loyalists when they attacked ports in South Carolina. At first, the **strategy,** or plan, worked and the British began winning battles. In 1780, they captured Charleston, South Carolina.

Because of Gálvez's attacks, some British troops were called away from the battles in the Carolinas to fight in the Gulf. Gálvez's capture of most of the British forts in the Gulf of Mexico also helped the Patriots. Gálvez's actions helped Spain regain control of Florida from the British.

1. **Look** at the battles that were fought in the South. **Explain** why Galvez's victories were important.

....

....

....

Battles, 1778–1781

map area

0   100 mi
0   100 km

Ohio River

Cahokia   Fort Vincennes   Yorktown

Kaskaskia   Guilford Court House

Cowpens   Kings Mountain

Camden

Eutaw Springs

N   W   E   S

Charleston

Savannah

Mississippi River

Natchez   Mobile

Baton Rouge   Pensacola

Gulf of Mexico

ATLANTIC OCEAN

KEY
United States
British victory
American victory
Spanish victory

The Fighting Spreads

Loyalists had helped the British gain control of Georgia and South Carolina. But their support was weaker than British leaders expected. Many southern farmers were Patriots, not Loyalists. Francis Marion, a southern Patriot, became famous for attacking the enemy with only a small group of men. Striking quickly, they retreated into the woods or swamps. These actions earned Marion the nickname Swamp Fox.

In 1780, General Nathanael Greene took command of the American army in the South. Greene had fewer soldiers than the British, so he avoided open battles. Instead, Greene's troops attacked and then retreated, again and again. This forced the British to chase the Patriots. British supplies dwindled, and the soldiers grew tired from searching for Greene's army.

Fighting took place in other regions, too. In 1779, an American named George Rogers Clark captured Fort Vincennes, which is in present-day Indiana. Much farther away, off the coast of Great Britain, John Paul Jones, an American sea captain, attacked a British ship. The two sides fought for several hours. "Will you surrender?" asked the British captain. Replied Jones, "I have not yet begun to fight!" When the battle finally ended, it was the British captain who surrendered to Jones.

Bonhomme Richard, *captained by John Paul Jones, defeats the British ship, the* Serapis.

2. ◉ **Cause and Effect**
John Paul Jones would not surrender to a British naval ship. **Describe** the effect Jones's victory might have had on soldiers in America.

....

....

....

....

....

....

This letter was written by Lafayette after the war.

James Armistead

African Americans Fight for Freedom

Throughout the war, African Americans fought for both the Patriots and the British. Early in the war, a British official offered to free any slaves who fought for Great Britain. Thousands of enslaved African Americans escaped and joined the British.

Many other African Americans fought on the side of the Patriots. Some of them, like Peter Salem, gained their freedom by fighting against the British. Salem fought at the battle of Bunker Hill and again at the battle of Saratoga.

More than half the soldiers in the First Rhode Island Regiment were African Americans. Some of the men in this regiment gained their freedom by fighting. Others were free men when they joined the unit.

Some African Americans, including James Armistead, worked as Patriot spies. Armistead, who was enslaved at the time, spied on British generals. He gathered information that helped win the last battle of the war at Yorktown, Virginia. After the war, Armistead changed his name to James Armistead Lafayette. This was to honor the Marquis de Lafayette, for whom he had spied, and who helped Armistead obtain his freedom.

3. In his letter, Lafayette wrote that Armistead should be freed from slavery. **Write** why you think Lafayette did this.

....

....

....

....

....

The Battle of Yorktown

By 1781, the troops of General Cornwallis, the British general in the South, were tired out. Nathanael Greene's strategy of fighting and retreating had worked. Cornwallis decided to rest his troops at Yorktown, Virginia, which is on a peninsula. A **peninsula** is a piece of land nearly surrounded by water.

Washington's army needed money. He contacted his friend, Haym Solomon, a Jewish man born in Poland and a member of the Sons of Liberty. Solomon raised the money. Washington then led American and French soldiers from New York to Yorktown. As the army attacked, French ships sailed into the Chesapeake Bay outside of Yorktown. They blocked the British navy from rescuing Cornwallis. The British troops were trapped.

On October 19, Cornwallis's army surrendered to Washington. As the disarmed British army was marched out of Yorktown, some say their band played a tune called "The World Turned Upside Down." It must have seemed that way, because the small new nation had just defeated powerful Great Britain.

5. This modern reenactment shows the ceremony of surrender of the British army after the battle of Yorktown. **Circle** the paragraph on this page that describes this scene.

4. ◉ **Categorize Write** the names of the groups of people who fought on the side of the Americans and the British.

Taking Sides

Americans	British

Ending the War

The United States had won the war. In 1782, Benjamin Franklin, John Adams, and John Jay met with British officials in Paris to **negotiate**, or reach an agreement on, a peace treaty. The following year, Great Britain and the United States signed the **Treaty of Paris.** This officially ended the war. In this treaty, Britain recognized American independence. Both sides agreed on the borders of the new nation. The United States now reached from Canada in the North, to the Mississippi River in the West, and to Spanish Florida in the South.

The new borders meant that many Native American lands were now part of the United States. What would happen there was just one of the issues now facing the new nation.

Got it?

6. ⊙ **Draw Conclusions** What advantages did the United States have over Great Britain that helped it to win the war?

....

....

....

7. ❓ You've just learned that the Treaty of Paris was signed by the United States and Great Britain. **Write** a letter to a friend in another state describing how you feel about independence.

my Story Ideas

....

....

....

⬛ **Stop!** I need help with ....

⏸ **Wait!** I have a question about ....

▶ **Go!** Now I know ....

Lesson 1

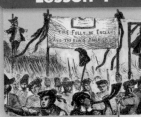

Tensions With Britain

- The colonists had no representatives in the British Parliament.
- Because they lacked representation, the colonists believed that new British taxes were unfair.
- The colonists worked together to protest unfair British taxes.

Lesson 2

The Colonists Rebel

- Tensions between the British and the American colonists led to the Boston Massacre and the Boston Tea Party.
- The colonists first fought against British soldiers at Lexington and Concord.

Lesson 3

Declaring Independence

- The Declaration of Independence established ideals of liberty, equality, and self-government for the new nation.
- Those who signed the Declaration risked their lives.

Lesson 4

On the Battlefield and at Home

- Early victories inspired the Patriots to keep on fighting.
- France and other nations supported the Patriots against the British.
- Native Americans were divided over which side they supported.

Lesson 5

Winning Independence

- After losing battles in the North, the British invaded the South.
- Washington's victory at Yorktown was the last major battle of the war.
- The Treaty of Paris established American independence.

Review and Assessment

Lesson 1

Tensions With Britain

1. **Write** a sentence explaining why each of the following people was important to the start of the American Revolution.

   a. Samuel Adams

   ....

   ....

   ....

   b. Mercy Otis Warren

   ....

   ....

   ....

Lesson 2

The Colonists Rebel

2. Use the numbers 1, 2, 3, and 4 to **arrange** the following events in the order that they happened.

   _____ Colonial leaders met at the First Continental Congress.

   _____ The Boston Massacre

   _____ Paul Revere's ride

   _____ Britain passed the Intolerable Acts.

Lesson 3

Declaring Independence

3. ◉ **Cause and Effect** In the chart below, **fill in** the missing effect.

   ┌─────────────────────────────────┐
   │ **Cause**   │
   │ Thomas Paine writes *Common Sense.* │
   └─────────────────────────────────┘
                    ↓
   ┌─────────────────────────────────┐
   │ **Effect**   │
   │   │
   │   │
   │   │
   └─────────────────────────────────┘

4. **Rewrite** the following sentence from the Declaration in your own words.

   "We hold these truths to be self-evident, that all men are created equal, that they are endowed by their creator with certain unalienable rights; that among these are life, liberty and the pursuit of happiness."

   ....

   ....

   ....

   ....

   ....

Lesson 4

On the Battlefield and at Home

5. Circle the correct answer.
What was one effect of the battle of Saratoga?

A. It cut New England off from the rest of the states.

B. It led France to form an alliance with the United States.

C. It led Spain to form an alliance with Britain.

D. It made Loyalists decide to move to the South.

6. List three problems the Continental army faced at Valley Forge.

....

....

....

7. Write how Washington's army was able to defeat the Hessians at the battle of Trenton.

....

....

....

Lesson 5

Winning Independence

8. What caused some African Americans to fight for the British?

....

....

....

9. Describe the role that the French played in the battle of Yorktown.

....

....

....

10. **What is worth fighting for?**
Read the following quotation.

"I know not what course others may take; but as for me, give me liberty or give me death!"

a. Who spoke these words?

....

b. What did the speaker think was worth fighting and dying for?

....

....

Go online to write and illustrate your own **myStory Book** using the **myStory Ideas** from this chapter.

What is worth fighting for?

The story of the American Revolution begins with colonists protesting unfair treatment by the British. In the Declaration of Independence the colonists stated the ideas they thought were worth fighting for. These included justice, equality, responsibility, and freedom.

Think about ways people choose to fight for these ideas. **List** your examples.

....

....

....

....

Draw an image that shows one of your examples.

....

....

While you're online, check out the **myStory Current Events** area where you can create your own book on a topic that's in the news.

A New Nation

What is the purpose of government?

Describe some of the rules you have to follow at school and at home. Then **explain** how these rules are helpful. What would life be like without these rules?

....

....

....

....

....

Visitors tour the Rotunda of the United States Capitol building.

Capitol Visitor Center
At the Nation's Legislature

my Story Video

Eleven-year-old Zana has seen the white dome of the United States Capitol building many times. After all, she lives nearby. But Zana has never seen the Capitol up close until today. "I can't believe how big it is," Zana marvels to her mother. "I'm surprised it's been standing for so long."

Construction on the Capitol began in 1793. One wing houses the U.S. Senate and the other the U.S. House of Representatives. The Capitol Complex serves as the center of the federal government. The Executive Branch is housed nearby in the White House and other office buildings.

Zana and her mother enter the newest addition to the historic complex, the U.S. Capitol Visitor Center. The Visitor Center is more than three-quarters the size of the Capitol itself. Zana takes a close look at a model of the Statue of Freedom that tops the Capitol dome. It stands for the freedoms that our government is required to protect, such as freedom of expression and freedom to practice one's religion.

Zana visits the United States Capitol building for the first time.

185

Zana sees statues, such as this one of Helen Keller, that states display in the U.S. Capitol.

Occasionally, members of the House and Senate meet together in the Capitol to hear a speech by the President.

Zana realizes that some parts of the Capitol are like a museum. Each state displays two statues in the Capitol. States can replace the statues whenever they want, so they are always changing. Zana likes one of the newer statues, from Alabama, of Helen Keller. "She's using a water pump," exclaims Zana, "and she looks like she's about my age."

Zana and her mom take a walking tour of the Capitol. Zana is impressed with the Rotunda, which is right in the middle of the Capitol. A massive frieze, or painted border, surrounds the room, depicting many important scenes from our nation's history.

On the tour, Zana also learns that this building isn't just for tourists and special ceremonies. The House of Representatives and the Senate meet here to conduct very important business. They create and vote on laws that help protect the rights of the people.

Zana and her mother on the Washington Mall, outside the U.S. Capitol

The frieze in the Rotunda circles the inside of the Capitol dome. Each scene shows an event in American history.

Senate pages must be at least 16 years old and have good grades.

"They meet right here to make and debate the laws of our land," she says, standing in the House gallery. "That congresswoman is introducing a bill. Will it make it through the steps it takes to become a law?"

Zana sees an office with the sign, *Speaker of the House.* "Some senators and representatives have their offices here," she realizes. Her tour guide explains that most of the 100 senators and 435 representatives have offices in buildings near the Capitol. Those buildings are linked to the Capitol by an underground subway.

Zana spies a very young worker. She asks her tour guide about the uniformed worker. The young man, she discovers, is a page.

"I think it would be really great to be a page," Zana tells her mom. "They get to run messages to and from the Senate, and they even get to raise and lower the flag on the Capitol." Zana's mother reminds her that pages have to be at least 16 years old. "That's okay," Zana says, "I'll wait."

After their tour, Zana looks back at the Capitol building. "When I grow up," she declares, "I'm not going to just drive by the Capitol, I'm going to drive to it because I'm going to work here." Her mother smiles. She knows that with Zana's determination, it will probably happen.

Think About It Based on this story, how do you think government helps citizens? As you read the chapter ahead, think about what Zana's trip to the Capitol tells you about the role government plays in our society.

Articles of Confederation

Envision It!

In 1785, the U.S. flag had 13 stripes for the original colonies and 13 stars for the number of states at that time.

The Second Continental Congress met to create a new government. John Hancock was one of the leaders of the Congress.

During the Revolution, the United States faced a difficult test. Could its citizens govern themselves? After years of British rule, many people did not want a government with too much power. Once the Second Continental Congress declared independence, its representatives worked together to create a government with limited control over the people.

The New Government

The plan that took shape was outlined in a document called the **Articles of Confederation.** A confederation is a union or partnership between states. Under the Articles, the only branch of the national government was Congress. This was a **legislative** branch, which means that it passed laws. For a new law to pass, at least nine out of the thirteen states had to vote for it.

Government under the Articles was different from our government today. The Articles did not provide for a **judicial** branch, or courts and judges, to decide what the laws mean. There was also no **executive** branch headed by a leader such as a President to carry out the laws. For the new government to take effect, all thirteen states had to **ratify,** or approve, the Articles of Confederation. They did so in 1781.

Draw your own version of the flag that symbolizes the United States just after the Revolutionary War.

UNLOCK THE BIG ?

I will know how the government was organized under the Articles of Confederation.

Vocabulary

Articles of Confederation	executive
	ratify
legislative	inflation
judicial	ordinance

The Articles reflected the states' long struggle against the power of the British king. The states wanted to avoid a strong central government. The new plan divided power between the states and the central government, but the states had more power. State leaders selected representatives to the national government. The functions of those representatives were limited, though. For example, Congress could not pass laws to collect taxes. It could only ask states to offer money. This made it a weak form of government.

1. ◉ **Summarize Write** a summary of the government under the Articles of Confederation.

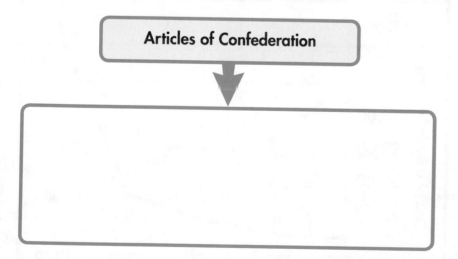

Articles of Confederation

A Weak National Government

Without the power to collect taxes, the nation lacked money. The American Revolution had left it in debt. The country could neither pay its own soldiers, nor repay the nations from which it had borrowed money for the war.

Even the money that the country did have was a problem. Today, the United States has one national currency. This currency, the dollar, is worth the same in every state. During the Revolution, each state had its own currency, and each currency was valued differently.

Congress had also printed its own paper money, called "continentals." Because the war caused inflation, continentals became nearly worthless. **Inflation** means that prices went up while money lost value. People couldn't buy as much with their money as they had in the past. State governments tried to control prices, but inflation continued.

The United States faced other weaknesses. It had no national army. Instead, each state loaned its troops to the national government to protect the country. Congress could not enforce laws about trade with other nations. Without such laws, the United States couldn't control or improve business. Some countries refused to take seriously a nation facing such challenges.

Money that was used in the United States in the early 1780s came in many forms. These bills were used in Rhode Island.

2. **Circle** the two years on the graph that show the period of greatest increase in the cost of a bushel of potatoes. **Write** the difference in price in the space below.

....

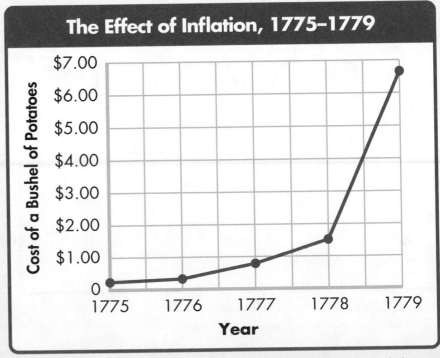

The Effect of Inflation, 1775–1779

Cost of a Bushel of Potatoes

$7.00
$6.00
$5.00
$4.00
$3.00
$2.00
$1.00
0

1775   1776   1777   1778   1779

Year

Source: Massachusetts Bureau of Statistics of Labor, 1885

To many Patriots, it looked as though the Articles of Confederation needed to be revised, or corrected. A group called the nationalists began to push for a stronger national government. The nationalists included leaders of the American Revolution such as George Washington and Benjamin Franklin.

A Tax Revolt

Though the national government could not collect taxes, the states could. In Massachusetts, the state decided to raise taxes that people paid on the property they owned. Desperate farmers protested. Those who could not pay were being sent to prison. Some even lost their lands.

One poor farmer, Daniel Shays, had been a captain during the Revolutionary War. In 1786, he was sued, or taken to court, for not paying his debts. Shays joined with a group of other farmers and soldiers who had also fought in the war. Armed with guns and other weapons, they sought to close the courts that sent farmers to prison. Shays' military record made him a natural leader. He became a leader of the movement known as Shays' Rebellion.

An early victory for the fighting farmers occurred in September 1786. Shays led a group of 700 men to close the highest court in Springfield, Massachusetts. Then on January 25, 1787, Shays led an attack on one of the national government's weapons depots. His army planned to steal guns, cannons, and other weapons. Because Congress did not have an army, the state militia stopped the attack. A militia is an army of ordinary citizens who are trained for battle. Shays retreated to Vermont.

The rebellion proved to be unsuccessful. However, it caused many people to fear that others would also try to take the law into their own hands. Calls for stronger government continued.

This painting shows Daniel Shays leading other farmers in the rebellion.

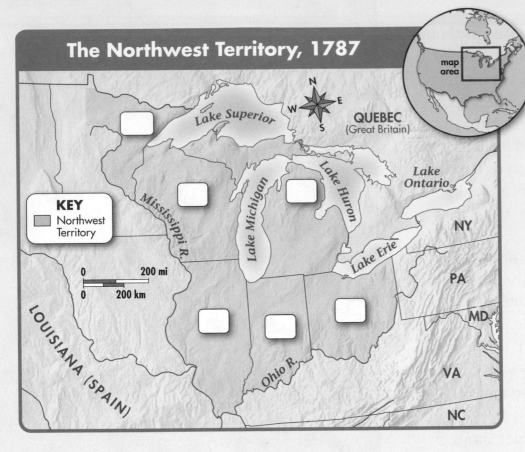

The Northwest Territory, 1787

KEY
Northwest Territory

0 ——— 200 mi
0 ——— 200 km

Lake Superior

QUEBEC
(Great Britain)

Lake Ontario

Lake Huron

Lake Michigan

Lake Erie

Mississippi R.

Ohio R.

LOUISIANA (SPAIN)

NY

PA

MD

VA

NC

map area

3. **Write** the abbreviations for the current states that grew out of the Northwest Territory in the spaces on the map.

New Lands for New States

One decision Congress faced was about the young nation's western lands. The Treaty of Paris, signed after the end of the war, gave the United States land stretching west from the Appalachian Mountains to the Mississippi River. The land north of the Ohio River was called the Northwest Territory.

Congress issued several **ordinances**, or laws, to describe how to organize the territory. The Land Ordinance of 1785 explained how the land would be divided. It also provided for public schools to be opened in the territory.

To describe how these lands could become states, Congress issued the Northwest Ordinance of 1787. A territory could ask to become a state when its population reached 60,000 free adult males. It also had to have a written constitution. Congress would then ratify the territory's statehood. The new state would have the same rights as any of the original 13 states.

The Northwest Ordinance had different effects on different people interested in the area. Because it made slavery against the law in the Northwest Territory, it helped to stop the spread of slavery north of the Ohio River. It guaranteed religious freedom.

It also stated that the United States would never take Native Americans' land without permission. However, many Native Americans still had to fight to keep settlers off their land.

The success of the Northwest Ordinance did not make people forget that the government had serious problems. The nation's debts, its worthless currency, and troubles such as Shays' Rebellion all showed the need for a stronger central government.

In May 1787, representatives from each state were called to Philadelphia for a meeting to revise the Articles of Confederation. The changes made during that meeting were much greater than anyone expected.

Got it?

4. **◉ Summarize** Why were Americans interested in having a weak national government?

....

....

....

....

5. **?** At the town museum, you read a letter from a traveler writing home in 1781. She describes the trouble she is having with paper money under the Articles of Confederation. What might the letter say?

my Story Ideas

....

....

....

▮ **Stop!** I need help with ....

❚❚ **Wait!** I have a question about ....

▶ **Go!** Now I know ....

Media and Technology

Search for Information on the Internet

One of the great things about the Internet is that it makes so much information available. The Internet connects you to libraries, databases, articles, and much more. You can search for both primary and secondary sources. When searching the Internet, however, you must keep asking yourself if the information you find is reliable. Just because a piece of information is found on the Internet, does not mean it is true. People and organizations put information on the Internet for many reasons. Governments, universities, museums, and encyclopedias often have their own Web sites. These are among the most reliable sites.

To find information on the Internet, you often use a search engine, which is a program that searches databases. Search engines let you type in a word or phrase. Then they present a list of sites that contain the word or phrase or information related to the word or phrase. Your school or public library may have prepared web directories that provide lists of reliable Web sites to help you search popular topics.

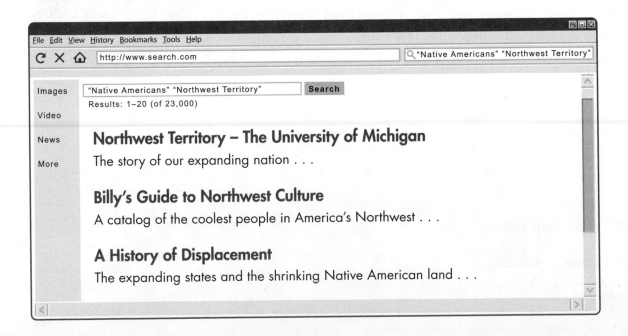

Learning Objective

I will know how to find accurate information on the Internet.

195

Suppose you want to find out more about the effects of the Northwest Ordinance on the Native Americans who lived in the Northwest Territory.

- You could type in "Native Americans" and "Northwest Territory" with quotation marks around each phrase.
- The quotation marks tell the search engine that you want to find the complete phrases "Northwest Territory" and "Native Americans" included on the Web page.

The Internet search engine on the previous page shows that 23,000 results were found. You will not need (or want!) to read all of these sites. How do you choose the right ones?

1. **Circle** one site that you know is probably from a reliable source.

2. Why is this site likely reliable?

   ....

3. Which site is probably the least reliable and why?

   ....

   ....

   ....

4. **Apply** Suppose that during your Internet research you learn that one of the groups that lived in the Northwest Territory were the Shawnee people. If you wanted to find out more about how the Shawnee people of Ohio were affected by the Northwest Ordinance, what would you type into a search engine?

   ....

   ....

Creating the Constitution

Thomas Jefferson and others used a numbered code to write secret letters during the Constitutional Convention.

In 1776, a group of American Patriots representing the different states signed the Declaration of Independence in Philadelphia. In May 1787, many of the same representatives, or **delegates**, returned to that city. This time, their goal was to form a stronger government. Some came to strengthen the Articles of Confederation. Others came to craft a completely new **constitution**, or written plan for government, for the young nation.

The Constitutional Convention

The meeting, known as the Constitutional Convention, included people who had steered the young nation toward independence. Benjamin Franklin was 81 by that time, the oldest person to take part. He suffered from poor health but was present for most of the convention. Franklin supported a stronger national government.

James Madison, also a member of the Continental Congress, firmly believed in a strong national government. During the convention, he took detailed notes that historians still consult today.

Patrick Henry, who had argued fiercely for independence, refused to attend the convention. He defended the Articles of Confederation and opposed taking power from the states.

George Washington, who had led the nation to victory during the Revolutionary War, also attended. Washington was elected president of the convention.

Benjamin Franklin

Key: 1=A   2=B   3=C   4=D   5=E
6=F   7=G   8=H   9=I   10=J   11=K
12=L   13=M   14=N   15=O   16=P   17=Q
18=R   19=S   20=T   21=U   22=V   23=W
24=X   25=Y   26=Z

12 5 20 ' 19 / 1 4 4 / 1 / 2 9 12 12 / 15 6 / 18 9 7 8 20 19

Use the above key to decode the message. Each number
equals a letter, and slashes show where new words begin.

UNLOCK THE BIG ?

I will know how the
Constitution was created and
the plan for government the
Constitution describes.

Vocabulary

delegate   separation of
constitution   powers
compromise   checks and
Preamble   balances
                veto

Alexander Hamilton had worked closely with George
Washington during the Revolution. Later, he became
a member of Congress and a lawyer. Hamilton agreed
that the central government created by the Articles of
Confederation was too weak.

1. **Read** the statements from each Patriot. **Write** C next to the
quote if the person supported a strong central government
and new Constitution, or A if the person supported the
Articles of Confederation.

Opinions About the Articles of Confederation

"Thirteen [states] pulling against each other and all tugging at the. . .head [central government] will soon bring ruin on the whole."—George Washington	
"Thus I consent, Sir, to this Constitution because I expect no better, and because I am not sure, that it is not the best."—Benjamin Franklin	
"Our rights and privileges are endangered, and the sovereignty [power] of the states [will] be relinquished [given away]."—Patrick Henry	
"This power [described in the Constitution] is calculated to annihilate [destroy] totally the state governments."—George Mason	

Ideas for Debate

The Constitutional Convention began on May 25, 1787. Its original goal was to improve the Articles of Confederation, but some delegates clearly had other plans.

Edmund Randolph, from Virginia, argued for a whole new form of government. He presented the Virginia Plan at the start of the convention. It called for an executive branch to carry out laws and a judicial branch to decide their meaning. Congress, the legislative branch, had a great deal of power in this plan. It would decide who served in the other two branches and would be made up of representatives from each state. States with larger populations would have more representatives in Congress. Therefore, they'd have more power in the government.

This plan was seen as a good starting point, except for one major point. Delegates from the smaller states did not like the idea of having less power than those in the larger states.

William Paterson of New Jersey, one of the smaller states, proposed a new plan, the New Jersey Plan. It was very similar to the Virginia Plan, except that it called for each state to have the same number of representatives. This would give all states equal power, no matter their size.

2. Delegates debated the Virginia and New Jersey plans. **Fill in** the parts of the two plans that are different.

The Virginia and New Jersey Plans

POPULATION 747,610

POPULATION 184,139

The Virginia Plan	The New Jersey Plan
Legislative Branch	Legislative Branch
Executive Branch Chosen by legislative branch	Executive Branch Chosen by legislative branch
Judicial Branch Chosen by legislative branch	Judicial Branch Chosen by legislative branch

The Great Compromise

The delegates could not agree on a new plan for government. Roger Sherman, from Connecticut, was one of the delegates with a new idea. He proposed that Congress be made up of two parts, or houses. In one house, the Senate, each state would have the same number of representatives. In the other, the House of Representatives, the number of representatives from each state would be in proportion to the state's population. Thus, each state would have equal power in the Senate. However, larger states would have more power in the House of Representatives.

The delegates debated for a month before agreeing to what became known as the Great Compromise. A **compromise** takes place when people on both sides of an issue give up something to reach an agreement.

Another difficult issue faced the convention. Southern states wanted their population counts to include the large numbers of enslaved people living in the South. This would increase their representation in the House of Representatives. However, they did not want enslaved people to be counted when it came to being taxed. Northern states, which had fewer enslaved workers, objected. The issue was settled with the Three-Fifths Compromise. States would count their enslaved people both for representation and for taxes. But only three of every five enslaved people would be counted.

Independence Hall in Philadelphia, where leaders met in 1787, still stands today.

We the People of the United States, in order to form a more perfect Union, establish Justice, insure domestic Tranquility, provide for the common defence, promote the general Welfare, and secure the Blessings of Liberty to ourselves and our Posterity, do ordain and establish this Constitution for the United States of America.

Article. I.

Section. 1. All legislative Powers herein granted shall be vested in a Congress of the United States, which shall consist of a Senate and House of Representatives.

Section. 2. The House of Representatives shall be composed of Members chosen every second Year by the People of the several States...

1787 copy of the Constitution of the United States

The Preamble of the Constitution

We the people of the United States, in order to form a more perfect Union, establish justice, insure domestic tranquility [peace], provide for the common defense [protection], promote the general welfare [well-being], and secure the blessings of liberty [freedom] to ourselves and our posterity [future], do ordain and establish this Constitution for the United States of America.

3. Read the words of the Preamble. **Circle** the first three words on the 1787 version. **Write** why you think these words are important.

....

....

....

....

A New Plan for Government

Delegates worked through the summer of 1787, writing the new plan for government. The **Preamble**, or introduction, expressed the main goals of the new constitution.

The Constitution set up a government with three branches. In contrast, the Articles of Confederation had only one branch of government. Under the new U.S. Constitution, the legislative branch would make the laws. It would be called Congress. The executive branch, led by the President, would put the laws into effect and make sure they were obeyed. The judicial branch would interpret the laws and make sure they followed the Constitution. This **separation of powers** meant that each branch of government would balance the power of the others.

The Constitution also set up a system of majority rule. This means that decisions are made by a majority, or more than half, of the people voting. For example, the majority of lawmakers must agree on a law before passing it.

The framers, or authors, of the Constitution wished to limit the power of government in other ways. They set up a system of **checks and balances.** In other words, each branch had ways of limiting the powers of the other branches. For example, Congress would pass laws, but the President would have to sign a law to make it official. In this way, no branch of the government could acquire too much power.

Limiting Government

The President can limit the power of Congress with a **veto,** or a refusal to sign a law. However, if two thirds of Congress wants a law, Congress can reject the veto. This is Congress's check on the power of the President.

The judicial branch can check the power of both Congress and the President. If the courts decide that the other branches are doing something against the Constitution, they can stop those actions. The President can check the power of the courts by choosing the justices and judges who serve in federal courts. Congress can check the power of the court by refusing to approve the choices of the President.

4. Fill in the chart with the missing checks and balances between the branches of government.

Checks and Balances

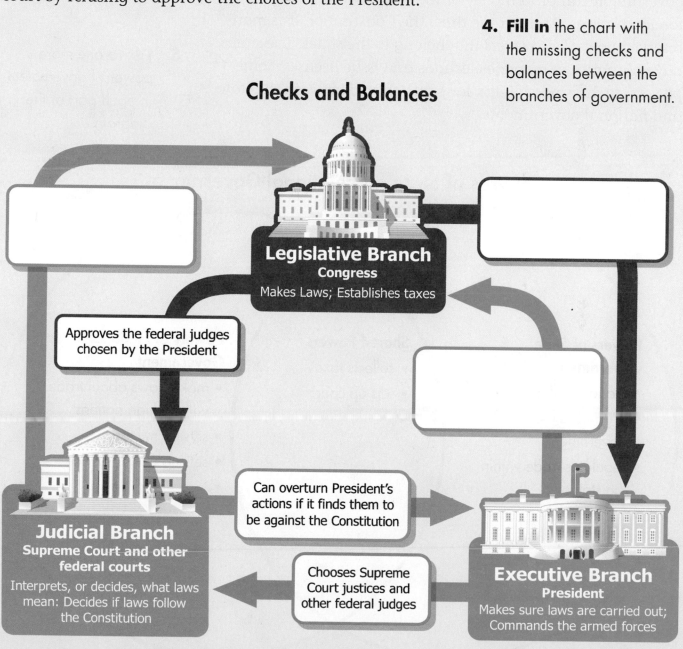

Legislative Branch
Congress
Makes Laws; Establishes taxes

Approves the federal judges chosen by the President

Can overturn President's actions if it finds them to be against the Constitution

Judicial Branch
Supreme Court and other federal courts
Interprets, or decides, what laws mean: Decides if laws follow the Constitution

Chooses Supreme Court justices and other federal judges

Executive Branch
President
Makes sure laws are carried out; Commands the armed forces

Powers of Government

As the delegates debated the Constitution, they asked questions. Would the new government take away all the power of the states? Would it become the kind of government from which they had just freed themselves? Would the President gain too much power and become a kind of king?

To avoid these dangers, the Constitution set up a federal system of government. The Articles of Confederation had given most of the power to the states. In a federal system, powers are divided between the national and state governments. For example, the Constitution explains that only the national government can print money or make laws about trade with foreign nations. At the same time, the Constitution lists many reserved powers, or powers that belong to the states. The states have authority to manage elections and issue licenses. Some powers, such as passing tax laws, are shared between the state and national governments.

5. **Write** one more power of government in each part of the diagram.

Powers of State and National Government

Powers of State Government
- manages elections
- organizes local government
- regulates trade within the states
-

Shared Powers
- collects taxes
- sets up courts
-

Powers of National Government
- makes laws about trade with foreign nations
- sets up military
- sets up postal service
-

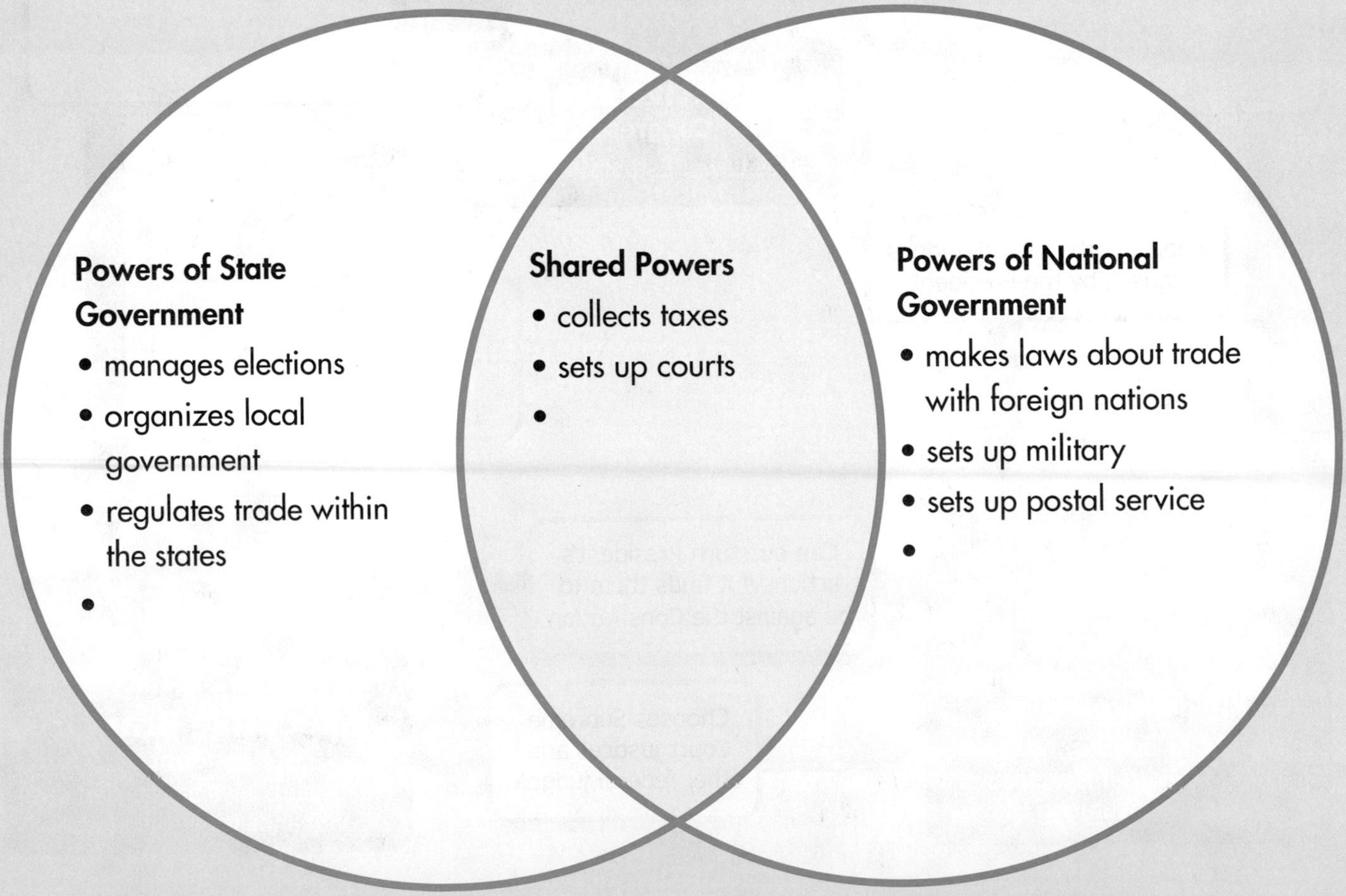

For some delegates, the new Constitution was not enough. Many believed firmly that the Constitution should include a list of the rights citizens have to protect their freedom. Others felt that the wording of the Preamble was enough. This debate would lead to one of the most important elements of the Constitution.

6. This picture shows a federal worker at the U.S. Bureau of Printing and Engraving. **Write** the power of government that is shown here.

....

7. ◉ **Compare and Contrast** Compare and contrast the main differences between the Articles of Confederation and the United States Constitution. Include in your answer how powers are shared and branches are divided under each plan for government.

....

....

....

....

8. ❓ The museum has a newspaper article from Philadelphia dated May, 1787. It tells about the arrival of delegates to the Constitutional Convention. Who is coming to town and how are they described?

my Story Ideas

....

....

....

⬛ **Stop!** I need help with ....

⏸ **Wait!** I have a question about ....

▶ **Go!** Now I know ....

The Bill of Rights

Today, the Great Seal of the United States features a bald eagle, the symbol of the country.

When the Constitutional Convention began, the delegates were divided between those who wanted to change the Articles of Confederation and those who wanted a new Constitution. By the end of the convention, even some delegates who supported the Constitution were having second thoughts.

The Nation Debates

When the new Constitution became public, the nation found itself divided. Citizens who supported it became known as **Federalists.** *Federal* refers to the kind of government the Constitution created. People who did not support the Constitution became known as **Anti-Federalists.**

The well-known Federalists Alexander Hamilton, James Madison, and John Jay joined the debate. They published essays in newspapers to explain why they backed a strong central government. Some essays pointed to the weaknesses of the Articles of Confederation. Others tried to reassure citizens that the new government protected the nation from the abuse of power. Later, the essays were collected in a book called *The Federalist.*

"A feeble [weak] executive implies a feeble execution of the government."

Alexander Hamilton

Draw the Great Seal with an animal that you think would have been a good symbol for the new country.

I will know that the Bill of Rights guarantees the individual rights of all citizens.

Vocabulary

Federalist   amendment
Anti-Federalist   due process
Bill of Rights

Anti-Federalists such as Patrick Henry and George Mason argued that the Constitution was flawed. They believed that it would be impossible for a federal government to pass laws that worked for all states. They also thought that a federal government would take power away from the states.

The Anti-Federalists, including Thomas Jefferson, made another strong argument. They believed that the Constitution needed a **Bill of Rights.** Such a statement, they argued, was vital to protect citizens' basic rights. These core rights included freedom of speech, freedom of religion, and trial by jury. Jefferson said,

"A bill of rights is what the people are entitled to against every government on earth."

"Your President may easily become king."

Patrick Henry

1. Based on the statements in the pictures on these two pages, **write** under each man's name whether he was a *Federalist* or an *Anti-Federalist*.

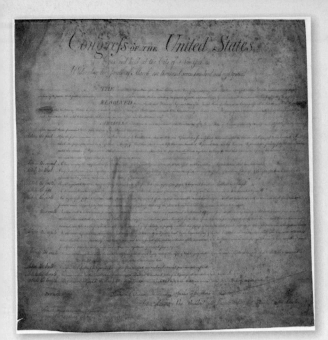

This copy of the Bill of Rights was created in 1790.

Ratifying the Constitution

On December 7, 1787, Delaware became the first state to ratify, or approve, the Constitution. Nine states needed to ratify it before the Constitution would become the law of the land. By the time Connecticut voted for it in early 1788, five states had ratified the Constitution. But the lack of a Bill of Rights remained a serious concern for many states.

In Massachusetts, leaders leaned towards voting against ratification of the Constitution. This made Federalists realize how important a Bill of Rights was to getting the Constitution passed. They pledged that Congress would allow **amendments,** or additions, that would add a bill of rights to the Constitution if Massachusetts ratified it. With this promise, Massachusetts voted to ratify.

This promise convinced the next three states to ratify. On June 21, 1788, New Hampshire became the ninth state to approve the Constitution. Leaders chose March 4, 1789, as the date the new Congress would meet and begin to govern. A few months later, Congress officially proposed ten amendments, which we know today as the Bill of Rights. By 1790, all thirteen states had ratified the Constitution of the United States.

2. **Circle** the date on the timeline when enough states had ratified the Constitution for it to take effect.

Ratifying the U.S. Constitution

December 7, 1787
Delaware

February 6, 1788
Massachusetts

May 23, 1788
South Carolina

July 26, 1788
New York

1788

December 18, 1787
New Jersey

January 9, 1788
Connecticut

April 28, 1788
Maryland

June 25, 1788
Virginia

December 12, 1787
Pennsylvania

January 2, 1788
Georgia

June 21, 1788
New Hampshire

Protecting Rights

Americans who fought for the Bill of Rights considered it so important because it spells out the individual rights of each citizen. Many people felt that unless their rights were stated, the government might take unfair advantage of its citizens. By promising to protect basic rights, the Constitution also served to protect the common good, or what is best for the whole United States.

Many of the most important freedoms that people wanted in the Constitution are in the First Amendment. These include the freedoms of religion, speech, and the press. The First Amendment also guarantees the right to assemble, or gather, peacefully and to express complaints about the government. Another important part of the Bill of Rights is its due process protections. **Due process** protects citizens' right to fair treatment through the judicial system. These are described in the Sixth, Seventh, and Eighth Amendments.

The Bill of Rights helps to limit the power of the federal government in other important ways. The Tenth Amendment says that the federal government only has the powers granted to it by the Constitution. All other powers belong to either the states or to the people.

3. **Describe** why you think people celebrated the ratification of the U.S. Constitution, as is seen in this New York City celebration.

....

....

....

....

....

November 21, 1789
North Carolina

1789

1790

May 29, 1790
Rhode Island

Ten Amendments

On September 25, 1789, just a few months after the Constitution took effect, the first national Congress officially proposed the Bill of Rights. The states approved these ten key amendments to the Constitution. On December 15, 1791, they went into effect. The Bill of Rights is summarized in the chart below.

4. ◉ **Summarize Circle** an amendment that you think is very important. **Explain** why.

....

....

....

The Bill of Rights

Amendments	Guaranteed Rights
First	Protects freedom of religion, speech, the press; the right to assemble peacefully; and the right to disagree with government decisions.
Second	Protects the right to own and bear firearms.
Third	Protects people's right not to house soldiers during peacetime.
Fourth	Protects people from having their property unfairly searched or taken.
Fifth	Guarantees that no one's life, liberty, or property can be taken unless decided by a court.
Sixth	In criminal cases, guarantees the right to a trial by a jury and to have a lawyer.
Seventh	In most civil cases, guarantees the right to a trial by a jury.
Eighth	Forbids very high bail, fines, and extraordinary punishment.
Ninth	Asserts that the people's rights are not limited to those stated in the Constitution.
Tenth	Asserts that all powers not stated as belonging to the federal government belong to the states or to the people.

The passage of the Bill of Rights established the idea that there are rights that are so important that they need to be written into the Constitution. The Bill of Rights was a guarantee that the American government recognized individual rights that must be protected. It has served as a model for governments all over the world.

5. **Draw** a picture to illustrate one of the rights in the First Amendment. **Write** a caption for your picture.

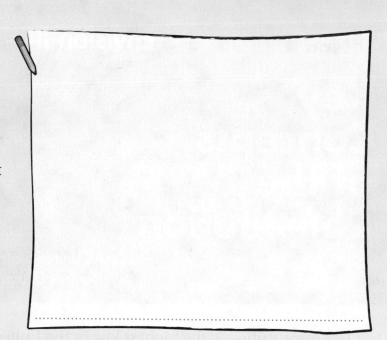

6. ◉ **Summarize** Why was the Bill of Rights so important that some states would not ratify the Constitution without its being included?

....

....

....

7. ❓ The museum has old posters from 1787. Some support the Federalist point of view and others support the Anti-Federalists. **Describe** what one of the posters says.

my Story Ideas

....

....

....

■ **Stop!** I need help with ....

❚❚ **Wait!** I have a question about ....

▶ **Go!** Now I know ....

Key Concepts of the Constitution

Envision It!

All United States coins have the motto, or saying, *E Pluribus Unum*. This is Latin for "out of many, one."

The Constitution is the highest law in the United States. It describes the powers of government and the rights of citizens. The first three words in the Constitution's Preamble are, "We the People." These words express **popular sovereignty** (SAHV run tee), the idea that power comes from the people. Thus, the United States is a **democracy**, or a government in which citizens have the power to make political decisions.

The Preamble describes the purpose of government, which is to provide citizens with a fair, safe, and peaceful way of life. The government of the United States still has these goals today.

A More Perfect Union

The Preamble explains that the Constitution was created to "form a more perfect union." Leaders hoped to strengthen and unify the country.

Under the Constitution, the nation has a strong federal government that shares powers with state governments. Each state has its own constitution, but each must obey the U.S. Constitution.

For government to work, citizens must accept the duties related to being a citizen. These duties are called **civic responsibilities.** They include being informed about current events, and voting.

Signs are displayed for candidates competing in local and national elections.

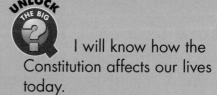
Explain why you think this is a good motto for the country.

Vocabulary

popular sovereignty

democracy

civic responsibility

rule of law

judicial review

Establish Justice

The Constitution rests on basic principles, or ideals. One of these is the **rule of law.** This means that the law protects citizens from a government's misuse of power. Another principle is "equality under the law." Everyone is considered equal, so the law applies equally to citizens and government officials. The Constitution seeks to treat all citizens with justice, or fairness. The rights and freedoms expressed in the Bill of Rights belong to every citizen equally. The government cannot take them away.

The judicial branch of government has the power of **judicial review.** This is the Supreme Court's duty to review laws and judge whether the laws follow the Constitution.

1. ◉ **Summarize Write** a brief summary in the space below of what you've learned about the Constitution so far.

Summarizing the Purpose of Our Government

A More Perfect Union	Establish Justice
States share power with the federal government. Individuals have civic responsibilities.	

Ensure Domestic Tranquility

Domestic tranquility refers to a safe and peaceful homeland. "Domestic" means home and family. "Tranquility" means peace or calm. The government has many agencies whose job it is to make sure Americans are safe as a nation and within their towns and homes.

The National Guard is a part of the military. Its job is to work within states and towns to protect and help citizens in times of emergency, such as natural disasters.

The Federal Bureau of Investigation, or FBI, is a government agency. The FBI investigates major crimes such as kidnapping and often assists other law enforcement agencies. It also gathers information about crime suspects and terrorists.

The National Park Service is in charge of our nation's parks and monuments, such as Grand Canyon National Park in Arizona and Everglades National Park in Florida. The Park Service's purpose is to preserve such places for the enjoyment and education of citizens.

The Environmental Protection Agency (EPA) makes and enforces rules that protect the environment. For example, it sets limits on air, land, and water pollution.

2. In this photograph, National Guard workers help to control damage from the Gulf of Mexico oil spill in 2010. **Write** how the National Guard helps to ensure domestic tranquility.

....

....

....

....

Provide for the Common Defense

The nation is defended, or protected, by men and women serving in the armed forces. The army protects the nation on land, and the navy defends the seas. The marines operate both on land and sea. The air force operates in the skies using jets, helicopters, and other aircraft. Along the nation's coastlines, the coast guard enforces the law, sometimes working as part of the navy. The coast guard also performs search-and-rescue missions to aid ships and people in danger. The National Guard serves as part of the army and the air force.

The Constitution limits the power of the military by dividing up control of the armed forces. Congress sets up and funds the military. The President leads it as commander in chief. Several civilian, or nonmilitary, officials under the President share control. The United States military has been called to duty in two world wars in the 20th century, as well as many smaller conflicts.

Four U.S. Navy aircraft, called F/A-18 Hornets, fly on a mission over Afghanistan.

3. **Add** where each branch of the military operates to the word web.

Military Branches of the U.S. Government

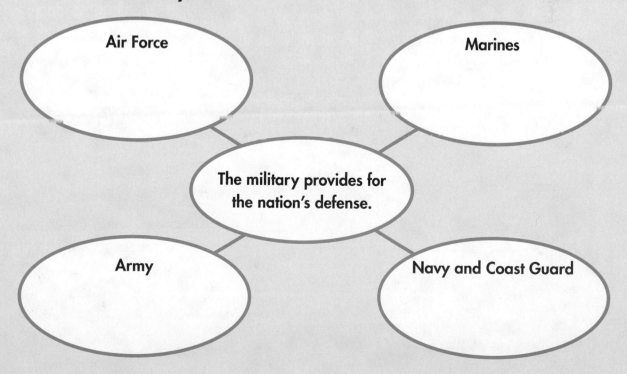

Air Force

Marines

The military provides for the nation's defense.

Army

Navy and Coast Guard

Promote the General Welfare

Many government agencies work for the welfare, or well-being, of Americans. The Food and Drug Administration makes sure that food and medicines are safe for public use. The Department of Transportation sets safety standards for automobiles. The National Institutes of Health help keep the public healthy by tracking outbreaks of disease such as the flu. The Centers for Disease Control also work to protect public health and prevent disease.

In addition, the federal government sets up special programs to help its citizens, especially people who are elderly, ill, or unemployed. Social Security is a program that gives financial benefits to people who have reached retirement age and to people who are out of work. Another government program, Medicaid, helps pay for health care for people who cannot afford it. Medicare provides health care to people over 65 years old, and the Children's Health Insurance Program works with states to ensure health care coverage for millions of children in the country.

4. Government agencies test and inspect products such as cars to ensure that they are safe. Why is this the responsibility of the federal government?

....

....

....

....

....

....

Secure Liberty

The ten amendments that make up the Bill of Rights all express what the Preamble calls "the Blessings of Liberty." *Liberty* means "freedom." For example, the Constitution protects a person's freedom to express an opinion in a newspaper. It also protects citizens' right to gather in public places and to own property. However, not all citizens have always enjoyed these freedoms. Throughout history, Americans have worked to give more citizens these blessings of liberty.

Women held protests demanding their right to vote. This rally took place at the White House in 1918.

Amending the Constitution

When the founding fathers wrote the Constitution, they allowed for it to be added to, or amended, over time. Several of these amendments have affected one of citizens' most important liberties, the right to vote.

Originally, only free white men who owned property were allowed to vote. African American men were not allowed to vote until the Fifteenth Amendment was ratified in 1870. That amendment says that no citizen can be denied the right to vote based on "race, color, or previous condition of servitude [former enslaved people]." Women were denied their right to vote in national elections until 1920, when the Nineteenth Amendment passed. The most recent amendment concerning voting rights is the Twenty-sixth Amendment, passed in 1971. It set 18 as the legal age limit for voting.

5. Amendments to the Constitution have expanded voting rights. **Fill in** the chart with the missing dates and amendments.

Voting Rights

Year	Amendment
1870	Fifteenth Amendment: African American males gain right to vote
1920	....
....	Twenty-sixth Amendment: Voting age lowered from 21 to 18

Fifteenth Amendment

The right of citizens to vote cannot be denied because of race.

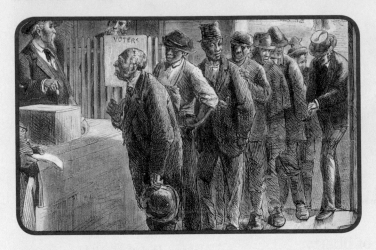

Twenty-fifth Amendment

If the President leaves office for any reason, the Vice President becomes President.

Twenty-sixth Amendment

Citizens 18 years of age or older may vote.

To amend the Constitution, the founding fathers set up a special, and rather difficult, amendment process. They wanted to ensure that only important additions would be made. The process begins when two thirds of Congress votes to propose an amendment. Three fourths of the states must then ratify the amendment. Only then is the amendment officially part of the Constitution.

Since the Constitution took effect, only 27 amendments have been made to it. These amendments reflect changes in people's attitudes or responses to new situations. The 27 amendments uphold the ideals expressed in the Preamble to the Constitution.

6. Compare and contrast the Fifteenth and Twenty-sixth amendments.

....
....
....
....
....
....

7. How many present-day states must ratify an amendment to make it part of the Constitution?

....

"Out of Many, One"

The motto *E Pluribus Unum* has special meaning for Americans. It means that out of 50 distinct states comes one United States. It suggests that despite our differences, we share certain principles, such as a strong belief in individual rights. These beliefs keep us united, though it is not always easy for one nation to include so many different people and opinions. However, to keep the nation strong and united, good citizens must go beyond their basic civic and political responsibilities to improve government and society. In other words, not only do citizens need to vote and exercise their rights, they need to take an active role in making the nation and their communities better. They can volunteer, suggest improvements, and even run for office.

On the Presidential Seal a bald eagle is pictured holding the motto "E Pluribus Unum."

Got it?

8. ◉ **Summarize Describe** two ways in which the Preamble to the Constitution affects our lives today.

....

....

....

9. ❓ During a hurricane, your town is in danger of flooding. Why would the President send the National Guard to help your town?   my Story Ideas

....

....

....

⬛ **Stop!** I need help with ....

⏸ **Wait!** I have a question about ....

▶ **Go!** Now I know ....

Study Guide

Lesson 1

Articles of Confederation

- The Northwest Ordinance expanded the borders of the United States.
- The Articles of Confederation created a weak central government.
- Many citizens called for a convention to change the Articles of Confederation.

Lesson 2

Creating the Constitution

- Many delegates at the Convention wanted to create a new constitution.
- The Great Compromise combined the Virginia Plan and the New Jersey Plan to create a legislative branch with two houses.
- The Constitution assigns powers to both federal and state governments.

Lesson 3

The Bill of Rights

- Federalists defended the Constitution and its strong federal government.
- Anti-Federalists criticized the Constitution for taking away power from the states.
- The Constitution was ratified after Federalists promised to add a Bill of Rights.

Lesson 4

Key Concepts of the Constitution

- The Preamble of the Constitution describes the purposes of government.
- National agencies help to carry out the goals in the Preamble.
- Amendments to the Constitution have allowed it to adapt to changing needs and ideas.

Review and Assessment

Lesson 1

Articles of Confederation

1. Why were many Americans satisfied with the Articles of Confederation?

   ....

   ....

   ....

2. Why did money cause confusion under the Articles of Confederation?

   ....

   ....

   ....

3. What was one effect of Shays' Rebellion?

   A. More farmers were sent to prison.

   B. More people called for a stronger national government.

   C. New state courts opened.

   D. The national government began collecting taxes.

4. In what way did the Northwest Ordinance affect Native Americans?

   ....

   ....

   ....

Lesson 2

Creating the Constitution

5. What was the Three-Fifths Compromise?

   ....

   ....

   ....

6. What check does the executive branch have over the legislative branch?

   ....

   ....

7. **Write** *V, NJ,* or *GC* next to the sentences that describe the Virginia Plan, the New Jersey Plan, or the Great Compromise.

   _____ Larger states would have more representatives in Congress.

   _____ Congress would have two houses, one with equal representation, and one with representation based on population.

   _____ Each state would have equal representation in Congress regardless of its population.

8. On a separate sheet of paper, **write** a short biography about one of the delegates discussed in the lesson. Include information such as his home state and contributions to the Constitutional Convention.

Lesson 3

The Bill of Rights

9. **⊙ Summarize** The Anti-Federalists had two main objections to the Constitution. What were they?

....

....

....

10. How did the Bill of Rights help the Constitution become ratified?

....

....

....

....

....

11. How does the Bill of Rights help citizens?

....

....

....

12. Fill in the blanks to complete the sentence.

By 1790, all 13 states had ....

the United States ....

Lesson 4

Key Concepts of the Constitution

13. **Draw** a line connecting each agency with the purpose it is meant to fulfill from the Preamble.

1. National Guard   A. "Provide for the Common Defense"

2. Armed Forces   B. "Promote the General Welfare"

3. Social Security   C. "Ensure Domestic Tranquility"

14. **? What is the purpose of government?**

Use the questions below to think more about this chapter's Big Question.

a. What purposes of government are stated in the Preamble to the Constitution?

....

....

....

b. How does the judicial branch help establish equal justice?

....

....

Go online to write and illustrate your own **myStory Book** using the **myStory Ideas** from this chapter.

What is the purpose of government?

The Constitution sets out how the government of the United States is structured and the rights and responsibilities of its citizens. As you go about your daily life, you are affected by many aspects of our constitutional government.

List some of the ways the U.S. Constitution and Bill of Rights affect your daily life and life in your community. **Explain** your choices.

....

....

....

....

Now **draw** an image that shows one way the Constitution affects your daily life.

While you're online, check out the **myStory Current Events** area where you can create your own book on a topic that's in the news.

myworldsocialstudies.com ▶ Understand ▶ my Story Book

221

The Young Nation Grows

How do leaders shape a nation?

Write the names of three leaders of our nation today. Then **describe** how you think one of them is shaping our nation.

....

....

....

....

....

President Jefferson sent the Lewis and Clark expedition west with the goal of reaching the Pacific Ocean, pictured here.

The Lewis and Clark Expedition:
Sacagawea's Unique Role

my Story Video

The Lewis and Clark expedition was the idea of President Thomas Jefferson. For years, he had been curious about the land in the West. After the United States bought the Louisiana Territory from France in 1803, Jefferson chose two men to explore it. Meriwether Lewis had been Jefferson's personal secretary. William Clark had been Lewis's commander in the army. These men hired soldiers who could hunt, trap, and pilot boats to help their exploration.

Jefferson wanted the team to learn about the land, meet Native Americans, and look for a water route to the Pacific Ocean. The expedition set out on May 14, 1804.

During the 8,000-mile journey, each member's skills helped the others on the expedition. But it was Sacagawea (sak uh juh WEE uh), a young Shoshone (shuh SHOWN) woman with a newborn baby, who gave what none of the others could. She spoke the languages of the Hidatsas and the Shoshones.

Thomas Jefferson chose Meriwether Lewis, his personal secretary, to be one of the expedition's leaders.

Lewis and Clark first met Charbonneau and Sacagawea when they stayed near Mandan and Hidatsa villages in the winter of 1804.

Sacagawea met her brother, Cameahwait, who provided the horses that carried the expedition over the Bitterroot Mountains.

Crossing the Rocky Mountains was just one part of the challenging 8,000-mile journey.

Starting from St. Louis, Missouri, Lewis and Clark led the expedition north on the Missouri River. The men paddled hard against the current. Waterfalls across the river forced them to carry their boats for miles around the obstacles. The two captains and several others kept journals of their travels. They noted sights and experiences, such as encounters with grizzly bears and other animals that they had never seen before.

During the winter of 1804–1805 the members of the expedition built a fort near Mandan and Hidatsa villages, in what is present-day North Dakota. There, they hired a French trapper named Charbonneau (shar BAW noh) and his Shoshone wife Sacagawea to join them. Lewis and Clark knew that Sacagawea's ability to speak Shoshone would help them, since they would soon enter Shoshone territory. When the group left in April, Sacagawea brought along her two-month-old baby. Sacagawea helped the expedition in many ways.

At one point, Charbonneau almost tipped over an expedition boat. Sacagawea saved important papers and instruments from being lost in the river. A week later, Lewis and Clark thanked her by naming a branch of a Montana river after her.

224

The expedition finally reached the Pacific Ocean in November 1805.

Having said good-bye to Charbonneau and Sacagawea, the expedition returned to St. Louis in September 1806.

Sacagawea's most unique contribution came later that summer. The expedition needed horses to cross the Bitterroot Range of the Rocky Mountains. Sacagawea knew she would be the one to talk with the Shoshone people. Imagine her surprise when she learned that the leader of the Shoshones was her own brother, Cameahwait (kah mee uh WAYT)!

Today, people fly all over the country to visit relatives. In 1805, however, "running into" a family member who lived so far away was unheard of. It was good luck for both Sacagawea and the expedition. As Sacagawea translated, Cameahwait's people agreed to supply the horses the expedition needed. Now, the group could continue over the Rockies on horseback.

Sacagawea and Charbonneau traveled with the expedition to the Pacific Ocean. There, she suggested a spot to spend the winter. The following spring, she and Charbonneau began the journey back east with Lewis and Clark. They left the group at the Mandan and Hidatsa villages. Later, they visited St. Louis, to see Clark and to have their child baptized.

The Lewis and Clark expedition might have succeeded without Sacagawea. But her skills were significant. Together with the other members of the expedition, she contributed to a journey that opened the West to future explorers and settlers.

Think About It Based on this story, in what ways did Sacagawea play a leadership role in the expedition? As you read the chapter ahead, think about what qualities make a leader and how leaders help to shape a nation.

Washington Takes Office

Envision It!

King George III of Great Britain wore royal robes. Compare the way he and George Washington (below) dressed.

Washington wore a plain brown suit to his inauguration in New York in 1789.

In April of 1789, George Washington left Mount Vernon, his home in Virginia, to travel to New York City for his inauguration. An **inauguration** is an official ceremony to make someone President. Standing on the balcony of Federal Hall, he placed one hand on a Bible. "I do solemnly swear [promise]," said Washington, "that I will faithfully execute the office of President of the United States, and will to the best of my ability, preserve, protect and defend the Constitution of the United States." With these words, George Washington became the first President of the United States.

The First President

Several months before, on February 4, 1789, the Electoral College had elected George Washington to be President. The **Electoral College** is a group of people chosen by each state to vote for the President and Vice President. The number of electors from each state equals its two senators plus the number of its members in the House of Representatives.

In the election of 1789, all of the electors voted for Washington. No President since then has been elected unanimously. John Adams, a long-time Patriot, was elected Vice President.

Write why you think these two leaders dressed so differently.

Vocabulary

inauguration

Electoral College

Cabinet

political party

tariff

Soon after Washington became President, Congress created different departments within the Executive Branch. For example, the Department of State was created to handle relations with other countries. The Department of the Treasury dealt with the nation's finances.

Washington chose one person called a secretary to run each of these departments. He picked Thomas Jefferson as the Secretary of State and Alexander Hamilton as the Secretary of the Treasury. Henry Knox, who had been in the army with Washington, became the Secretary of War. As the Attorney General, Edmund Randolph advised Washington on legal issues.

This group of advisors became known as the President's **Cabinet.** They met often to help Washington govern. The creation of the Cabinet is an example of a practice begun by Washington that continued after he left office.

1. This chart names the men in Washington's Cabinet and describes their responsibilities. **Write** their job titles in the blank spaces.

The Cabinet

Name	Thomas Jefferson	Alexander Hamilton	Henry Knox	Edmund Randolph
Position	Secretary of State			
Responsibilities	Handles relations with other countries	Deals with national money matters	Conducts war and protects the nation	Handles legal issues and law enforcement

The First Political Parties

Two of the members of Washington's Cabinet, Alexander Hamilton and Thomas Jefferson, had many disagreements. Hamilton, the Secretary of the Treasury, believed in a powerful national government. He thought the country needed a strong economy, based on trade and industry. Thomas Jefferson, on the other hand, believed the economy should be based on farming. He did not think the national government should be allowed to become too powerful. He worried that such a powerful government might take away people's rights.

The followers of Jefferson and Hamilton became the country's first political parties. A **political party** is a group of people who have the same beliefs about government. Members of political parties work to elect their candidates to government offices. Hamilton's followers were called Federalists, and Jefferson's party became known as the Democratic-Republicans.

George Washington with his first Cabinet; from left to right: Washington, Knox, Hamilton, Jefferson, and Randolph

George Washington and some other early leaders opposed political parties. Washington thought they were harmful. He wanted the people in his Cabinet to work together as a united government. He even published a speech in which he warned against "the baneful [harmful] effects of the Spirit of Party."

2. ⊙ **Generalize** Based on the information in the text and in the chart on the next page, **write** a generalization about the kinds of people who might have supported each party.

....

....

....

Building a Strong Economy

An important issue that Jefferson and Hamilton argued about was the idea of a national bank. Hamilton wanted a national bank to hold the government's money and to lend it money, if needed. Jefferson opposed the idea. He thought the federal government did not have the power to create a national bank. Washington listened to Hamilton. The bank was set up in 1791.

The national bank issued bank notes, or paper money, that were accepted throughout the nation. In 1792, the U.S. Mint was created to make coins. With bank notes and coins, the nation now had a standard currency. This made it much easier for people in different states to trade with each other.

As Secretary of the Treasury, Hamilton took other actions to build a strong economy. He had the federal government pay its war debts. Hamilton also supported **tariffs**, which are taxes on imported goods. Tariffs raise the prices of goods from other countries. They encourage people to buy goods made in their own country.

Hamilton supported high tariffs for two reasons. First, the tariffs would raise money for the federal government. Second, tariffs helped American businesses. Jefferson opposed high tariffs because they raised prices for farmers and others. Southerners also argued that a high tariff would help the North, where most industries were located. In the end, the tariff was the only part of Hamilton's plan for the economy that Congress did not accept.

This copper one-cent coin was issued by the U.S. Mint in 1793. Today, fewer than five coins of this kind exist.

The First Political Parties

	Federalists (followed Hamilton)	Democratic-Republicans (followed Jefferson)
Economy	Wanted the economy to be based on trade and factories	Wanted the economy based on farming and small crafts
National Bank	Supported the idea of a national bank; thought it would help the nation grow	Opposed the idea of a national bank; thought the government did not have the right to create it

An aerial view of our nation's capital, Washington, D.C., originally designed by Pierre-Charles L'Enfant

Benjamin Banneker, surveyor of the land

A New Capital

In 1790, leaders wanted a new city that would be the center of the government and not part of an existing commercial center, such as Philadelphia or New York City. George Washington chose its location. The nation's capital would be built on the Potomac River between Maryland and Virginia. It would not be part of either state.

Although they disagreed on many issues, Jefferson and Hamilton compromised on others. Hamilton wanted the nation's capital to be his home city of New York. Hamilton had compromised on the Potomac River location after Jefferson had agreed to Hamilton's plan for paying off war debts.

The capital city was named Washington, District of Columbia (D.C.), in part to honor George Washington. Pierre-Charles L'Enfant, a French engineer, designed the city with wide streets that led to important buildings and monuments. Andrew Ellicott and Benjamin Banneker, a free African American, served as surveyors for the city. A surveyor measures land.

John Adams was elected the country's second President in 1796. In 1800, when the federal government moved to Washington, D.C., many buildings were not yet finished.

The President's Palace, which was later named the White House, was one of those unfinished buildings. Adams and his wife, Abigail, moved in anyway. The plaster was still wet on some walls, and many rooms were unfinished.

In a letter to her daughter, Abigail Adams wrote,

" . . . there is not a single apartment [room] finished, . . . We have not the least fence, yard, or other convenience, without, and the great unfinished audience room I made a drying room of, to hang up the clothes in."

Despite these rough living conditions, John and Abigail Adams made this new building the official home of the President of the United States.

Abigail Adams

Got it?

3. ⊙ **Generalize** Based on the information you have read in this lesson, **write** a generalization about President Washington's actions while in office.

....

....

4. ❓ President George Washington knew he needed help running the new government. As Washington's aide, help draft a letter to Alexander Hamilton. Tell Hamilton how the government will be set up and offer him a job in the Cabinet.

my Story Ideas

....

....

....

◻ **Stop!** I need help with ....

❙❙ **Wait!** I have a question about ....

▶ **Go!** Now I know ....

Media and Technology

Evaluate Web Sites

Where would you look if you were writing a report about the first Cabinet of the United States and you needed good sources of information? You would probably use a search engine to find Web sites about your topic. To be sure they contain accurate and reliable information, you would need to evaluate the Web sites.

File Edit View History Bookmarks Tools Help

First U.S. Cabinet

Search Results

1. **U.S.** Senate: Art & History Home > Historical Minutes > 1787–1800 . . .
   www.USsenate.gov

2. **United States Cabinet**
   www.student.encyclopedia.com

3. A 'Balanced' **First Cabinet**
   www.jeffersoncabinet.org

4. **First Cabinet** – Bad choices
   www.badcabinet.blog.com

5. Kitchen **Cabinets**: Beautiful Cabinets for Your Home
   www.greatcabinet.com

Learn

Look at the list of sources above. Circle the Web sites that end in *.gov* and *.org*. Sites that end in *.gov* are government Web sites. These are usually good sources of information. Sites that end in *.org* are nonprofit organizations. These can offer good information, but might not be reliable if the organization expresses a point of view. Read carefully before deciding.

Cross out the *blog.com* Web site. Blogs are usually created by a single individual and are not accurate sources.

Web sites that end in *.com* are commercial sites, which try to make money. However, online encyclopedias are often reliable and accurate sources of information and provide summaries about a topic. Underline the *.com* that is an encyclopedia.

Try it!

Practice

Look at the list of Web sites again. Then **answer** the questions below.

1. Which source might give you a summary of the members of the first Cabinet and a description of their jobs? How do you know?

....

....

2. Which source is trying to sell something? How do you know?

....

3. Which source might have accurate information but is about a different period than your report? How do you know?

....

....

4. Which source most likely contains one person's opinion? How do you know?

....

....

5. **Apply** Choose a topic from Lesson 1. **Write** the topic below. Use a search engine to find three reliable Web sites about your topic. **Write** the URLs (addresses) of those three Web sites below.

Topic: ....

....

....

....

Jefferson and the Louisiana Purchase

Envision It!

Sacagawea (spoke Hidatsa and Shoshone)

3

Charbonneau (spoke French and Hidatsa)

If Meriwether Lewis wanted to speak to Cameahwait, his message would need to be translated.

In 1791, the Union added its fourteenth state, Vermont. As the nation grew, people began to feel that there was not enough fertile land in the East. They started looking for land west of the Appalachian Mountains to build new lives.

Moving West

Daniel Boone was an experienced woodsman and pioneer in the Appalachian Mountains region. A **pioneer** is someone who settles a new place before others. Boone, like other pioneers, helped create new settlements in Kentucky and other western territories.

In 1769, Boone and several others had followed a Native American trail through the Appalachians from Virginia to Kentucky. The trail snaked through the Cumberland Gap, a narrow passage in the mountains. Boone helped clear the trail, which was later called the Wilderness Road. This made it easier for people to move west.

1. **Look** at the drawing of the Wilderness Road. **Draw** the route of the Wilderness Road between Blockhouse and Boonesborough.

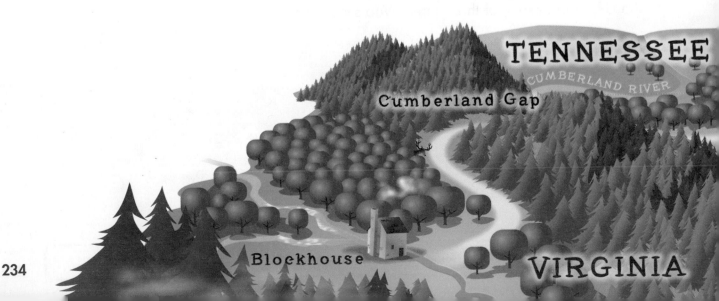

TENNESSEE

CUMBERLAND RIVER

Cumberland Gap

Blockhouse

VIRGINIA

Meriwether Lewis
(spoke English
and French)

Cameahwait
(spoke
Shoshone)

Number the speakers in the order they would use to pass a message from Lewis to Cameahwait.

UNLOCK THE BIG ?

I will know that Jefferson's actions, especially the purchase of the Louisiana Territory, changed where and how people in North America lived.

Vocabulary

pioneer

frontier

interpreter

Life on the **frontier**, the edge of settlement, was hard. Pioneers cleared land, built houses, grew their own food, and made their own clothes. In spite of these hardships, settlers continued moving west. Kentucky became the fifteenth state in 1792. By 1800, more than 300,000 settlers traveled the Wilderness Road into Kentucky and the Midwest.

Jefferson Becomes President

Changes were also taking place in Washington, D.C. During Adams's presidency, the United States and France came into conflict. When President Adams cut off trade with France, the Democratic-Republicans criticized his tough stance. Congress then passed a series of laws called the Alien and Sedition Acts. These laws limited free speech, a free press, and the freedom of "aliens," or immigrants.

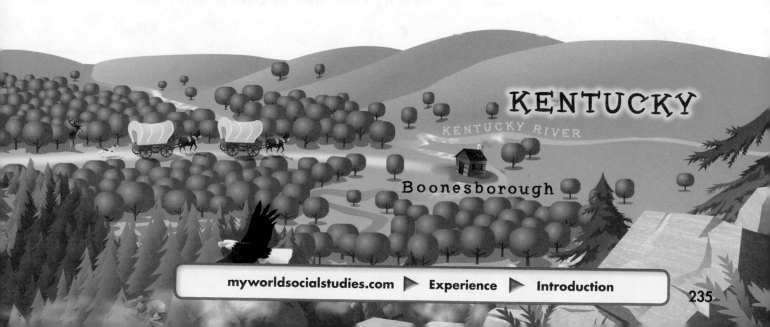

KENTUCKY

KENTUCKY RIVER

Boonesborough

Thomas Jefferson, head of the Democratic-Republicans, fought against the Alien and Sedition Acts. His party thought they were unconstitutional because they violated individual rights. Jefferson was elected President in 1800.

When Adams lost, it was the first time that one party had given up power to the other. Jefferson filled government jobs with Democratic-Republicans. His actions began a trend that continues today whenever a member of a different political party is elected President.

The Louisiana Purchase

For many years, the land west of the Mississippi River had been claimed by Spain. In 1800, however, France took over this territory. President Jefferson worried that France might try to stop Americans from using the port of New Orleans. The settlers west of the Appalachian Mountains relied on the Mississippi River to ship goods south to the port. From there, the goods were sent to cities on the East Coast.

Jefferson sent James Monroe to France to try to buy the port of New Orleans and some land nearby. At first, Napoleon Bonaparte, the leader of France, did not want to sell New Orleans. But France was fighting a war against Britain and needed money. So, Napoleon surprised the Americans. He offered to sell the entire Louisiana Territory.

The Louisiana Territory stretched from the Mississippi River to the Rocky Mountains. It would double the size of the United States. It would provide rich natural resources and help the nation develop its economy. Monroe quickly agreed to buy it for about $15 million. When Jefferson learned how much land was involved, he grew concerned.

2. ◎ **Generalize Circle** a detail in the text that supports this generalization: The Louisiana Purchase changed the nation.

3. **Look** at the chart. **Circle** the reason France offered to sell the Louisiana territory to the United States.

Events Leading to Louisiana Purchase

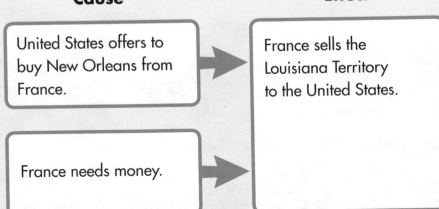

Cause	Effect
United States offers to buy New Orleans from France.	France sells the Louisiana Territory to the United States.
France needs money.	

Did a U.S. President have the power to buy new lands? Jefferson believed in a strict interpretation of the Constitution. The Constitution does not mention buying territory. However, he found a way to explain the purchase: the Constitution gives the President the power to negotiate treaties, or agreements with other countries. In 1803, the United States completed the purchase of the Louisiana Territory from France.

Compass and leather pouch used on the Lewis and Clark expedition

Exploring the West

Jefferson was curious about the new territory beyond the Mississippi River. He decided to send an expedition into the Louisiana Territory. Jefferson chose Meriwether Lewis and William Clark to lead the expedition. He gave the expedition three goals. First, they were to explore the Missouri and Columbia rivers to see if they could find a water route to the Pacific Ocean. Second, they were to meet and learn about the Native Americans who lived in the region. Third, they were to study and take notes on the landforms, plants, and animals they found.

In May 1804, Lewis and Clark and more than 30 others left St. Louis, Missouri. Later, a French trapper named Charbonneau and his Shoshone wife, Sacagawea, joined them as guides and interpreters. An **interpreter** translates what people are saying into other languages. Sacagawea explained to Native Americans that they met that their mission was peaceful.

Hardships and Successes

The expedition traveled more than 8,000 miles during its two-and-a-half-year journey. The explorers faced all kinds of weather, from blizzards to scorching heat. In addition to exploring the mountains and plains of the West, the expedition encountered dangerous animals, such as grizzly bears and mountain lions. They saw huge herds of bison and pronghorns, and groups of prairie dogs.

Finally, in November 1805, the explorers caught their first glimpse of the Pacific Ocean. When they arrived, Clark wrote in his journal "Ocean in view! O! the joy." After spending the winter on the West Coast, Lewis, Clark, and the others returned to St. Louis in September 1806. They had succeeded in exploring the nation's new territory.

4. **Look** at the map. **Write** the names of the rivers that Lewis and Clark followed to reach the Pacific Ocean.

....

....

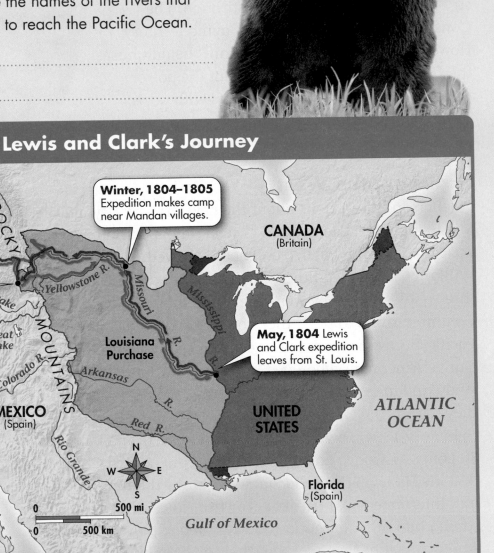

Lewis and Clark's Journey

November, 1805
The expedition reaches the Pacific Ocean.

Winter, 1804–1805
Expedition makes camp near Mandan villages.

August, 1805 Expedition meets Sacagawea's brother Cameahwait, who is chief of the Shoshone.

May, 1804 Lewis and Clark expedition leaves from St. Louis.

CANADA (Britain)

Columbia R.

ROCKY

Yellowstone R.

Snake R.

Missouri R.

Mississippi R.

Great Salt Lake

Louisiana Purchase

PACIFIC OCEAN

Colorado R.

Arkansas R.

MOUNTAINS

MEXICO (Spain)

Red R.

Rio Grande

UNITED STATES

ATLANTIC OCEAN

Florida (Spain)

Gulf of Mexico

N
W   E
S

KEY
- United States in 1803
- Louisiana Purchase
- Disputed territory
- ← Westward route of Lewis and Clark, 1804–1805
- → Eastward route of Lewis and Clark, 1806

0   500 mi
0   500 km

Lewis and Clark made maps and kept detailed journals of the land, people, and animals they saw. They even brought back new varieties of plants and animals for Jefferson to examine. Lewis and Clark did not find a water route across the continent, but they reached the Pacific Ocean. Their journey paved the way for future explorers and settlers from the United States.

One such explorer of the new territory was Zebulon Pike. With a small group, he followed the Arkansas River to present-day Colorado. There, he saw a great mountain that today is known as Pikes Peak.

5. **Fill in** the chart with Lewis and Clark's accomplishments.

Lewis and Clark's Accomplishments

6. ◉ **Sequence List** in sequential order four key events that led to the Louisiana Purchase.

....

....

....

7. **?** Help President Jefferson by drafting a letter to Meriwether Lewis and William Clark, asking them to explore the newly purchased Louisiana Territory. **Explain** the goals of the trip.

my Story Ideas

....

....

....

....

■ **Stop!** I need help with ....

❙❙ **Wait!** I have a question about ....

▶ **Go!** Now I know ....

The War of 1812

Envision It!

This cartoon is from 1809. King George III is on the left. Napoleon is on the right. Jefferson is in the middle.

Have you ever been caught in the middle when two friends were fighting? In some ways, that is what happened to the United States in the early 1800s. France and Great Britain were at war. The United States wanted to stay neutral, but the warring countries made that nearly impossible.

Leading Up to War

In this war, neither side wanted its enemy to trade with the United States. Both France and Great Britain threatened to attack American ships and take their cargo. Great Britain also blockaded French ports so the United States could not ship goods to and from France.

Great Britain also angered the United States when it began capturing sailors from American ships. The **impressment** of these sailors meant that they were forced to work on British ships. Many of these sailors were United States citizens. Americans believed the British had no right to take these men.

Great Britain and the United States were also in conflict over the Northwest Territory. After the American Revolution, the British had agreed to leave the area. But in the early 1800s, British soldiers remained in what is now Canada, which Great Britain controlled. Americans believed that these soldiers were supplying weapons to Native Americans.

Combat between French and British ships, 1806

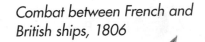

_____

_____

_____

_____

_____

_____

Explain the meaning of the cartoon. What do you think is happening?

Vocabulary

impressment   casualty

anthem   nationalism

Tecumseh (tuh KUM suh), a Shawnee leader, and his brother, known as the Prophet, were working to unite Native Americans. If Native Americans fought together, they might be able to drive settlers out of the Northwest Territory.

By the fall of 1811, many Native Americans supported Tecumseh. They gathered near the Tippecanoe River in Indiana Territory. Tecumseh was away, recruiting other Native Americans. The Prophet decided to attack nearby United States troops. William Henry Harrison, the governor of the Northwest Territory, led American soldiers against the Prophet. The battle was seen as a victory for the United States. Afterward, Tecumseh joined British allies in Canada.

1. Fill in the blanks to complete the sequence chart.

Conflicts in Northwest Territory

```
British give weapons to          William Henry Harrison
Native Americans.          ──→    defeats the Native
      │                           Americans.
      ↓                              ↑      │
Tecumseh unites Native ───────────────┘     ↓
Americans against settlers.       ...................joins
                                  ...................allies
                                  in Canada.
```

War With Great Britain Begins

In 1809, James Madison became President. He tried to keep the nation neutral. However, a group of congressmen called the War Hawks argued in favor of war against Great Britain. Henry Clay from South Carolina was a leader of this group. Most of the War Hawks lived in the West and the South.

One reason the War Hawks wanted a war was because of the British attacks on American ships. They also believed that the United States could force the British out of Canada. If the British left Canada, they thought, the United States would have more land for settlers and fewer conflicts with Native Americans. In June 1812, President Madison gave in to the War Hawks. Congress declared war on Great Britain.

The War at Sea

Early in the war, the United States tried several times to invade Canada, but did not succeed. However, the small United States Navy did win some important victories over the powerful British navy. The American warship USS *Constitution* defeated a British warship. The wooden sides of the *Constitution* were so thick that British cannonballs seemed to bounce off them. For this, the ship, which still exists today, earned the nickname "Old Ironsides."

Another important naval victory was fought on Lake Erie, which is one of the Great Lakes. Oliver Hazard Perry commanded American ships in a battle that lasted several hours. At the end of it, Perry sent a message to General William Henry Harrison. In it, Perry said, "We have met the enemy and they are ours."

USS *Constitution*

2. ◉ **Generalize** The United States had some early naval victories in the War of 1812. **Write** a generalization about the United States Navy during the war.

....

....

242

Battles on Land

In August 1814, the British attacked Washington, D.C. President Madison and other leaders were forced to flee the city. Dolley Madison, the President's wife, did not have time to pack much at all. But she would not leave without one important item, namely, a famous portrait of George Washington. After she and others escaped, the British set fire to the White House, Capitol, Treasury, and other important government buildings.

Next, the British tried to capture the city of Baltimore, Maryland. On September 13, a fleet sailed toward Fort McHenry, which stood on an island in the harbor and was defended by American troops. The British bombarded Fort McHenry during the night. The Americans refused to surrender the fort. Finally, the British gave up.

Francis Scott Key, an American lawyer, watched the battle through the night. At sunrise, he saw the American flag still flying at the fort. Inspired, he wrote a poem about the battle. Later, his poem, "The Star-Spangled Banner," was set to music and became the U.S. national anthem. An **anthem** is a song of praise.

Dolley Madison as First Lady

Oh, say can you see by the dawn's early light
What so proudly we hailed at the twilight's last gleaming?
Whose broad stripes and bright stars through the perilous fight,
O'er the ramparts we watched were so gallantly streaming?
And the rocket's red glare, the bombs bursting in air,
Gave proof through the night that our flag was still there.
Oh, say does that star-spangled banner yet wave
O'er the land of the free and the home of the brave?

3. Francis Scott Key wrote the lyrics of the national anthem during the War of 1812. **Circle** the words that describe the United States.

243

Fighting for New Orleans

By the end of 1814, the United States and Great Britain had been fighting for more than two years. Neither side was winning. They agreed to end the war. They signed a peace treaty in the city of Ghent, Belgium, in December. News of the treaty took several weeks to make it across the Atlantic Ocean to the soldiers still fighting in the United States.

In January 1815, before news of the peace had reached them, the British attacked the port of New Orleans, Louisiana. American general Andrew Jackson defended the city. He led an army of soldiers from southern states, including pirates and free African Americans. Jackson's troops fought hard and forced the British to surrender. During this battle, the British suffered more than 2,000 **casualties**, or people who were injured or killed. The Americans had only 71 casualties.

Though the war was already over, the victory at the battle of New Orleans made Andrew Jackson a national hero. His soldiers gave him the nickname "Old Hickory" because they thought he was as tough as hickory wood.

4. **Look** at this painting of the battle of New Orleans and study the map. **Write** why both sides fought to control New Orleans.

....

....

....

....

Mississippi River

New Orleans

The Return of Peace

The Treaty of Ghent, which ended the war, simply returned things to the way they were before the conflict. When the war between Britain and France ended in 1815, so did American problems with British naval policies.

One major effect of the War of 1812 was that many Americans felt more confident about their new nation. The battle of New Orleans had been a victory. The United States had stood up to Great Britain, the most powerful nation on Earth. Some people have even called the War of 1812 "the second war of independence." It created strong feelings of patriotism and **nationalism,** or pride in the nation. It made many Americans feel more united than ever.

Got it?

5. ◉ **Cause and Effect Write** three effects of the War of 1812.

....

....

....

....

6. ❓ President Madison does not want to go to war with Great Britain, but in 1812, he asks Congress to declare war anyway. Help President Madison draft a letter to Henry Clay, explaining why he has decided to fight.

my Story Ideas

....

....

....

⬛ **Stop!** I need help with ....

⏸ **Wait!** I have a question about ....

▶ **Go!** Now I know ....

Native Americans and the Trail of Tears

Envision It!

The Cherokees may have carried baskets like this when they were forced to leave their homeland.

President James Monroe, 1817

1. ◎ **Generalize Write** a generalization about President Monroe's foreign policy.

....

....

....

....

After the War of 1812, the United States entered what some people called an "Era of Good Feelings." People felt proud of their country and disagreed about fewer national issues than they had before.

The Monroe Doctrine

James Monroe became President in 1817. Although people within the country felt united, President Monroe faced tough issues of foreign policy. **Foreign policy** is the actions a government takes in relation to other governments and nations. At the time, Russia claimed territory in present-day Alaska. Monroe did not want Russia expanding its land claims near the United States. Also, several former Spanish colonies had recently become independent countries. Monroe worried that Spain might try to invade or reclaim those former colonies.

In 1823, Monroe made an important speech to the Congress of the United States. Known as the **Monroe Doctrine**, his message warned European nations to stay out of the Western Hemisphere. "The American continents," Monroe said, "are . . . not to be considered as subject for future colonization by any European powers."

UNLOCK THE BIG ?

I will know that Andrew Jackson's actions shaped the United States and forced thousands of Native Americans to leave their homes.

Vocabulary

foreign policy   suffrage

Monroe   Trail of Tears
Doctrine

Conflict Over Florida

Florida was also a source of conflict between the United States and Spain. In 1817, Spain ruled Florida and a large part of what is today the southwestern United States. For years, many enslaved Africans had escaped to Florida. Some of them lived with the Seminole people. Americans believed that Seminoles were attacking settlers in Georgia.

Monroe sent Andrew Jackson, the hero of the War of 1812, to stop the Seminoles. Jackson not only defeated the Seminoles, but he also captured the city of Pensacola. Because of these attacks, Spain decided that Florida was too difficult to defend. In 1819, Spain sold Florida to the United States for $5 million.

Jackson's victory in Florida made him popular. Jackson had grown up on the Carolina frontier. Ordinary people, especially those in the West, felt he was one of them. As western territories became states, western voters played a key role in national elections.

2. **Look** at the map of land claims in 1817. **Circle** the land that the United States gained in 1819.

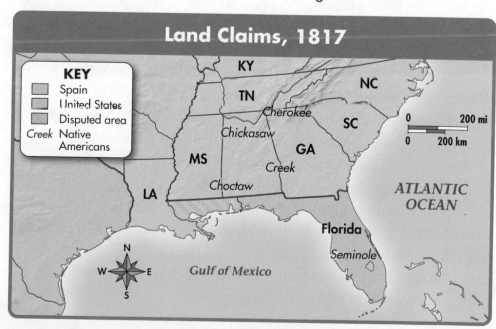

Land Claims, 1817

KEY
- Spain
- United States
- Disputed area
- *Creek* Native Americans

KY
TN
Cherokee
Chickasaw
SC
GA
MS
Creek
Choctaw
LA
NC
Florida
Seminole
ATLANTIC OCEAN
Gulf of Mexico

0   200 mi
0   200 km

N W E S

President Jackson

When the U.S. Constitution was first written, only white men who owned property were able to vote. As new states joined the Union, they gave **suffrage**, or the right to vote, to all white men whether they owned property or not. In the 1820s, other states also dropped the property requirement. This change in the law affected later elections as more white men began to vote.

Andrew Jackson ran for President in 1824 and lost. He ran again in 1828. This time, with the help of new voters from southern and western states, he won. Jackson was the first U.S. President to come from a region west of the Appalachians. When he was inaugurated, about 20,000 people came to Washington, D.C., to celebrate the election of the "People's President."

Once in office, Jackson aimed many of his policies at helping ordinary citizens. He closed the Bank of the United States because he believed it favored the rich. He also supported lower tariffs, or taxes on imports. Lower taxes on imports would mean lower prices, which Jackson thought would help ordinary people.

3. Crowds came to see President-elect Jackson as he traveled to his inauguration. **Circle** in the text things that people liked about Jackson.

Native Americans Fight for Their Homes

In the 1820s and 1830s, the Cherokees, Creeks, Chickasaws, Choctaws, and Seminoles lived in the Southeast. In many ways, the Cherokees lived as the white settlers near them did. They farmed, traded, and lived in towns. A Cherokee named Sequoyah (sih KWOI uh) had developed an alphabet for the Cherokee language. The Cherokees used it to create a newspaper, the *Cherokee Phoenix*. Today, you can read a version of the *Cherokee Phoenix* online.

Many settlers were moving west during these years. As they searched for new places to live, they began to move onto the land that belonged to Native Americans in the Southeast. The settlers believed they had a right to the land. President Jackson agreed with them.

In 1830, Congress passed the Indian Removal Act. This law said that Native Americans in the Southeast had to move to a territory west of the Mississippi River. This territory, called Indian Territory, was in present-day Oklahoma.

Many Native Americans tried to fight the new law. The Seminoles, led by Chief Osceola [ahs ee OH luh], battled against the United States Army for years before being defeated. Eventually, Chief Osceola was captured, and the Seminoles were forced to move.

4. Study the map below. Which Native Americans had to travel the farthest from their homelands to reach Indian Territory?

....

....

....

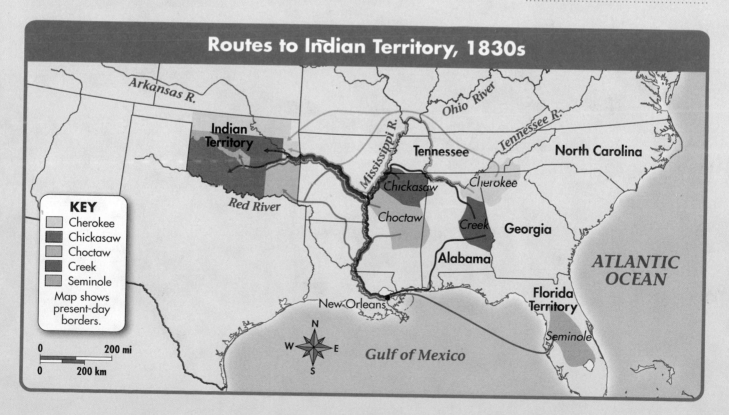

Routes to Indian Territory, 1830s

KEY
- Cherokee
- Chickasaw
- Choctaw
- Creek
- Seminole

Map shows present-day borders.

0   200 mi
0   200 km

Arkansas R.
Ohio River
Indian Territory
Mississippi R.
Tennessee R.
Tennessee
North Carolina
Chickasaw
Cherokee
Red River
Choctaw
Creek
Georgia
Alabama
ATLANTIC OCEAN
New Orleans
Florida Territory
N W E S
Gulf of Mexico
Seminole

The Trail of Tears

The Cherokees used the courts to fight the Indian Removal Act. One of their leaders, John Ross, took the case to the Supreme Court. John Marshall, the Chief Justice of the Supreme Court, agreed with Ross. He said that it was illegal to force the Cherokees to move.

Andrew Jackson ignored Chief Justice Marshall's decision. Jackson supposedly said, "John Marshall has made his decision. Now let him enforce it." However, the decision could only be enforced by the executive branch: the President. So the Cherokees were forced to move.

Between 1838 and 1839, the U.S. Army forced about 15,000 Cherokees to travel about 1,000 miles to Indian Territory. Some of them rode on horseback or in wagons, but most walked. Thrust from their home environments, the people were not prepared to face natural events and a harsh winter on the trail. Many cold, hungry Cherokees fell ill. By the end of the journey, nearly one fourth of them had died. The journey of Native American groups to Indian Territory became known as the **Trail of Tears.**

5. This painting shows the Cherokees traveling on the Trail of Tears. **Circle** details that show the people are being forced to move.

6. Write how each Native American leader worked to help his people.

Native Americans Fight for Their Land

Leader	Sequoyah	Chief Osceola	John Ross
How He Helped His People	Developed Cherokee writing system		

Got it?

7. ◎ **Generalize** Write a generalization about how President Andrew Jackson's policies changed life for Native Americans.

....

....

....

8. **Write** a letter to a friend that explains why the Cherokee leader John Ross took his people's case to the Supreme Court.

my Story Ideas

....

....

....

⬛ **Stop!** I need help with ....

⏸ **Wait!** I have a question about ....

▶ **Go!** Now I know ....

Women and African Americans Fight for Freedom

Envision It!

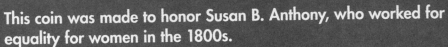

This coin was made to honor Susan B. Anthony, who worked for equality for women in the 1800s.

1. Analyze the line graph. About how many more immigrants came to the United States in 1850 than in 1840?

....

....

....

The United States was changing quickly in the mid-1800s. Immigrants flocked to America from Europe. An immigrant is a person who moves from one place to live in another. Between 1840 and 1860, millions of immigrants arrived. More than one third of them came from Ireland.

New Groups Arrive

In Ireland, potatoes were an important food source. In the 1840s, much of the country's potato crop failed to grow. More than a million people died in the Irish Potato Famine. A **famine** is a severe food shortage. To escape the famine, many Irish people left their country.

Irish immigrants traveled by ship to East Coast ports, such as New York and Boston. When they arrived, many of them didn't have enough money to go any farther. They stayed in the cities, taking any jobs they could find. Many Irish women worked as servants. Many Irish men worked in factories or built railroads or canals.

Immigration to the United States

Number of Immigrants vs. Year

Source: Historical Statistics of the United States, U.S. Department of Commerce

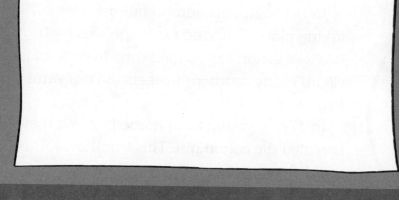

Draw a coin to honor a woman who has achieved something today.

UNLOCK THE BIG ?

I will know that women and African Americans worked to change laws and improve American society in the mid-1800s.

Vocabulary

famine

abolition

reform

Large numbers of immigrants also came from Germany. A revolution in Germany in 1848 caused many people to leave that country because of its new government. When they arrived in the United States, many Germans traveled to the Midwest. Some bought land and started farming.

In the mid-1800s, factories sprang up across the Northeast and the Midwest. Some German immigrants found jobs in factories in midwestern cities, such as Chicago, Milwaukee, and Cincinnati. Germans and immigrants from other countries provided the labor that helped factories to grow in many cities.

2. ◉ **Generalize** Many people settled in New York City in the 1800s, as this painting shows. **Write** a generalization about life in New York City during this time.

....

....

....

....

....

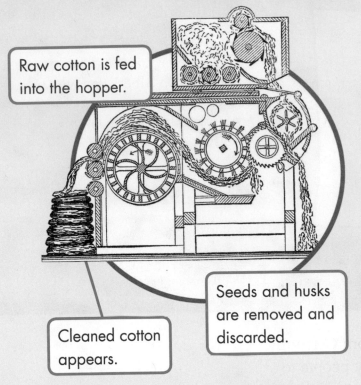

Raw cotton is fed into the hopper.

Seeds and husks are removed and discarded.

Cleaned cotton appears.

Cross-section of Eli Whitney's cotton gin

Slavery Spreads West

In the South, economic changes were taking place. Demand for cotton was high. Because cotton took a long time to pick and clean, many southern farmers did not want to grow it.

In 1792 a young man named Eli Whitney invented the cotton gin. This small machine could clean as much cotton in one day as 50 people could clean by hand. Suddenly, growing cotton became profitable. Cotton plantations sprang up in states such as Mississippi and Alabama. The plantations relied on slaves to pick the cotton. As cotton farming moved farther west, so did slavery.

Working to End Slavery

In 1808, the United States stopped the importation of enslaved people from foreign countries. Despite this, the number of enslaved people in the United States continued to grow. The **abolition** movement, the fight to abolish or end slavery, also grew. Its supporters, called *abolitionists*, attacked slavery in speeches and articles as a terrible wrong that had to end.

Sojourner Truth, who had been enslaved in New York, became a famous abolitionist. She traveled the country making speeches against slavery. She also spoke in favor of women's rights.

White abolitionist William Lloyd Garrison started an anti-slavery newspaper, *The Liberator*, in Boston in 1831. He said:

3. Circle the words in Garrison's quote that reveal his strong political feelings.

"I will be as harsh as truth and as uncompromising [determined] as justice. On this subject, I do not wish to think or speak, or write with moderation [restraint] . . . and I will be heard."

—William Lloyd Garrison

Frederick Douglass was another important abolitionist. He had escaped from slavery in the South. Douglass gave many speeches about his experiences. He said,

"I appear before [you] this evening as a thief and a robber. I stole this head, these limbs, this body from my master and ran off with them."

—Frederick Douglass

Frederick Douglass

Sojourner Truth

As more people realized how badly enslaved people were treated, calls to abolish slavery grew stronger. Abolitionists felt that their efforts to free slaves was linked to the fight for freedom that had begun in the 1770s. The Declaration of Independence stated that "all men are created equal." Abolitionists worked to extend equality to African Americans, whose rights were being denied because of slavery and discrimination.

Women Work for Reform

In the early 1800s, women had few rights. Married women could not own property. Everything they had belonged to their husbands. Women could not vote, and most women could not go to college.

The types of jobs that women held usually paid very little. The working conditions in the textile mills and clothing shops that hired women were harsh. Women who worked in them often toiled in poorly ventilated and overcrowded rooms. Some women worked for as long as 12 hours a day.

4. ◉ **Make Inferences** Sojourner Truth and Frederick Douglass spoke out against slavery. Why do you think African Americans were convincing speakers for abolition?

....

....

....

....

....

....

In spite of these limits, women began to work to **reform**, or improve, their society. Many women promoted temperance, or stopping the drinking of alcohol. They also strove to make education available to more girls. One reformer, Emma Willard, opened a school for female students in Troy, New York, that offered college courses.

Many women were abolitionists. As they became involved in the abolitionist movement, they recognized the injustices they also faced as women. Susan B. Anthony was a crusader for women's rights, temperance, and abolition. Anthony eventually became the president of an organization that fought for women's voting rights, or suffrage.

Two other women, Lucretia Mott and Elizabeth Cady Stanton, were also abolitionists who began to fight for women's rights. In 1848, Stanton and Mott called a convention in Seneca Falls, New York, to talk about equality for women. Nearly 300 people attended.

Seneca Falls Resolutions

- . . . all laws . . . which place [a woman] in a position inferior to that of a man . . . [have] no force or authority.

- . . . it is the duty of the women of this country to secure to themselves their sacred right to elective franchise [the right to vote].

Elizabeth Cady Stanton addressed the first women's rights convention in Seneca Falls, New York, on June 20, 1848.

The Seneca Falls Convention

At the Seneca Falls Convention, Stanton read a statement called the Declaration of Sentiments, which was based on the Declaration of Independence. It said,

"We hold these truths to be self-evident, that all men and women are created equal."

— from the Declaration of Sentiments

Participants also discussed a series of resolutions, or decisions. The convention began the women's rights movement in the United States. Like the abolition movement, it would grow and eventually improve the lives of many Americans.

Got it?

5. ◉ **Generalize** Give three facts to support the generalization that many women worked to reform society in the mid-1800s.

....

....

....

6. ❓ You have volunteered to help write pamphlets to advertise the Seneca Falls Convention. What would the cover of your pamphlet say and what pictures would it show?

my Story Ideas

....

....

....

....

◻ **Stop!** I need help with ....

❚❚ **Wait!** I have a question about ....

▷ **Go!** Now I know ....

Study Guide

Lesson 1

Washington Takes Office

- George Washington became the first U.S. President in 1789.
- Washington's chosen advisors became the first Cabinet.
- The first political parties were the Federalists, led by Alexander Hamilton, and the Democratic-Republicans, led by Thomas Jefferson.

Lesson 2

Jefferson and the Louisiana Purchase

- The United States bought the Louisiana Territory from France in 1803.
- Jefferson sent the Lewis and Clark expedition to explore the territory.
- The expedition traveled to the Pacific Ocean, learning about unfamiliar plants and animals and meeting Native Americans on the way.

Lesson 3

The War of 1812

- In response to British raids on American shipping and British support for Native American attacks, the United States declared war against Great Britain in 1812.
- Neither side won the war, but they signed a peace treaty in 1814.

Lesson 4

Native Americans and the Trail of Tears

- Andrew Jackson was elected in 1828 as the "People's President."
- Jackson forced Native Americans to leave their homelands.
- The forced removal of Native Americans from the southeast U.S. to the Indian Territory became known as the Trail of Tears.

Lesson 5

Women and African Americans Fight for Freedom

- European immigrants came to the United States in the mid-1800s.
- The cotton gin increased cotton farming, causing slavery to increase.
- Abolitionists worked to end slavery.
- Women played key roles in reform movements, such as women's rights.

Review and Assessment

Lesson 1

Washington Takes Office

1. **Circle** the correct answer.

   Which of the following was created during Washington's time in office?

   A. the Trail of Tears

   B. the national anthem

   C. the cotton gin

   D. the first Bank of the United States

2. The opinions below belonged to either Thomas Jefferson or Alexander Hamilton. **Write** a *J* or an *H* to identify which man held each opinion.

   _____ The states should have more power than the federal government.

   _____ The country needs a national bank.

   _____ The federal government should be stronger than the states.

   _____ The American economy should be based on farming.

3. **Write** a description of Thomas Jefferson's responsibilities as Secretary of State.

   ....

   ....

   ....

Lesson 2

Jefferson and the Louisiana Purchase

4. ◉ **Generalize** Provide an example that supports this generalization: The Louisiana Purchase benefited the United States.

   ....

   ....

5. **Think** about the goals for the Lewis and Clark expedition. What was one goal they accomplished?

   ....

   ....

Lesson 3

The War of 1812

6. **Write** two causes of the War of 1812.

   ....

   ....

   ....

7. What event led Francis Scott to write "The Star-Spangled Banner"?

   ....

   ....

Lesson 4

Native Americans and the Trail of Tears

8. How was the "Era of Good Feelings" different from previous periods?

....

....

....

9. What effect did the new western states have on the election of 1828?

....

....

....

10. Identify one cause and one effect of the Indian Removal Act.

....

....

....

....

Lesson 5

Women and African Americans Fight for Freedom

11. Where did many Irish immigrants to the United States settle in the mid-1800s?

....

12. Write one similarity and one difference between Sojourner Truth and William Lloyd Garrison.

....

....

....

13. **How do leaders shape a nation?**

Look at the picture below. **Write** a sentence that tells how the first President and Cabinet helped shape the United States.

....

....

....

myworldsocialstudies.com ▶ **Understand** ▶ **Vocabulary Review**

Go online to write and illustrate your own **myStory Book** using the **myStory Ideas** from this chapter.

How do leaders shape a nation?

In the early 1800s, the United States was growing. Political leaders such as George Washington, Thomas Jefferson, and Andrew Jackson took actions that shaped the nation. Their personal qualities also convinced citizens to trust their leadership.

Write a letter to the editor of a newspaper. **Explain** what qualities are important for a candidate for national office.

....

....

....

....

....

....

....

....

....

....

While you're online, check out the **myStory Current Events** area where you can create your own book on a topic that's in the news.

Moving West

THE BIG ? What are the costs and benefits of growth?

Suppose you are moving to a new home far away. What might be some of the benefits of the move? What might be the costs, or the things you would not look forward to?

....

....

....

....

Wagon tracks, Whitman Mission National Historic Site, Washington

Narcissa Whitman
Oregon Trail Pioneer

my Story Video

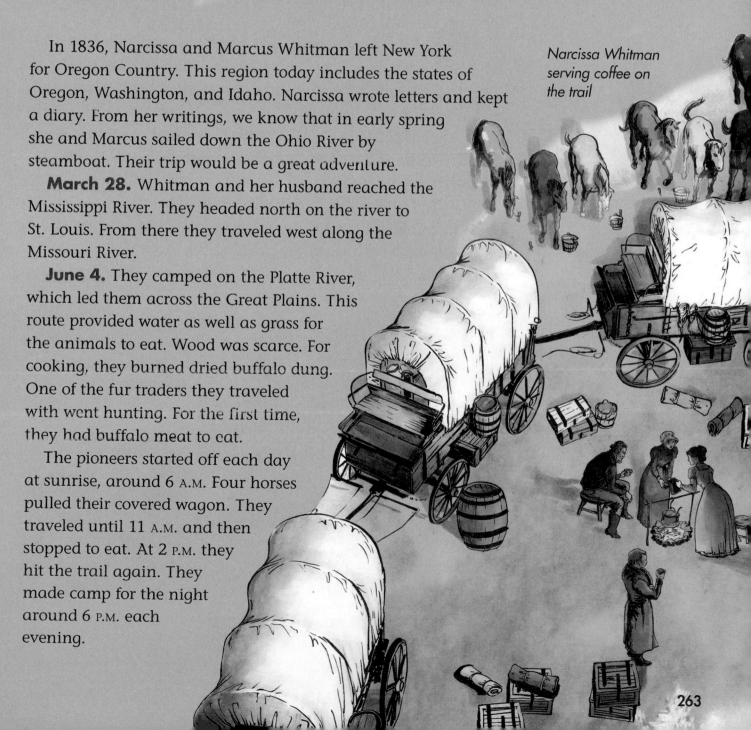

Narcissa Whitman serving coffee on the trail

In 1836, Narcissa and Marcus Whitman left New York for Oregon Country. This region today includes the states of Oregon, Washington, and Idaho. Narcissa wrote letters and kept a diary. From her writings, we know that in early spring she and Marcus sailed down the Ohio River by steamboat. Their trip would be a great adventure.

March 28. Whitman and her husband reached the Mississippi River. They headed north on the river to St. Louis. From there they traveled west along the Missouri River.

June 4. They camped on the Platte River, which led them across the Great Plains. This route provided water as well as grass for the animals to eat. Wood was scarce. For cooking, they burned dried buffalo dung. One of the fur traders they traveled with went hunting. For the first time, they had buffalo meat to eat.

The pioneers started off each day at sunrise, around 6 A.M. Four horses pulled their covered wagon. They traveled until 11 A.M. and then stopped to eat. At 2 P.M. they hit the trail again. They made camp for the night around 6 P.M. each evening.

One of the hunters from the wagon train brought back buffalo meat for the travelers to eat.

Narcissa Whitman found fording rivers and streams a challenge. Wagons could get swept away and animals drowned.

June 27. Narcissa Whitman said it was easier traveling here, on bare earth, than it was on the roads back East. Crossing streams, though, was hard. First someone had to swim across with a rope. Then they loaded their bags into a canoe, tied the rope to it, and pulled the load across the stream.

By now they were eating buffalo meat all the time. "We have meat and tea in the morn," Whitman wrote, "and tea and meat at noon."

July 16. The Whitmans were in the Rocky Mountains. Narcissa told of meeting a group of Native Americans. She was quite pleased with the greeting she received from the women. They gave her a hearty handshake and a big kiss.

The axle of a covered wagon snapped going over rough terrain.

The Whitmans struggled up steep trails while crossing the Rocky Mountains.

At last the Whitmans reached Walla Walla. Later, they would settle near the fort. Their home became a station on the Oregon Trail.

July 28. The trail through the mountains was steep and rough. Mountain streams and woods offered a change in the travelers' diet. They now had fish and antelope to eat.

August 5. The Whitmans covered 10 miles this day, arriving at camp after dark. Narcissa complained about the swamps they passed through. She wrote, "We were so swarmed with mosquitoes as to be scarcely able to see." They were in the Oregon Country now, following the Snake River.

August 15. The Whitmans abandoned their wagon. The mountains ahead were too steep. They were left with their horses to ride and a cart pulled by mules. Crossing the Snake River caused a scare when the cart tipped over. The travelers managed to save the mules from drowning.

August 29. The Whitmans crossed the Blue Mountains in northeast Oregon and got their first glimpse of Mount Hood.

September 1. The long, hard westward journey came to an end. The Whitmans arrived at Fort Walla Walla in present-day Washington. Narcissa enjoyed a muskmelon, "The first, I think, I ever saw or tasted." She was soon ready for her next adventure.

Think About It Based on this story, do you think the trip west was worth the effort it took to get there? As you read the chapter ahead, think about what Narcissa Whitman's story tells you about the costs and benefits faced by the westward pioneers.

Inventions, Roads, and Railroads

Envision It!

You are in a hurry and you have a long way to go. Would you walk or would you ride a bicycle?

People in business want to make a profit. A **profit** is the money a business earns after all its expenses are paid. One way to increase profits is to reduce the amount of time it takes to produce goods. Another way is by lowering costs of materials or labor. In the early 1800s, new inventions and better transportation helped businesses make a profit.

New Inventions

The cotton gin, invented by Eli Whitney in 1792, helped to greatly increase cotton production. Other machines also helped farmers. In 1831, Cyrus McCormick invented a mechanical reaper. His horse-drawn machine made cutting grain easier. Farmers no longer had to cut their wheat or barley with a scythe. A scythe is a hand tool with a long, curved blade. The reaper let farmers plant more land and grow more grain.

Mechanical reaper cutting grain

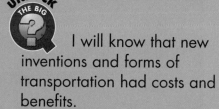

I will know that new inventions and forms of transportation had costs and benefits.

A bicycle works the same way as some machines. List other machines that help us do things faster and easier.

Vocabulary

profit   canal

mass production

Industrial Revolution

Another invention made sewing easier. Women often made all the clothes for their family by hand. In 1846, Elias Howe invented the sewing machine. By 1860, Americans were buying more than 100,000 sewing machines a year. This machine greatly reduced the time it took to sew a piece of clothing.

Samuel F.B. Morse took advantage of new ideas about electricity to invent machines that could be used to send messages. In 1844, he sent the first electric telegraph message. He also developed a code of dots and dashes, called Morse code, for sending the messages over wires. Before the telegraph, letters traveled by horse or boat. The telegraph started a revolution in the way information was shared. Cell phones and the Internet are two of the latest products of that revolution.

1. **Fill in** the missing cause in the cause-and-effect chart.

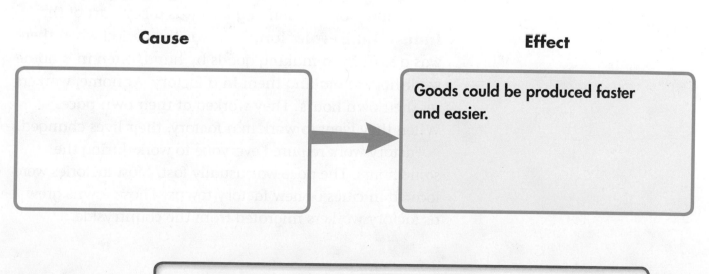

Cause

Effect

Goods could be produced faster and easier.

Young women and girls work in a factory.

2. ⊙ **Fact and Opinion**
Write one fact and one opinion about what you see in this picture of a cotton factory.

....
....
....
....
....
....

A New Way to Work

Some new ideas changed the way people worked. In the late 1700s, Eli Whitney was hired by the United States government to produce thousands of muskets. At the time, skilled workers made one gun at a time. All the parts of the gun fit nicely together, but only in that one gun. Whitney thought, why not make parts that would fit any gun? He used the idea of interchangeable parts, or parts that are the exact same shape and size, to make many goods at the same time. This process is known as **mass production.**

In Whitney's system of interchangeable parts, any part of one gun could be changed for that same part in another gun. Now a worker, using the right tools, could make the same part over and over again. Each part would be exactly like the next.

The mass production of goods was a key part of the **Industrial Revolution.** This was the period when there was a shift from making goods by hand, often in a home workshop, to making them in a factory. At home, workers set their own hours. They worked at their own pace. When they went to work in a factory, their lives changed.

Factory work required everyone to work during the same hours. The pace was usually fast. Most factories were located in cities or new factory towns. Those towns grew as factory workers migrated from the countryside.

Factories and Factory Towns

Some of the earliest American factories produced cotton textiles, or cloth. A skilled mechanic from Britain, Samuel Slater, helped make this possible. The Industrial Revolution had started in Britain in the late 1700s. The British had invented machines to spin yarn and weave it into cloth. They tried to keep the design of those machines secret. Slater learned how to build a spinning machine. He brought this knowledge with him to the United States.

In 1793, Slater helped build a factory in Rhode Island. He designed the factory's machines. Powered by flowing river water, they spun fibers into yarn. Francis Cabot Lowell of Massachusetts learned how to make weaving machines. He opened a large factory in 1811. There he brought the machines for spinning and weaving fibers into cloth together in one factory, or mill.

Lowell's factory relied mainly on young women from all over New England to run the machines. Known as "mill girls," they worked ten or more hours a day, with a half-hour each for breakfast and dinner. Most lived in rented rooms near the factory. In the 1850s, French-Canadian and Irish immigrants moved into many of these factory jobs.

3. In the 1830s, textile mills lined the Merrimack and Concord rivers in Lowell, Massachusetts. Why do you think mills were built on rivers?

....

....

....

....

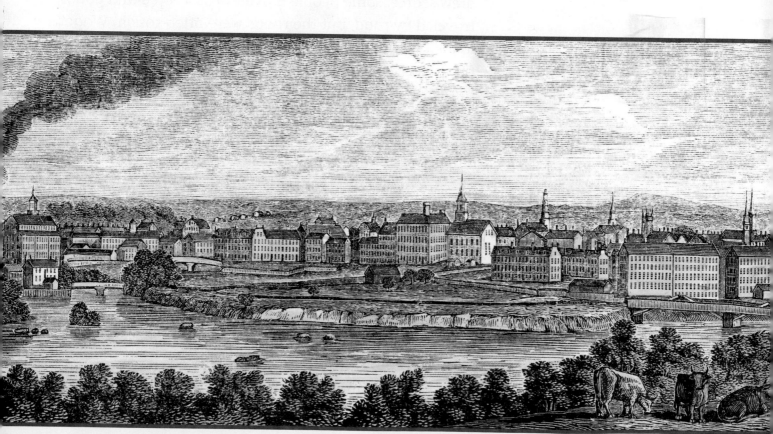

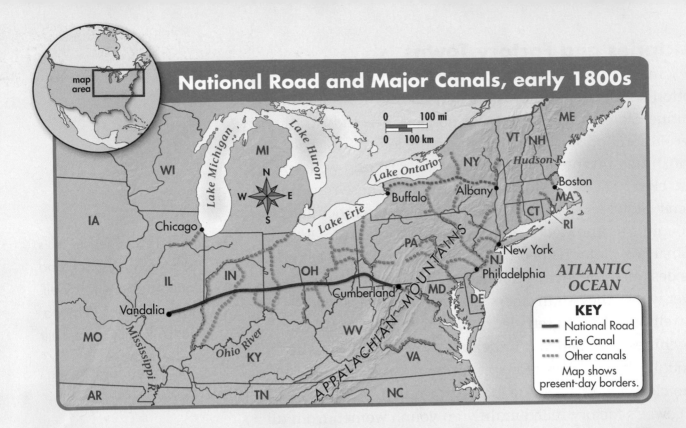

National Road and Major Canals, early 1800s

KEY
— National Road
···· Erie Canal
···· Other canals
Map shows present-day borders.

4. Write the towns where the National Road began and ended.

....

....

....

Better Transportation

The young nation had many natural resources. Its land, water, and minerals allowed the population to grow and businesses to thrive. When farmland in the East grew scarce, some people moved west. People and goods traveled by road, but the roads were often rough. Wagons loaded with goods moved slowly. Roads were expensive to build and maintain, too.

In 1811, the federal government started building the National Road. It was finished in 1837. This 66-foot-wide highway ran from Cumberland, Maryland, to Vandalia, Illinois. It became a main route for settlers heading across the Appalachian Mountains into the Ohio Valley.

Farmers in the West grew cotton, tobacco, corn, and wheat. They also raised cattle and hogs. Eastern cities shipped tools and other manufactured goods to the West. Early on, goods were shipped between eastern and western markets on flatboats, or cargo boats with flat bottoms. The flatboats floated on rivers that drained into the Mississippi River and the boats ended up in New Orleans, Louisiana. Sailing ships carried the goods from New Orleans, around Florida, and then up the East Coast. Shipping goods required a long and costly journey.

Flatboats were useful for traveling downstream but they could not easily travel upstream against a river's current. An American engineer named Robert Fulton found a way to solve this problem. He designed and built the *Clermont*, a boat powered by a steam engine. In August 1807, the *Clermont* traveled up the Hudson River from New York City to Albany in 32 hours. The same 150-mile trip took sailing ships four days. Steamboats soon carried freight up and down rivers.

The Erie Canal

Even with these improvements, the movement of goods and people remained slow. To travel from New York City to Chicago in 1800 took around six weeks by horse and wagon. By 1830, the time had been cut in half. What made the difference? It was the Erie Canal. A **canal** is a human-made waterway.

Workers began digging the Erie Canal in 1817. By 1825, it was open for business. It ran from Albany to Buffalo, New York, a distance of 363 miles. The Erie Canal linked the Hudson River to Lake Erie. Now a family heading west from New York City could travel the whole way by water. They went up the Hudson River, along the Erie Canal, and across one or more of the Great Lakes.

The Erie Canal carried many settlers west. It also carried freight faster and cheaper than other ways. It took 8 days instead of 20 to get from Buffalo to New York City. The cost to ship a ton of freight dropped from $100 to $10. Farmers in the Ohio Valley started shipping grain and other bulk goods east by this new route. The success of the Erie Canal led to a flurry of canal building. For a while, the country had "canal fever."

5. The boats traveling on the Erie Canal in this picture do not have an engine. **Circle** what powers these boats.

The First Railroads

Roads, rivers, and canals kept improving transportation. Speed increased. Costs fell. Then along came the railroads. They were expensive to build and run, but they would revolutionize the way people and goods were moved.

The earliest railroads were horse-drawn carts that ran on rails. They could not compete with the Erie Canal though. Why not replace the horse with a steam engine?

The first true railroad in the United States was the Baltimore & Ohio, or B&O. It laid its first 13 miles of track over a steep and twisting route. In the summer of 1830, the Tom Thumb, a small but mighty steam engine, made the first run. Pulling a cart with some 40 passengers, the Tom Thumb made the outbound trip with no trouble. It proved that a steam engine could operate over hilly terrain.

The Tom Thumb

6. **Fill in** the chart with the missing advantages and disadvantages.

Transportation in the Early 1800s

Form of Transportation	Advantages	Disadvantages
Road	• can go anywhere • direct route from west to east	• .... • ....
Canal	• .... •	• route must follow waterways • costly to build
Railroad	• .... •	• .... • ....

Settling Along the Routes

Railroad tracks could be laid nearly anywhere. No longer did travelers and freight have to follow rivers or canals. Farm products could travel directly to market. Investors understood what that meant. They poured money into railroad companies, expecting to make a profit. They believed railroads would continue to grow and prosper, and they were right.

New towns sprang up along the tracks. These settlements attracted even more migrants and businesses to the West. By the 1850s, rail companies had laid more than 9,000 miles of track. Tracks were even being laid across the Mississippi River. In the coming decade, the Atlantic and Pacific oceans would be linked by rail.

Got it?

7. ◉ **Cause and Effect** What effects did mass production in factories have on workers' lives?

....

....

....

8. ❓ As a volunteer at an archaeology dig along the Erie Canal, you find a shovel and some horseshoes. **Think** about what these items tell about building the canal. **Write** a report to the dig leader describing your finds and their possible meaning.

my Story Ideas

....

....

....

⬛ **Stop!** I need help with ....

⏸ **Wait!** I have a question about ....

▶ **Go!** Now I know ....

Give an Effective Presentation

The picture below shows the *Clermont*, the steamboat that made a famous trip on the Hudson River in 1807. If you gave a presentation about Robert Fulton, this image could help you. Using visual aids, such as paintings, graphs, and other organizers, can provide information about your topic's appearance, size, uses, and time period. They can also help your audience better understand your topic.

Here are some other keys to an effective presentation:

1. Know your audience. Think about how much they know, and give them information in a form that they can follow. Your presentation should have an introduction, several main ideas, and a conclusion.

2. Be prepared. Practice your presentation in front of a mirror or in front of a friend or family member. Then practice some more.

3. Do not simply read your presentation. Know everything you want to say ahead of time. Write key points on notecards as reminders. When possible, talk directly to your audience.

4. Speak loudly. Your voice must reach the person farthest away from you. Don't rush. Pause to take a breath between ideas.

Suppose you wanted to give a presentation about Robert Fulton.
Answer the following questions.

1. Your audience would likely be your classmates. How would your presentation be different if you gave it to a first-grade class?

....

....

2. Your introduction should grab the audience's attention. What could you say to introduce Robert Fulton?

....

....

3. **Circle** some things in the picture that you might need to explain to your audience. How could you use this picture to make your presentation more interesting?

....

....

4. What else could you do to make your presentation effective?

....

....

5. **Apply** Reread the information about Samuel Slater in this chapter. How could you start a presentation about Slater in a way that would grab the attention of your audience?

....

....

....

Lesson 2

The Lone Star State

from sea to shining sea

This is a line from the song "America the Beautiful."

Stephen Austin

During the early 1800s, American pioneers kept moving west. The rich, cheap farmland of the interior drew them, despite the hardships of frontier life. They had the "frontier spirit." Thousands of settlers brought that spirit to Texas.

Americans in Texas

In the 1820s, Texas was a part of Mexico. Yet few Mexicans had settled there. The government of Mexico wanted people to live there, work the land, and become loyal citizens. It granted Stephen Austin the right to bring American families into Texas.

Austin and other land agents found people easily. Land cost much less in this part of Mexico than in the United States. By 1832, some 20,000 American settlers had moved to Texas. These settlers far outnumbered Tejanos (teh HAH nohz) in Mexico. Tejanos are Spanish-speaking people living in Texas.

Many of the settlers grew cotton. Many others started ranches. Texas had long been cattle country. Mexican cowboys, or **vaqueros** (vah KER ohz), were known for their skill at handling cattle and riding horses. They taught the settlers many Mexican ranching techniques.

1. ◉ **Cause and Effect Fill in** the effect in this chart.

Cause	Effect
Mexico invites people to settle in Texas. →	

UNLOCK THE BIG ?

I will know that achieving independence and statehood had costs and benefits for Texas.

Vocabulary

vaquero   manifest destiny

annex

Missouri Compromise

Draw a map or picture that describes the phrase "from sea to shining sea."

The Texas settlers missed the freedoms they had left behind in the United States. They complained about the Mexican government's strict control over its citizens. They wanted more open trade with the United States. They also wanted slavery made legal in Texas. The settlers, who came mainly from the South, had brought thousands of slaves with them. However, Mexico had banned slavery in 1829.

By 1835, many Texans, both settlers and Tejanos, had decided they should be independent of Mexico and prepared to govern themselves. That fall, armed Texans clashed with government troops. The Texas Revolution had begun.

Northern Mexico, 1835

map area

U.S. TERRITORY

MEXICO

PACIFIC OCEAN

N W E S

0   400 mi
0   400 km

2. **Look** at a present-day map of the United States. **Write** the name of two states that were once part of Mexico.

....

....

Defending the Alamo

Key

A Main plaza   **E** Soldiers' barracks

B Cattle pen   **F** Chapel

C Main gate   **G** Hospital

D Officers' housing   **X** ....

Battle of the Alamo

A general, Antonio Lopez de Santa Anna, was president of Mexico. In early 1836, he led an army of several thousand men into Texas to end the revolt. He headed toward San Antonio. There, some 180 Texans prepared to defend themselves at a walled fortress called the Alamo.

Those few Texans held off Santa Anna's army for nearly two weeks. Finally, on March 6, the Mexican forces stormed the Alamo. Fierce hand-to-hand fighting followed. By the end of the battle of the Alamo, all of the defenders were killed. They included Davy Crockett and James Bowie, two famous men of the frontier. Around 600 Mexican soldiers were killed or wounded.

3. The Texans placed cannons on the roof of the chapel and the hospital, and at each corner of the Alamo. **Mark** those positions with an **X.** Add this information to the key.

Texas Independence

Meanwhile, on March 2, 1836, Texan leaders declared independence. They drew up a constitution and formed a government. The leaders chose Sam Houston to take command of the Texas army. That army included a unit of Tejano soldiers, led by Juan Seguín (hwan suh GEEN). They would soon join a major battle.

Houston had a hard job ahead of him. Santa Anna's army was sweeping across Texas. By April, Santa Anna had Houston's army on the run. It looked as if the Texas Revolution would soon be over. But the Texans stopped their retreat at the San Jacinto (juh SIN toh) River, near Galveston Bay. It was time to make a bold move. Houston launched a surprise attack on Santa Anna.

On April 21, the Texas cavalry and foot soldiers quietly approached the enemy camp. Then they charged, yelling, "Remember the Alamo!" The battle of San Jacinto was over quickly. The Texans defeated the Mexican army and captured Santa Anna. They forced him to sign a treaty giving Texas its independence.

In September 1836, Texans voted to make Sam Houston president of the Republic of Texas. Stephen Austin became its secretary of state. Texas was now an independent country.

Texas's flag, adopted in 1839, has a single star. Today, Texas is still known as the Lone Star State.

4. This painting shows the surrender of Santa Anna, dressed in a private soldier's uniform, to Sam Houston, who was wounded in the battle. **Label** both men, including the countries they fought for.

279

Tensions Over Texas

Texas had gained its independence. Now what? Most Texans thought the United States would **annex** Texas, or take it over and make it a state. But many Americans did not support that move. They were concerned about the spread of slavery.

In 1820, Congress passed the **Missouri Compromise.** That law brought two states into the Union. Maine would be a free state, where slavery would not be allowed. Missouri would be a slave state, where slavery was allowed. The law also banned slavery in the rest of the Louisiana Purchase. Disagreements over slavery in the states grew. States in the South relied on enslaved Africans as a source of labor. States in the North wanted an end to slavery. Northerners did not want to add Texas to the Union as a slave state.

Tensions also flared over **manifest destiny**, or the idea that the United States had a right to add territory until it reached the Pacific Ocean. In 1845, just before James K. Polk took office as President, Congress voted to annex Texas. Texas became a state later that year. Mexicans protested, since in spite of the treaty signed by Santa Anna, they still saw Texas as part of Mexico. In addition, Texans claimed that their southern border was a river, the Rio Grande. Mexicans said the border was farther north.

The Texas Revolution and Mexican War

1836
Texans declare independence, March 2; Battle of the Alamo ends, March 6; Battle of San Jacinto, April 21

1832
20,000 American settlers living in Texas

1832   **1834**   **1836**   **1838**

1835
Armed Texans clash with Mexican government troops

War With Mexico

In January 1846, President Polk sent an army led by General Zachary Taylor into the border region. In April, Mexican troops crossed the Rio Grande and attacked a small American force. That action triggered the Mexican War. In his war message to Congress on May 11, Polk said,

"Mexico has passed the boundary of the United States, has invaded our territory and shed American blood upon the American soil."

The war lasted just a few months. American soldiers swept into Mexico's northern territory and took Santa Fe, New Mexico. Two months earlier, American settlers in California had started their own revolt. By the time American forces arrived, the settlers had attacked Mexican troops and declared California to be an independent republic. Their rebellion became known as the Bear Flag Revolt because of the grizzly bear on their flag.

By 1847, all of northern Mexico was in American hands. But the main battles of the war took place to the south. Polk sent another general, Winfield Scott, to invade Mexico by sea. Scott's forces captured Mexico City on September 14. The war's main fighting was over. The effects of the war, however, meant lasting boundary changes for both the United States and Mexico.

5. **Write** how many years passed between when Texas declared independence and when it gained statehood. ....

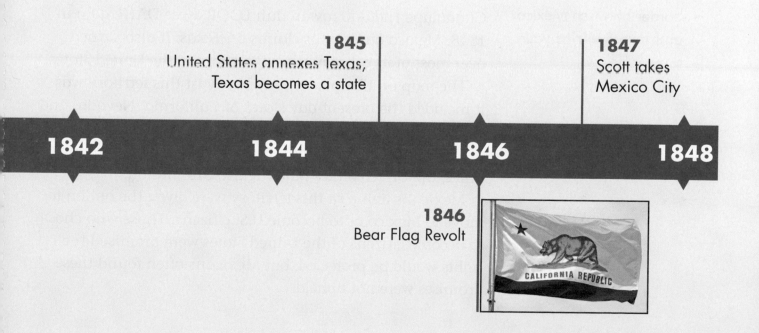

1845
United States annexes Texas;
Texas becomes a state

1847
Scott takes
Mexico City

1842　　**1844**　　**1846**　　**1848**

1846
Bear Flag Revolt

CALIFORNIA REPUBLIC

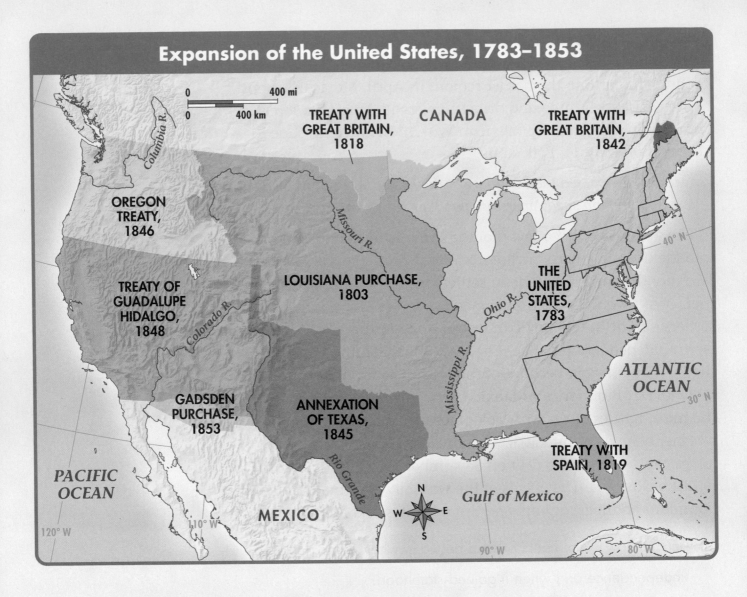

Expansion of the United States, 1783–1853

TREATY WITH GREAT BRITAIN, 1818

CANADA

TREATY WITH GREAT BRITAIN, 1842

OREGON TREATY, 1846

TREATY OF GUADALUPE HIDALGO, 1848

LOUISIANA PURCHASE, 1803

THE UNITED STATES, 1783

GADSDEN PURCHASE, 1853

ANNEXATION OF TEXAS, 1845

TREATY WITH SPAIN, 1819

PACIFIC OCEAN

ATLANTIC OCEAN

Gulf of Mexico

MEXICO

Columbia R.

Missouri R.

Ohio R.

Mississippi R.

Colorado R.

Rio Grande

0   400 mi
0   400 km

40° N

30° N

120° W   110° W   90° W   80° W

6. According to the map, which river forms the border between Mexico and Texas? **Write** your answer below.

....

Winning the Peace

The Mexican War ended officially with the Treaty of Guadalupe Hidalgo (gwah duh LOOP ay ee DAHL goh) in 1848. Mexico gave up its claims on Texas. It also turned over most of its other northern territory to the United States.

The map on this page shows how vast this territory was. It included the present-day states of California, Nevada, and Utah, most of New Mexico and Arizona, and smaller parts of Wyoming and Colorado. For more than 525,000 square miles, the United States paid Mexico $15 million.

Mexicans living in this territory were given the option to move to Mexico or to become U.S. citizens. Those who chose to become citizens of the United States were promised their rights would be protected, but Mexicans often found these promises were not upheld.

In 1853, the United States acquired another chunk of land. Called the Gadsden Purchase, it completed the present-day southern boundaries of New Mexico and Arizona. For this, the United States paid Mexico $10 million.

The lands gained as a result of the Mexican War filled out the American Southwest. In doing so, Americans achieved their goal of manifest destiny for the United States. The country now stretched from the Atlantic Ocean to the Pacific Ocean. The United States could now claim to reach "from sea to shining sea."

Got it?

7. **⊙ Fact and Opinion Write** an example of a fact from the section on Texas Independence. Then **write** an opinion about that fact.

....

....

....

....

8. **?** When you join an archaeology dig at the Alamo in San Antonio, Texas, you see many tourists visiting the site. Why is this fort so important to Texans?

my Story Ideas

....

....

....

....

Stop! I need help with ....

Wait! I have a question about ....

Go! Now I know ....

Trails to the West

Envision It!

This is part of an old trail to the West. Over time, wagon wheels wore down the rock, creating these ruts.

Hundreds of thousands of people followed trails west between 1840 and 1860. Most left from the town of Independence, Missouri. There they joined a **wagon train,** or a line of wagons traveling as a group, to places such as California or Oregon. To get there, they had to cross the vast Great Plains and the towering Rocky Mountains. The journey, which was up to 2,000 miles long, was a test of courage and strength.

The Westward Trail

A few migrants rode horses along the trail. But many pioneers heading west walked much of the way because their wagons were already heavy with supplies. Riding in the wagon would put more strain on the oxen or mules pulling it. Travelers knew the value of those animals.

Pioneers also brought other animals west, including cows for milk and chickens for eggs. For meat, the settlers hunted wild animals. Families packed their wagons with barrels of water, butter churns, shovels, axes, and other supplies. Experienced migrants knew to take along only what they would need for the trip. Anything else would end as trash along the trail.

A wagon train crosses the Great Plains.

UNLOCK THE BIG ? I will know that traveling on the westward trails had costs and benefits.

Vocabulary

wagon train

prairie schooner

persecution

Draw the vehicle that you think made these ruts in the trail in the mid-1800s.

Not all overland wagons were alike. Some were simply farm wagons with cloth covers. The typical covered wagon on the westward trail was called a **prairie schooner.** Named after a type of sailing ship, the prairie schooner was designed for the trip west. Built solidly for the long and dangerous journey, the prairie schooner was tough enough to travel over rough ground. Its cover kept out the sun, wind, and rain. Its large wheels kept the wooden bed of the wagon out of the mud. The bed itself was made watertight, to float like a boat across slow-flowing rivers.

Some pioneers did not survive the journey west. Disease, accidents, and cold weather took lives. Native Americans rarely attacked wagon trains. Usually they came to trade.

Details About Traveling West

Main Idea
Prairie schooners were built to withstand the long trip west.

Supporting Detail

Supporting Detail

Supporting Detail

1. **Fill in** three details to support the main idea.

The Oregon Country

In the early 1840s, many pioneers headed for Oregon Country. This region included the present states of Oregon, Washington, and Idaho, as well as lands to the north. In 1846, the United States and Great Britain split the region. The southern part, where most Americans had settled, went to the United States. It was called the Oregon Territory.

Oregon drew settlers for several reasons. Married couples could claim 640 acres of rich farmland there for free. Oregon also had rivers, mountains, and ancient forests. This was a wilderness region, and that, too, attracted people with the frontier spirit. Fur traders had worked the area for many years.

Among the earliest settlers were Marcus and Narcissa Whitman. They were missionaries who settled in present-day Washington in 1836. The Whitmans taught Native Americans about Christianity. They also encouraged others to move there. In 1843, Marcus Whitman led about 1,000 migrants to Oregon after returning to the East. Their settlement became a stopping place along the main route to Oregon called the Oregon Trail.

Narcissa Whitman

Transportation, Then and Now

2. Which vehicle should be able to climb a mountain more easily?

....

Circle the statistic in the chart that supports your answer.

	Prairie Schooner	Sport Utility Vehicle (SUV)
Length	10 feet	16 feet
Width	4 feet	6 feet
Height	10 feet	6 feet
Wheelbase	5 feet	$9\frac{1}{2}$ feet
Weight	1,300 pounds	4,455 pounds
Power	4–6 oxen or 6–10 mules	210 horsepower gasoline engine

Sources: http://www.historicoregoncity.org/HOC/index.php?option=com_content&view=article& id=156&Itemid=75 and http://www.fordvehicles.com/suvs/explorer/compare/

"Oregon or Bust!"

For settlers, the Oregon Trail was 2,000 miles of rough travel. It was an exhausting trip. But many pioneers had the attitude "Oregon or bust"! That meant, "I'll make it to Oregon or die trying." The Oregon Trail started in Independence, Missouri. Pioneers gathered there in the spring. They bought any supplies they needed, including prairie schooners, and signed up with the leader of a wagon train.

Once the new grass on the prairie was high enough to feed their animals, the migrants left. They followed the Platte River westward across the dry, flat Great Plains. Then they headed into the Rocky Mountains. The closer they came to Oregon, the harder and more dangerous the trail became. Wagons inched along cliff ledges and struggled up steep mountain tracks.

Wagon trains traveled about 12 to 15 miles a day, on average. Moving fast, a wagon train might make the trip in four months. But settlers often spent six months on the trail. A longer trip might mean disaster. An early snow in the mountains could block the passes. Settlers trapped by mountain storms might die before they reached the Oregon Territory.

3. **Write** how the parts of the prairie schooner helped travelers.

Prairie Schooner

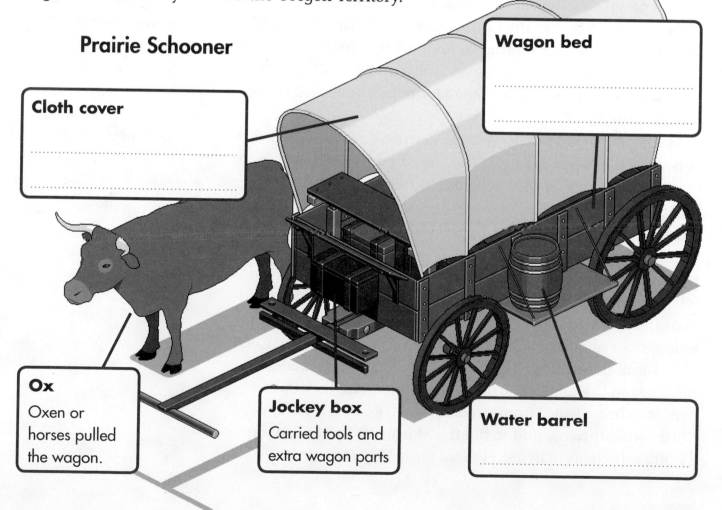

Cloth cover

Wagon bed

Ox
Oxen or horses pulled the wagon.

Jockey box
Carried tools and extra wagon parts

Water barrel

The Mormon Trail

One group of settlers moved west to seek religious freedom. They were members of the Church of Jesus Christ of Latter-day Saints, also known as Mormons. Joseph Smith founded the church in 1830 in New York State. Smith and his followers soon moved to Ohio. From there, some Mormons established homes in Missouri and Illinois.

Many people did not accept the Mormons' religious beliefs. Wherever the Mormons went, they faced **persecution,** or poor treatment because of their religion. In Illinois in 1844, a mob killed Joseph Smith. His followers decided it was time to find a place where they could worship freely.

In 1846, the church's new leader, Brigham Young, led 150 Mormons west from Illinois. Like other migrants, the Mormons followed the Platte River across the Great Plains. They stopped near the Great Salt Lake in what is now Utah. The route they followed for about 1,300 miles is known as the Mormon Trail.

In Utah, they founded Salt Lake City. Thousands more migrated to the area. To farm in this dry region, they built canals to bring water from streams in the Rocky Mountains. Their farms thrived, and so did the Mormons. By 1860, about 40,000 settlers were living in more than 150 communities.

4. **Label** two geographic features in this painting of Salt Lake City, Utah. Then **write** why you think the Mormons chose this location for their settlement.

....

....

....

....

....

Trails to the Southwest

The Santa Fe Trail was about 900 miles long. A wagon train could make the trip to what was then Mexico in about two months. However, few settlers crossed the Great Plains by this route. It was a trail followed mainly by traders. Starting in 1821, they used it to move cargo to and from Santa Fe.

In Independence, Missouri, traders loaded up Conestoga wagons with manufactured goods. These wagons were rugged and twice the size of the prairie schooners. They could haul five tons of cargo.

From Missouri, the traders headed for Santa Fe where they sold their cargo of cloth, tools, jewelry, religious objects, and other items. The traders took mules, silver, furs, and other goods back to Missouri. The early traders along this route could make great profits. Mexicans paid well for American goods. Furs and silver sold well in Missouri.

After the Mexican War, big freight-hauling companies pushed many of the smaller traders out of business. Native Americans also increased their attacks during this time. They resented the loss of their territory to Texan settlers.

5. ◎ **Fact and Opinion**
Write an *F* for Fact or an *O* for Opinion on the line next to each of the following statements.

.... The Mormon Trail was the most difficult of the westward trails.

.... The Oregon Trail was longer than the Santa Fe Trail.

.... Traders returned from Santa Fe with silver.

.... Women worked harder than men on the westward trails.

The Governors' Palace in Santa Fe

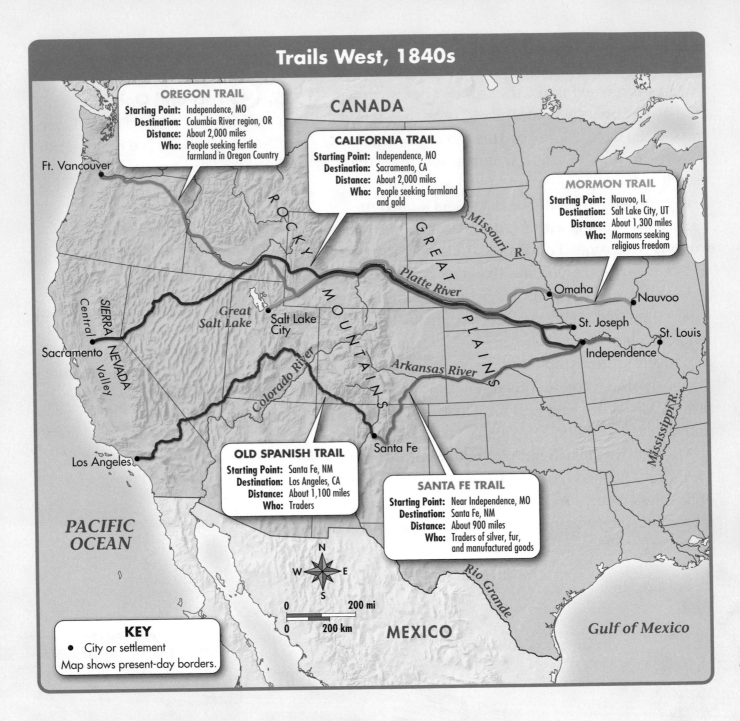

Trails West, 1840s

OREGON TRAIL
Starting Point: Independence, MO
Destination: Columbia River region, OR
Distance: About 2,000 miles
Who: People seeking fertile farmland in Oregon Country

CALIFORNIA TRAIL
Starting Point: Independence, MO
Destination: Sacramento, CA
Distance: About 2,000 miles
Who: People seeking farmland and gold

MORMON TRAIL
Starting Point: Nauvoo, IL
Destination: Salt Lake City, UT
Distance: About 1,300 miles
Who: Mormons seeking religious freedom

OLD SPANISH TRAIL
Starting Point: Santa Fe, NM
Destination: Los Angeles, CA
Distance: About 1,100 miles
Who: Traders

SANTA FE TRAIL
Starting Point: Near Independence, MO
Destination: Santa Fe, NM
Distance: About 900 miles
Who: Traders of silver, fur, and manufactured goods

CANADA

Ft. Vancouver

ROCKY MOUNTAINS

GREAT PLAINS

Missouri R.

Platte River

Omaha

Nauvoo

St. Joseph

St. Louis

Independence

Great Salt Lake

Salt Lake City

SIERRA NEVADA

Central Valley

Sacramento

Colorado River

Arkansas River

Santa Fe

Los Angeles

PACIFIC OCEAN

Rio Grande

Mississippi R.

MEXICO

Gulf of Mexico

N W E S

0   200 mi
0   200 km

KEY
• City or settlement
Map shows present-day borders.

6. Travelers used different trails on their journeys west. On a separate sheet of paper, **create** a chart to compare and contrast the routes listed on the map. Include starting and ending points, and landforms and bodies of water encountered.

Reaching California

In 1829, a Mexican trader forged a new trail from Santa Fe to California. Traders could earn money in California markets selling woolen goods from New Mexico. In return, they brought horses and mules from California back to New Mexico. The trail, later called the Old Spanish Trail, followed a series of Native American and early explorers' trails. It crossed the deserts and mountains of Mexico's northern territory and ended in the small frontier town of Los Angeles.

The Old Spanish Trail was too rough for wagons. Traders instead packed their mules with goods to make the challenging trip to California. Often, they traded with Native Americans along the way.

Unlike traders, settlers usually traveled to California from Missouri on the California Trail. After climbing the eastern Rocky Mountains, the trails for California and Oregon split near the Snake River. The California Trail went southwest from there, crossing the high mountains of the Sierra Nevada. It ended at Sacramento, today the capital of California. Before the 1840s, most settlers took the path to Oregon. But a new discovery would change this settlement pattern.

Got it?

7. ⊙ **Compare and Contrast** What was the main difference between the Santa Fe and Old Spanish trails and the other major trails to the West?

....

....

....

8. ❓ On an archaeology dig on a section of the Oregon Trail, you help dig up an abandoned wagon. It is about 10 feet long, much smaller than you thought it would be. How does knowing the size of the wagon help you imagine the pioneers' journey?

my Story Ideas

....

....

....

◻ **Stop!** I need help with ....

❙❙ **Wait!** I have a question about ....

▶ **Go!** Now I know ....

The California Gold Rush

Many miners in California found gold dust and small chunks of gold in streams flowing out of the mountains.

In the 1840s, farmers in California found little competition for land. The Native American population was around 150,000 and falling. Only about 7,000 Mexicans and other whites lived there. Then gold was discovered.

Gold Fever

Gold is a yellow metal, soft enough to be formed into beautiful objects. It will not tarnish, or discolor. It is also scarce. For these reasons, it has great value. The possibility of finding lots of gold can excite people. The California gold rush proved that. A **gold rush** is a rapid flood of people into an area where gold has been discovered.

It all started in January 1848. A carpenter was building a sawmill on a river in California. One day, he found some chunks of gold in the river. He and the mill owner, John Sutter, tried to keep the gold a secret. However, by August, some 4,000 gold seekers had set up tents and shacks on Sutter's property. They all hoped to strike it rich.

More fortune seekers were on the way. In December 1848, President Polk announced the discovery of gold to Congress. The news spread fast. In 1849, more than 80,000 people left their jobs, homes, and families to go to California. The miners were called "forty-niners" and came from as far away as Europe, China, and Australia. All of them had "gold fever."

Posters such as this one used unreal images and promises to draw people to San Francisco.

I will know that the California gold rush had costs and benefits.

Vocabulary

gold rush
entrepreneur
discrimination
Pony Express

To make coins, the gold was melted, shaped, and stamped with a design. **Design** and **draw** a $5 gold coin.

Thousands of Americans from the East arrived by boat. Some sailed all the way around South America and up the Pacific Coast to the port of San Francisco. Others sailed first to Central America. They had to cross the thick, hot jungle to the Pacific. There they boarded ships to finish their voyage. About 40,000 more crossed the Great Plains in a steady stream of wagon trains along the California Trail.

1. This picture shows how San Francisco looked in 1849. **Write** a caption that describes San Francisco at this time.

Population of San Francisco, 1847–1860	
Year	Population
1847	460
1848	850
1849	5,000
1850	25,000
1852	36,000
1856	50,000
1860	57,000

Source: http://www.sfgenealogy.com/sf/history/hgpop.htm; San Francisco: 1846–1856, From Hamlet to City (Lotchin, 1979)

Searching for Gold

By 1853, the gold rush had drawn more than 250,000 people to California. The gold fields attracted people from all over the world. White Americans, African Americans, Chinese, Latinos, and others staked out claims to land.

Mining for gold was fairly simple at first. Fast-moving mountain streams had washed a lot of gold out of the rock. The gold had settled to the bottom of streams farther down the slopes. Miners "panned" for gold in spots where the current slowed. After scooping up gravel with a flat pan, the heavier particles of gold, if any, dropped to the bottom of the pan.

Other tools included the sluice. Miners ran stream water through this long, sloping wooden box. Wooden bars across the bottom of the box kept the lighter material moving along. Any gold stayed on the bottom.

Gold mining could be dangerous, however. Miners often worked in freezing streams. They suffered from disease and poor diet. Accidents were common. Furthermore, while some miners struck it rich, many more did not.

In 1848 and 1849, miners in California produced 76 tons of gold. After 1850, less gold was found in streambeds. Soon much of the mining was done mechanically. Mining companies brought in rock-crushing mills to find gold on a large scale. Miners who failed to find their fortunes on their own often went to work for these big companies.

Miners use a sluice to find gold.

2. **Contrast** this picture of San Francisco in 1860 with the one on the previous page. What differences do you see?

....

....

....

The Profit Motive

Where there were gold miners, there were profits to be made. In fact, some of the largest gold-rush fortunes were made by people who never even lifted a pan or a pick. They were the merchants who sold the pans, picks, shovels, kettles, tents, blankets, clothing, and food to the miners.

Supplies were scarce in mining country, and demand was great. As a result, merchants were able to charge high prices for their products. A gold-mining pan that cost around 20 cents in the East might cost $8 or more in California.

One Jewish entrepreneur (ahn truh pruh NUR), Levi Strauss, opened a store in San Francisco in 1853. An **entrepreneur** is someone who takes risks to start a business. Strauss sold cloth, linens, and clothing to miners and others. Later, he produced a new kind of work pants made of blue denim held together with copper rivets, or tiny bolts. The pants became known as Levi's jeans.

Another entrepreneur provided services in a mining camp. Luzena Stanley Wilson opened a hotel in which miners could also get a meal. With the money she earned, she and her husband started a successful store. She explained,

"We made money fast. In six months we had ten thousand dollars invested in the hotel and store and we owned a stock of goods worth perhaps ten thousand more."

—Luzena Stanley Wilson

The Levi Strauss building in San Francisco

Chinese immigrants came to California to mine gold.

California Becomes a State

Many gold seekers left for home after a few months, but many more stayed. As a result, California's population soared. In 1850, just two years after gold was found, California had enough people to become the nation's thirty-first state.

With all the immigrant miners, the new state had a diverse mix of residents. Some Americans, however, did not like the competition. Mexican and Chinese miners worked hard and found a lot of gold. Both groups faced **discrimination**, or unfair treatment.

In 1850, the California government passed a law taxing foreign miners $20 a month. Many Mexicans were forced out of the gold fields when they could not pay the tax. Some, perhaps most, of them were actually Mexican Americans. The treaty settling the Mexican War had made them citizens, so the tax on foreign miners should not have applied to them. Later, the state passed a new Foreign Miner's Tax on Chinese immigrants as well.

By 1860, the country needed a fast way to get mail out to California. The **Pony Express** was a system of carrying mail by horse. Riders left St. Joseph, Missouri, at full gallop. Every 10–15 miles they stopped to get a fresh horse. Then they raced on. Their goal was the next station, 70 to 100 miles west. There they passed the mailbag to the next rider, who carried the mail at full speed to yet another station.

3. Read the timeline, and then **write** information about California's history to complete it.

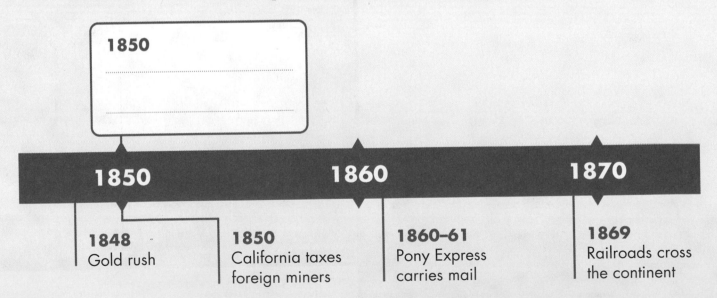

1850

....

....

1850

1860

1870

1848
Gold rush

1850
California taxes foreign miners

1860–61
Pony Express carries mail

1869
Railroads cross the continent

It took about 10 days for the mail to reach the state of California. Pony Express service ended in 1861, after telegraph lines reached California.

The gold rush had a huge impact on California. Besides mining, residents of the state developed lumber companies, ranches, and huge farms. By 1869, rails were laid all the way across the continent. California businesses could now ship many of their products east by train. The state's economy boomed.

The California state flag

Got it?

4. ⊙ **Fact and Opinion** Write an opinion that you think someone outside of California might have had about the forty-niners.

....

....

....

5. ❓ Your archaeology team has researched a gold-rush town. They ask you to write a description of the town to be printed on a sign for visitors.

my Story Ideas

....

....

....

....

⬛ **Stop!** I need help with ....

⏸ **Wait!** I have a question about ....

▶ **Go!** Now I know ....

Lesson 1

Inventions, Roads, and Railroads

- New ideas and inventions helped businesses make profits.
- New roads and canals, along with the invention of the steamboat, moved settlers and goods more quickly and cheaply to the West.
- Railroads, although expensive to build, brought benefits in speed and cost.

Lesson 2

The Lone Star State

- In the 1830s, many Americans settled in Texas to farm and ranch.
- In 1836, Texans declared and won independence from Mexico.
- American annexation of Texas led to the Mexican War. The treaty ending the war gave all of northern Mexico to the United States.

Lesson 3

Trails to the West

- In the 1840s, thousands of settlers headed west in covered wagons.
- The pioneers mainly followed the Oregon Trail, the Mormon Trail, and the California Trail across the Great Plains and Rocky Mountains.
- Traders used the Santa Fe Trail and Old Spanish Trail to move cargo.

Lesson 4

The California Gold Rush

- The discovery of gold in California in 1848 set off a huge gold rush.
- Miners used pans, sluices, picks, and other tools to find gold.
- Entrepreneurs made big profits selling goods and services to miners.
- California's population grew. It become a state in 1850.

Review and Assessment

Lesson 1

Inventions, Roads, and Railroads

1. **Circle** the correct answer.
   How did mass production change how goods were made?

   A. Goods were made in factories.

   B. Goods were made at a slower pace.

   C. Goods were made at home.

   D. Goods were made out of wood.

2. Why did Americans keep trying to improve transportation?

   ....

   ....

   ....

Lesson 2

The Lone Star State

3. **Fill in** the correct answers.

   The .... captured Santa

   Anna at the battle of ....

4. How did the Treaty of Guadalupe Hidalgo complete America's goal of manifest destiny?

   ....

   ....

Lesson 3

Trails to the West

5. Why were animals important to the survival of pioneers on the westward trails?

   ....

   ....

   ....

6. How were the Oregon, Mormon, and California trails all similar?

   ....

   ....

   ....

7. Where did traders exchange American cloth for Mexican silver?

   ....

8. Use a separate sheet of paper to create a map showing two of the routes that pioneers and/or traders followed west. **Draw** the physical features and waterways along the routes and **label** each trail and its most important features, including starting and ending points.

Lesson 4

The California Gold Rush

9. **⊙ Fact and Opinion** Place an *F* next to each fact. Place an *O* next to each opinion.

_____ The trip by ship to California was more difficult than the trip by overland wagon.

_____ In 1849, more than 80,000 people migrated to California.

_____ Levi Strauss opened a store in San Francisco in 1853.

_____ Miners should not have left their families in the East to hunt for gold.

10. Why were the gold seekers called "forty-niners"?

....

....

....

11. Why did merchants take the risk of moving to California to open shops?

....

....

....

....

12. **?** **What are the costs and benefits of growth?**

Use the picture and questions below to think more about this chapter's Big Question.

a. How did the expansion of railroads benefit the economy?

....

....

b. Why might some people object to having trains passing by their homes?

....

....

c. Did Americans in the mid-1800s think the benefits of growth outweighed its costs? Use the railroads to support your answer.

....

....

....

....

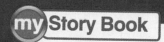
Go online to write and illustrate your own **myStory Book** using the **myStory Ideas** from this chapter.

What are the costs and benefits of growth?

As a young nation, the United States controlled vast amounts of land. As the eastern states became more populated and crowded, farmers, miners, and ranchers moved west to take over the land.

What are the benefits of developing new regions of land today? What are the costs? **Think** about the impact of growth both on the economy and the environment as you **write** your answer.

....

....

....

Now **draw** an image that shows either a cost or benefit of developing new land.

While you're online, check out the **myStory Current Events** area where you can create your own book on a topic that's in the news.

 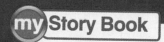

Civil War and Reconstruction

 my Story Spark

THE BIG ?

What is worth fighting for?

Describe a time when you wanted to stand up for another person. Then **write** to explain how and why you handled the situation in the way that you did.

....

....

....

....

....

This memorial in Boston honors an African American regiment from Massachusetts that fought bravely during the Civil War.

Gettysburg National Battlefield
Fighting for a Cause

my Story Video

Eleven-year-old Trent is a history buff. He especially likes studying wars and battles. He is excited to be visiting Gettysburg National Battlefield in Pennsylvania, the site of one of the most important battles of the Civil War.

Trent enters the visitor's center, where he views the collection of guns, ammunition, and other artifacts of the battle. He studies the uniforms on display. "They look hot," says Trent, "especially since this battle took place during the summer."

Trent next visits the Gettysburg Cyclorama. Painted in the 1880s, this 360-degree painting shows how the battle unfolded. For three days in July 1863, the Union Army held off the Confederate soldiers led by Robert E. Lee. "It looks like they fought on farm land," says Trent. "I didn't realize normal people and their homes were impacted by the fighting."

Trent is eager to see the battlefield for himself. "Hi Trent, are you ready for our tour?" asks Renae, a Battlefield Guide. "I sure am!" says Trent. The two of them head out to the battlefield.

Trent is happy to be visiting the site of the battle of Gettysburg.

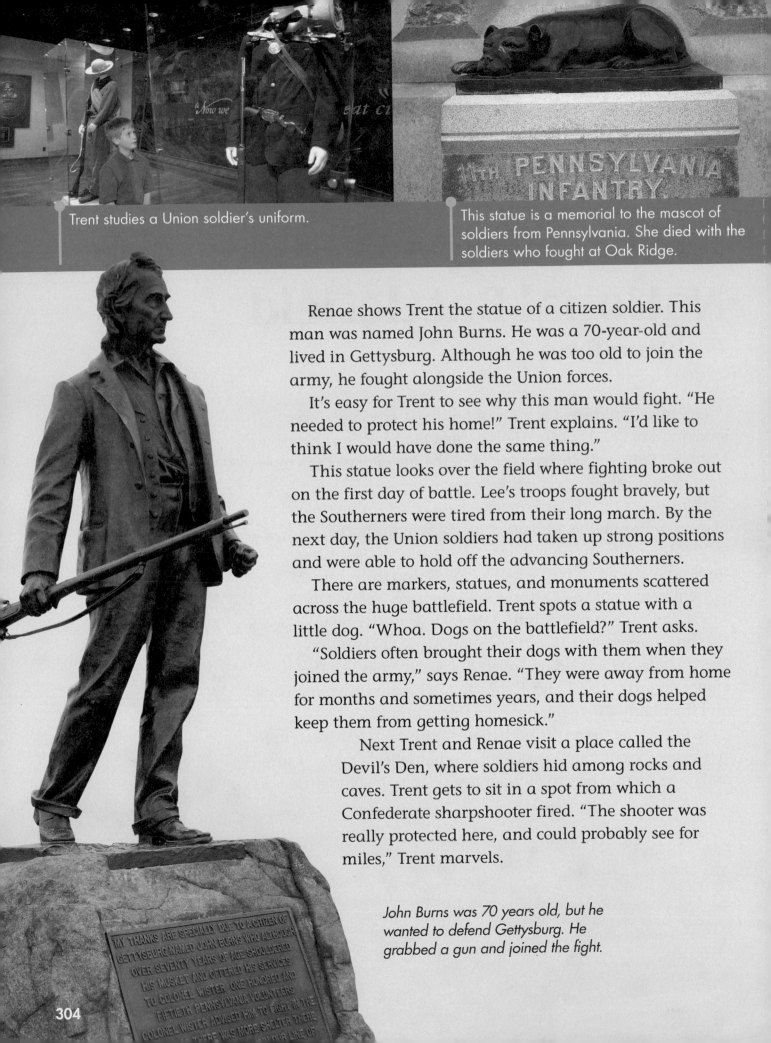

Trent studies a Union soldier's uniform.

This statue is a memorial to the mascot of soldiers from Pennsylvania. She died with the soldiers who fought at Oak Ridge.

Renae shows Trent the statue of a citizen soldier. This man was named John Burns. He was a 70-year-old and lived in Gettysburg. Although he was too old to join the army, he fought alongside the Union forces.

It's easy for Trent to see why this man would fight. "He needed to protect his home!" Trent explains. "I'd like to think I would have done the same thing."

This statue looks over the field where fighting broke out on the first day of battle. Lee's troops fought bravely, but the Southerners were tired from their long march. By the next day, the Union soldiers had taken up strong positions and were able to hold off the advancing Southerners.

There are markers, statues, and monuments scattered across the huge battlefield. Trent spots a statue with a little dog. "Whoa. Dogs on the battlefield?" Trent asks.

"Soldiers often brought their dogs with them when they joined the army," says Renae. "They were away from home for months and sometimes years, and their dogs helped keep them from getting homesick."

Next Trent and Renae visit a place called the Devil's Den, where soldiers hid among rocks and caves. Trent gets to sit in a spot from which a Confederate sharpshooter fired. "The shooter was really protected here, and could probably see for miles," Trent marvels.

John Burns was 70 years old, but he wanted to defend Gettysburg. He grabbed a gun and joined the fight.

304

These rocks, called the Devil's Den, offered protection to Confederate shooters.

Thousands of grave markers identify those who died at Gettysburg.

Renae tells Trent about the battle of Little Round Top. The Confederates attacked this hill and nearly broke the Union lines. Union soldiers charged down the hill against the attacking Confederates. "Why did they follow their leader down a hill against hundreds of armed soldiers?" Trent asks. "Well," Renae explains, "their leader, Joshua Chamberlain, was well liked and bravely fought alongside them."

Their next stop is the place where the battle ended on July 3. Trent is amazed at the rows of cannons. Renae explains that both Union and Confederate forces fired hundreds of cannons. But the Confederate soldiers could not defeat the Union army. Eventually, General Lee retreated.

Trent ends his visit to Gettysburg with a trip to Soldiers' National Cemetery. He walks among the grave markers and wonders about the thousands of men who lost their lives. He stops before a small stone plaque and reads the inscription: "Four score and seven years ago our fathers brought forth on this continent a new nation conceived in liberty, and dedicated to the proposition that all men are created equal."

As Trent reads the Gettysburg Address, the famous speech delivered by President Lincoln, he begins to understand what some of the soldiers at Gettysburg may have been fighting for. "It was for our freedom," he decides. "All of our freedom. I'd say that is something worth fighting for!"

Think About It Based on this story, why do you think both sides in the battle fought so fiercely? As you read the chapter ahead, think about the things people were willing to fight for.

Struggles Over Slavery

Envision It!

Different geography created different economies in the North and the South.

The song "The Battle Cry of Freedom" was popular during the U.S. Civil War. Both sides were fighting for freedom but disagreed about what *freedom* meant. Their fight was the bloodiest in U.S. history. What divided our nation so deeply? Read on to find out.

The North and South Grow Apart

The North and South had developed quite differently due to differences in geography. Much of the South is low and level with rich soil. The climate is warm and sunny for much of the year. Big farms called **plantations** developed. In the 1800s, most Southerners lived on plantations or in small towns. Many of the farmworkers were enslaved people. Although only about one third of the farmers owned slaves, the Southern economy depended upon their work.

The United States, 1860

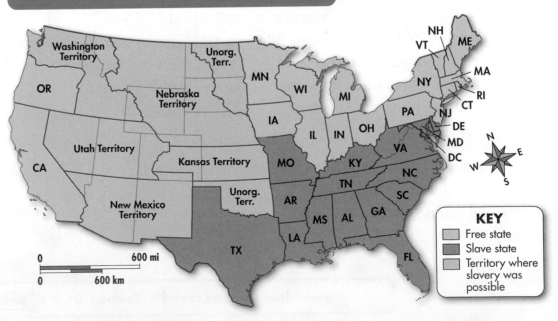

KEY
- Free state
- Slave state
- Territory where slavery was possible

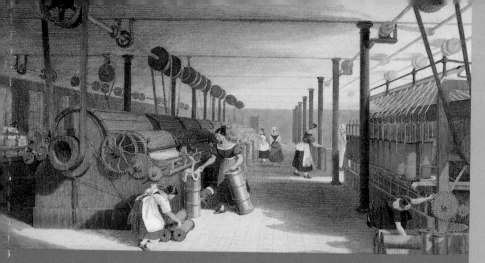

Put an *S* on the picture that represents the South and an *N* on the picture that represents the North.

Vocabulary

plantation
Union
states' rights
compromise

Underground
Railroad
abolitionist
secession
Confederacy

The geography of the Northeast is very different from that of the South. The Northeast has hills, mountains, and lakes. The climate is cold and snowy in the winter. In places, the ground is rocky, so farming is not easy. Northeast resources include coal for making steel. In the 1800s, many Northerners worked in factories. More and more people crowded into large towns and cities. Most big cities had good harbors, so shipping raw materials to factories and finished goods from factories was easy.

The South did not have as many ports as the North. However, the southern port of New Orleans was important to both the South and North. People far inland could ship goods down the Mississippi River to New Orleans and then around the world.

These differences in geography led to differences in economies and ways of life. The North had many workers, and so did not rely on enslaved people. These and other issues led to conflict.

1. **Generalize Write** a generalization based on the data in this graph.

....

....

....

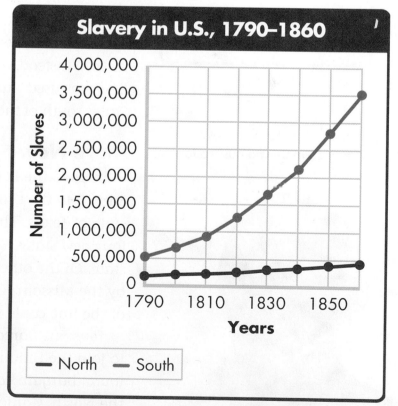

Slavery in U.S., 1790–1860

Number of Slaves

4,000,000
3,500,000
3,000,000
2,500,000
2,000,000
1,500,000
1,000,000
500,000
0

1790 1810 1830 1850

Years

— North — South

Source: University of Virginia Library

2. Write to explain the main ideas of each law below.

Missouri Compromise
- Missouri would be a slave state.
- ....
  ....
- ....
  ....
  ....

Compromise of 1850
- California would be admitted as a free state.
- ....
  ....
  ....

Daniel Webster was a Northern Congressman who pushed for the Compromise of 1850.

Tough Compromises

At the end of the American Revolution, the United States had obtained from Britain the large region we now call the Midwest. Known then as the Northwest Territory, it more than doubled the size of the country.

Congress passed a law called the Northwest Ordinance of 1787. It outlined how new states could be formed as the country grew. Once admitted to the **Union**, as the United States was often called, a new state would have the same rights as other states.

Slavery was prohibited in this territory. This sparked arguments. Many wanted the same number of slave states, where slavery was allowed, and free states, where it was illegal. They feared that if there were more representatives in Congress for either side, it might threaten **states' rights**, the rights of states to make their own local laws.

In 1819, Missouri asked to join the Union as a slave state. That would upset the balance in Congress. A compromise was worked out. A **compromise** is when each side gives in a little to reach an agreement. A law known as the Missouri Compromise was passed in 1820.

According to the Missouri Compromise, Missouri could be a slave state and Maine would join the Union as a free state. Also, not all states formed from the Northwest Territory would be free. Instead, an imaginary line, called the Mason-Dixon line, was used. States north of the line would be free states. States south of the line could allow slavery if they wished.

More New States

In 1845 the Republic of Texas was annexed (united or joined) to the United States. Part of the republic became the state of Texas. The rest of the territory was to be divided into four new states. Texas was admitted to the Union as a slave state. Of the other four new states, those north of the line set by the Missouri Compromise would be free. But those south of the line could vote on whether to allow slavery.

Tensions flared again in 1849 when California applied to join the Union as a free state. The country made another tough bargain called the Compromise of 1850. To satisfy the North, California was admitted as a free state. To satisfy the South, the North agreed to the Fugitive Slave Law.

Changes in Slave-Free States and Territories, 1820–1854

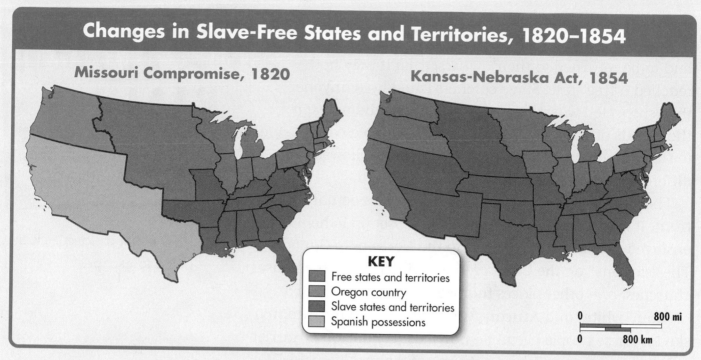

Missouri Compromise, 1820

Kansas-Nebraska Act, 1854

KEY
- Free states and territories
- Oregon country
- Slave states and territories
- Spanish possessions

0   800 mi
0   800 km

A fugitive is someone who escapes and runs away. The Fugitive Slave Law said that escaped slaves must be returned to their owners, even if they had reached a free state. Daniel Webster and other members of Congress from the North hoped that this law would keep the country united.

In 1854 Nebraska was split into the Nebraska Territory and Kansas Territory. Under the Kansas-Nebraska Act, the people of each territory could vote to decide if they would allow slavery.

"Bleeding Kansas"

A majority vote would decide whether Kansas would be free or allow slavery. Northerners opposed to slavery rushed to Kansas to vote. Southerners also rushed to Kansas to vote for slavery.

When the votes were counted, the pro-slavery side had won. The Kansas Territory would allow slavery.

Northerners demanded that the vote be thrown out. Southerners argued that the vote should stand. Most people who lived in Kansas wanted peace, but leaders on both sides stirred up trouble. People clashed all over the Kansas Territory. By 1856, this violence had earned the territory the sad name "Bleeding Kansas."

3. **Look** at the maps. **Write** how the Kansas-Nebraska Act affected the spread of slavery.

....

....

....

....

In "Bleeding Kansas," anti-slavery forces prepared to attack supporters of slavery.

309

Escape to Freedom

According to the Fugitive Slave Law, escaped slaves had to be returned to their owners, even if they had reached a free state. Slave catchers could hold anyone they suspected was a runaway slave. This did not stop thousands of enslaved people from trying to escape to freedom, however. The fugitives usually followed different routes on the Underground Railroad.

The **Underground Railroad** was not an actual train. It was an organized, secret system set up to help enslaved people escape, mostly to the North or to Canada. The "stations" on the Underground Railroad were the houses, churches, and other places fugitive slaves hid and rested.

Many whites and African Americans helped the escaping slaves. These people became known as "conductors." Harriet Tubman, an escaped slave, was one of the most famous conductors. At great personal risk, Tubman made repeated trips south to lead more people to freedom. Tubman's route was one of three major routes that went through New Jersey.

Because the Underground Railroad was secret, no one knows how many slaves escaped—probably only a few thousand each year between 1840 and 1860. This seems like a lot of people, but in the 1860s, nearly 4 million people in the United States were enslaved. However, stories of the Underground Railroad filled slave owners with fear. It deepened the division between the North and the South.

People escaping used maps like the one below. They also relied on "conductors," such as Harriet Tubman, at right.

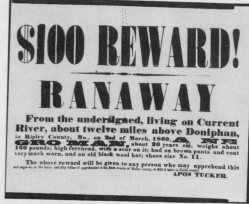

4. How might a slave pick a place to escape?

....

....

....

SCALE OF MILES

Starting Down the Road to War

The North and South became further divided. In Boston, William Lloyd Garrison published a newspaper called *The Liberator*. Garrison was an **abolitionist**, someone who wanted to abolish, or get rid of, slavery. He attacked slavery in his paper, and he also helped found the American Anti-Slavery Society. In the South, writers and speakers argued for states' rights and the freedom to keep their way of life.

Women played a big role in fighting slavery. Sojourner Truth was an African American woman who had been enslaved in New York, but she was freed when New York outlawed slavery. In 1843, she joined the abolition movement. Harriet Beecher Stowe published a novel called *Uncle Tom's Cabin*. This book described the cruelties of slavery and convinced many people to oppose it.

Anger Grows

One event that made people angry was the case of an enslaved man named Dred Scott from Missouri. Scott's owner had taken him to two free states, Illinois and Wisconsin, before returning to Missouri. When Scott's owner died, Scott claimed he was free because he had lived in free states. In 1857, the Supreme Court ruled that Scott had no rights because African Americans were not citizens.

Then, in 1859, abolitionist John Brown attacked Harper's Ferry, Virginia. Brown had fought in Bleeding Kansas. Now he wanted to attack slavery supporters in Virginia, but he needed weapons. He decided to steal weapons the army had stored at Harper's Ferry. Brown and 22 other men raided Harper's Ferry on October 16, but soldiers stopped them. Brown was caught, tried, and hanged. John Brown's raid did not succeed, but it showed that the fight over slavery was getting fiercer.

5. Tell whether or not you would have approved of John Brown's raid.

....

....

....

6. ⊚ **Sequence Fill in** the missing items to show the sequence of events leading to the Civil War.

1820 Missouri Compromise

↓

Compromise of 1850/ Fugitive Slave Law

↓

1854

↓

1857

↓

1859

John Brown

311

The Election of 1860

Abraham Lincoln opposed slavery and wanted to keep it from spreading to new territories and states. "I hate it because of the monstrous injustice," he said in 1854. The Republican Party in Illinois chose Lincoln to run for the U.S. Senate in 1858. Lincoln's opponent, Democratic Senator Stephen Douglas (seated to the left of Lincoln below) disagreed. He believed that each state had the right to decide whether or not to allow slavery. Douglas won that election, but Lincoln's arguments in a series of famous debates with Douglas made him a leader of the new Republican Party.

The 1860 presidential election had three candidates. The Democratic Party had split in two. The Northern Democrats chose Stephen Douglas. The Southern Democrats chose John Breckenridge. The Republicans chose Abraham Lincoln.

The election reflected the sharp divide between North and South. Lincoln won, taking many Northern votes. But he did not win any electoral votes in the Southern states because voters there worried that he would end slavery if elected.

While running for the U.S. Senate in 1858, Lincoln had said:

> "'A house divided against itself cannot stand.' I believe this government cannot endure permanently half slave and half free. I do not expect the Union to be dissolved . . . but I do expect it will cease to be divided. It will become all one thing, or all the other."

This was a frightening prediction. Soon, Lincoln and his fellow Americans would find out if the Union could survive.

7. If you could ask Lincoln a question, what would it be?

....

....

....

....

Abraham Lincoln, standing, argued for stopping the spread of slavery during the Lincoln-Douglas debates.

The South Breaks Away

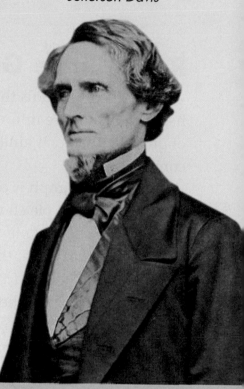

Confederate President Jefferson Davis

Even before the election, some Southern leaders had talked about **secession**, or separating, from the Union. Many Southerners wanted their own country. After Lincoln's election, South Carolina became the first to secede.

Other states followed. By March, 1861, Alabama, Florida, Mississippi, Georgia, Louisiana, and Texas had also seceded. These states formed their own government, called the Confederate States of America, also known as the **Confederacy**. *Confederacy*, like *Union*, means "joined together."

The Confederate leaders wrote a constitution and elected Jefferson Davis as President. They seized forts across the South, except Fort Sumter in Charleston Harbor in South Carolina.

States that remained loyal to the U.S. government were still called the Union. A civil war between the Union and Confederacy now seemed certain. The word *civil* refers to citizens, so a civil war is a war among citizens of the same country.

Got it?

8. ◉ **Cause and Effect Write** what issues and regional differences made the Missouri Compromise and Compromise of 1850 necessary.

....

....

....

....

9. ❓ **Write** a sentence from the viewpoint of presidential candidate Abraham Lincoln, telling what he would be willing to fight for.

my Story Ideas

....

....

⬛ **Stop!** I need help with ....

⏸ **Wait!** I have a question about ....

▶ **Go!** Now I know ....

Read Circle Graphs

Graphs are visuals that show information in a way that helps you compare information. There are many kinds of graphs, and each kind shows a different way to make comparisons.

One kind of graph is a **circle graph.** Circle graphs are also sometimes called pie charts, as they are round and divided into wedges, like slices of pie.

With a circle graph, the entire circle is the whole and the wedges are the parts. This kind of graph makes it easy to compare the parts to the whole and to other parts. Reading a circle graph can help you interpret numbers and facts.

To read a circle graph, first look at the title to understand what the graph is about. Next, read the words in the graph to find out what each part shows. The title of the circle graph below is *Union and Confederate Casualties*. This graph compares the Union and Confederate armies. Within the section for each army, it shows the number of casualties, or soldiers killed or wounded. You can see how the number of casualties compares to the total number of soldiers for each army.

Union and Confederate Forces and Casualties

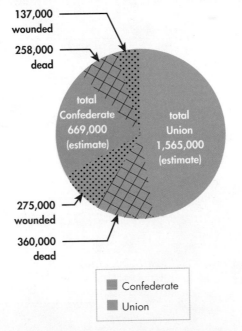

137,000 wounded

258,000 dead

total Confederate 669,000 (estimate)

total Union 1,565,000 (estimate)

275,000 wounded

360,000 dead

■ Confederate
■ Union

Source: Navy Department Library War Casualty Statistics

Here is another circle graph. You can see there are more parts in this graph. The number of parts is determined by what is being shown. This is a graph of how many battles were fought in several states.

The chapter mentions key battles, but there were hundreds of others. There were 16 states with 1 to 11 battles each. The states in this graph all had 15 or more battles. You can see right away which states had the most battles. Circle graphs are good for making comparisons clear.

States With 15 or More Civil War Battles

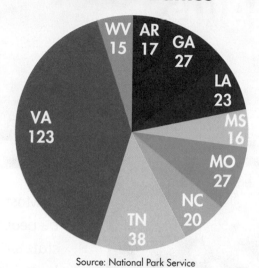

Source: National Park Service

Use the two circle graphs to answer these questions.

1. Which side had a larger army?

....

2. Which side had the greater number of casualties?

....

3. How many states had 15 or more battles? ....

4. Which state saw the most fighting?

....

5. How does the second graph help explain the first graph?

....

....

6. Apply How could you use a circle graph to show what your day is like?

....

....

Lesson 2

The War Begins

Envision It!

Union soldier

The U.S. Civil War split the nation and often split communities and families, as well.

Most leaders of the Confederacy expected the secession to be peaceful. They believed deciding to secede was one of a state's rights. They didn't think their actions would lead to a long, bloody war. They were very wrong.

The First Shots

A Union force controlled Fort Sumter in South Carolina. It was in a Confederate state, so Confederate President Jefferson Davis thought the Union force should surrender the fort. He sent South Carolina's governor to ask the Union soldiers to leave the fort, but they refused.

On April 8, 1861, the governor learned that Lincoln was sending a ship to resupply the fort. Jefferson Davis sent soldiers to help the governor.

On April 11, the Confederates again asked the Union soldiers to leave. Again, they refused. At 4:30 A.M. on April 12, Confederate forces began to fire on the fort. The next day, with no supplies left, the Union force surrendered the fort to the Confederates. No one had been killed, but the Civil War had begun.

Confederate forces fired on Fort Sumter on April 12, 1861. This event touched off the Civil War.

Confederate soldier

UNLOCK THE BIG ?

I will know the strategies and key battles in the first years of the Civil War.

Write what you think each soldier might say to the other about why they are fighting.

Vocabulary

enlist

blockade

The Civil War Begins

Lincoln responded to the attack on Fort Sumter by raising an army. Virginia, Arkansas, Tennessee, and North Carolina joined the Confederacy. The Confederacy now had 11 states; the Union consisted of 23. Men on both sides eagerly enlisted. To **enlist** is to join the military. After all, it was an important cause. The North wanted to preserve the unity of the United States as a whole. The North also didn't want to lose access to the Mississippi River. The South was fighting for states' rights and a way of life.

The First Battle of Bull Run

At first, it seemed that the war *would* be over soon—and the Confederates would win. Lincoln sent 35,000 troops against the Confederate capital, Richmond, Virginia. On July 21, 1861, they met Confederate troops at a stream called Bull Run. The Union soldiers did well at first. But the Confederates stood their ground, inspired by a general named Thomas Jackson. "There stands Jackson like a stone wall," declared another Confederate general. This earned the general the nickname "Stonewall" Jackson. When Southern reinforcements arrived, the overwhelmed Union soldiers fled.

1. ◎ **Sequence Put** the events on these pages in the correct sequence.

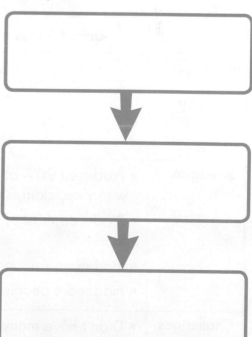

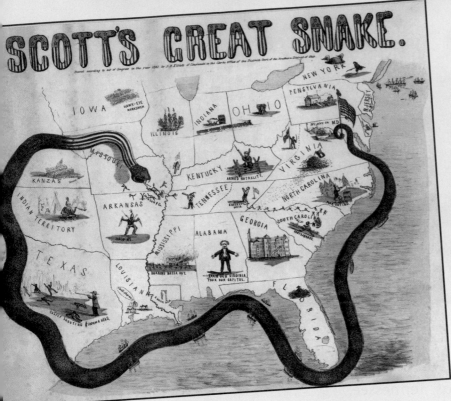

SCOTT'S GREAT SNAKE.

General Scott's plan was to wrap around the South and "squeeze" it, like a giant snake.

Lincoln Versus Davis

Abraham Lincoln, the President of the Union, and Jefferson Davis, the President of the Confederacy, were both skilled leaders. Both were born in Kentucky, but Davis had moved to Mississippi and Lincoln had moved to Illinois. Lincoln trained as a lawyer. Davis, a West Point graduate, became an army officer. Both served in Washington, D.C.

Lincoln and Davis faced different challenges as the war began. The South had fewer resources than the North, but it had better military leaders and stronger reasons to fight.

The two men were different in their war time strategies, too. Lincoln sought advice from General Winfield Scott, a Mexican War veteran.

2. ◎ **Compare and Contrast Complete** this chart to compare the Union and the Confederacy.

The Union and the Confederacy		
	United States of America	**Confederate States of America**
President		
Strategy		
Strengths	• Produced 90% of the country's weapons, cloth, shoes, and iron • Produced most of the country's food • Had more railroads and roads • Had more people	• Had more experienced hunters and soldiers • Had a history of producing great military leaders • Believed they were fighting for freedom • Were fighting for—and on—their own land
Challenges	• Didn't have many war veterans • Didn't have as many talented military leaders	• Lacked big manufacturing centers • Had fewer railroads

Scott planned a three-part strategy. First, the Union would form a naval blockade of the coasts. A **blockade** is a barrier of troops or ships to keep people and supplies from moving in and out of an area. Under a blockade, the South would not be able to ship cotton to European countries and wouldn't have money to pay for the war.

Second, Scott planned to take control of the Mississippi River. This would cut the Confederacy in half. Third, Scott planned to attack the Confederacy from the east and west. He called his strategy the Anaconda Plan because it would squeeze the Confederacy like an anaconda, a huge snake.

Davis had his own strategy. First, he planned to defend Confederate land until the North gave up. Southerners believed that Union troops would quit fighting because they weren't defending their own land. Second, Davis believed the British would help because they needed Southern cotton. Davis was wrong. Britain offered no help to either side.

New Tools of War

Wars often result in the invention of new tools and technologies. During the Civil War, guns were improved. The new guns could shoot farther and more accurately. Both Union and Confederate soldiers used early versions of the hand grenade. The Confederacy built a submarine, a ship that could travel under water.

The Confederates created another new weapon: the ironclad. It was a ship covered, or clad, in iron, so cannonballs simply bounced off it. To make the ironclad, the Confederates covered an old Union ship, the *Merrimack*, with iron plates. They named it the *Virginia*. The *Virginia* successfully sank several Union ships. The Union built its own ironclad, the *Monitor*, which fought the *Virginia*. Since both ships were ironclads, they were unable to cause serious damage to each other.

3. **Write** a newspaper headline for the battle of the *Monitor* and the *Virginia*.

....

....

....

....

Brilliant Confederate Generals

While the Union had far greater resources than the Confederacy, the South had brilliant generals, especially Thomas "Stonewall" Jackson and Robert E. Lee. These generals often outsmarted Union forces many times larger than their own.

In 1862, Union General George McClellan hoped to capture the Confederate capital of Richmond, Virginia. McClellan planned to sail his troops to a place on the coast of Virginia, to avoid the Confederate army in northern Virginia. At first, it seemed as though McClellan's plan would work. However, Stonewall Jackson was fighting so successfully in Virginia's Shenandoah Valley that extra Union troops had to be sent there. There was no help for McClellan. Robert E. Lee then badly defeated McClellan's forces at Richmond. Some people feared that the Confederates would now move on Washington, D.C.

With each Confederate success, there was more pressure on Lincoln. Northerners had expected a swift, easy victory. It was beginning to look like the war might be long, and people began to question Lincoln's decision to fight.

4. The painting below is of the Battle of Antietam. **Write** a newspaper headline to go with this painting.

....

....

General Robert E. Lee was respected by people on both sides, even during the war.

320

The Battle of Antietam

The Union needed a victory. It got one on September 17, 1862, at the Battle of Antietam (an TEET um). This battle was the single bloodiest day in the war. In the end, about 23,000 men lay dead or wounded, evenly divided between North and South. This horrific battle led Lincoln to make a decision that would change the war and the country.

Got it?

5. ⊙ **Main Idea and Details** **Fill in** this chart to show the purpose, or main idea, of the Anaconda Plan. Then fill in details to show how the plan would work.

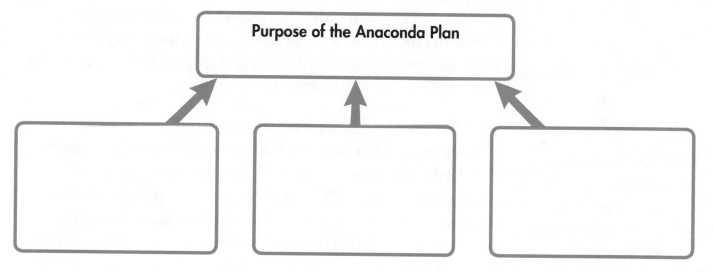

Purpose of the Anaconda Plan

6. **Write** a short dialogue between Lincoln and Davis about why they are willing to fight.

my Story Ideas

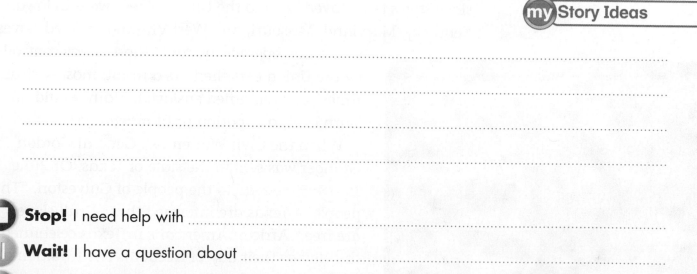

....

....

....

....

Stop! I need help with ....

Wait! I have a question about ....

Go! Now I know ....

Life During the Civil War

Mathew Brady used the new technology of photography to record the people and events of the Civil War.

The U.S. Civil War didn't start as a war to end slavery. President Lincoln just wanted to keep the country together. By 1862, however, Lincoln's thinking had changed. He said, "Slavery must die that the nation might live."

The Emancipation Proclamation

Some of Lincoln's advisors said ending slavery would divide the North and unite the South. They were right. But Lincoln was determined. On January 1, 1863, he issued a **proclamation**, or official announcement. It called for the **emancipation**, or setting free, of slaves. Lincoln's Emancipation Proclamation freed slaves in states at war with the Union.

The proclamation did not end slavery in the border states, slave states that stayed loyal to the Union. These were Delaware, Kentucky, Maryland, Missouri, and West Virginia. It freed slaves in the Confederacy, but only those areas controlled by the Union benefited. As a result, most African Americans remained enslaved. Many would not learn of emancipation until much later.

When the Civil War ended, General Gordon Granger was sent to the state of Texas. On June 19, 1865, he read to the people of Galveston, "The people of Texas are informed that . . . all slaves are free." African Americans in Texas celebrated this day as their day of freedom. The tradition of celebrating on this day spread quickly to other states. This day is now known as **Juneteenth**.

1. **Write** the feelings shown in this painting of African Americans learning they were free.

....

....

UNLOCK THE BIG ?

I will know the importance of the Emancipation Proclamation and the roles of different groups in the Civil War.

Vocabulary

proclamation

emancipation

Juneteenth

Why do you think these cannons are near a river?

A Diverse Army

Although the Emancipation Proclamation did not end all slavery, it did change the war. African American abolitionist Frederick Douglass supported Lincoln and encouraged other African Americans to help the Union. Large numbers of them responded by joining the Union Army.

By the end of the war, about 179,000 African American men had served as soldiers in the Union army. African Americans helped the war effort in other ways, too. They served as carpenters, cooks, guards, workers, nurses, scouts, spies, and doctors. African American women served as nurses, spies, and scouts. Harriet Tubman became the most famous African American scout.

Many recent immigrants also enlisted. Many German, Irish, British, and Canadian soldiers joined in the fight. They hoped to prove their loyalty to their new country.

About 20,000 Native Americans served in either the Confederate or Union armies. Some Native American nations, such as the Cherokee, were divided. General Ely S. Parker, a Seneca, wrote the surrender document that General Robert E. Lee signed at the end of the war. Parker later told how, during the surrender, Lee said to him, "I am glad to see a real American here." Parker replied to the general, "We are all Americans."

2. About what percentage of the Union Army was made up of immigrants?

Union Army

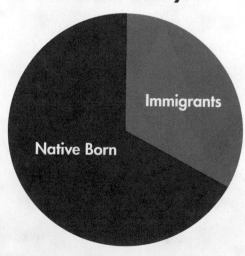

Immigrants

Native Born

A Soldier's Life

The average age of a Civil War soldier was 25. However, boys as young as 12 went into battle as drummer boys. For young soldiers and old, life on the Civil War battlefields was dirty, dangerous, and difficult.

Battles were horrible, but long, boring waits between battles were hard, too. Most battles were in the South, where summers were very hot. Soldiers almost always traveled on foot and might march up to 25 miles a day. The supplies in their backpacks weighed as much as 50 pounds. Marching proved even more difficult for Confederate soldiers. The Union blockade kept supplies from reaching the Southerners, so soldiers could not replace worn out shoes. They often marched and fought in bare feet.

Food was a problem, too. It was rarely fresh. The armies supplied beef and pork. Both were preserved so they did not spoil. Fresh pork had been salted to become "salt pork." Beef was pickled, or preserved in water and spices. In addition, the troops had beans and biscuits. These biscuits were tough flour-and-water biscuits called "hardtack." To survive, troops raided local farms to steal fresh fruits and vegetables.

3. Soldiers were away from home for long periods during the war. What does this photo tell you about how families solved this?

....

....

A Confederate soldier's hat, shoes, and gloves

324

Sick and Wounded

In the mid-1800s, the idea that germs caused disease was a new and untested theory. Most doctors hadn't heard of it. Many doctors never washed their hands or medical instruments.

A wounded soldier who made it to a hospital might be put in a bed in which someone just died of fever—without the sheets being changed. Infections were common and disease spread quickly. There were few medicines and no antibiotics. Twice as many soldiers died of disease as died of gunshot wounds.

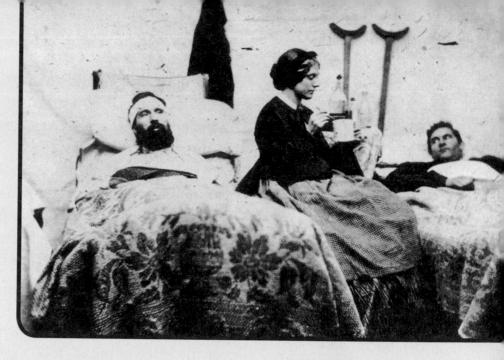

Civil War nurse caring for the wounded at a field hospital

Caring for the Soldiers

At this time, there were almost no nursing schools in the United States. Most nurses learned as they worked, and most were volunteers. One nurse described a field hospital this way: ". . . just across the lawn there are some of the worst cases & the sight & sounds we have to encounter daily are most distressing. I am mightily afraid we shall have some sort of infectious fever here for it is impossible to keep the place clean & there is a bad smell everywhere."

Clara Barton was the most famous of the volunteer nurses. She went out to where the soldiers were. Barton said her place was "anywhere between the bullet and the battlefield." At the battle of Antietam, as the cannons boomed, she held the operating table steady for the surgeon. She became known as "the Angel of the Battlefield." After the war, in 1881, she founded the American Red Cross.

Hundreds of women helped on both sides. Juliet Opie Hopkins from Alabama cared for Confederate soldiers. In 1861 she sold all her property and gave the money to the Confederacy to establish hospitals. She organized medical services in Richmond, Virginia, and then for the whole state of Alabama. Hopkins was shot twice while rescuing wounded men on the battlefield.

4. **Write** two things you might do to help nurse soldiers.

....

....

....

....

On the Home Front

Not all women could work on the battlefield. Most stayed home and took care of the families. They filled the jobs that had been held by men. They ran stores and planted crops. In addition, they worried.

Women in the South often had to move their families and belongings, as homes and towns were destroyed. They also had to deal with shortages of supplies caused by the North's blockade. Prices increased sharply. The average Southern family's monthly food bill rose from $6.65 just before the war to $68 by 1863. Almost no one could afford food. In April of that year, hundreds of women in Richmond, Virginia, rioted to protest the rise in prices. Women in other Southern cities rioted over the price of bread, too.

When they could, women hid their livestock as the armies came through. Hungry soldiers would kill and eat all the chickens and pigs. Of course, the army would take any other food they could find, too. Often, after an army had passed through, the civilians were left starving. This was the case when the Union army marched through the South.

Women also hid possessions from the enemy soldiers. These included items that had been in their families for generations.

In a letter dated August 23, 1862, a Virginia woman complained to her sister about hard times and high prices:

"Times are very hard here every thing is scarce and high . . . corn is selling for ten dollars, bacon 45 cents per pound . . . . We cannot get a yard of calico for less than one dollar."

5. List three things you would take with you if you had to escape before an enemy army came.

....

....

....

A Southern family flees the approaching Union army.

People in the North read about the war. Many sent husbands or sons to fight. In the South, families struggled with the direct effects of the war's destruction.

Women in Wartime

Women on both sides contributed to the war effort. In addition to being nurses on the battlefield or keeping farms and family businesses running, they sewed clothing and made bandages. They sold personal possessions to raise money and sent food to the armies.

Some women traveled with their soldier husbands and sons, cooking for them, nursing them, and helping them. A few women even became soldiers. Frances Clalin, for example, disguised herself as a man so that she could fight in the Union army.

Sojourner Truth, an African American and former slave, had worked for abolition before the war and would work for women's rights after the war. During the war, she gathered supplies for African American regiments. A popular speaker, she often told stories of her life as an enslaved person.

Some women became spies. Women had clever ways to carry secret documents, such as maps and messages. Documents and even weapons could be hidden under the large hoop skirts they wore.

Belle Boyd, nicknamed "La Belle Rebelle," was one of the most famous female Confederate spies. Union soldiers arrested her six times, but she kept spying for the Confederates. After one arrest, Boyd communicated to a Confederate by hiding messages inside rubber balls and throwing them between the bars of her cell windows!

I have borne thirteen children, and seen most all sold off to slavery, and when I cried out with my mother's grief, none but Jesus heard me!
—Sojourner Truth

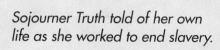

Sojourner Truth told of her own life as she worked to end slavery.

327

Bringing the War Home

New technology changed the way the war was fought, but it also changed the way people at home experienced the war. People still got news from the battlefield through the "old" technology of soldiers' letters and newspapers.

For the first time, people back home also got to see something of what these soldiers were living through. A new technology, photography, made this possible. The Civil War was the first war to be "taken home" in images. Mathew Brady thought it was important to photograph the war.

People still learn from Brady's photographs showing the details of war. He took pictures of soldiers posing, resting, and cooking. Brady and other photographers also took photos of field hospitals, weapons, and dead bodies on the battlefield. Their photos appeared in newspapers and special exhibits.

6. **Write** how you think seeing photographs of the war might have changed people's feelings about war.

....

....

....

....

Civil War photographers and their camera and portable darkroom

Camera technology was not well developed at the time. Cameras were large and heavy. All the preparation and developing had to be done in the dark, so the photographers used a "darkroom" wagon. Photographs at that time were taken on specially treated glass plates. The glass plates had to be handled carefully as the wagon bumped through the countryside and across battlefields. Some people claim that as a result of all the letters home and all the photographs, civilians knew more about the Civil War than about any war before.

Mathew Brady spent his own money, buying equipment and hiring assistants, to capture the war in photographs.

Got it?

7.  **Sequence** Put these events in the correct sequence: Emancipation Proclamation, Juneteeth holiday created, First Battle of Bull Run, Clara Barton starts the Red Cross, Battle of Antietam.

....

....

....

....

8. **Write** a letter from the point of view of a Confederate soldier telling his family about his experiences.

my Story Ideas

....

....

....

....

Stop! I need help with ....

Wait! I have a question about ....

Go! Now I know ....

Lesson 4

The War Ends

By April 1865, the Confederate capital, Richmond, Virginia, lay in ruins.

President Lincoln regularly met with Union officers at their military camps.

People were eager to see the Civil War end, and both sides became more aggressive. All major battles had been in the South, but in July 1863, for the first time, Lee led his forces north of the Mason-Dixon line. This line had come to represent the division between free and slave states. The Confederates marched toward Gettysburg, Pennsylvania.

Union Victory at Gettysburg

The Battle of Gettysburg was one of the most important battles of the war. It lasted three brutal days and was a turning point in the war.

General George Meade led the Union troops. On July 1, 1863, after a successful Confederate attack, Union soldiers retreated. However, the weary Confederates were unable to follow and gain the victory.

On July 2, fresh Union troops arrived. The Confederates attacked again, but this time the Union troops held their ground. The fighting was fierce.

On July 3, the Confederate forces fired more than 150 cannons. Northern cannons roared back. Commanded by General George Pickett, thousands of Confederate troops attacked. But "Pickett's Charge," as it was called, was a disaster. By the time it ended, more than 5,000 Confederate soldiers lay dead or wounded. The Union had won.

The Battle of Gettysburg was a key victory for the Union, but the victory came at a steep cost. More than 23,000 Union soldiers and 28,000 Confederate soldiers were dead or wounded.

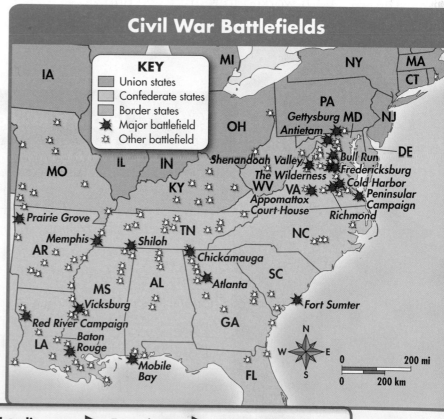
Vocabulary

siege
total war
assassinate

Write, in the space above, what you think the picture suggests about the outcome of the war.

Union Victory at Vicksburg

The Confederates held a strong position at Vicksburg, Mississippi. They had turned back all previous Union attacks. But controlling Vicksburg meant controlling the Mississippi River, so the Union wanted to take Vicksburg.

Union General Ulysses S. Grant attacked Vicksburg from two directions at once, but the Confederates successfully defended Vicksburg. Grant attacked again and again, from the east and then, crossing the river, from the south. But direct attack continued to fail. So Grant laid siege.

A **siege** is a military blockade designed to make a city surrender. The siege lasted 48 days. People in Vicksburg dug caves into the hillside to escape fire from Union cannons. Confederate soldiers and civilians faced starvation. Vicksburg surrendered on July 4, 1863. The tide had finally turned in favor of the Union.

1. ◎ **Summarize Write** a sentence summarizing what the map shows about Civil War battles.

....

....

Civil War Battlefields

KEY
■ Union states
■ Confederate states
■ Border states
✸ Major battlefield
✿ Other battlefield

IA
MI
NY
MA
CT
PA
Gettysburg MD
NJ
Antietam
OH
DE
Shenandoah Valley
Bull Run
IL
IN
The Wilderness
Fredericksburg
MO
KY
WV
VA
Cold Harbor
Peninsular
Appomattox
Campaign
Court-House
Richmond
Prairie Grove
TN
NC
Memphis
Shiloh
AR
Chickamauga
SC
AL
Atlanta
MS
Fort Sumter
Vicksburg
GA
Red River Campaign
Baton
Rouge
LA
Mobile
Bay
FL

N
W   E
S

0   200 mi
0   200 km

Grant Versus Lee

President Lincoln once said of Ulysses S. Grant, "I can't spare this man. He fights." Grant proved to be the fighter the Union needed. In March of 1864, Lincoln promoted Grant and gave him control over the entire Union army. Grant was famous for his aggressive fighting style and for being relentless. He would just keep sending in more men until the other side ran out of food or ammunition.

Robert E. Lee, the chief commander of the Confederate troops, faced a terrible decision when the Civil War broke out. Lee loved the United States and was an officer in the U.S. Army. His father had fought alongside George Washington. However, he felt tied to Virginia. He resigned from the Union army and sided with the South.

As a general, Lee was famous for his brilliant military tactics. He was skilled, smart, and daring on the battlefield. He was also known as a gentleman. He was a soldier with refined manners. He used strategy rather than brute force. He inspired his troops, because they respected him so much.

Grant and Lee were alike in many ways. Both had received their military training at the U.S. Military Academy at West Point. Both had served in the Mexican-American War. Both were brilliant military leaders. After the war, both worked to reunite the nation.

2. **Write** how Lee and Grant were similar.

....

....

....

....

....

Grant and Lee		
	Ulysses S. Grant	**Robert E. Lee**
Birthplace	Ohio	Virginia
Education	U.S. Military Academy at West Point	U.S. Military Academy at West Point
Prior Military Service	Mexican-American War	Mexican-American War
Military Rank	General	General
Side	North	South

Sherman in Georgia

Union General William Tecumseh Sherman played a major role in ending the war. Sherman's idea was that war should be as horrible as possible, so the enemy would stop fighting. He didn't just attack military targets; he worked to destroy the South economically, so it could no longer support an army. Sherman's approach came to be known as **total war.**

Leading 100,000 Union troops, Sherman began his invasion of Georgia in May 1864. He headed first for Atlanta. Confederate troops tried to stop Sherman's advance but were driven back by the huge number of Union soldiers.

Sherman began a siege of the city of Atlanta. By September 2, Sherman's forces controlled the city. They destroyed Atlanta's railroad center to disrupt the South's transportation system.

Sherman ordered everyone to leave and then burned much of the city. Union soldiers also took all the food and supplies they could find. Atlanta could no longer offer help to the Confederate army.

From Atlanta, Sherman headed for Savannah on the coast. With 62,000 soldiers, he cut a path of destruction across Georgia. This campaign came to be called "Sherman's March to the Sea." Union troops destroyed everything that might help the South keep fighting. Sherman gave his soldiers only bread to force them to raid villages for food.

Confederate soldiers continued to follow and fight Sherman's forces. They couldn't win, but they reduced the amount of damage done by the Union forces.

On December 21, 1864, Savannah fell without a fight. Union soldiers had caused $100 million worth of damage in their march across Georgia. They then turned north, marching into South Carolina, causing even more destruction in the state where the war began.

Sherman's forces tore up railroad tracks and burned towns as they marched across the South.

3. **Circle** the part of Sherman's route known as his March to the Sea.

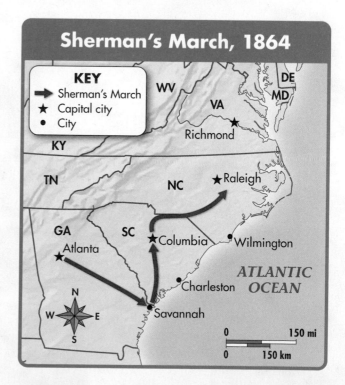

Sherman's path after Atlanta

333

The Road to Appomattox

Union forces were closing in on Lee's army in Virginia. On April 2, 1865, General Lee sent a message to Jefferson Davis that the Confederates should leave Richmond, Virginia. The next day, Union troops entered the city. The Union had captured the capital of the Confederacy! When President Lincoln arrived to tour Richmond, the city's former slaves cheered him.

Exhausted and starving, Lee's army of 55,000 men tried to escape west. Grant's force of about 113,000 soldiers trapped them. Grant met Lee in one last battle near the village of Appomattox Court House, Virginia, and once again defeated the weary Confederates. The end had come. The Civil War was over.

On April 9, 1865, General Grant and General Lee met at a farmhouse at Appomattox to discuss the terms of surrender. Among the many Union officers who witnessed the surrender was Ely S. Parker. A Seneca lawyer and Union officer, he had helped write up the terms of surrender.

4. Label Generals Lee and Grant in the painting.

Grant and Lee sign the terms of surrender at Appomattox Court House. Ely S. Parker is on the left, next to the fireplace.

Costs of the Civil War (in millions of 1860 Dollars)

	South	North	Total
Government expenditures	1,032	2,302	3,334
Physical destruction	1,487	0	1,487
Costs of the war			

5. Add up the costs of the war.

Grant wanted the healing of the nation to start right away. He didn't take Confederate soldiers prisoner. Instead, he allowed Lee's soldiers to go free. In addition, the Union allowed the Southerners to keep their personal weapons and any horses they had. Grant also offered to give Lee's men food from Union supplies. Lee accepted. As Lee returned to his men, the Union soldiers cheered and fired their rifles, to celebrate their victory over the South. Grant silenced them, saying, "The war is over; the rebels are our countrymen again."

The Cost of the Civil War

The Civil War was the most destructive war in our history. The human costs were very high. About 620,000 people died. Families were torn apart, as some members sided with the Union and others with the Confederacy. The governments of both sides spent billions to fight the war.

Other economic costs were shattering as well. Towns, farms, and industries in the South were ruined. Factories in the North that had relied on Southern cotton were in trouble. However, the economy of the South suffered far greater losses, particularly because the enslaved people on whom the economy depended were now freed.

There are many ways to think about the price that was paid. But no matter how the costs are estimated, the Civil War had a tremendous human and economic cost.

In spite of the destruction, Lincoln still hoped for the healing of the nation. After news of the Confederate surrender reached Washington, D.C., Lincoln appeared before a crowd and asked a band to play "Dixie," one of the battle songs of the Confederacy. "I have always thought 'Dixie' one of the best tunes I ever heard," he told the crowd.

Civil War Currency

"We here highly resolve that these dead shall not have died in vain, that this nation under God shall have a new birth of freedom, and that government of the people, by the people, for the people shall not perish from the earth."

—Abraham Lincoln, from the "Gettysburg Address"

6. Underline the words in this excerpt that describe democracy.

A reward was offered for the capture of Lincoln's assassin, John Wilkes Booth.

The Gettysburg Address

Abraham Lincoln left us a beautiful summary of why so many had to die in this terrible war. He wrote it a year and a half before the war ended.

In 1863, thousands of Americans had been killed at Gettysburg, so the battlefield was made into a national cemetery to honor them. On November 19, 1863, about 15,000 people gathered for the ceremony to establish the cemetery. At this event, President Lincoln gave what has become one of America's most famous speeches.

Lincoln's speech, now known as the Gettysburg Address, began with the words "Four score and seven years ago our fathers brought forth upon this continent a new nation." (A score is 20.) Lincoln was reminding people that it had been 87 years since the Declaration of Independence. The fight was about preserving the nation and about self government.

In the Address, Lincoln also praised the soldiers who had given their lives to keep the dream of America alive. It reminded Americans that there was still more work to be done, but also why the work was important.

A Terrible Loss for the Nation

Friday evening, April 14, 1865, President Lincoln and his wife, Mary, attended a play at Ford's Theater. During the play, the audience was surprised to hear a gunshot. This was followed by Mary Lincoln's screams. President Lincoln had been shot!

The bullet had entered the back of the president's head, and he was unconscious. He died a few hours later, on the morning of April 15.

Lincoln was **assassinated**, or murdered for political reasons, by John Wilkes Booth, a 26-year-old actor who supported the Confederacy. Booth escaped from the theater. But federal troops found him later in a Virginia barn. He refused to surrender. The soldiers shot and killed him. Booth had not worked alone, and Lincoln was not the only target. The whole group of plotters was captured, tried, and hanged.

A funeral train took Lincoln's body to his hometown of Springfield, Illinois, to be buried. People paid their respects along the route as the train traveled from Washington to Springfield. It was a tragic loss for the nation. But, before he died, Lincoln had achieved his goal. He had saved the Union.

Statue of Lincoln in the Lincoln Memorial, Washington, D.C.

7. ◉ **Main Idea and Details Fill in** the missing details that support the main idea.

Main Idea
The war turned in the Union's favor.

Detail

Detail

Detail

8. ❓ **Explain** how not punishing the South relates to the Union's reason for fighting.

my Story Ideas

....

....

⬜ **Stop!** I need help with ....

⏸ **Wait!** I have a question about ....

▶ **Go!** Now I know ....

Reconstruction

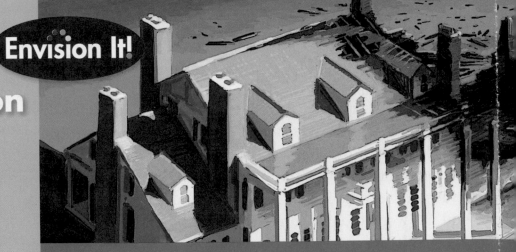

Envision It!

After the Civil War, the South was in ruins. Several plans were created to help repair and rebuild the region.

After President Lincoln's assassination, Vice President Andrew Johnson became President. Johnson wanted to carry out Lincoln's plan for **Reconstruction**, the rebuilding and healing of the country. However, Johnson lacked Lincoln's skill at dealing with people. He and Congress fought fiercely.

Lincoln and Johnson wanted to pardon Southerners who swore loyalty to the United States and promised to obey the country's laws. They would also welcome states back into the Union if they outlawed slavery and asked to be let back in. Congress thought these plans were too gentle and felt that the South should be punished for having seceded. However, Congress did want to help newly freed African Americans, called freedmen.

Congress and Reconstruction

The Republicans who controlled Congress didn't trust Johnson. He was a Southerner and had been a Democrat before becoming Lincoln's vice president. Members of Congress began developing a new plan of Reconstruction. They passed the Civil Rights Act of 1866 to grant freedmen full legal equality. Congress then passed several Reconstruction Acts between 1867 and 1868.

Like much of the South, Richmond, Virginia, had been destroyed during the Civil War.

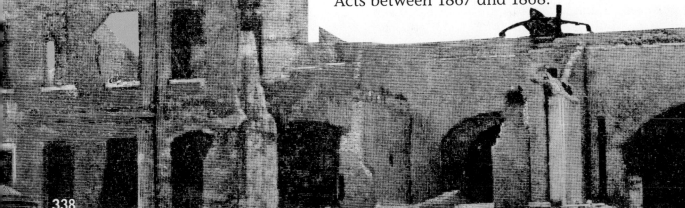

List in the empty box things that would need to be reconstructed after the war.

UNLOCK THE BIG ?

I will know the different plans for Reconstruction and the effects of new amendments to the Constitution.

Vocabulary

Reconstruction   segregation
amendment   black codes
impeachment   sharecropping
carpetbaggers

The Acts divided the former Confederate states into military districts. The President sent federal troops to the South to keep order and enforce emancipation of slaves. The Acts required Southern states to write new state constitutions giving African American men the right to vote. The Acts prevented former Confederate leaders from voting or holding elected office. Congress also passed three new amendments to the Constitution. An **amendment** is a change or addition. You will read about these amendments later in this lesson.

Johnson opposed many of Congress's actions. He argued that the Reconstruction Acts were against the law because they had been passed without the Southern states being represented in Congress. He said passing laws with half the country unrepresented was unconstitutional. Johnson used his veto power to try to stop Congress. However, Congress was able to override Johnson's vetoes. Congress continued to make its own plans.

Angry about Johnson's attempts to block their laws, the Republicans in Congress tried to impeach Johnson. **Impeachment** is the bringing of charges of wrongdoing against an elected official by the House of Representatives. If an impeached President is found guilty in a Senate trial, he can be removed from office. In May 1868 the Senate found Johnson not guilty. However, Johnson's ability to lead the nation had been seriously weakened.

1. **Write** who supported the idea in each part of the Venn diagram.

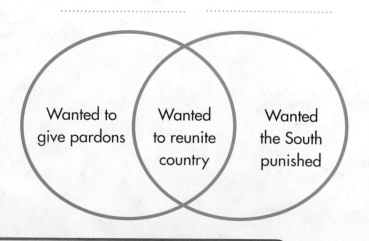

Wanted to give pardons | Wanted to reunite country | Wanted the South punished

Rebuilding the South

Reconstruction had many successes. The Freedmen's Bureau had been created by President Lincoln to help freed slaves and refugees of the war. Congress strengthened the Bureau to help the 4 million recently freed slaves.

The Freedmen's Bureau built schools and hospitals. It hired African American and white teachers from the South and North. New leaders raised taxes to help rebuild roads and railroads, and to establish a free education system. Many industries were expanded, to provide more jobs.

For the first time, African Americans became elected officials. In Mississippi, two African Americans were elected to the U.S. Senate. In 1870, Hiram R. Revels won the Senate seat that Jefferson Davis once held. In 1874, Blanche K. Bruce was elected to the Senate. Twenty other African Americans were elected to the House of Representatives.

Some Southerners resented the new state governments that had been forced on them. Others disliked the Northerners who moved South to start businesses. Because they often carried their possessions in cloth suitcases called carpetbags, these newcomers were called "**carpetbaggers.**" Some carpetbaggers came to help, but many came to take advantage of the South's ruined condition. Southerners who supported Reconstruction were given the insulting nickname "scalawags."

People also disliked the new taxes. Many Southerners had a hard time paying these taxes because they were trying to rebuild their farms and homes.

Reconstruction also had some failures; segregation was one of these. **Segregation** is the separation of people, usually by race. Schools, hospitals, theaters, railroad cars, even whole towns were segregated.

Right after the war, some Southern states passed **black codes.** These laws denied African American men the right to vote. It kept them from owning guns or taking certain types of jobs. The Civil Rights Act was designed to protect African Americans from these codes.

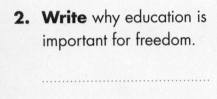

Schools were opened to help African Americans learn new skills.

2. Write why education is important for freedom.

....

....

....

....

New Amendments

Ending slavery was one of the first steps in Reconstruction—and the most important. The Emancipation Proclamation had not ended all slavery. The Republicans in Congress now wanted slavery to be illegal everywhere in the United States.

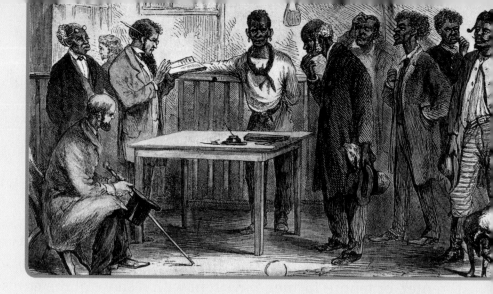

African American men voting

Congress passed the Thirteenth Amendment on January 31, 1865. It abolished slavery. The Fourteenth Amendment was approved in July 1868. It guaranteed equality under the law for all citizens—and it gave Congress the power to enforce this guarantee. It also ruled that important Confederate leaders could not be elected to political office.

The Fifteenth Amendment, passed by Congress in 1869 and approved by the states in February 1870, gave all male citizens the right to vote without regard to race. It was a big step forward for formerly enslaved African Americans.

Before being allowed back into the Union, former Confederate states had to accept all three amendments. Eventually, all did. By July 15, 1870, all the former Confederate states had been allowed back into the Union.

3. ◉ **Summarize** what each of the three new amendments did.

13th Amendment	14th Amendment	15th Amendment
ended slavery.		

After Reconstruction

After Reconstruction, the South remained the poorest section of the country. Rebuilding was slow. Poverty was widespread. African Americans lost much of the political power they had gained during Reconstruction. Northern whites began to lose interest in the problems of the South.

Many African Americans and poor whites in the South became trapped in a system called sharecropping. **Sharecropping** is a system in which someone who owns land lets someone else "rent" the land to farm it. The renter, or tenant farmer, pays rent with a share of the crops he or she raises. The renter then uses the rest of the crops to feed the family or sell for income.

In the South, sharecropping was run in a way that often kept people in debt. Landowners would charge high interest on money tenant farmers borrowed for seeds and tools. It was often impossible to pay off the debt. It was rare for sharecroppers to save enough to buy their own land.

4. Write what a sharecropper might say about sharecropping.

....

....

....

....

....

Negative Reaction

During Reconstruction, some white Southerners objected to rights for African Americans. A few formed a group called the Ku Klux Klan. This group used terror to restore white control. They burned African American schools and homes. They attacked African Americans who tried to vote. Congress passed laws against the group and its activities. However, the Klan continued its activity for years.

In 1877, the federal government withdrew the last federal troops from the South. White Southern Democrats regained power in state governments. They passed new laws known as Jim Crow laws that reinforced segregation.

Other laws kept African Americans from voting. Some states charged a poll tax, or payment, to vote. Many African Americans couldn't afford the poll tax.

Many formerly enslaved people now worked as sharecroppers.

Some states required African Americans to take a reading test before they could vote. Under slavery, many had not been allowed to learn to read or write, and so they failed the test.

A "grandfather clause" was added to some state constitutions. It said that men could vote only if their father or grandfather had voted before 1867. This "grandfather clause" kept most African Americans from voting, because they had not gained the right to vote until 1870. It would be a long time before most African Americans enjoyed the civil rights they should have as citizens.

Got it?

5. ◉ **Sequence Place** these events in the correct sequence on the timeline: 13th, 14th, and 15th Amendments, Civil Rights Act, first Reconstruction Act.

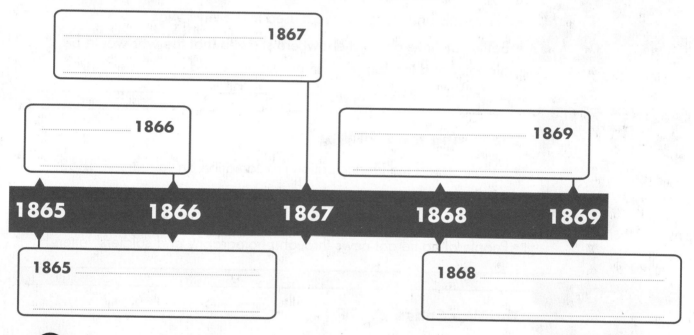

6. As a result of the war, you are now freed from slavery. In a letter **my Story Ideas** to a friend, **write** about how things have changed for you because of the war.

....

....

● **Stop!** I need help with ....

❚❚ **Wait!** I have a question about ....

▶ **Go!** Now I know ....

Study Guide

Lesson 1

Struggles Over Slavery

- The North and South disagreed sharply over the spread of slavery.
- The Underground Railroad helped enslaved people to escape from the South.
- Lincoln was elected President and Southern states seceded.

Lesson 2

The War Begins

- The Civil War began when the South attacked Fort Sumter.
- New tools and weapons were used in the Civil War.
- Battles at Antietam and elsewhere showed that the war would be bloodier and last longer than people expected.

Lesson 3

Life During the Civil War

- Lincoln issued the Emancipation Proclamation on January 1, 1863.
- African Americans, Native Americans, immigrants, and women contributed to the war in many ways.
- People at home got news through photographs and soldiers' letters.

Lesson 4

The War Ends

- Union victories at Gettysburg and Vicksburg were turning points.
- The costs of war grew with total war in the South.
- On April 9, 1865, Lee surrendered, and five days later Lincoln was assassinated.

Lesson 5

Reconstruction

- National leaders made different plans for Reconstruction.
- Congress passed laws to support newly freed African Americans.
- New Southern "Jim Crow" laws denied African Americans many rights.

Chapter 9
Review and Assessment

Lesson 1

Struggles Over Slavery

1. How did the economies of the North and the South differ?

....

....

....

2. **Write** a sentence explaining the following:

a. Why people were concerned about new states coming into the Union

....

....

....

b. How the Missouri Compromise addressed this concern

....

....

3. What was the Underground Railroad?

....

....

4. What event led to Southern states seceding?

....

....

Lesson 2

The War Begins

5. How did the Civil War start?

....

....

6. What was the goal of the Anaconda Plan?

....

7. ◉ **Sequence** Use the numbers 1, 2, 3 to arrange the following events in time order.

_____ The First Battle of Bull Run

_____ The Battle of Antietam

_____ Southern states secede

Lesson 3

Life During the Civil War

8. **Circle** the letters that show what the Emancipation Proclamation did.

A. freed slaves in the Confederate states

B. ended slavery in the entire country

C. allowed slavery in the border states

D. ended the Civil War

9. What happened as a result of the Northern blockade of Southern ports?

....

....

....

Lesson 4

The War Ends

10. Give two reasons why the Battle of Gettysburg was important.

....

....

....

11. Sherman's approach to fighting became known as total war. What is total war?

....

....

....

....

12. Complete this Venn diagram to compare and contrast Lee and Grant.

Lee   Both   Grant

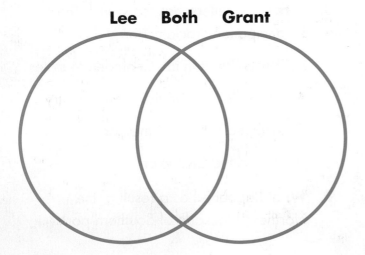

Lesson 5

Reconstruction

13. List three effects of Reconstruction on the South.

a. ....

....

b. ....

....

c. ....

14. **?** **What is worth fighting for?**

Use the question below to think more about the chapter's Essential Question.

What reason did each side have for going to war?

....

....

....

....

....

Go online to write and illustrate your own **myStory Book** using the **myStory Ideas** from this chapter.

 my Story Book

What is worth fighting for?

After the Civil War, Americans counted their losses, including those who died in the war, the property destroyed, and the money it had cost. Yet for many Americans fighting for what they believed in was worth the cost.

Think about the challenges you face in doing the right thing. **Write** about how you know when something good is worth standing up for.

....

....

....

....

Not all fighting is done with weapons. Hard work and good deeds are other ways to fight. **Create** a poster that shares your opinion of something worth fighting for.

While you're online, check out the **myStory Current Events** area where you can create your own book on a topic that's in the news.

The Declaration of Independence

In Congress, July 4, 1776
The Unanimous Declaration of the Thirteen
United States of America

The first part of the Declaration of Independence is called the Preamble. A preamble is an introduction, or the part that comes before the main message. The Preamble states why the Declaration was written.

The second paragraph lists the basic rights that all people should have. The founders called these **unalienable** rights, meaning that these rights cannot be taken or given away. If a government cannot protect these rights, the people must change the government or create a new one.

1. According to the Declaration, what are three "unalienable rights?" **Circle** these words in the text.

The third paragraph introduces the List of Grievances. Each part of this list begins with the words, "He has …." These words refer to King George III's actions in the colonies. To prove that the king had abused his power over the colonies, this list of 27 complaints described how the British government and the king had treated the colonists.

When in the Course of human events it becomes necessary for one people to dissolve the political bands which have connected them with another, and to assume among the powers of the earth, the separate and equal station to which the Laws of nature and of nature's God entitle them, a decent respect to the opinions of mankind requires that they should declare the causes which impel them to the separation.

We hold these truths to be self-evident, that all men are created equal, that they are endowed by their Creator with certain unalienable Rights, that among these are Life, Liberty and the Pursuit of Happiness. That to secure these rights, Governments are instituted among Men, deriving their just powers from the consent of the governed; That whenever any Form of Government becomes destructive of these ends it is the Right of the People to alter or to abolish it, and to institute new Government, laying its foundation on such principles and organizing its powers in such form, as to them shall seem most likely to effect their Safety and Happiness. Prudence, indeed, will dictate that Governments long established should not be changed for light and transient causes; and accordingly all experience hath shown, that mankind are more disposed to suffer, while evils are sufferable, than to right themselves by abolishing the forms to which they are accustomed. But when a long train of abuses and usurpations, pursuing invariably the same Object evinces a design to reduce them under absolute Despotism, it is their right, it is their duty, to throw off such Government, and to provide new Guards for their future security.

Such has been the patient sufferance of these Colonies; and such is now the necessity which constrains them to alter their former Systems of Government. The history of the present King of Great Britain is a history of repeated injuries and usurpations, all having in direct object the establishment of an absolute Tyranny over these States. To prove this, let Facts be submitted to a candid world.

He has refused his Assent to Laws, the most wholesome and necessary for the public good.

He has forbidden his Governors to pass Laws of immediate and pressing importance, unless suspended in their operation till his

Assent should be obtained; and when so suspended, he has utterly neglected to attend to them.

He has refused to pass other Laws for the accommodation of large districts of people, unless those people would relinquish the right of Representation in the Legislature, a right inestimable to them and formidable to tyrants only.

He has called together legislative bodies at places unusual, uncomfortable, and distant from the depository of their Public Records, for the sole purpose of fatiguing them into compliance with his measures.

He has dissolved Representative Houses repeatedly, for opposing with manly firmness his invasions on the rights of the people.

He has refused for a long time, after such dissolutions, to cause others to be elected; whereby the Legislative powers, incapable of Annihilation, have returned to the People at large for their exercise; the State remaining in the mean time exposed to all the dangers of invasions from without, and convulsions within.

He has endeavored to prevent the population of these States; for that purpose obstructing the Laws for Naturalization of Foreigners; refusing to pass others to encourage their migration hither, and raising the conditions of new Appropriations of Lands.

He has obstructed the Administration of Justice, by refusing his Assent to Laws for establishing Judiciary powers.

He has made Judges dependent on his Will alone for the tenure of their offices, and the amount and payment of their salaries.

He has erected a multitude of New Offices, and sent hither swarms of Officers to harass our people and eat out their substance.

He has kept among us in time of peace, Standing Armies, without the Consent of our legislatures.

He has affected to render the Military independent of, and superior to, the Civil Power.

He has combined with others to subject us to a jurisdiction foreign to our constitutions, and unacknowledged by our laws; giving his Assent to their Acts of pretended Legislation:

For quartering large bodies of armed troops among us;

For protecting them, by a mock Trial, from punishment for any Murders which they should commit on the Inhabitants of these States;

In the List of Grievances the colonists complain that they have no say in choosing the laws that govern them. They say that King George III is not concerned about their safety and happiness. They list the times when the king denied them the right to representation. The colonists also state that the king has interfered with judges, with the court system, and with foreigners who want to become citizens.

2. There are many words in the Declaration that may be unfamiliar to you. **Circle** three words you do not know. Look the words up in the dictionary. **Write** one word and its meaning on the lines below.

....

....

....

....

....

....

....

....

This page continues the colonists' long List of Grievances.

3. In your own words, briefly sum up three grievances.

....

....

....

4. Match each word from the Declaration with its meaning. Use a dictionary if you need help with a word.

abolishing	tried to achieve
plundered	changing
suspending	doing away with
altering	stopping for a time
endeavored	robbed

Statement of Independence

After listing their many grievances, the signers begin their statement of independence. Because the king has refused to correct the problems, he is an unfair ruler. Therefore, he is not fit to rule the free people of America.

For cutting off our Trade with all parts of the world;

For imposing Taxes on us without our Consent;

For depriving us, in many cases, of the benefits of Trial by Jury;

For transporting us beyond Seas to be tried for pretended offenses;

For abolishing the free System of English Laws in a neighboring Province, establishing therein an Arbitrary government, and enlarging its Boundaries so as to render it at once an example and fit instrument for introducing the same absolute rule into these Colonies;

For taking away our Charters, abolishing our most valuable Laws, and altering fundamentally the Forms of our Governments;

For suspending our own Legislatures, and declaring themselves invested with Power to legislate for us in all cases whatsoever.

He has abdicated Government here, by declaring us out of his Protection, and waging War against us.

He has plundered our seas, ravaged our Coasts, burned our towns, and destroyed the lives of our people.

He is at this time transporting large Armies of foreign mercenaries to complete the works of death, desolation and tyranny, already begun with circumstances of Cruelty and perfidy scarcely paralleled in the most barbarous ages, and totally unworthy the Head of a civilized nation.

He has constrained our fellow Citizens taken Captive on the high Seas to bear Arms against their Country, to become the executioners of their friends and Brethren, or to fall themselves by their Hands.

He has excited domestic insurrections amongst us, and has endeavored to bring on the inhabitants of our frontiers the merciless Indian Savages whose known rule of warfare, is an undistinguished destruction of all ages, sexes, and conditions.

In every stage of these Oppressions We have Petitioned for Redress in the most humble terms. Our repeated Petitions have been answered only by repeated injury. A Prince, whose character is thus marked by every act which may define a Tyrant, is unfit to be the ruler of a free People.

Nor have We been wanting in attentions to our British brethren. We have warned them from time to time of attempts by their legislature to extend an unwarrantable jurisdiction over us. We have reminded them of the circumstances of our emigration and settlement here. We have appealed to their native justice and magnanimity, and we have conjured them by the ties of our common kindred to disavow these usurpations, which, would inevitably interrupt our connections and correspondence. They too have been deaf to the voice of justice and of consanguinity. We must, therefore, acquiesce in the necessity, which denounces our Separation, and hold them, as we hold the rest of mankind, Enemies in War, in Peace Friends.

We, therefore, the Representatives of the United States of America, in General Congress, Assembled, appealing to the Supreme Judge of the world for the rectitude of our intentions, do, in the Name, and by the Authority of the good People of these Colonies, solemnly publish and declare, That these United Colonies are, and of right ought to be Free and Independent States; that they are Absolved from all Allegiance to the British Crown, and that all political connection between them and the State of Great Britain, is and ought to be totally dissolved, and that as Free and Independent States, they have full Power to levy War, conclude Peace, contract Alliances, establish Commerce, and to do all other Acts and Things which Independent States may of right do. And for the support of this Declaration, with a firm reliance on the protection of Divine Providence, we mutually pledge to each other our Lives, our Fortunes, and our sacred Honor.

New Hampshire:
Josiah Bartlett
William Whipple
Matthew Thornton

Massachusetts Bay:
John Hancock
Samuel Adams
John Adams
Robert Treat Paine
Elbridge Gerry

Rhode Island:
Stephan Hopkins
William Ellery

Connecticut:
Roger Sherman
Samuel Huntington
William Williams
  Oliver Wolcott

New York:
William Floyd
Philip Livingston
Francis Lewis
Lewis Morris

New Jersey:
Richard Stockton
John Witherspoon
Francis Hopkinson
John Hart
Abraham Clark

Delaware:
Caesar Rodney
George Read
Thomas M'Kean

Maryland:
Samuel Chase
William Paca
Thomas Stone
Charles Carroll of
  Carrollton

Virginia:
George Wythe
Richard Henry Lee
Thomas Jefferson
Benjamin Harrison
Thomas Nelson, Jr.
Francis Lightfoot Lee
Carter Braxton

Pennsylvania:
Robert Morris
Benjamin Rush
Benjamin Franklin
John Morton
George Clymer
James Smith
George Taylor
James Wilson
George Ross

North Carolina:
William Hooper
Joseph Hewes
John Penn

South Carolina:
Edward Rutledge
Thomas Heyward, Jr.
Thomas Lynch, Jr.
Arthur Middleton

Georgia:
Button Gwinnett
Lyman Hall
George Walton

In this paragraph, the signers point out that they have asked the British people for help many times. The colonists hoped the British would listen to them because they have so much in common. The British people, however, paid no attention to their demand for justice. This is another reason for why the colonies must break away from Great Britain.

In the last paragraph, the members of the Continental Congress declare that the thirteen colonies are no longer colonies. They are now a free nation with no ties to Great Britain. The United States now has all the powers of other independent countries.

5. List three powers that the signers claim the new nation now has.

....

....

....

....

....

6. The signers promised to support the Declaration of Independence and each other with their lives, their fortunes, and their honor. On a separate sheet of paper, tell what you think this means. Then explain why it was a brave thing to do.

United States Constitution

This **Preamble** gives the reasons for writing and having a Constitution. The Constitution will form a stronger and more united nation. It will lead to peace, justice, and liberty and will defend American citizens. Finally, it will improve the lives of people.

Section 1. Congress
The legislative branch of government makes the country's laws. Called the Congress, it has two parts, or houses: the House of Representatives and the Senate.

Section 2. The House of Representatives
Members of the House of Representatives are elected every two years. Representatives must be 25 years old and U.S. citizens. They must also live in the states that elect them.

The number of Representatives for each state is based on the population, or number of people who live there.

1. Why do some states have more Representatives in Congress than other states?

....

....

....

....

Over the years, the Constitution has been altered, or changed. These altered parts are shown here in crossed out type.

PREAMBLE

We the People of the United States, in Order to form a more perfect Union, establish Justice, insure domestic Tranquility, provide for the common defence, promote the general Welfare, and secure the Blessings of Liberty to ourselves and our Posterity, do ordain and establish this Constitution for the United States of America.

ARTICLE I
The Legislative Branch

Section 1.
All legislative Powers herein granted shall be vested in a Congress of the United States, which shall consist of a Senate and House of Representatives.

Section 2.
1. The House of Representatives shall be composed of Members chosen every second Year by the People of the several States, and the Electors in each State shall have the Qualifications requisite for Electors of the most numerous Branch of the State Legislature.
2. No Person shall be a Representative who shall not have attained to the age of twenty-five Years, and been seven Years a Citizen of the United States, and who shall not, when elected, be an Inhabitant of that State in which he shall be chosen.
3. ~~Representatives and direct Taxes shall be apportioned among the several States which may be included within this Union, according to their respective Numbers, which shall be determined by adding to the whole Number of free Persons, including those bound to Service for a Term of Years and excluding Indians not taxed, three fifths of all other Persons.~~ The actual Enumeration shall be made within three Years after the first Meeting of the Congress of the United States, and within every subsequent Term of ten Years, in such Manner as they shall by Law direct. The Number of Representatives shall not exceed one for every thirty Thousand, but each State shall have at Least one Representative; and, until such enumeration shall be made, the State of New Hampshire shall be entitled to choose three, Massachusetts eight, Rhode Island and Providence Plantations one, Connecticut five, New York six, New Jersey four, Pennsylvania eight, Delaware one, Maryland six, Virginia ten, North Carolina five, South Carolina five, and Georgia three.

4. When vacancies happen in the Representation from any State, the Executive Authority thereof shall issue Writs of Election to fill such Vacancies.

5. The House of Representatives shall choose their Speaker and other Officers; and shall have the sole Power of Impeachment.

Section 3.

1. The Senate of the United States shall be composed of two Senators from each State ~~chosen by the Legislature~~ thereof for six Years; and each Senator shall have one Vote.

2. Immediately after they shall be assembled in Consequences of the first Election, they shall be divided, as equally as may be, into three Classes. The Seats of the Senators of the first Class shall be vacated at the Expiration of the second Year; of the second Class, at the Expiration of the fourth Year; and of the third Class, at the Expiration of the sixth Year; so that one-third may be chosen every second Year; ~~and if Vacancies happen by Resignation, or otherwise, during the Recess of the Legislature of any State, the Executive thereof may make temporary Appointments until the next Meeting of the Legislature, which shall then fill such Vacancies.~~

3. No Person shall be a Senator who shall not have attained to the Age of thirty Years, and been nine Years a Citizen of the United States, and who shall not, when elected, be an Inhabitant of that State for which he shall be chosen.

4. The Vice President of the United States shall be President of the Senate but shall have no Vote, unless they be equally divided.

5. The Senate shall choose their other Officers, and also a President pro tempore, in the Absence of the Vice President, or when he shall exercise the Office of President of the United States.

6. The Senate shall have the sole Power to try all Impeachments. When sitting for that Purpose, they shall be on Oath or Affirmation. When the President of the United States is tried, the Chief Justice shall preside: And no Person shall be convicted without the Concurrence of two thirds of the Members present.

7. Judgment in Cases of Impeachment shall not extend further than to removal from Office, and disqualification to hold and enjoy any Office of honor, Trust, or Profit under the United States: but the Party convicted shall nevertheless be liable and subject to Indictment, Trial, Judgment and Punishment, according to Law.

A state governor calls a special election to fill an empty seat in the House of Representatives.

Members of the House of Representatives choose their own leaders. They also have the power to impeach, or accuse, government officials of crimes.

Section 3. Senate
Each state has two Senators. A Senator serves a six-year term.

At first, each state legislature elected its two Senators. The Seventeenth Amendment changed that. Today the voters of each state elect their Senators.

Senators must be 30 years old and U.S. citizens. They must also live in the states they represent.

2. How is the length of a Senator's term different from a Representative's term?

....

....

The Vice President is the officer in charge of the Senate but only votes to break a tie. When the Vice President is absent, a temporary leader (President Pro Tempore) leads the Senate.

The Senate holds impeachment trials. When the President is impeached, the Chief Justice of the Supreme Court is the judge. A two-thirds vote is needed to convict. Once convicted, an official can be removed from office. Other courts of law can impose other punishments.

SECTION 4. Elections and Meetings of Congress

The state legislatures determine the times, places, and method of holding elections for senators and representatives.

SECTION 5. Rules for Congress

The Senate and House of Representatives judge the fairness of the elections and the qualifications of its own members. At least half of the members must be present to do business. Each house may determine the rules of its proceedings and punish its member for disorderly behavior. Each house of Congress shall keep a record of its proceedings, and from time to time publish the record.

3. Why is it important for Congress to publish a record of what they do?

....

....

....

....

....

SECTION 6. Rights and Restrictions of Members of Congress

The senators and representatives shall receive payment for their services to be paid out of the Treasury of the United States. Members of Congress cannot be arrested during their attendance at the session of Congress, except for a very serious crime, and they cannot be arrested for anything they say in Congress. No person can have a government job while serving as a member of Congress.

Section 4.

1. The Times, Places and Manner of holding Elections for Senators and Representatives, shall be prescribed in each State by the Legislature thereof; but the Congress may at any time by law make or alter such Regulations, except as to the Places of choosing Senators.

2. The Congress shall assemble at least once in every Year, and such Meeting shall be on the first Monday in December, unless they shall by Law appoint a different Day.

Section 5.

1. Each House shall be the Judge of the Elections, Returns and Qualifications of its own Members, and a Majority of each shall constitute a Quorum to do Business; but a smaller Number may adjourn from day to day, and may be authorized to compel the Attendance of absent Members, in such Manner, and under such Penalties, as each House may provide.

2. Each House may determine the Rules of its Proceedings, punish its Members for disorderly Behavior, and, with the Concurrence of two thirds, expel a Member.

3. Each House shall keep a Journal of its Proceedings, and from time to time publish the same, excepting such Parts as may in their Judgment require Secrecy; and the Yeas and Nays of the Members of either House on any question shall, at the Desire of one fifth of those Present, be entered on the Journal.

4. Neither House, during the Session of Congress, shall, without the Consent of the other, adjourn for more than three days, nor to any other Place than that in which the two Houses shall be sitting.

Section 6.

1. The Senators and Representatives shall receive a Compensation for their Services, to be ascertained by Law, and paid out of the Treasury of the United States. They shall in all Cases, except Treason, Felony, and Breach of the Peace, be privileged from Arrest during their Attendance at the Session of their respective Houses, and in going to and returning from the same; and for any Speech or Debate in either House, they shall not be questioned in any other Place.

2. No Senator or Representative shall, during the Time for which he was elected, be appointed to any civil Office under the Authority of the United States, which shall have been created, or the Emoluments whereof shall have been increased during such time; and no Person holding any Office under the United States, shall be a Member of either House during his Continuance in Office.

Section 7.

1. All Bills for raising Revenue shall originate in the House of Representatives; but the Senate may propose or concur with amendments as on other Bills.

2. Every Bill which shall have passed the House of Representatives and the Senate, shall, before it become a law, be presented to the President of the United States: If he approve, he shall sign it, but if not he shall return it, with his Objections to that House in which it shall have originated, who shall enter the Objections at large on their Journal, and proceed to reconsider it. If after such Reconsideration two thirds of the House shall agree to pass the Bill, it shall be sent, together with the Objections, to the other House, by which it shall likewise be reconsidered, and if approved by two thirds of that House, it shall become a Law. But in all such Cases the Votes of both Houses shall be determined by Yeas and Nays, and the Names of the Persons voting for and against the Bill shall be entered on the Journal of each House respectively. If any Bill shall not be returned by the President within ten Days (Sunday excepted) after it shall have been presented to him, the Same shall be a law, in like Manner as if he had signed it, unless the Congress by their Adjournment, prevent its Return, in which Case it shall not be a Law.

3. Every Order, Resolution, or Vote to which the Concurrence of the Senate and House of Representatives may be necessary (except on a question of adjournment) shall be presented to the President of the United States; and before the Same shall take Effect, shall be approved by him, or, being disapproved by him, shall be repassed by two thirds of the Senate and House of Representatives, according to the Rules and Limitations prescribed in the Case of a Bill.

Section 8.

The Congress shall have Power

1. To lay and collect Taxes, Duties, Imposts and Excises to pay the Debts and provide for the common Defence and general Welfare of the United States; but all Duties, Imposts and Excises, shall be uniform throughout the United States;

2. To borrow Money on the credit of the United States;

3. To regulate Commerce with foreign Nations, and among the several States, and with the Indian Tribes;

4. To establish an uniform Rule of Naturalization, and uniform Laws on the subject of Bankruptcies throughout the United States;

SECTION 7. How Laws are Made

All bills for raising money shall begin in the House of Representatives. The Senate may suggest or agree with amendments to these tax bills, as with other bills.

Every bill which has passed the House of Representatives and the Senate must be presented to the President of the United States before it becomes a law. If the President approves of the bill the President shall sign it. If the President does not approve, then the bill may be vetoed. The President then sends it back to the house in which it began, with an explanation of the objections. That house writes the objections on their record, and begins to reconsider it. If two-thirds of each house agrees to pass the bill, it shall become a law. If any bill is neither signed nor vetoed by the President within ten days, (except for Sundays) after it has been sent to the President, the bill shall be a law. If Congress adjourns before ten days have passed, the bill does not become a law.

SECTION 8. Powers of Congress

Among the powers of Congress listed in Section 8 are:

- establish and collect taxes on imported and exported goods and on goods sold within the country. Congress also shall pay the debts and provide for the defense and general welfare of the United States. All federal taxes shall be the same throughout the United States.

- borrow money on the credit of the United States;

- make laws about trade with other countries, among the states, and with the American Indian tribes;

- establish one procedure by which a person from another country can become a legal citizen of the United States;

- protect the works of scientists, artists, authors, and inventors;

- create federal courts lower than the Supreme Court;

- declare war;
- establish and support an army and navy;
- organize and train a National Guard and call them up in times of emergency;
- govern the capital and military sites of the United States; and
- make all laws necessary to carry out the powers of Congress.

4. The last clause of Section 8 is called "the elastic clause" because it stretches the power of Congress. Why do you think it was added to the Constitution?

....

....

....

....

....

....

5. To coin Money, regulate the Value thereof, and of foreign Coin, and fix the Standard of Weights and Measures;

6. To provide for the Punishment of counterfeiting the Securities and current Coin of the United States;

7. To establish Post Offices and post Roads;

8. To promote the Progress of Science and useful Arts, by securing, for limited Times to Authors and Inventors the exclusive Right to their respective Writings and Discoveries;

9. To constitute Tribunals inferior to the supreme Court;

10. To define and punish Piracies and Felonies committed on the high Seas, and Offences against the Law of nations;

11. To declare War, grant Letters of Marque and Reprisal, and make Rules concerning Captures on Land and Water;

12. To raise and support Armies; but no Appropriation of Money to that Use shall be for a longer Term than two Years;

13. To provide and maintain a Navy;

14. To make Rules for the Government and Regulation of the land and naval Forces;

15. To provide for calling forth the Militia to execute the Laws of the Union, suppress Insurrections and repel Invasions;

16. To provide for organizing, arming, and disciplining the Militia, and for governing such Part of them as may be employed in the Service of the United States, reserving to the States respectively the Appointment of the Officers, and the Authority of training the Militia according to the discipline prescribed by Congress;

17. To exercise exclusive Legislation in all Cases whatsoever, over such District (not exceeding ten Miles square) as may, by Cession of Particular States, and the Acceptance of Congress, become the Seat of the Government of the United States, and to exercise like Authority over all Places purchased by the Consent of the Legislature of the State in which the Same shall be, for the Erection of Forts, Magazines, Arsenals, Dockyards and other needful Buildings;—And

18. To make all Laws which shall be necessary and proper for carrying into Execution the foregoing Powers and all other Powers vested by this Constitution in the Government of the United States, or in any Department or Officer thereof.

Section 9.

1. The Migration or Importation of such Persons as any of the States now existing shall think proper to admit, shall not be prohibited by the Congress prior to the Year one thousand eight hundred and eight, but a Tax or duty may be imposed on such Importation, not exceeding ten dollars for each Person.

2. The Privilege of the Writ of Habeas Corpus shall not be suspended, unless when in Cases of Rebellion or Invasion the public safety may require it.

3. No Bill of Attainder or ex post facto Law shall be passed.

4. No Capitation, or other direct, Tax shall be laid, ~~unless in Proportion to the Census of Enumeration hereinbefore directed to be taken.~~

5. No Tax or Duty shall be laid on Articles exported from any State.

6. No Preference shall be given by any Regulation of Commerce or Revenue to the Ports of one State over those of another: nor shall Vessels bound to, or from, one State, be obliged to enter, clear or pay Duties in another.

7. No Money shall be drawn from the Treasury, but in Consequence of Appropriations made by Law; and a regular Statement and Account of the Receipts and Expenditures of all public Money shall be published from time to time.

8. No Title of Nobility shall be granted by the United States: And no Person holding any Office of Profit or Trust under them, shall, without the Consent of the Congress, accept of any present, Emolument, Office, or Title, of any kind whatever, from any King, Prince, or foreign State.

Section 10.

1. No State shall enter into any Treaty, Alliance, or Confederation; grant Letters of Marque and Reprisal; coin Money; emit Bills of Credit; make any Thing but gold and silver Coin a Tender in Payment of Debts; pass any Bill of Attainder, ex post facto Law, or Law impairing the Obligation of Contracts, or grant any Title of Nobility.

2. No State shall, without the Consent of the Congress, lay any Imposts or Duties on Imports or Exports, except what may be absolutely necessary for executing its inspection Laws; and the net Produce of all Duties and Imposts, laid by any State on Imports or Exports, shall be for the Use of the Treasury of the United States; and all such Laws shall be subject to the Revision and Control of the Congress.

SECTION 9: Powers Denied to Congress

Congress cannot

- stop slaves from being brought into the United States until 1808;
- arrest and jail people without charging them with a crime, except during an emergency;
- punish a person without a trial; punish a person for something that was not a crime when he or she did it;
- pass a direct tax, such as an income tax, unless it is in proportion to the population;
- tax goods sent out of a state;
- give the seaports of one state an advantage over another state's ports; let one state tax the ships of another state;
- spend money without passing a law to make it legal; spend money without keeping good records;
- give titles, such as king and queen, to anyone; allow federal workers to accept gifts or titles from foreign governments.

5. Why do you think the writers included the last clause of Section 9?

....
....
....
....
....
....

Section 10: Powers Denied to the States

After listing what Congress is not allowed to do, the Constitution tells what powers are denied to the states.

State governments do not have the power to

- make treaties with foreign countries; print money; do anything that Section 9 of the Constitution says the federal government cannot
- tax goods sent into or out of a state unless Congress agrees;
- keep armed forces or go to war; make agreements with other states or foreign governments unless Congress agrees;

6. What problems might arise if one state went to war with a foreign country?

....

....

....

....

....

Article 2 describes the executive branch.

Section 1. Office of President and Vice President

The president has power to execute, or carry out, the laws of the United States.
Electors from each state choose the President. Today, these electors are called the Electoral College and are chosen by the voters.

Before 1804, the person with the most electoral votes became President. The person with the next-highest number became Vice President. The Twelfth Amendment changed this way of electing presidents.

3. No State shall, without the Consent of Congress, lay any Duty of Tonnage, keep Troops, or Ships of War in time of Peace, enter into any Agreement or Compact with another State, or with a foreign Power, or engage in War, unless actually invaded, or in such imminent Danger as will not admit of delay.

ARTICLE II
The Executive Branch

Section 1.

1. The executive Power shall be vested in a President of the United States of America. He shall hold his Office during the Term of four Years, and, together with the Vice President, chosen for the same Term, be elected as follows:

2. Each State shall appoint, in such Manner as the Legislature thereof may direct, a Number of Electors, equal to the whole Number of Senators and Representatives to which the State may be entitled in the Congress: but no Senator or Representative, or Person holding an Office of Trust or Profit, under the United States, shall be appointed an Elector.

3. The Electors shall meet in their respective States, and vote by Ballot for two Persons, of whom one at least shall not be an Inhabitant of the same State with themselves. And they shall make a List of all the Persons voted for, and of the Number of Votes for each; which List they shall sign and certify, and transmit sealed to the Seat of the Government of the United States, directed to the President of the Senate. The President of the Senate shall, in the Presence of the Senate and House of Representatives, open all the Certificates, and the Votes shall then be counted. The Person having the greatest Number of Votes shall be the President, if such Number be a majority of the whole Number of Electors appointed; and if there be more than one who have such Majority, and have an equal Number of Votes, then, the House of Representatives shall immediately choose by Ballot one of them for President; and if no Person have a Majority, then from the five highest on the List the said House shall in like Manner choose the President. But in choosing the President, the Votes shall be taken by States, the Representatives from each State having one Vote; a quorum for this Purpose shall consist of a Member or Members from two thirds of the States, and a Majority of all the States shall be necessary to a Choice. In every Case, after

~~the Choice of the President, the Person having the greatest Number of Votes of the Electors shall be the Vice President. But if there should remain two or more who have equal Votes, the Senate shall choose from them by Ballot the Vice President.~~

4. The Congress may determine the Time of choosing the Electors, and the Day on which they shall give their Votes; which Day shall be the same throughout the United States.

5. No Person except a natural born Citizen, or a Citizen of the United States, at the time of the Adoption of this Constitution, shall be eligible to the Office of President; neither shall any person be eligible to that Office who shall not have attained to the Age of thirty-five Years, and been fourteen Years a Resident within the United States.

6. ~~In Case of the Removal of the President from Office, or of his Death, Resignation, or Inability to discharge the Powers and Duties of the said Office, the Same shall devolve on the Vice President, and the Congress may by Law provide for the Case of Removal, Death, Resignation or Inability, both of the President and Vice President, declaring what Officer shall then act as President, and such Officer shall act accordingly, until the Disability be removed, or a President shall be elected.~~

7. The President shall, at stated Times, receive for his Services, a Compensation, which shall neither be increased nor diminished during the Period for which he shall have been elected, and he shall not receive within that Period any other Emolument from the United States, or any of them.

8. Before he enter on the Execution of his Office, he shall take the following Oath or Affirmation: "I do solemnly swear (or affirm) that I will faithfully execute the Office of President of the United States, and will to the best of my Ability, preserve, protect and defend the Constitution of the United States."

Section 2.

1. The President shall be Commander in Chief of the Army and Navy of the United States, and of the Militia of the several States, when called into the actual Service of the United States; he may require the Opinion, in writing, of the principal Officer in each of the executive Departments, upon any Subject relating to the Duties of their respective Offices, and he shall have Power to Grant Reprieves and Pardons for Offences against the United States, except in Cases of Impeachment.

Congress decides when electors are chosen and when they vote for President. Americans now vote for the electors on Election Day, the Tuesday after the first Monday in November.

To become President, a person must be born in the United States and be a citizen. Presidents also have to be at least 35 years old and have lived in the United States for at least 14 years.

If a President dies or leaves office for any reason, the Vice President becomes President. If there is no Vice-President, Congress decides on the next President. (In 1967, the Twenty-fifth Amendment changed how these offices are filled.)

7. Why is it important to agree on how to replace the President or Vice President if one should suddenly die or leave office?

....

....

....

....

The President's salary cannot be raised or lowered while he is in office. The President cannot accept other money or gifts while in office.

Before taking office, the President must swear to preserve, protect, and defend the Constitution.

SECTION 2. Powers of the President
The President is in charge of the armed forces and National Guard. The President can ask for the advice and opinions of those in charge of government departments. (Today we call these advisers the President's Cabinet.) The President can pardon, or free, people convicted of federal crimes.

The President can make treaties, but two-thirds of the Senate must approve them. The President, with Senate approval, can name Supreme Court judges, ambassadors, and other important officials.

8. What is the Senate's ability to approve or reject treaties an example of?

....

....

SECTION 3. Duties of the President
From time to time, the President must talk to Congress about the condition of the nation. (Today we call this speech the State of the Union address. It is given once a year in late January.) In an emergency, the President can call on Congress to meet. The President also meets with foreign leaders, makes sure the nation's laws are carried out, and signs the orders of military officers.

SECTION 4. Removal From Office
The President, Vice-President, and other high officials can be impeached. If proved guilty, they are removed from office.

2. He shall have Power, by and with the Advice and Consent of the Senate, to make Treaties, provided two thirds of the Senators present concur; and he shall nominate, and by and with the Advice and Consent of the Senate, shall appoint Ambassadors, other public Ministers and Consuls, Judges of the supreme Court, and all other Officers of the United States, whose Appointments are not herein otherwise provided for, and which shall be established by Law: but the Congress may by Law vest the Appointment of such inferior Officers, as they think proper, in the President alone, in the Courts of Law, or in the Heads of Departments.

3. The President shall have Power to fill up all Vacancies that may happen during the Recess of the Senate, by granting Commissions which shall expire at the End of their next Session.

Section 3.

He shall from time to time give to the Congress Information of the State of the Union, and recommend to their Consideration such Measures as he shall judge necessary and expedient; he may, on extraordinary Occasions, convene both Houses, or either of them, and in Case of Disagreement between them, with Respect to the Time of Adjournment, he may adjourn them to such Time as he shall think proper; he shall receive Ambassadors and other public Ministers; he shall take Care that the Laws be faithfully executed, and shall Commission all the Officers of the United States.

Section 4.

The President, Vice President and all Civil Officers of the United States, shall be removed from Office on Impeachment for and Conviction of, Treason, Bribery, or other high Crimes and Misdemeanors.

ARTICLE III
The Judicial Branch

Section 1.

The judicial Power of the United States, shall be vested in one supreme Court, and in such inferior Courts as the Congress may from time to time ordain and establish. The Judges, both of the supreme and inferior Courts, shall hold their Offices during good Behavior, and shall, at stated Times, receive for their Services, a Compensation, which shall not be diminished during their Continuance in Office.

Section 2.

1. The judicial Power shall extend to all Cases, in Law and Equity, arising under this Constitution, the Laws of the United States, and Treaties made, or which shall be made, under their Authority;— to all Cases affecting Ambassadors, other public ministers, and Consuls;— to all Cases of Admiralty and maritime Jurisdiction;— to Controversies to which the United States shall be a Party;— to Controversies between two or more States;— between a State and Citizens of another State;— between Citizens of different States;— between Citizens of the same State claiming Lands under Grants of different States, and between a State, or the Citizens thereof, and foreign States, Citizens, or Subjects.

2. In all Cases affecting Ambassadors, other public Ministers and Consuls, and those in which a State shall be a Party, the supreme Court shall have original Jurisdiction. In all the other Cases before mentioned, the supreme Court shall have appellate Jurisdiction, both as to Law and Fact, with such Exceptions, and under such Regulations as the Congress shall make.

3. The trial of all Crimes, except in Cases of Impeachment, shall be by Jury; and such Trial shall be held in the State where the said Crimes shall have been committed; but when not committed within any State, the Trial shall be at such Place or Places as the Congress may by Law have directed.

SECTION 3. The Crime of Treason

Treason is waging war against the United States or helping its enemies. To be found guilty of treason, a person must confess to the crime; or, two people must have seen the crime committed.

10. Name the three branches of the federal government described in Articles 1, 2, and 3.

....

....

....

Congress decides the punishment for a traitor. The traitor's family cannot also be punished for the crime if they are innocent.

Article 4 deals with relationships between the states.

SECTION 1. Recognition by Each State

Each state must respect the laws and court decisions of the other states.

SECTION 2. Rights of Citizens in Other States

Citizens keep all their rights when visiting other states.

A person charged with a crime who flees to another state must be returned to the state in which the crime took place.

A slave who escapes to another state must be returned to his or her owner. (The Thirteenth Amendment outlawed slavery.)

SECTION 3. New States

Congress may let new states join the United States. New states cannot be formed from the land of existing states unless Congress approves.

Congress has the power to make laws to govern territories of the United States.

Section 3.

1. Treason against the United States shall consist only in levying War against them, or in adhering to their Enemies, giving them Aid and Comfort. No Person shall be convicted of Treason unless on the Testimony of two Witnesses to the same overt Act, or on Confession in open Court.
2. The Congress shall have Power to declare the Punishment of Treason, but no Attainder of Treason shall work Corruption of Blood, or Forfeiture except during the Life of the Person attainted.

ARTICLE IV
Relations Among the States

Section 1.

Full Faith and Credit shall be given in each State to the public Acts, Records, and judicial Proceedings of every other State. And the Congress may by general Laws prescribe the Manner in which such Acts, Records and Proceedings shall be proved, and the Effect thereof.

Section 2.

1. The Citizens of each State shall be entitled to all Privileges and Immunities of Citizens in the several States.
2. A Person charged in any State with Treason, Felony, or other Crime, who shall flee from justice, and be found in another State, shall on Demand of the executive Authority of the State from which he fled, be delivered up, to be removed to the State having Jurisdiction of the Crime.
3. No Person held to Service or Labor in one State, under the Laws thereof, escaping into another, shall, in Consequence of any Law or Regulation therein, be discharged from Service or Labor, but shall be delivered up on Claim of the Party to whom such Service or Labor may be due.

Section 3.

1. New States may be admitted by the Congress into this Union; but no new State shall be formed or erected within the Jurisdiction of any other State; nor any State be formed by the Junction of two or more States, or Parts of States, without the Consent of the Legislatures of the States concerned as well as of the Congress.

2. The Congress shall have Power to dispose of and make all needful Rules and Regulations respecting the Territory or other Property belonging to the United States; and nothing in this Constitution shall be so construed as to Prejudice any Claims of the United States, or of any particular State.

Section 4.

The United States shall guarantee to every State in this Union a Republican Form of Government, and shall protect each of them against Invasion; and on Application of the Legislature, or of the Executive (when the Legislature cannot be convened) against domestic Violence.

ARTICLE V
Amending the Constitution

The Congress, whenever two thirds of both Houses shall deem it necessary, shall propose Amendments to this Constitution, or, on the Application of the Legislatures of two thirds of the several States, shall call a Convention for proposing Amendments, which, in either Case, shall be valid to all Intents and Purposes, as Part of this Constitution, when ratified by the Legislatures of three fourths of the several States, or by Conventions in three fourths thereof, as the one or the other Mode of Ratification may be proposed by the Congress; Provided that no Amendment which may be made prior to the Year One thousand eight hundred and eight shall in any Manner affect the first and fourth Clauses in the Ninth section of the first Article; and that no State, without its Consent, shall be deprived of its equal Suffrage in the Senate.

ARTICLE VI
Debts, Federal Supremacy, Oaths of Office

Section 1.

All Debts contracted and Engagements entered into, before the Adoption of this Constitution, shall be as valid against the United States under this Constitution, as under the Confederation.

Section 2.

This Constitution, and the Laws of the United States which shall be made in Pursuance thereof; and all Treaties made, or which shall be made, under the Authority of the United States, shall be the supreme Law of the Land; and the Judges in every State shall be bound thereby, anything in the constitution or Laws of any State to the Contrary notwithstanding.

12. "The power under the Constitution will always be in the people," wrote George Washington in 1787. Explain what you think he meant.

....

....

....

....

....

....

....

Section 3.

The Senators and Representatives before mentioned, and the Members of the several State legislatures, and all executive and judicial Officers, both of the United States and of the several States, shall be bound by Oath or Affirmation, to support this Constitution; but no religious Test shall ever be required as a Qualification to any Office or public Trust under the United States.

ARTICLE VII
Ratifying the Constitution

The ratification of the Conventions of nine States, shall be sufficient for the Establishment of this Constitution between the States so ratifying the same.

Done in Convention by the Unanimous Consent of the States present the Seventeenth Day of September in the Year of our Lord one thousand seven hundred and Eighty-seven and of the Independence of the United States of America the twelfth. In witness whereof We have hereunto subscribed our Names.

Attest:
William Jackson,
  Secretary
George Washington,
  President and Deputy
  from Virginia

New Hampshire
John Langdon
Nicholas Gilman

Massachusetts
Nathaniel Gorham
Rufus King

Connecticut
William Samuel
  Johnson
Roger Sherman

New York
Alexander Hamilton

New Jersey
William Livingston
David Brearley
William Paterson
Jonathan Dayton

Pennsylvania
Benjamin Franklin
Thomas Mifflin
Robert Morris
George Clymer
Thomas FitzSimons
Jared Ingersoll
James Wilson
Gouverneur Morris

Delaware
George Read
Gunning Bedford, Jr.
John Dickinson
Richard Bassett
Jacob Broom

Maryland
James McHenry
Dan of St. Thomas
  Jennifer
Daniel Carroll

Virginia
John Blair
James Madison, Jr.

North Carolina
William Blount
Richard Dobbs Spaight
Hugh Williamson

South Carolina
John Rutledge
Charles
  Cotesworth Pinckney
Charles Pinckney
Pierce Butler

Georgia
William Few Abraham
  Baldwin

AMENDMENTS

Amendment 1

Congress shall make no law respecting an establishment of religion, or prohibiting the free exercise thereof, or abridging the freedom of speech, or of the press; or the right of the people peaceably to assemble, and to petition the Government for a redress of grievances.

Amendment 2

A well-regulated Militia being necessary to the security of a free State, the right of the people to keep and bear Arms, shall not be infringed.

Amendment 3

No Soldier shall, in time of peace be quartered in any house, without the consent of the Owner, nor, in time of war, but in a manner to be prescribed by law.

Amendment 4

The right of the people to be secure in their persons, houses, papers, and effects, against unreasonable searches and seizures, shall not be violated, and no Warrants shall issue, but upon probable cause, supported by Oath or affirmation, and particularly describing the place to be searched, and the persons or things to be seized.

Amendment 5

No person shall be held to answer for a capital, or otherwise infamous crime, unless on a presentment or indictment of a Grand Jury, except in cases arising in the land or naval forces, or in the Militia, when in actual service in time of War, or public danger; nor shall any person be subject for the same offence to be twice put in jeopardy of life or limb; nor shall be compelled in any criminal case to be a witness against himself, nor be deprived of life, liberty, or property, without due process of law; nor shall private property be taken for public use, without just compensation.

The first ten amendments to the Constitution are called the Bill of Rights.

First Amendment—1791
Freedom of Religion and Speech
Congress cannot set up an official religion or stop people from practicing a religion. Congress cannot stop people or newspapers from saying what they want. People can gather peacefully to complain to the government.

Second Amendment—1791
Right to Have Firearms
People have the right to own and carry guns.

Third Amendment—1791
Right Not to House Soldiers
During peacetime, citizens do not have to house soldiers.

Fourth Amendment—1791
Search and Arrest Warrant
People or homes cannot be searched without reason. A search warrant is needed to search a house.

Fifth Amendment—1791
Rights of People Accused of Crimes
Only a grand jury can accuse people of a serious crime. No one can be tried twice for the same crime if found not guilty. People cannot be forced to testify against themselves.

13. Write the amendment number that protects each right.

_____ to speak freely

_____ to be protected against unreasonable searches.

_____ to not be put on trial twice for the same crime

Sixth Amendment—1791
Right to a Jury Trial
People have the right to a fast trial by a jury and to hear the charges and evidence against them. They also have the right to a lawyer and to call witnesses in their own defense.

Seventh Amendment—1791
Right to a Jury Trial in a Civil Case
In a civil, or noncriminal case, a person also has the right to a trial by jury.

Eighth Amendment—1791
Protection from Unfair Punishment
A person accused of a crime cannot be forced to pay a very high bail. A person convicted of a crime cannot be asked to pay an unfairly high fine or be punished in a cruel or unusual way.

Ninth Amendment—1791
Other Rights
People have other rights that are not specifically mentioned in the Constitution.

Tenth Amendment—1791
Powers of the States and the People
Some powers are not given to the federal government or denied to states. These rights belong to the states or to the people.

Eleventh Amendment—1795
Limits on Rights to Sue States
People from another state or foreign country cannot sue a state.

Amendment 6
In all criminal prosecutions, the accused shall enjoy the right to a speedy and public trial, by an impartial jury of the State and district wherein the crime shall have been committed, which district shall have been previously ascertained by law, and to be informed of the nature and cause of the accusation; to be confronted with the witnesses against him; to have compulsory process for obtaining witnesses in his favor, and to have the Assistance of Counsel for his defence.

Amendment 7
In Suits at common law, where the value in controversy shall exceed twenty dollars, the right of trial by jury shall be preserved, and no fact tried by a jury, shall be otherwise re-examined in any Court of the United States, than according to the rules of the common law.

Amendment 8
Excessive bail shall not be required, nor excessive fines imposed, nor cruel and unusual punishment inflicted.

Amendment 9
The enumeration in the Constitution, of certain rights, shall not be construed to deny or disparage others retained by the people.

Amendment 10
The powers not delegated to the United States by the Constitution, nor prohibited by it to the States, are reserved to the States respectively, or to the people.

Amendment 11
The Judicial power of the United States shall not be construed to extend to any suit in law or equity, commenced or prosecuted against one of the United States by Citizens of another State, or by Citizens or Subjects of any Foreign State.

Amendment 12

The Electors shall meet in their respective States and vote by ballot for President and Vice President, one of whom, at least, shall not be an inhabitant of the same State with themselves; they shall name in their ballots the person voted for as President, and in distinct ballots the person voted for as Vice President, and they shall make distinct lists of all persons voted for as President, and of all persons voted for as Vice President, and of the number of votes for each, which lists they shall sign and certify, and transmit sealed to the seat of the government of the United States, directed to the President of the Senate;— The President of the Senate shall, in the presence of the Senate and the House of Representatives, open all the certificates and the votes shall then be counted;— the person having the greatest Number of votes for President shall be the President, if such number be a majority of the whole number of Electors appointed; and if no person have such a majority, then, from the persons having the highest numbers not exceeding three on the list of those voted for as President, the House of Representatives shall choose immediately, by ballot, the President. But in choosing the President, the votes shall be taken by States, the representation from each State having one vote; a quorum for this purpose shall consist of a member or members from two thirds of the States, and a majority of all the States shall be necessary to a choice. And if the House of Representatives shall not choose a President whenever the right of choice shall devolve upon them, before the fourth day of March next following, then the Vice President shall act as President, as in case of death or other constitutional disability of the President. The person having the greatest number of votes as Vice President, shall be the Vice President, if such number be a majority of the whole number of Electors appointed, and if no person have a majority, then from the two highest numbers on the list, the Senate shall choose the Vice President; a quorum for the purpose shall consist of two thirds of the whole number of Senators, a majority of the whole number shall be necessary to a choice. But no person constitutionally ineligible to the office of President shall be eligible to that of Vice-President of the United States.

Twelfth Amendment—1804
Election of President and Vice President

This Amendment changed the way the Electoral College chooses the President and Vice-President. Before this amendment, candidates for President and Vice-President ran separately, and each elector had two votes—one for President and one for Vice President. The candidate receiving the most votes became President, and the runner-up became Vice President.

Under this Amendment, a candidate for President and a candidate for Vice President must run together. Each elector has only one vote, and the pair of candidates that receives more than half the electoral votes become the President and Vice President. If no one receives a majority of the electoral votes, the House of Representatives votes for the President from a list of the top three vote-getters. In this situation, each state has one vote, and the candidate must receive more than half of the votes to become President.

If the Representatives fail to elect a President by March 4 (later changed to January 20), the Vice President serves as President. If no candidate receives at least half the electoral votes for Vice President, the names of the two top vote getters are sent to the Senate. The Senators then vote on the names, and the person receiving more than half the votes becomes Vice President.

Thirteenth Amendment—1865
Abolition of Slavery

The United States outlaws slavery.

Congress can pass any laws that are needed to carry out this amendment.

Fourteenth Amendment—1868
Rights of Citizens

People born in the United States are citizens of both the United States and of the state in which they live. States must treat their citizens equally. States cannot deny their citizens the rights outlined in the Bill of Rights.

This section of the amendment made former slaves citizens of both the United States and their home state.

Based on its population, each state has a certain number of Representatives in Congress. The number of Representatives from a state might be lowered, however, if the state does not let certain citizens vote.

This section tried to force states in the South to let former slaves vote.

14. Why would a state not want to have its number of Representatives in Congress cut?

....

....

....

....

....

Amendment 13

Section 1. Neither slavery nor involuntary servitude, except as a punishment for crime whereof the party shall have been duly convicted, shall exist within the United States, or any place subject to their jurisdiction.

Section 2. Congress shall have power to enforce this article by appropriate legislation.

Amendment 14

Section 1. All persons born or naturalized in the United States and subject to the jurisdiction thereof, are citizens of the United States and of the State wherein they reside. No State shall make or enforce any law which shall abridge the privileges or immunities of citizens of the United States; nor shall any State deprive any person of life, liberty, or property, without due process of law; nor deny to any person within its jurisdiction the equal protection of the laws.

Section 2. Representatives shall be apportioned among the several States according to their respective numbers, counting the whole number of persons in each State, excluding Indians not taxed. But when the right to vote at any election for the choice of electors for President and Vice President of the United States, Representatives in Congress, the Executive and Judicial officers of a State, or the members of the Legislature thereof, is denied to any of the male inhabitants of such State, being twenty-one years of age and citizens of the United States, or in any way abridged, except for participation in rebellion, or other crime, the basis of representation therein shall be reduced in the proportion which the number of such male citizens shall bear to the whole number of male citizens twenty-one years of age in such State.

Section 3. No person shall be a Senator or Representative in Congress, or elector of President and Vice President, or hold any office, civil or military, under the United States, or under any State, who, having previously taken an oath, as a member of Congress, or as an officer of the United States, or as a member of any State legislature, or as an executive or judicial officer of any State, to support the Constitution of the United States, shall have engaged in insurrection or rebellion against the same, or given aid or comfort to the enemies thereof. But Congress may, by a vote of two thirds of each House, remove such disability.

Section 4. The validity of the public debt of the United States, authorized by law, including debts incurred for payment of pensions and bounties for services in suppressing insurrection or rebellion, shall not be questioned. But neither the United States nor any State shall assume or pay any debt or obligation incurred in aid of insurrection or rebellion against the United States, or any claim for the loss or emancipation of any slave; but all such debts, obligations and claims shall be held illegal and void.

Section 5. The Congress shall have power to enforce, by appropriate legislation, the provisions of this article.

Amendment 15

Section 1. The right of citizens of the United States to vote shall not be denied or abridged by the United States or by any State on account of race, color, or previous condition of servitude.

Section 2. The Congress shall have power to enforce this article by appropriate legislation.

Officials who took part in the Civil War against the United States cannot hold federal or state office. Congress can remove this provision by a two-thirds vote.

The United States will pay back the money it borrowed to fight the Civil War. The money that the South borrowed to fight the Civil War will not be paid back to lenders. The former owners of slaves will not be paid for the slaves that were set free.

Congress can pass any necessary laws to enforce this article.

15. List two ways in which the Fourteenth Amendment tended to punish white Southerners.

....

....

....

....

....

....

....

....

Fifteenth Amendment—1870
Voting Rights
The federal and state government cannot stop people from voting based on race or color. Former slaves must be allowed to vote.

Sixteenth Amendment—1913
Income Tax
Congress has the power to collect an income tax regardless of the population of a state. (Originally, Section 9 of Article 1 of the Constitution had denied this power to Congress.)

Seventeenth Amendment—1913
Direct Election of Senators
The voters of each state will elect their senators directly. (Originally, Article 1, Section 3 said state legislatures would elect senators.)

A state can hold a special election to fill an empty Senate seat. Until then, the governor can appoint a senator to fill an empty seat.

Eighteenth Amendment—1919
Prohibition
Making, importing, or selling alcoholic drinks is illegal in the United States. This was called Prohibition because the Amendment prohibited, or outlawed, the use of alcohol.

Congress and the states can make any laws to prohibit alcohol.

This amendment becomes part of the Constitution if it is approved within seven years.

This Amendment was repealed, or cancelled, in 1933 by the Twenty-first Amendment.

16. Write the amendment number that did each of the following:
_____ let the Federal Government collect income tax
_____ guaranteed voting rights for African- Americans
_____ outlawed the sale of alcohol
_____ abolished slavery
_____ let voters elect their senators

Amendment 16
The Congress shall have power to lay and collect taxes on incomes, from whatever source derived, without apportionment among the several States, and without regard to any census or enumeration.

Amendment 17
The Senate of the United States shall be composed of two Senators from each State, elected by the people thereof, for six years; and each Senator shall have one vote. The electors in each State shall have the qualifications requisite for electors of the most numerous branch of the State legislatures.

When vacancies happen in the representation of any State in the Senate, the executive authority of such State shall issue writs of election to fill such vacancies: Provided, That the legislature of any State may empower the executive thereof to make temporary appointments until the people fill the vacancies by election as the legislature may direct.

This amendment shall not be so construed as to affect the election or term of any Senator chosen before it becomes valid as part of the Constitution.

Amendment 18
Section 1. After one year from the ratification of this article the manufacture, sale, or transportation of intoxicating liquors within, the importation thereof into, or the exportation thereof from the United States and all territory subject to the jurisdiction thereof for beverage purposes is hereby prohibited.

Section 2. The Congress and the several States shall have concurrent power to enforce this article by appropriate legislation.

Section 3. This article shall be inoperative unless it shall have been ratified as an amendment to the Constitution by the legislatures of the several States, as provided in the Constitution, within seven years of the date of the submission hereof to the States by Congress.

Amendment 19

The right of citizens of the United States to vote shall not be denied or abridged by the United States or by any State on account of sex.

Congress shall have power to enforce this article by appropriate legislation.

Amendment 20

Section 1. The terms of the President and Vice President shall end at noon on the 20th day of January, and the terms of Senators and Representatives at noon on the 3d day of January, of the years in which such terms would have ended if this article had not been ratified; and the terms of their successors shall then begin.

Section 2. The Congress shall assemble at least once in every year, and such meeting shall begin at noon on the 3d day of January, unless they shall by law appoint a different day.

Section 3. If, at the time fixed for the beginning of the term of the President, the President elect shall have died, the Vice President elect shall become President. If a President shall not have been chosen before the time fixed for the beginning of his term, or if the President-elect shall have failed to qualify, then the Vice President elect shall act as President until a President shall have qualified; and the Congress may by law provide for the case wherein neither a President elect nor a Vice President elect shall have qualified, declaring who shall then act as President, or the manner in which one who is to act shall be selected, and such person shall act accordingly until a President or Vice President shall have qualified.

Section 4. The Congress may by law provide for the case of the death of any of the persons from whom the House of Representatives may choose a President whenever the right of choice shall have devolved upon them, and for the case of the death of any of the persons from whom the Senate may choose a Vice President whenever the right of choice shall have devolved upon them.

Section 5. Sections 1 and 2 shall take effect on the 15th day of October following the ratification of this article.

Section 6. This article shall be inoperative unless it shall have been ratified as an amendment to the Constitution by the legislatures of three fourths of the several States within seven years from the date of its submission.

Nineteenth Amendment—1920
Women's Right to Vote

No government can stop people from voting because of their sex.

Congress can pass necessary laws to carry out this amendment.

Twentieth Amendment—1933
Terms of Office

The term of a new President begins on January 20. This date is called Inauguration Day. Members of Congress take office on January 3. (Originally their terms began on March 4.)

Congress must meet at least once a year. They should first meet on January 3, unless they chose a different day.

If a candidate for President does not win a majority of votes in the Electoral College and dies while the election is being decided in the House, Congress has the power to pass laws to resolve the problem. Congress has similar power if a candidate for Vice President dies while the election is being decided in the Senate.

Sections 1 and 2 of this amendment take effect on the fifteenth day of October after the amendment becomes part of the Constitution.

This amendment has to be approved by three-fourths of the states within seven years.

17. How long was the Eighteenth Amendment in effect in the United States?

....

18. Do you think a President should be limited to just two terms in office? Why or why not?

....

....

....

....

....

....

....

Amendment 21

Section 1. The eighteenth article of amendment to the Constitution of the United States is hereby repealed.

Section 2. The transportation or importation into any State, Territory, or possession of the United States for delivery or use therein of intoxicating liquors, in violation of the laws thereof, is hereby prohibited.

Section 3. This article shall be inoperative unless it shall have been ratified as an amendment to the Constitution by conventions in the several States, as provided in the Constitution, within seven years from the date of the submission hereof to the States by the Congress.

Amendment 22

Section 1. No person shall be elected to the office of the President more than twice, and no person who has held the office of President, or acted as President, for more than two years of a term to which some other person was elected President shall be elected to the office of the President more than once. But this Article shall not apply to any person holding the office of President, when this Article was proposed by the Congress, and shall not prevent any person who may be holding the office of President, or acting as President, during the term within which this Article becomes operative from holding the office of President or acting as President during the remainder of such term.

Section 2. This article shall be inoperative unless it shall have been ratified as an amendment to the Constitution by the legislatures of three fourths of the several states within seven years from the date of its submission to the States by the Congress.

Amendment 23

Section 1. The District constituting the seat of Government of the United States shall appoint in such manner as the Congress may direct:

A number of electors of President and Vice President equal to the whole number of Senators and Representatives in Congress to which the District would be entitled if it were a State, but in no event more than the least populous State; they shall be in addition to those appointed by the States, they shall be considered, for the purposes of the election of President and Vice President, to be electors appointed by a State; and they shall meet in the District and perform such duties as provided by the twelfth article of amendment.

Amendment 24

Section 1. The right of citizens of the United States to vote in any primary or other election for President or Vice President, for electors for President or Vice President, or for Senator or Representative in Congress, shall not be denied or abridged by the United States or any State by reason of failure to pay any poll tax or other tax.

Section 2. The Congress shall have power to enforce this article by appropriate legislation.

Amendment 25

Section 1. In case of the removal of the President from office or of his death or resignation, the Vice President shall become President.

Section 2. Whenever there is a vacancy in the office of the Vice President, the President shall nominate a Vice President who shall take office upon confirmation by a majority vote of both Houses of Congress.

Section 3. Whenever the President transmits to the President pro tempore of the Senate and the Speaker of the House of Representatives his written declaration that he is unable to discharge the powers and duties of his office, and until he transmits to them a written declaration to the contrary, such powers and duties shall be discharged by the Vice President as Acting President.

Twenty-third Amendment—1961 Presidential Elections for District of Columbia

People living in Washington, D.C. have the right to vote in presidential elections. Washington D.C. can never have more electoral votes than the state with the smallest number of people.

Twenty-fourth Amendment—1964 Outlawing of Poll Tax

No one can be stopped from voting in a federal election because he or she has not paid a poll tax or any other kind of tax.

Congress can make laws to carry out this amendment.

Twenty-fifth Amendment—1967 Presidential Succession

If the President dies or resigns, the Vice President becomes President.

If the office of Vice President is empty, the President appoints a new Vice President.

When the President is unable to carry out the duties of the office, Congress should be informed. The Vice President then serves as Acting President. The President may resume the duties of the office after informing Congress.

If the Vice President and half the President's top advisers, or Cabinet, inform Congress that the President cannot carry out his or her duties, the Vice President become Acting President. If the President informs Congress that he or she is able to carry out these duties, the President returns to office. However, after four days, if the Vice President and half the Cabinet again tell Congress that the President cannot carry out his or her duties, the President does not return to office. Instead, Congress must decide within 21 days whether the President is able to carry out his or her or duties. If two-thirds of Congress votes that the President cannot continue in office, the Vice President becomes Acting President. If two-thirds do not vote in this way, the President remains in office.

**Twenty-sixth Amendment—1971
Votes for Eighteen-Year-Olds**

People who are eighteen years old have the right to vote in federal and state elections.

Congress can pass laws to carry out this amendment.

Over the years, amendments to the Constitution have improved our democracy by expanding voting rights to more and more citizens.

19. Write the number of the amendment that:

_____ gave votes to women

_____ gave votes to citizens in Washington , D.C.

_____ gave votes to eighteen-year-olds

_____ outlawed taxes that blocked voting

**Twenty-seventh Amendment—1992
Limits on Congressional Salary Changes**

Laws that increase the salaries of Senators and Representatives do not take effect immediately. They take effect after the next election of the House of Representatives.

Section 4. Whenever the Vice President and a majority of either the principal officers of the executive departments or of such other body as Congress may by law provide, transmit to the President pro tempore of the Senate and the Speaker of the House of Representatives their written declaration that the President is unable to discharge the powers and duties of his office, the Vice President shall immediately assume the powers and duties of the office as Acting President.

Thereafter, when the President transmits to the President pro tempore of the Senate and the Speaker of the House of Representatives his written declaration that no inability exists, he shall resume the powers and duties of his office unless the Vice President and a majority of either the principal officers of the executive department or of such other body as Congress may by law provide, transmit within four days to the President pro tempore of the Senate and the Speaker of the House of Representatives their written declaration that the President is unable to discharge the powers and duties of his office. Thereupon Congress shall decide the issue, assembling within forty-eight hours for that purpose if not in session. If the Congress, within twenty-one days after receipt of the latter written declaration, or, if Congress is not in session, within twenty-one days after Congress is required to assemble, determines by two-thirds vote of both Houses that the President is unable to discharge the powers and duties of his office, the Vice President shall continue to discharge the same as Acting President; otherwise, the President shall resume the powers and duties of his office.

Amendment 26

Section 1. The right of citizens of the United States, who are eighteen years of age or older, to vote shall not be denied or abridged by the United States or by any State on account of age.

Section 2. The Congress shall have the power to enforce this article by appropriate legislation.

27th Amendment

No law varying the compensation for the services of the Senators and Representatives, shall take effect, until an election of Representatives shall have intervened.

The United States of America, Political

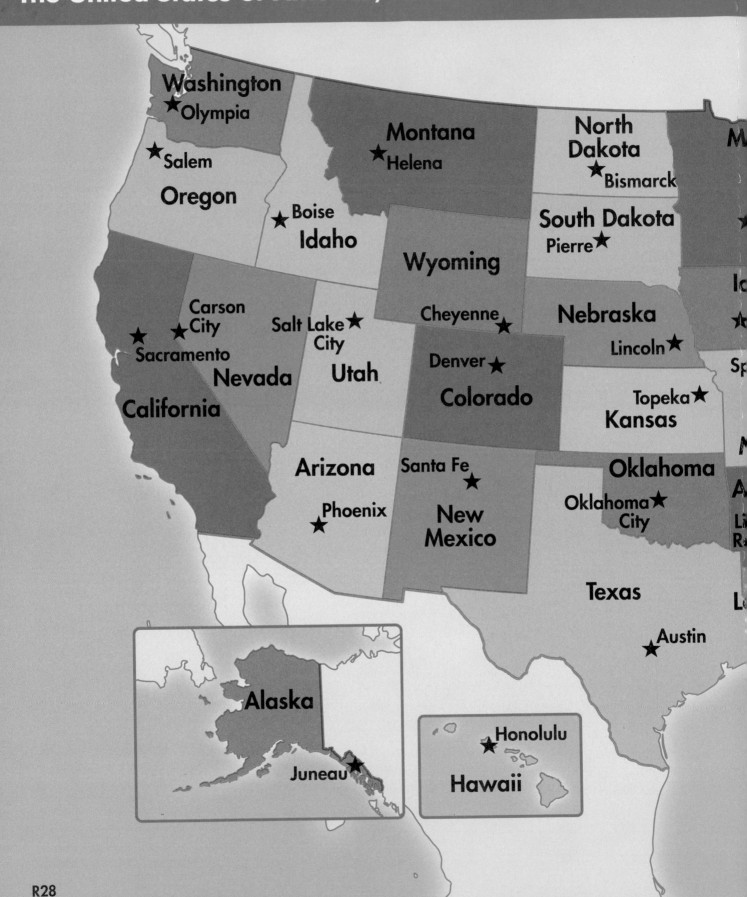

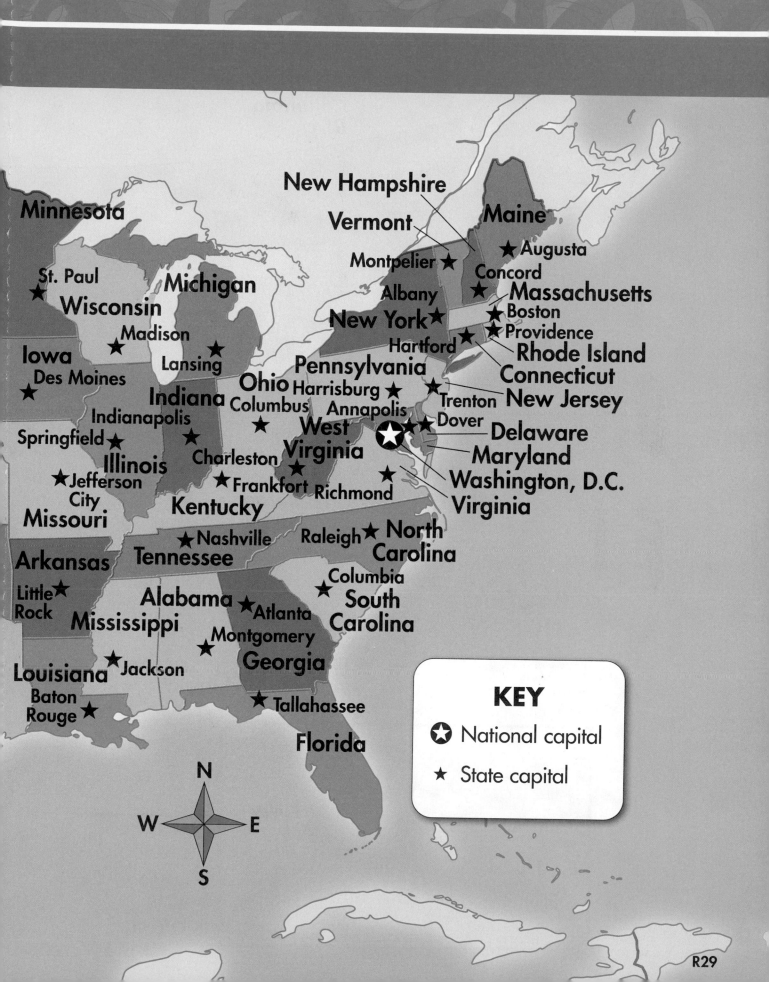

New Hampshire

Vermont

Maine

Minnesota

★ Augusta

Montpelier ★

Concord

St. Paul
★

Michigan

Albany

Massachusetts

Wisconsin

★ Boston

Madison

New York ★

★ Providence

Iowa

★

Lansing

Hartford

★

Rhode Island

Des Moines
★

★

Pennsylvania

★ Connecticut

Indiana

Harrisburg ★

Trenton ★ New Jersey

Indianapolis

Columbus

Annapolis

Dover

Springfield ★

★

West
Virginia

★★

Delaware

Ohio

Illinois

Charleston

★

Maryland

★Jefferson
City

★Frankfort

Richmond

★

Washington, D.C.

Missouri

Kentucky

Virginia

★ Nashville

Raleigh ★ North
Carolina

Arkansas

Tennessee

Columbia

Little★
Rock

Alabama

★

South
Carolina

Mississippi

★Atlanta

Montgomery

Louisiana

★Jackson

Georgia

Baton
Rouge ★

★ Tallahassee

Florida

N

W   E

S

KEY

⭐ National capital

★ State capital

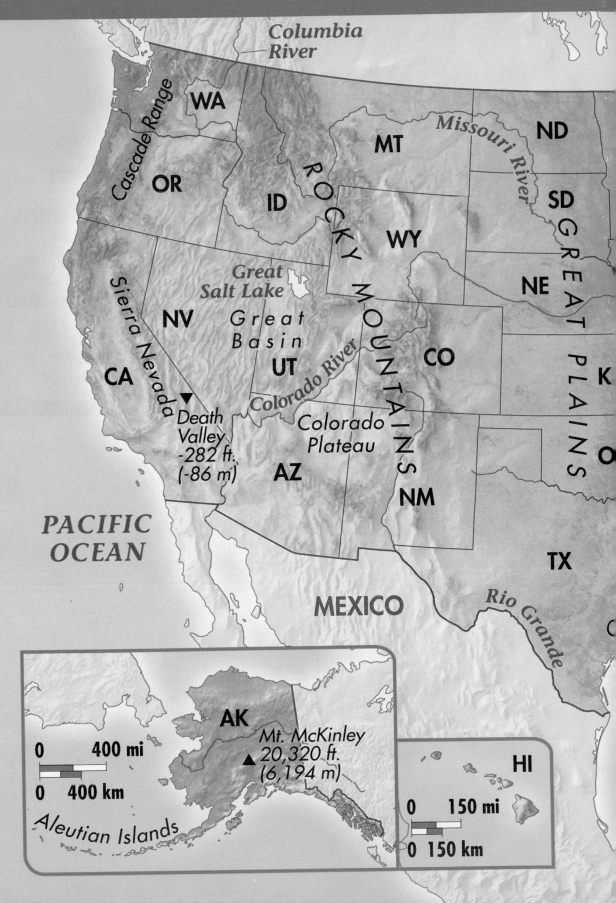

Columbia River

WA

Cascade Range

OR

ID

MT

Missouri River

ND

SD

ROCKY MOUNTAINS

WY

NE

GREAT PLAINS

K

Great Salt Lake

Great Basin

Sierra Nevada

NV

UT

Colorado River

CO

CA

▼ Death Valley
-282 ft.
(-86 m)

Colorado Plateau

AZ

NM

O

PACIFIC OCEAN

TX

MEXICO

Rio Grande

AK

Mt. McKinley
▲ 20,320 ft.
(6,194 m)

0   400 mi

0   400 km

Aleutian Islands

HI

0   150 mi

0   150 km

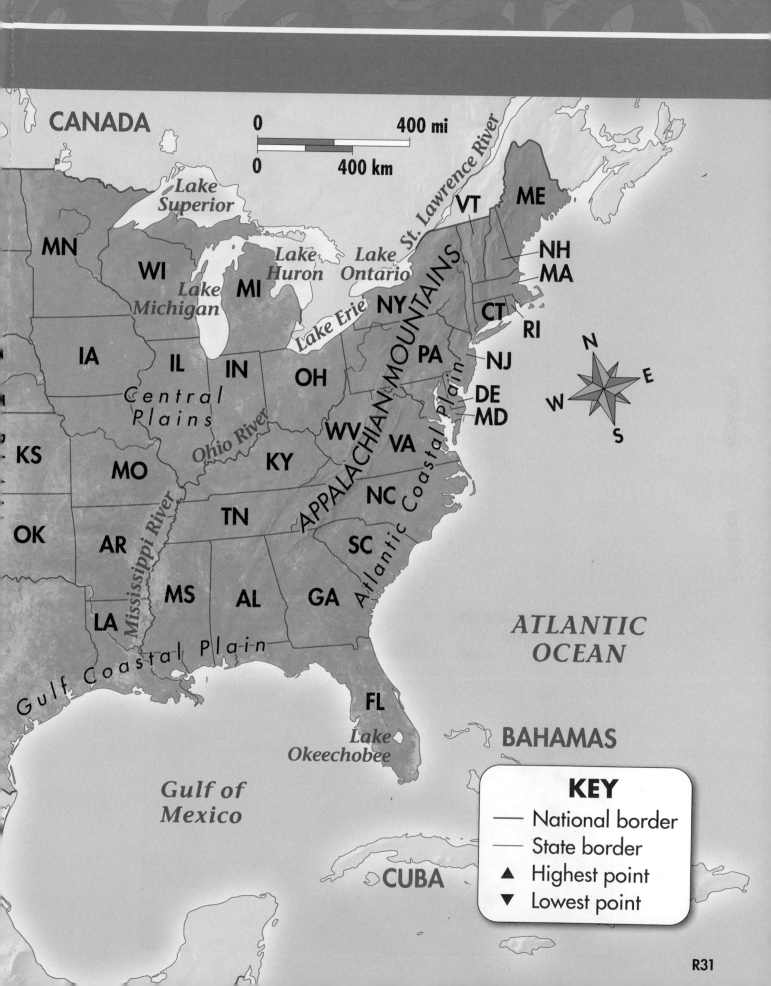

CANADA

0 — 400 mi
0 — 400 km

Lake Superior

Lake Huron

Lake Michigan

Lake Ontario

Lake Erie

St. Lawrence River

MN
WI
MI
IA
IL
IN
OH
KS
MO
KY
OK
AR
TN
MS
AL
LA
GA
SC
NC
VA
WV
PA
NY
VT
ME
NH
MA
CT
RI
NJ
DE
MD
FL

Central Plains

Ohio River

Mississippi River

APPALACHIAN MOUNTAINS

Atlantic Coastal Plain

Gulf Coastal Plain

Lake Okeechobee

Gulf of Mexico

ATLANTIC OCEAN

BAHAMAS

CUBA

N
E
S
W

KEY
— National border
— State border
▲ Highest point
▼ Lowest point

The World

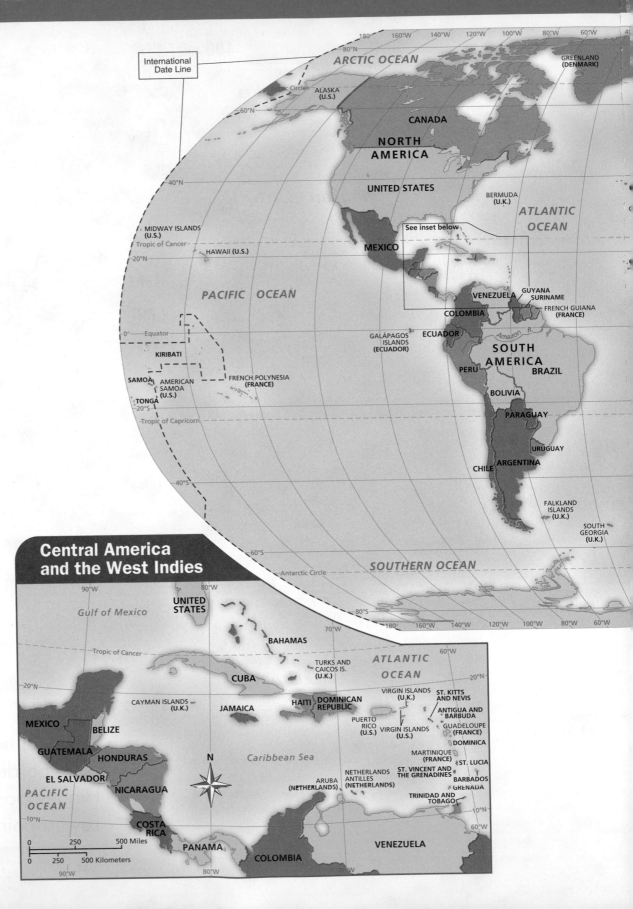

International Date Line

ARCTIC OCEAN

GREENLAND (DENMARK)

Arctic Circle

ALASKA (U.S.)

CANADA

NORTH AMERICA

UNITED STATES

BERMUDA (U.K.)

ATLANTIC OCEAN

MIDWAY ISLANDS (U.S.)

Tropic of Cancer

HAWAII (U.S.)

MEXICO

See inset below

PACIFIC OCEAN

VENEZUELA

GUYANA
SURINAME

FRENCH GUIANA (FRANCE)

COLOMBIA

GALÁPAGOS ISLANDS (ECUADOR)

ECUADOR

SOUTH AMERICA

Amazon R.

Equator

KIRIBATI

PERU

BRAZIL

SAMOA

AMERICAN SAMOA (U.S.)

FRENCH POLYNESIA (FRANCE)

BOLIVIA

TONGA

PARAGUAY

URUGUAY

CHILE

ARGENTINA

FALKLAND ISLANDS (U.K.)

SOUTH GEORGIA (U.K.)

SOUTHERN OCEAN

Antarctic Circle

Central America and the West Indies

Gulf of Mexico

UNITED STATES

BAHAMAS

Tropic of Cancer

TURKS AND CAICOS IS. (U.K.)

ATLANTIC OCEAN

CUBA

MEXICO

CAYMAN ISLANDS (U.K.)

JAMAICA

HAITI

DOMINICAN REPUBLIC

VIRGIN ISLANDS (U.K.)

ST. KITTS AND NEVIS

BELIZE

PUERTO RICO (U.S.)

VIRGIN ISLANDS (U.S.)

ANTIGUA AND BARBUDA

GUADELOUPE (FRANCE)

GUATEMALA

DOMINICA

HONDURAS

N

Caribbean Sea

MARTINIQUE (FRANCE)

ST. LUCIA

EL SALVADOR

NETHERLANDS ANTILLES (NETHERLANDS)

ST. VINCENT AND THE GRENADINES

BARBADOS

PACIFIC OCEAN

NICARAGUA

ARUBA (NETHERLANDS)

GRENADA

TRINIDAD AND TOBAGO

COSTA RICA

0   250   500 Miles
0   250   500 Kilometers

PANAMA

COLOMBIA

VENEZUELA

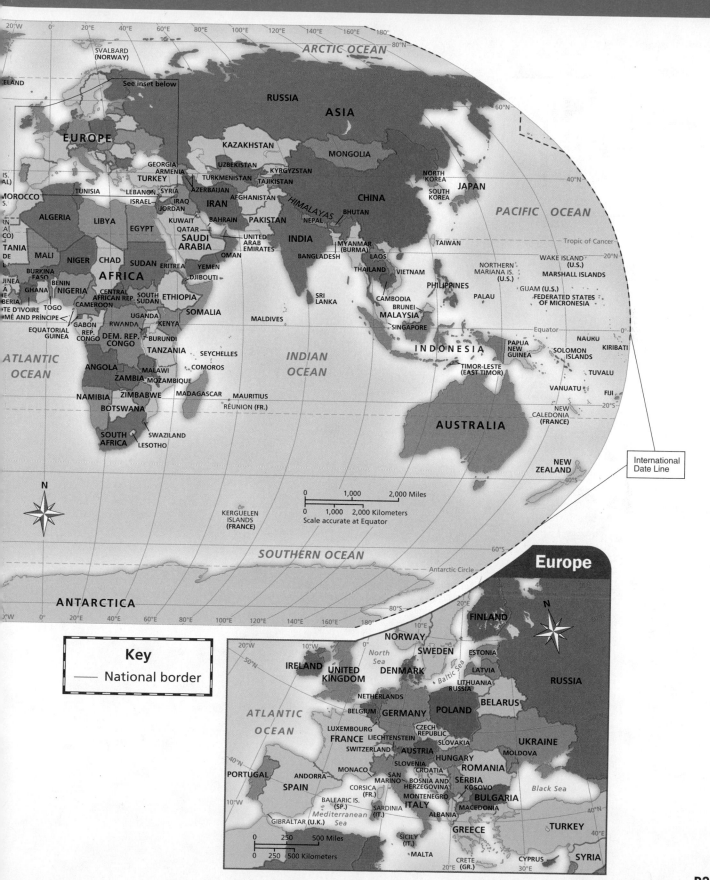

ARCTIC OCEAN

80°N

RUSSIA

ASIA

60°N

SVALBARD
(NORWAY)

ELAND

See inset below

EUROPE

KAZAKHSTAN

MONGOLIA

40°N

IS.
AL)

GEORGIA
ARMENIA
TURKEY

UZBEKISTAN

KYRGYZSTAN

NORTH
KOREA

JAPAN

PACIFIC OCEAN

IS.

MOROCCO
S.

TUNISIA

TURKMENISTAN

TAJIKISTAN

LEBANON SYRIA
ISRAEL

AZERBAIJAN
AFGHANISTAN

HIMALAYAS

CHINA

SOUTH
KOREA

RN
A
CO)

ALGERIA

LIBYA

EGYPT

JORDAN

IRAN

PAKISTAN

BHUTAN

NEPAL

TAIWAN

Tropic of Cancer

20°N

KUWAIT
QATAR

BAHRAIN

INDIA

MYANMAR
(BURMA)

TANIA
L

MALI

NIGER

CHAD

SUDAN

SAUDI
ARABIA

UNITED
ARAB
EMIRATES

OMAN

BANGLADESH

LAOS

WAKE ISLAND
(U.S.)

AFRICA

ERITREA

YEMEN

THAILAND

VIETNAM

NORTHERN
MARIANA IS.
(U.S.)

MARSHALL ISLANDS

INEA
A
E
BERIA
TE D'IVOIRE
MÉ AND PRÍNCIPE

BURKINA
FASO

BENIN

GHANA NIGERIA

TOGO

CENTRAL
AFRICAN REP.

CAMEROON

DJIBOUTI

SOUTH
SUDAN

ETHIOPIA

SOMALIA

SRI
LANKA

MALDIVES

CAMBODIA

BRUNEI

MALAYSIA

SINGAPORE

PHILIPPINES

PALAU

GUAM (U.S.)

FEDERATED STATES
OF MICRONESIA

EQUATORIAL
GUINEA

GABON
REP.
CONGO

RWANDA

DEM. REP.
CONGO

UGANDA

BURUNDI

KENYA

Equator

NAURU

KIRIBATI

0°

ATLANTIC
OCEAN

ANGOLA

TANZANIA

ZAMBIA

MALAWI

SEYCHELLES

COMOROS

INDIAN
OCEAN

INDONESIA

PAPUA
NEW
GUINEA

SOLOMON
ISLANDS

TUVALU

MOZAMBIQUE

TIMOR-LESTE
(EAST TIMOR)

NAMIBIA

ZIMBABWE

MADAGASCAR

MAURITIUS

RÉUNION (FR.)

VANUATU

NEW
CALEDONIA
(FRANCE)

FIJI

20°S

BOTSWANA

AUSTRALIA

SOUTH
AFRICA

SWAZILAND

LESOTHO

International
Date Line

N

NEW
ZEALAND

40°S

0
0

1,000

1,000

2,000 Miles

2,000 Kilometers

Scale accurate at Equator

60°S

KERGUELEN
ISLANDS
(FRANCE)

Antarctic Circle

SOUTHERN OCEAN

ANTARCTICA

°W

0°

20°E

40°E

60°E

80°E

100°E

120°E

140°E

160°E

80°S

180°

Key

— National border

Europe

N

FINLAND

20°W

10°W

0°

10°E

NORWAY

SWEDEN

North
Sea

ESTONIA

Baltic Sea

LATVIA

RUSSIA

IRELAND

UNITED
KINGDOM

DENMARK

LITHUANIA

RUSSIA

ATLANTIC

NETHERLANDS

GERMANY

POLAND

BELARUS

OCEAN

BELGIUM

LUXEMBOURG

CZECH
REPUBLIC

UKRAINE

FRANCE

LIECHTENSTEIN

SLOVAKIA

MOLDOVA

SWITZERLAND

AUSTRIA

HUNGARY

ROMANIA

SLOVENIA

PORTUGAL

ANDORRA

MONACO

SAN
MARINO

CROATIA

BOSNIA AND
HERZEGOVINA

SERBIA

KOSOVO

SPAIN

CORSICA
(FR.)

ITALY

MONTENEGRO

BULGARIA

Black Sea

BALEARIC IS.
(SP.)

SARDINIA
(IT.)

ALBANIA

MACEDONIA

40°N

GIBRALTAR (U.K.)

Mediterranean
Sea

GREECE

TURKEY

0

250

500 Miles

SICILY
(IT.)

0

250

500 Kilometers

MALTA

CRETE
(GR.)

20°E

CYPRUS

SYRIA

40°N

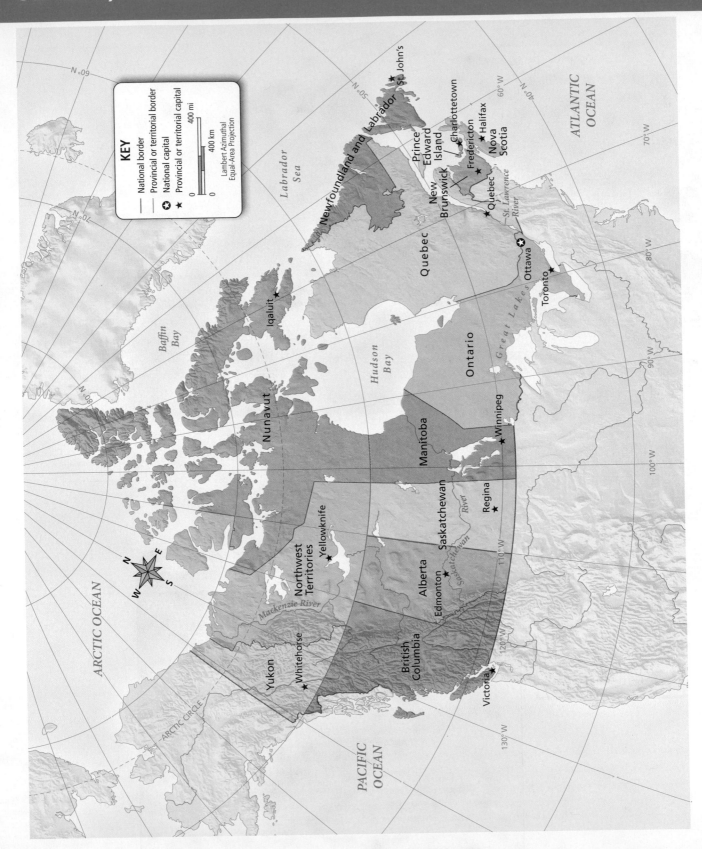

KEY
- National border
- Provincial or territorial border
- ✪ National capital
- ★ Provincial or territorial capital

400 mi
0
400 km
0
Lambert Azimuthal
Equal-Area Projection

ATLANTIC OCEAN

St. John's

Labrador Sea

Newfoundland and Labrador

Charlottetown
Prince Edward Island
Fredericton
Halifax
New Brunswick
Nova Scotia
Quebec
St. Lawrence River
Ottawa
Toronto

Quebec

Baffin Bay

Iqaluit

Hudson Bay

Ontario
Great Lakes

Nunavut

Manitoba
Winnipeg

Saskatchewan
River
Regina

Yellowknife
Northwest Territories

Alberta
Edmonton
Saskatchewan River

British Columbia

Mackenzie River

Yukon
Whitehorse

ARCTIC OCEAN

ARCTIC CIRCLE

Victoria

PACIFIC OCEAN

N
E
W
S

60°N
50°N
40°W
60°W
70°W
70°N
80°W
80°N
90°W
100°W
110°W
120°W
130°W

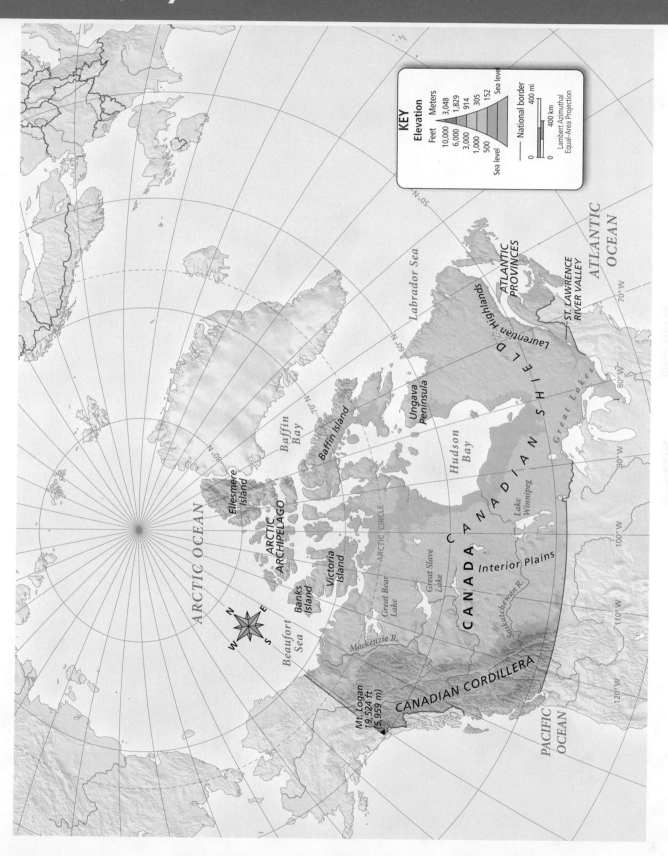

KEY

Elevation

Feet	Meters
10,000	3,048
6,000	1,829
3,000	914
1,000	305
500	152
Sea level	Sea level

— National border

Lambert Azimuthal
Equal-Area Projection

ARCTIC OCEAN

ATLANTIC OCEAN

PACIFIC OCEAN

Labrador Sea

Baffin Bay

Baffin Island

Ellesmere Island

ARCTIC ARCHIPELAGO

Victoria Island

Banks Island

Beaufort Sea

ATLANTIC PROVINCES

ST. LAWRENCE RIVER VALLEY

Laurentian Highlands

Ungava Peninsula

Hudson Bay

CANADIAN SHIELD

CANADA

Great Lakes

Lake Winnipeg

Interior Plains

Great Slave Lake

Great Bear Lake

Saskatchewan R.

Mackenzie R.

ARCTIC CIRCLE

CANADIAN CORDILLERA

Mt. Logan
19,524 ft
(5,959 m)

Mexico, Political

Caribbean Sea

Gulf of Mexico

PACIFIC OCEAN

Gulf of California

Rio Grande

TROPIC OF CANCER

Tijuana

Ciudad Juárez

Torreón

Monterrey

San Nicolás de Guadalupe

Zapopan

León

Guadalajara

Toluca

Nezahualcóyotl

Mexico City

Puebla

80° W

90° W

100° W

110° W

30° N

20° N

KEY

National border

⬤ Capital city

◯ Other city

300 mi

300 km

Lambert Conformal Conic Projection

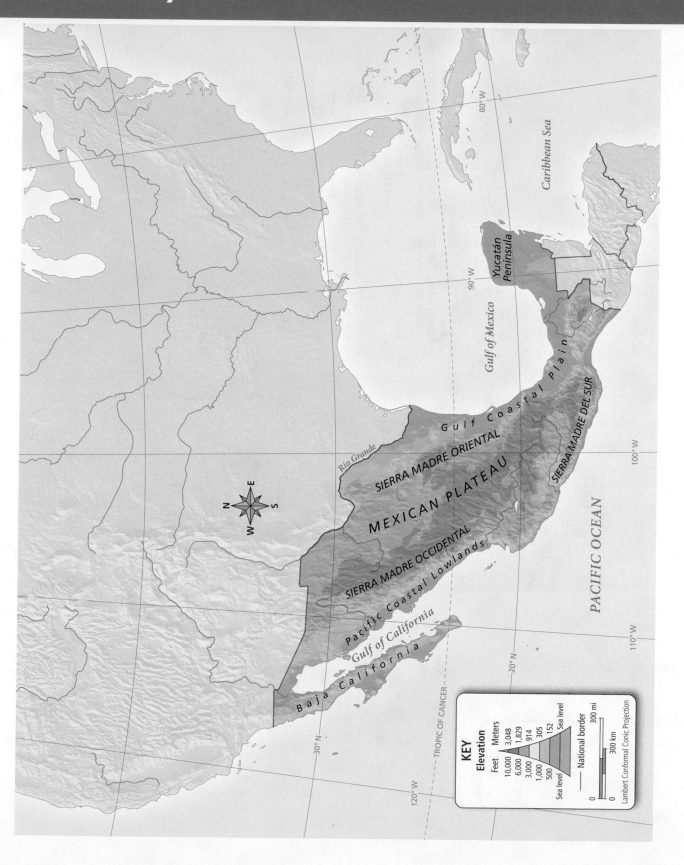

Caribbean Sea

80° W

Yucatán Peninsula

90° W

Gulf of Mexico

Gulf Coastal Plain

Rio Grande

SIERRA MADRE ORIENTAL

SIERRA MADRE DEL SUR

MEXICAN PLATEAU

100° W

SIERRA MADRE OCCIDENTAL

PACIFIC OCEAN

Pacific Coastal Lowlands

110° W

20° N

Gulf of California

Baja California

TROPIC OF CANCER

30° N

120° W

KEY

Elevation

Feet	Meters
10,000	3,048
6,000	1,829
3,000	914
1,000	305
500	152
Sea level	Sea level

National border

300 mi

300 km

Lambert Conformal Conic Projection

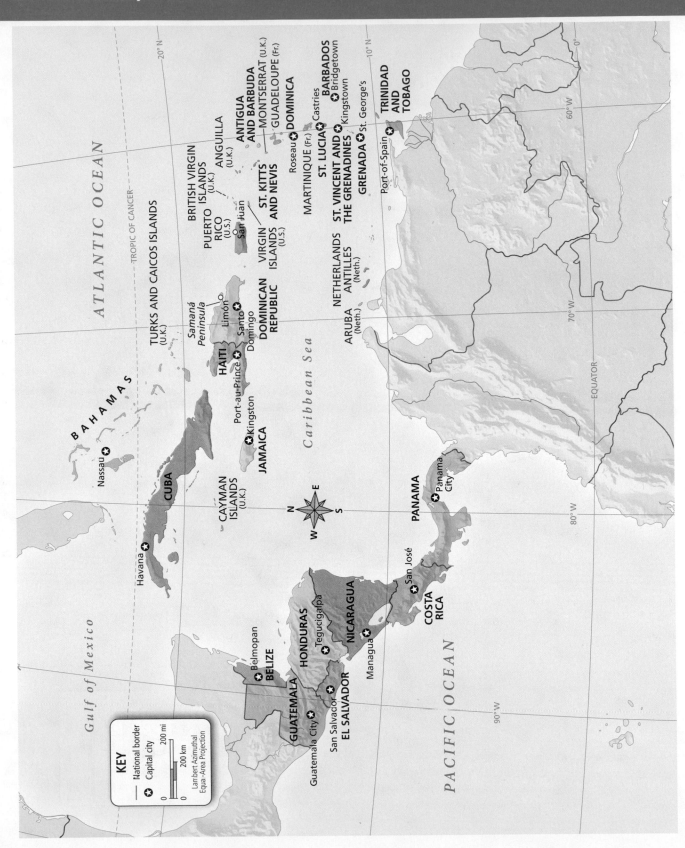

ATLANTIC OCEAN

TROPIC OF CANCER

TURKS AND CAICOS ISLANDS (U.K.)

BRITISH VIRGIN ISLANDS (U.K.)

ANGUILLA (U.K.)

ANTIGUA AND BARBUDA

MONTSERRAT (U.K.)

GUADELOUPE (Fr.)

PUERTO RICO (U.S.)

San Juan

VIRGIN ISLANDS (U.S.)

ST. KITTS AND NEVIS

DOMINICA

Roseau

MARTINIQUE (Fr.)

ST. LUCIA ✪ Castries

BARBADOS ✪ Bridgetown

ST. VINCENT AND THE GRENADINES

GRENADA ✪ St. George's

Kingstown

TRINIDAD AND TOBAGO

Port-of-Spain ✪

NETHERLANDS ANTILLES (Neth.)

ARUBA (Neth.)

Samaná Peninsula

Limón

Santo Domingo

DOMINICAN REPUBLIC

HAITI

Port-au-Prince

Kingston

JAMAICA

Caribbean Sea

BAHAMAS

Nassau ✪

CUBA

CAYMAN ISLANDS (U.K.)

Havana ✪

Gulf of Mexico

PANAMA

Panama City ✪

San José ✪

COSTA RICA

NICARAGUA

HONDURAS

Tegucigalpa ✪

Managua ✪

Belmopan ✪

BELIZE

GUATEMALA

Guatemala City ✪

San Salvador ✪

EL SALVADOR

PACIFIC OCEAN

EQUATOR

N E W S

KEY
— National border
✪ Capital city

200 mi
0
200 km
0

Lambert Azimuthal Equa-Area Projection

20° N

10° N

0°

60° W

70° W

80° W

90° W

Glossary

A

abolition (ab/uə lih/shən) The act of ending or abolishing something, such as slavery.

abolitionist (ab/ə lih/shən ist) A person who works to end or get rid of something, especially slavery.

adapt (ə dapt/) To change in order to live in a new place.

agriculture (ag/ rih kul/ chər) The system of growing crops for food.

alliance (ə lī/ əns) A formal agreement of friendship between countries.

ally (ə lī/) A nation that is a military partner.

amendment (ə mend/ mənt) A change or improvement.

ancestor (an/ses/ tər) A group or family member who lived in the past.

annex (ə neks/) To take territory and join it to a state or country.

anthem (an/ thəm) A patriotic song used to express praise or loyalty to a nation.

Anti-Federalist (an/ tī/ fed/ ər əl ist) A person who opposed the passage of the U.S. Constitution.

Articles of Confederation (ärt/ i kəls əv kən fed/ ər ā/ shən) The first plan for government of the United States.

artisan (ärt/ ə zən) A worker skilled in a trade, usually done by hand.

assassinate (ə sas/ən āt/) To murder someone famous or powerful, usually for political reasons.

astrolabe (as/ tr<lo> lāb) An instrument used in navigation.

B

bank account (bank ə kount/) The money an individual puts into a bank.

barter (bät/ ə) To trade goods or services for other goods or services without using money.

Bill of Rights (bil/ əv rīts/) Amendments to the U.S. Constitution that protect citizens' basic rights.

bison (bī/ sən) A large animal that once roamed the Great Plains.

black codes (blak kōdz) A group of laws passed in the late 1800s that denied African American men the right to vote, kept African Americans from owning guns or taking certain types of jobs.

blockade (blä kād/) A barrier of troops or ships to keep people and supplies from moving in and out of an area.

boycott (boi/ kät/) To refuse to use or buy something.

C

Cabinet (kab/ ə nit) The group of advisors to the U.S. President.

canal (kə nal/) A human-made waterway.

Pronunciation Key

a in hat	ō in open	'l in cattle
ā in age	ô in order	'n in sudden
ä in father	o͞o in tool	th in weather
e in let	u in cup	zh in measure
ē in equal	ʉ in reverse	
i in it	ə a in ago	
ī in ice	e in agent	
o in hot	o in collect	
	u in focus	

candidate (kan′ d ə dāt′) A person who runs for a particular job or office.

caravel (kar′ ə vel′) A small, fast sailing ship created by the Portuguese in the 1400s.

carpetbaggers (kär′pət bag′ərz) Northerners who went to the South after the Civil War to start businesses and make money.

cash crop (kash kräp) A crop that is grown to sell, rather than to be used by the grower.

casualty (kazh′ o͞o əl tē) A person who is injured or killed in war.

checks and balances (cheks and bal′ əns es) The separation of powers in a democracy that gives each branch of government—the legislative, executive, and judicial—some form of authority over the others.

circumnavigate (sʉr′ kəm nav′ ə gāt) To travel completely around.

citizen (sit′ ə zən) A member of a city, state, or town, who has legal rights and responsibilities.

civic responsibility (siv′ ik ri spän′ sə bil′ ə tē) The duties related to being a citizen.

civilization (siv′ ə lə zā′ shən) A complex culture that has made advances in learning, as well as in systems of government, religion, economics, and the arts.

class (klas) A societal group.

class structure (klas struck′ chər) The organization of people in a society according to wealth and power

climate (klī′ mət) The usual pattern of weather in a place over a period of time.

colony (käl′ ə nē) A settlement far away from the country that rules it.

Columbian Exchange (kə lum′ bē ən eks chānj′) The movement of people, animals, plants, and cultures between the Eastern and Western hemispheres.

commerce (käm′ ərs) The buying and selling of products on a large scale.

common good (käm′ən good) The benefit, or good, of all.

compass rose (kum′pəs rōz) A symbol on a map that shows directions.

competition (käm′pə tish′ən) The struggle between two or more businesses for the money of consumers.

compromise (käm′ prə mīz′) A situation when groups on each side of an issue each give in a little to reach an agreement.

Confederacy (kən′fed ər ə sē′) Together, the Southern states that left the United States and formed their own nation; the Confederate States of America.

conquistador (kän kwis′ tə dôr′) A conqueror.

constitution (kän′ stə too′ shən) A written plan for government that describes the principles and organization of a nation.

Continental army (känt′′n ent′′l ar′mē) An army of paid soldiers from the thirteen colonies.

council (koun′səl) A decision-making body that makes decisions for the good of the group.

credit card (kred′it kärd) A card that a person uses to borrow the money to buy goods and services; the cardholder then pays the total amount later by a set due date.

culture (kul′ chər) A system of beliefs and ways of living that are special to a certain group, including their language, religion, government, and arts.

D

debt (det) Money owed.

delegate (del′ ə ght) A representative.

demand (di mand′) Consumers' desire to buy a particular good or service.

democracy (di mäk′rə sē) A government in which citizens have the power to make political decisions.

devastation (dev′ə stā′shən) Great harm.

discrimination (di skrim′ i nā′ shən) Unfair treatment.

dissent (di sent′) Disagreement.

diverse (də vʉrs′) Showing much variety.

drought (drout) A long period without rain.

due process (dōō prä′ses′) A citizen's right to fair treatment through the judicial system.

E

economy (i kän′ ə mē) The system by which a group makes, uses, and shares or distributes goods and services.

effigy (ef′ i jē) A rough model or dummy of a person.

Electoral College (ē lek′ tər əl käl′ ij) The group of people chosen by each state to vote for the U.S. president and vice president.

elevation (el′ə vā′shən) The distance above or below sea level.

elevation map (el′ə vā′shən map) A map that shows physical characteristics of a land area.

emancipation (ē man′sə pā′shən) The freeing of a group from slavery.

empire (em′ pīr′) A group of nations or peoples ruled by a single authority.

encomienda (en kō m ē en′ də) A gift of land by the king of Spain, which gave a person control over the land and the people living there.

enlist (en list′) To join the military.

entrepreneur (än trə prə nʉr′) Someone who takes a risk to start a business.

epidemic (ep′ ə dem′ ik) An outbreak of disease affecting many people at the same time.

executive branch (eg zek′yōō tiv branch) The branch of government that carries out the laws; the U.S. President and his or her administration.

expedition (eks pə djsb′ ən) An organized group of people taking a journey for a purpose.

export (ek′ spôrt) A product sent from one country to another to be sold.

F

famine (fam′ in) A severe shortage of food.

federalism (fed′ər əl iz′əm) The distribution of power in a government between a central government and local governments, such as states.

Federalist (fed′ ər əl ist) A person who supported the passage of the U.S. Constitution.

foreign policy (fôr′ in päl ə sē) The actions a government takes in relation to other governments and nations.

free market economy (frē mär′kit i kän′ə mē) An economic system in which private people and companies, and not the government, own factories and stores.

frontier (frun tir′) An undeveloped region on the edge of settled territory.

G

gold rush (gōld rush) The quick movement of people to a place where gold has been discovered.

government (guv′ ərn mənt) The system by which nations and other groups make laws and carry out the affairs of citizens.

H

historical map (his tôr′ik əl map) A map that shows information about the past.

House of Burgesses (hous uv bʉr′ jəs əs) The first legislative body in the American colonies; in Virginia, this body included representatives elected by the colony's landowners.

hunter-gatherer (hunt′ ər gath′ ə ə) Someone who hunts animals and collects wild plants for food.

I

import (im′ pôrt) A product brought into a country to be sold.

impressment (im pres′ mənt) The act of being forced to serve in the armed forces

inauguration (in ô′ gyə rā′ shən) An official ceremony to make someone president.

indentured servant (in den′ chəd sʉr′ vənt) A person who agrees to work for a set period of time without pay, in exchange for necessities such as transportation, food, clothing, and shelter.

independence (in′ dē pen′ dəns) Freedom from rule by others.

individual rights (in′də vij′o͞o əl rīts) The right of all citizens to decide how to live their lives.

Industrial Revolution (in dus′trē əl rev′ə lo͞o′shən) The period when there was a shift from making goods by hand at home to making them in a factory.

inflation (in flā′ shən) A steady rise in prices that occurs as money loses value and things cost more.

interest (in′trist) A small fee paid to bank customers in exchange for allowing the bank to use their money; a fee charged by banks for borrowing money.

interpreter (in tʉr′ prə tər) A person who can translate from one language to another.

investor (in ves′ tôr) A person who risks money in a business, hoping to earn a profit.

irrigation (ir ə gā′ shən) The practice of bringing water to fields, usually by means of ditches and channels.

J

judicial (joo dish′ əl branch) The branch of government that interprets the laws; the U.S. Supreme Court and other courts.

judicial review (joo dish′ əl ri vyoo′) The power of the courts to decide whether actions are lawful.

Juneteenth (joon tenth′) The celebration of the day when enslaved African Americans were freed during the Civil War.

K

King Philip's War (king fil′ips wär) A conflict between the colonists and the Wampanoag tribe, lead by Metacom, who was called King Philip by the settlers. Metacom suffered a terrible defeat in this war.

L

latitude (lat′ə tood′) Lines that measure the distance north and south from the equator.

league (lēg) A group made up of different nations that share the same goals.

legislative (lej′ is slāt tiv′) The branch of government that makes laws; the U.S. Congress.

locator map (lō′kā′ tər map) A simple map that shows where the area in which an accompanying map is located.

longitude (län′jə tood) Lines that measure the distances east and west of the prime meridian.

Loyalist (loi′ əl ist) An American colonist who remained loyal to Great Britain.

M

manifest destiny (man′ ə fest des′ tə nē) The belief that the United States had a right to add territory until it reached the Pacific Ocean.

manufacture (man′yoo fak′chər) To make goods.

map key (map kē) A map legend; the boxed list showing what the symbols or colors on a map represent.

marketplace (mär′kit plās′) A place in which buyers and sellers meet to exchange goods and services.

martial law (mär′shəl lô) Military rule.

mass production (mas′ prə duk′ shən) To produce many things at once, usually with machinery.

massacre (mas′ ə kər) The killing of many people.

Mayflower Compact (mā ′ flou′ ər kəm pakt′) An agreement made by the Pilgrims to govern themselves and make just laws.

mercantilism (mʉr′ kən til iz′ əm) Economic ideas popular in the 1600s and 1700s which suggested that governments should limit imports but increase manufacturing and exports.

mercenary (mʉr′ sə ner′ ē) A soldier who is paid to fight for another country.

merchant (mur′ chənt) A person who buys and sells goods.

Middle Passage (mid′ ′l pas′ ij) The part of the triangular trade route in which captured and enslaved Africans were sent by ship, under terrible conditions, to be sold in the Americas.

migrate (mī′ grāt′) To move.

militia (mə lish′ ə) A volunteer army.

missionary (mish′ ən er′ ē) A person sent to a new land to spread his or her religion.

Missouri Compromise (mi zoor′ē käm′prə mīz′) A law passed by Congress in 1820 that allowed Maine to enter the Union as a free state while Missouri entered the Union as a slave state.

monarch (män′ərk) A ruler.

Monroe Doctrine (mən rō′ däk′trin) A policy made by President James Monroe warning European nations to stay out of the Americas.

morale (mə ral′) Spirits.

nationalism (nash′ ə nəl iz′ əm) The belief that your country and its culture are better than others′.

navigation (nav ə gā′ shən) The process of charting a course for a ship or an aircraft.

negotiate (nih gō′ shē āt′) To try to reach an agreement.

neutral (noo′ trəl) Not taking sides.

nomad (nō′ mad′) A person who travels from place to place in order to survive.

Northwest Passage (nôrth′ west pas′ ij) A mythical shortcut by water from the Atlantic to the Pacific Ocean.

opportunity cost (äp ər too′nə tē kôst) Something that must be given up in order to get the thing you want.

ordinance (ôrd′ ′n əns) A law.

Patriot (pā′ trē ət) An American colonist who strongly opposed British rule.

patron (Pā′ trən) A person who supports the work of another person or organization, often with money.

peninsula (pə nin′ sə lə) A piece of land almost surrounded by water, but still attached to the mainland.

persecution (pur′sə kyoo′shən) Poor treatment of a person or group based on their religion.

petition (pə tish′ən) A written request for rights or benefits.

physical map (fiz′i kəl map) A map that shows geographic features of a place, such as mountains and valleys and bodies of waters.

pilgrim (pil′ grəm) A person who makes a journey for religious regions.

pioneer (pī′ ə nir′) A person who settles a new place before others.

plantation (plan tā′shən) A large farm, especially in the southern United States, that usually grows one kind of crop.

political map (pə lit′i kəl map) A map that shows information such as borders, capitals, and important cities.

political party (pə lit′i kəl pär′ tē) A group of people who have similar beliefs about government.

Pontiac's Rebellion (pän′tē aks′ ri bel′yən) An attack on British settlers in the Ohio River valley led by an Ottawan leader named Pontiac. The British crushed the rebellion.

Pony Express (pō′ nē ek spres′) Mail service to California provided by riders on swift horses.

popular sovereignty (päp′ yə lər säv′ rən tē) The idea that the power of government comes from the consent of the people.

population density map (päp′yə lā′shən den sə tē′ map) A map that shows how many people live in an area.

prairie schooner (prer′ ē skoo′ nər) A covered wagon with large wheels, used for transportation to the West.

Preamble (prē′ am′ bəl) The introduction to the Constitution of the United States of America.

Proclamation of 1763 (präk′lə mā′shən əv 1763) An order by King George III of England that blocked colonists from settling lands west of the Appalachian Mountains.

profit (präf′it) The money a business earns after all its expenses are paid.

proprietor (prə prī′ ə tə r) A person who owns property or a business.

Puritan (pyoor′i tən) An early settler who left England so he or she could practice a religion freely.

Q

quarter (kwôrt′ ər) To provide lodging or shelter for a person.

R

ratify (rat′ ə fī′) To approve.

raw material (rô mə tir′ ē əl) Resources that are used to manufacture products.

rebellion (ri bel′ yən) A revolt or an armed uprising.

Reconstruction (rē′kən struk′shən) The period when laws were passed that sought to rebuild and heal the northern and southern regions of the United States after the Civil War.

reform (ri fôrm′) Change for the better.

region (rē′ jən) An area defined by its common features.

repeal (ri pēl′) To cancel or end something.

representative (rep′ rə zen′ tə tiv) A person chosen to act on behalf of others.

representative democracy (rep′ rə zen′ tə tiv di mäk′rə sē) A system of government in which the citizens elect people to act on their behalf.

retreat (ri trēt′) To move away from an enemy.

right (rīt) A freedom established by law.

rule of law (rool əv lô) The principle that the law applies to everyone, equally.

satellite map (sat/'l īt/ map) A map that shows a picture of what an area looks like from space.

scale (skāl) A ruler that shows distances on a map.

scarcity (sker/sə tē) A shortage.

secession (si sesh/ən) The separation of a state from nation.

segregation (seg/rə gā/shən) The division of groups of people, usually by race.

separation of powers (sep/ ə rā/ shən əv pou/ ərz) The plan to divide the powers and duties of government into separate branches.

sharecropping (sher/krap/ing) A system in which someone who owns land lets someone else "rent" the land to farm it.

siege (sēj) A military blockade and extended attack designed to make a city or other location surrender.

slave trade (slāv/ trād) The capture, enslavement, buying, and selling of people for profit.

slavery (slā/ vər ē) The practice of owning and controlling people against their will.

specialize (spesh/əl īz/) To make one product, rather than many different ones.

states' rights (stāts rīts) The right of each U.S. state to make its own local laws.

strategy (stra/ tə jē) A plan.

suffrage (səf/ rij) The right to vote.

supply (sə plī/) The amount of goods or services available for a consumer to buy.

tariff (tar/ if) A tax on imports.

technology (tek näl/ ə jē) The use of scientific knowledge or new tools to improve how things are done.

topographic map (top/ə graf/ik map) A map that shows the elevation of an area.

total war (tōt/'l wär) A method of warfare that seeks to destroy civilian as well as military targets to force a surrender.

trading post (trād/ ing pōst) A store set up in a distant place to allow trade to take place.

Trail of Tears (trāl əv terz) The forced march of 15,000 Cherokee in 1838, traveling from the American southeast to Indian Territory in present-day Oklahoma.

translator (trans/ lāt/ ər) A person who can give the meaning of one language in another language.

treason (trē/ ən) The crime of betraying one's country.

treaty (trēt/ ē) A formal agreement between countries.

Treaty of Paris (TREE tee uv P/ RIS) A formal agreement between the United States and Great Britain in which Great Britain recognized the United States as an independent country.

triangular trade route (trī an/ gyə lər trād root) Trade routes between Africa, the Americas, and Europe, in which ships carried cash crops, manufactured goods, and enslaved people.

Underground Railroad (un′dər ground′rāl′rōd′) Before the Civil War, a series of secret routes out of the South along which escaped slaves traveled to freedom in the North.

Union (yōōn′yən) The United States; also the Northern States that remained part of the nation and fought against the Confederacy in the Civil War.

uprising (up′rī zing′) A rebellion.

vaquero (vä ker′ō) A Mexican cowboy.

veto (vē′ tō) To refuse to approve something.

wagon train (wag′ ən trān) A line of wagons traveling as a group.

Index

The index lists the pages on which topics appear in this book. Page numbers followed by *m* refer to maps. Page numbers followed by *p* refer to photographs. Page numbers followed by a *c* refer to charts or graphs. **Bold** page numbers indicate vocabulary definitions.

Credits

Text Acknowledgements

Grateful acknowledgement is made to the following for copyrighted material:

210 "I, Too" from *The Selected Poems of Langston Hughes* by Langston Hughes. Copyright © 1926 by Alfred A. Knopf, Inc. Renewed copyright © 1954 by Langston Hughes. Used by permission of Alfred A. Knopf, a division of Random House, Inc. and Harold Ober Associates, Inc.

220 *The Grapes of Wrath* by John Steinbeck, copyright (c) 1939, renewed (c) 1967 by John Steinbeck.

Note: Every effort has been made to locate the copyright owners of the material produced in this component. Omissions brought to our attention will be corrected in subsequent editions.

Illustrations

xiv, SSH1, SSH3, SSH4, SSH5, SSH6 Dan Santat; **4, 26** Luigi Galante; **6, 104, 152** Joe LeMonnier; **20, 44, 338** Scott Dawson; **31, 32, 33,** CVR Craig Phillips; **52, 58** Victor Rivas; **SSH24, 74, 201, 234** Dave Cockburn; **CVR1, 101, 102, 103** Keith Robinson; **106, 154, 286** James Palmer; **141, 142, 143** Tin Salamunic; **150, 194, 197, 198** Robin Storesund; **157, 180** John Walker; **159, 172, 180** Rick Whipple; **223, 224, 225** Dennis Juan Ma; **234** Kim Herbst; **263, 264, 265** Raul Allen; **276** Roger Chouinard; **278** Frank Ippolito; **287** Supertotto.

Maps

XNR Productions, Inc.

Photographs

Every effort has been made to secure permission and provide appropriate credit for photographic material. The publisher deeply regrets any omission and pledges to correct errors called to its attention in subsequent editions.

Unless otherwise acknowledged, all photographs are the property of Pearson Education, Inc.

Photo locators denoted as follows: Top (T), Center (C), Bottom (B), Left (L), Right (R), Background (Bkgd).

Cover

CVR1 (B) ©Nikreates/Alamy, (BC) Stockbyte/Thinkstock, (BL) Robert F. Sisson/National Geographic/Getty Images; **CVR2** (C) Hemera/Thinkstock, (CL) Library of Congress Prints and Photographs Division/Library of Congress

Front Matter

v (BR) July Flower, 2010/Shutterstock; **vi** (BL) Garry Gay/Getty Images; **vii** (B) ©The Granger Collection, NY; **viii** (BL) The Granger Collection, NY **x** (B) The Granger Collection, NY; **xi** (BR) Marty Lederhandler/©Associated Press; **xii** (BL) ©The Granger Collection, NY; **xiii** (BR) Jupiterimages/Thinkstock

Text

SSH10 (BL) Tony Arruza/Getty Images; **SSH11** (TL) age fotostock/SuperStock, (BL) IndexStock/SuperStock, (BR) Peter Arnold, Inc/Alamy Images; **SSH20** Jack Sullivan/Alamy Images; **SSH22** Don Smetzer/PhotoEdit, Inc., Jeff Greenberg/PhotoEdit, Inc., Kayte Deioma/PhotoEdit, Inc., Photos to Go/Photolibrary; **SSH23** ©Quang Ho/Shutterstock, Hemera/Thinkstock, Ian Murray/Photographer's Choice/Getty Images, Thomas Northcut/Thinkstock; **SSH27** Erick Nguyen/Alamy Images; **SSH31** Phil Coale/©Associated Press; **SSH32** (BC) Glyn Jones/Corbis/Jupiter Images, (BR) Stewart Cohen/Blend Images/Getty Images, (BL) Visions of America, LLC/Alamy Images; **SSH33** (B) Alex Wong/Getty Images; **SSH34** (T) Jeff Greenberg/PhotoEdit, Inc.; **4** (T) Gary718, 2010/Shutterstock; **7** (B) National Geographic Society/Corbis; **8** (B) Dean Pennala, 2010/Shutterstock; **10** (B) George Catlin/The Bridgeman Art Library/Getty Images; **12** (BL) Danita Delimont/Gallo Images/Getty Images, (T) Peter Dennis/©DK Images; **14** (B) The Granger Collection, NY; **15** (R) July Flower, 2010/Shutterstock; **16** (TL) Jeff Vanuga/NRCS/USDA; **18** (TR) ©Paul Chesley/Stone/Getty Images, (B) Lawrence Migdale/Alamy Images; **19** (BR) Peter Newark American Pictures/Bridgeman Art Library; **21** (TR) pf/Alamy; **22** (T) Sioux Indian Council, 1852 (colour litho), Eastman, Captain Seth (1808–75)/Private Collection/Peter Newark American Pictures/Bridgeman Art Library; **24** (B) Corbis; **25** (TR) Alan Keohane/Courtesy of the Hopi Learning Centre, Arizona/©DK Images; **26** (B) Lawrence Migdale/Alamy Images, (C) Danita Delimont/Gallo Images/Getty Images; **28** (B) Alan Keohane/Courtesy of the Hopi Learning Centre, Arizona/©DK Images, (T) Peter Dennis/©DK Images; **30** (Bkgrd) Bill Hatcher/National Geographic/Getty Images; **34** (TR) Garry Gay/Getty Images, (CR) Hulton Archive/Getty Images; **36** (C) Garry Gay/Getty Images, (BL) The British Library/AGE Fotostock, (TL, TC) The Trustees of the British Museum/Art Resource, NY; **37** (BR) Steven Governo/©Associated Press, (TL) The British Library/AGE Fotostock; **38** (TL) ©DK Images, (B) Robert Harding Travel/PhotoLibrary Group, Inc.; **39** (TL) DEA/G. Dagli Orti/Getty Images; **40** (TL) National Maritime Museum, London/The Image Works, Inc.; **42** (R) ©DK Images, (L) Hulton Archive/Getty Images; **44** (BL) Peter Newark American Pictures/Bridgeman Art Library; **46** (T) The Art Gallery Collection/Alamy Images; **47** (TR) ©The Granger Collection, NY; **49** (TR) Bridgeman Art Library; **50** (BL) Rolf Richardson/HIP/